SURVIVAL OF THE FATTEST 4

An alternative review of the
'97-98 football season

Compiled and edited by

David Jenkins
&
Judi Holly

Red Card
Publishing

Survival of the Fattest 4
An alternative review of the '97-98 football season

Copyright © 1998 Red Card Publishing Ltd

Front cover illustration by
David Banks

First published in 1998 by
RED CARD PUBLISHING LIMITED
23 Hamilton Road
Brighton
BN1 5DL

British Library Cataloguing in Publication Data.
A catalogue record for this book is available from the British Library

ISBN 0 9526610 47

Printed and bound in Great Britain by
Mackays of Chatham Plc

For Derek Anderson
1963-1998

Joker, arguer, Gooner.

But mostly, just friend.

CONTENTS

CONTENTS, CONT.

ROLL OF HONOUR

Our thanks go to this book's contributors who managed to send in the articles which appear in theses pages. Apologies to those we've missed and also to the thousands of other un-named contributors and helpers. It's not much consolation, but *you* know who you are!

The 69er	Anna Merriman, Craig Jack
A Kick up the R's	Anthony Hobbs, Dave Thomas
A Large Scotch	Kevin, Gary Bright, Adrian Plimmer, Rob Palmer
A Slice of Kilner Pie	Phil Humphreys
The Abbey Rabbit	Steve Jillings
The Adams Family	Andy & Jon Dickinson, Dave Chapman
All Aboard the Wagon Train	Matthew Porter
Amber Nectar	Geoff Bradley, Les Motherby
Another View From The Tower	The ed
Another Vintage Liverpool Perf.	Andy Hampson, Roy Gilfoyle
Bamber's Right Foot	Hayden Jones
Beesotted	David Lane
Bert Trautman's Helmet	Noel Bayley
Better Red Than Dead	James Vizard
Beyond The Boundary	Pete Mason
Black Arab	The Eternal Optimist, Mr Angry
The Blue Eagle	Jason Skinner, Robert Searle
Bob Lord's Sausage	Rob & Steve Winkley, Steve Anderson
Brian Moore's Head	Simon Baker, Chris Lynham, Eddy Alcorn, Prof Tarquin Zoological-Garden
Build A Bonfire	Terry Brannigan, Gail Brannigan
The Chelsea Independent	Danny Stewart
The Cider'Ed	Ed Hayes, Ben Jones, MTE, Mark Man
City Gent	Richard Halfpenny, John Watmough
Clap Yr. Hands, Stamp Yr. Feet	Matthew Bentote, Ron Mgr, Vic A Rage
Cock A Doodle Doo	Martin Cloake
Come in No. 7, Your Time is Up	Marcus Allin, Chris White
Community Service	Jerry Tosswell
Curious Blue	Darren Luke
Deranged Ferret	Gary Parle, Kevin Stow
Exceedingly Good Pies	Mark Wilbrahim, Matt Smith, S Elvidge
Exiled!	Andy Burton, Gordon Buchan, Adrian Smith
Ferry Across The Wensum	Jim Emerson, Andrew Fuller
Fly Me To The Moon	Rob Nichols, Sharon Caddell, Bob Fisher
Follow The Yellow Brick Road	Keith Parnill, Steve Hartshorn

The Gooner .... Mike Francis
Grorty Dick .... Glynis Wright
Hanging On The Telephone .... Mick, Mini, Wights
The Hanging Sheep .... Chris Stringer
The Hatchet .... Chris Bainbridge, Jeff Hoyle, Tony Dallas
Heaven 11 .... Simon & Jonnie Blackburn, Peter Stevens
Heroes And Villains .... Dave Woodhall
Hey Big Spender .... Mark Aldridge, Shadow, Simon Evans
Highbury High .... Ian Trevett, Tony Madden,
The Holy Trinity .... Steve Whitehouse, Steve Hood, Rob Rodway
In Dublin's Fair City .... Paul Wheeler
It's the Hope I Can't Stand .... Nic Wiseman, Mark Egan
Jackanory .... Geraint Jones
January 3rd, '88 .... Steve Bone, Michael Whitcombe
Keegan Was Crap Really .... Alan Caldwell, Phil Martin, Karen Wright
Kicker Conspiracy .... Jim Park, 'Ed Lines'
King Of The Kippax .... Ged Isaacs, Dave Wallace
Land of Sheep and Glory .... Matthew Potts, Daniel MacLennan
The Latic Fanatic .... Andrew Werrill
Leyton Orientear .... Jamie Stripe, Tom Davies, Stephen Harris
Loadsamoney .... Paul Loftus
Mad As A Hatter .... Keith Hayward
Man Utd Are On The Tele Again Ian 'Duke' Lindsay, Dave Greenwood
Many Miles From Home .... David Stainton
Monkey Business .... Paul Mullen
Moulin Rouge .... Matt Norcliffe, Steve Exley
New Frontiers .... Chris Forth, Dave Wake
No More Pie In The Sky .... Ivan 'Bart' Bainbridge, Julie 'Joolz'
                                                    Bainbridge, 'The Band'
No-One Likes Us .... The Albatross, The Jocko, Alex Hall
The Number Nine .... Steve Wraith, Rob Wraith, John Wraith
The Oatcake .... Martin Smith
On The Terraces .... Marc Williams
One More Point .... Cris Lehmann, Wags, Safety, Tony Dobson
One Nil Down Two One Up ...... Daniel Gilson, Mike Collins, Tony Willis
One Team In Bristol .... Rob Humphries
The Onion Bag .... Jon Wainwright
Over Land And Sea .... Gary Firmager
The Pie....................................... Steve & Sue Westby, Neil McGowan
Pie Muncher .... Ken Robinson, Steve Brennan
Rage On .... Beavis, Boris, Mr G Love
Red All Over The Land.............. John Pearman
Route One .... Malcolm Brackley

Rub Of The Greens .... David Pay, Steve Nicholson
The Seadog Bites Back .... James Hunter
Seaside Saga .... Jackie Mooney
The Second Of May .... Hazel Potter, Ian Marriott
The Sheeping Giant .... Richard 'Dai Shovett' Sympson, Gavin
Evans, Bryn & Tom Law
Shrimp Season .... Ian Kemp, Derek Murr
Sky Blue Army .... David Rose
Son Of A Ref .... Harry G, Paul Singleton
Speke From The Harbour .... Mark Staniford
Spitting Feathers .... Graham Lightfoot
Stand Up .... Ross Wilkinson, Nicola Hanson
The Sunderland Fanatic .... Robert Stein
Super Dario Land .... Jules Hornbrook
Talk Of The Tyne .... Kev Fletcher, Michael Swan
The Lion Roars .... Carl Prosser, Paul Casella
The Tea Party .... Dave Espley, Martin Frost
There's Only One F In Fulham ... David Lloyd, John Gordon
The Thin Blue Line .... Andrew Turton
Those Were The Days .... Philip Ham, Steven Mellen
The Tricky Tree .... Andy Lowe, Neil Shaw
Tripe 'N' Trotters .... Chris 'n' Dave, Gary Parkinson
The Ugly Inside .... Clive Foley, Nick Illingworth
United We Stand .... Steve Black, Andy Mitten
The Vale Park Beano .... Biffo
Voice Of The Valley .... Rick Everitt
Wake Up Blue .... James Brown, Steve Caffrey, Dave Branwood
War of the Monster Trucks .... Sir Stanley Headfire, Nick Riley, Paul
Taylor, Andy Selman
The Water in Majorca .... Darron Kirkby
We Are Leeds .... Steve Abbott
What A Load Of Cobblers .... Rob Marshall
When Skies Are Grey .... Phil Redmond, Graham Ennis, Dave
Swaffield
When You're Smiling .... Geoff, Tom, Jock Lobster
Where's The Money Gone? .... Daniel King, 'Peter Graham's Bandy Legs',
Robbie Bear, Phillip 'Feethams' Bear
White Love .... Dick Smiley, Ray Burke, Paul Hanley
Yellow Belly .... Rob Bradley
Yellow fever .... Daniel Curtis
Yooo Reds .... Mark Richardson
The Zulu .... Dave Small, Dave Thomas

RANTING FROM THE EDS

Once again a big thank you to everyone that bought the book last year and thus enabled this fourth edition of *Survival of the Fattest* to float effortlessly out of Red Card Towers. (If only...)

Publishing on a shoestring budget and with the distraction of the World Cup can make for, shall we say, a few 'why the hell are we doing this?' moments. And never more so than when nursing a Stella '16 World Cup cans for the price of 8' hangover and trying to rationalise why, for the third time in the nineties, international football has failed to offer any respite from seemingly endless domestic woes. (Those last four words are journalist-speak for 'follows a crap team!')

We do this book because four years ago it seemed like a good idea at the time. It'll never win any literary prizes, it'd never pass the quality control checks of a big publishing house and we're pretty sure that it will never grace the shelves of any boardroom in the country. But we do know that it's an honest book, written by passionate football people and enjoyed by a lot of folk. And that's reason enough to continue.

However, with the growth in the divide between the 'haves' and 'have nots' showing no signs of abating, then it can only be a few years before football's structure is changed so completely that the type of comment put forth in this book is compromised for ever. If you don't believe us then read the *Beesotted* article, which shocked both of us, and also take a good look at *Yellow Fever*, which highlights the isolation that many supporters of 'small' clubs now feel. But don't get us wrong, we're not advocating the death of the Premiership. The problem is that the balance is wrong. How many more football clubs are going to be laid open to 'businessmen' keen to cash in on this media-inspired frenzy?

Yet everyone's to blame. From ego-bloated chairmen, to incompetent administrators and blue-rinsed councillors, through to trendy politicians and 'new generation' football fans and pundits. But at the end of the day (Brian), football is parochial. Few of the game's power brokers - the Premier League, its chairmen, the media owners, sponsors and players' agents - could care less about life outside the top flight. And on the whole, fans are no better. It is our tendency towards small-mindedness, our insularity about our particular team that causes the problems, but at the same time gives rise to the passion. No-one *really* gives a toss about Doncaster. No-one really gives a toss about whether Arsenal stay at Highbury or move to King's Cross. No-one really gives a toss about Ken Bates' ticketing policies or West Ham's price rises for the forthcoming season (although *Over Land & Sea* and *On The Terraces* are particularly vocal on this subject). No-one really, except the people that follow that club (and maybe you too, since you're reading this book). Mind you, it would be great if people did.

Of course there are exceptions. *Everyone* supposedly gives a toss about Posh's bloke...

Enjoy the book.

THE 69'ER

Swindon Town

For the supporters of Swindon Town this season, knowledge of horses was essential. It was a story partly of fetlocks and hooves, but mostly of donkeys and shirehorses. And the benefit of knowing which way round the horse should go became rapidly clear.

After a dismal finish to the '96-97 season (witness the much-repeated statistics of our run-in: P10, W1, D2, L7, F2, A24), it was a surprise when '97-98 started brightly. Far from being the donkey his fee suggested, new striker Chris Hay from Celtic banged in 13 goals in 20 games, with a particularly impressive hat-

80P

Issue 28
April 1998

The 69er

THE SWINDON TOWN FANZINE

McMAHON + HUNT MUST GO

trick against Port Vale, and he was the catalyst for ten wins in the opening 18 league games. October saw us nose top after a 1-0 win at Portsmouth, when 'keeper Steve Mildenhall kept us in the game despite suffering a cut to his scrotum, and *The 69er* was pretty much roundly booed for a depressing opening issue of the season.

But this status as favourite was all a desperate sham. Come the beginning of December (when we still looked to some like a decent each-way bet) we had not beaten a side in the upper half of the table. By the end of February we were still harking back to Oxford on December 7th - the last time we'd scored more than two goals in a game. In fact, we only managed that feat once more (away at QPR) and not one single time did we beat anyone who finally ended in the top ten. Our five away wins came against the sides who finished 24th, 23rd, 21st, 20th and 19th respectively. It was enough to make you turn to drink.

Yet listen to the people at the club and you'd think we were over-achieving in relation to our size; listen to manager Steve McMahon and chairman Rikki Hunt (who signs his letters 'Rikki' with a big circle over the last 'i') and you'd think that the football you'd been watching was entertaining; listen and you would get the impression that it was an unrepresentative "minority of morons" who were venting their spleen by shouting for the manager's head. And of course, all those who decided to vote with their feet were "quitters."

The truth was much harder to swallow. From December the season was a miserable, pathetic shambles. Poor performances were topped, for some, by the home defeat in the FA Cup at the hands of non-league Stevenage. Others picked out the six and five-nil defeats away at Middlesbrough and Norwich while many just bemoaned the sheer mind-numbing tedium of the displays. In the home defeat to West Brom we even witnessed the sorry sight of two Town players throwing punches at each other. Among the complainers were those who'd begged McMahon to stay when he considered quitting in April. In the final 20 games of the season we managed to concede 34 goals and score just 10, becoming the footballing equivalent of the lamest nag in the field.

Hay's goals all but dried up: he scored just one in the last 19 matches. Remedies included sending him back to Scotland because he was home-sick and booking him an appointment with Eileen Drewery. Perhaps he just didn't fancy the going. Predictably, the downturn in his form and our overall results from December coincided with the departure of target man Wayne Allison to Huddersfield. And though we continued to hoof the ball upfield as if he were still there, the gap he left remained until April when we signed 31-year-old Iffy Onuora, a player who'd spent virtually his entire career outside the top two divisions, as our replacement target man.

Was it coincidence that the downward slide began earlier than it did last season? And when will it begin next?

It was the manner of the defeats, rather than the losing, which we objected to. Most of the displays were an unadulterated shambles. Where Ardiles and Hoddle built a creative midfield and a team which played entertaining football, even when it was losing, McMahon has built a combative one that played like a two-legged horse unsure of which direction to take. Even when we won, which wasn't often, the performance wasn't up to the standard we had come to expect. Predictably, our disciplinary record was again one of the worst in the Football League. What else could be expected from a team which included a man who had allegedly bitten a policeman's ear and a manager who was dismissed from the dugout at Port Vale for ear-bashing the referee over a missed backpass; a boss who was hauled up before a disciplinary committee for allegedly verbally abusing a referee at one of his son's matches. The committee accepted McMahon's explanation that he had merely been giving the referee some advice.

No, there was little evidence of the artistic past here. What we had was a team of pugilists and hoofers: not one true creative player amongst them. And McMahon consistently failed to motivate any of them. If there were show-ponies (Mark Walters and Philippe Cuervo), they were often left on the bench. A classic example of this was the 0-6 defeat at Middlesbrough when Cuervo was allegedly told he was not playing because McMahon "wanted to keep the defence tight." It came from the horse's mouth alright: McMahon kept announcing that he didn't know what else he could do or say to change things. As the manager, if *he* didn't, then who the hell did? The games were dismal, effortless and passionless and the banners came out.

"Neigh," went Rikki and brandished a huge vote of confidence in McMahon like a nosebag to the hungry. The disappointing thing was that he meant it. He even said that he would *never* sack him. McMahon himself sunk further into the dugout, bald pate shining in the watery spring sun and refused to take any of the responsibility for performances, blaming poor finances for limited forays into the transfer market. Lack of money undoubtedly does have an ongoing impact, but it should not be too heavily stressed. He might equally have argued that using his lucky horseshoe was the wrong way to get up. Good, creative teams have been built on a shoestring before: the important thing for Swindon Town to realise is that Steve McMahon does not know how.

And what of '98-99? There is no air of anticipation, no revelling in news of new signings, because there is no reason to suppose things will improve. McMahon asked us to judge him on his own team and not on Gorman's legacy. Well, he has his team now and it is not good enough.

The abiding memory of the season came in the form of a particularly depressing trip to Maine Road and another 6-0 defeat. No, losing wasn't the highlight, but seeing a police horse performing its toilet in front of us was. I am still amazed by the speed of dilation of that horse's rectum and the scale that the dilation eventually reached, not to mention the volume of what came out. That was the horse's arse and that really was as good as it got.

Above: Beckham takes his dog for a walk, and the Rottweiler pups.

Source: Red All Over The Land

A KICK UP THE R'S

Queen's Park Rangers

In early August last year, the pubs around Shepherds Bush were full of characteristically attractive Queens Park Rangers fans in characteristically ill-fitting shirts indulging in characteristically intelligent discourse about our prospects for the season. Whilst the start of our second term in Division One was probably greeted with a touch more healthy cynicism than our first, there were still many who were prepared to indulge in ale-fuelled 'religious fundamentalist nutter' style proclamations about our promotion chances:

"We're stronger than last year...", "No one can defeat us...", "As good as the best in the division...". Predictably enough, the heavy hand of realism was about to slap us firmly in the face and the comfy chair of optimism was soon to be cruelly pulled away from behind us. St. Paul (Parker), the patron saint of solid defences, was already packing his bags to leave and, far away, the relegation wolves were being released. Have I gone too far? You get the idea, anyway. A dull 0-0 draw with Ipswich on the first day followed by defeat at Tranmere would tell us everything we would need to know about the season ahead. Soon enough, the effects of the London Pride started to wear off and things were back to normal:

"Can't get any worse...", "Could be an outside bet for a play-off place, possibly...", "As good as Norwich, I should think..."

By mid-September, a chill wind blew around the Roy Wegerle staircases of the South Africa Road stand. Manager Stewart Houston, taking time off from his role as Skeletor in the stage version of *Masters of the Universe*, had somehow conspired to win Manager of the Month on the back of 'crushing' single-goal victories over the likes of Crewe and Portsmouth. On the training ground, Bruce Rioch was busy indulging in some friendly kick-boxing with the players and on the terraces (OK, OK, in the seats then); the early season euphoria had completely evaporated:

"We're not very good, but whisper it quietly and perhaps no-one will find out..."

For their part, the players were busy writing themselves into tomorrow's football metaphors. How long, one wonders, before Barry Davies uses a line like, "he was clean through there with only the 'keeper to beat, but somehow managed to Mike Sheron it into the upper tier...", or, "It seemed like a harmless enough ball into the box, but the 'keeper and defender somehow got into a bit of a Karl Ready, resulting in this corner..."

By November, with the team fighting off the pitch instead of on it, the-man-with-the-daft-hair, chairman Chris Wright, had seen enough. With a rocky shareholders meeting approaching, in which he would have to explain why Loftus Road PLC shares were now so worthless that the price was being quoted in Italian lira, he decided that Houston and Rioch needed a gentle push onto their swords.

Perhaps it was the accident the club says it was, but I must say I'd respect Chris Wright even more if I could be certain that Bruce Rioch finding out about his dismissal via Ceefax was a deliberate act on the part of the club. Most supporters I know don't want handshakes and "thanks for the hard work" platitudes when managers leave. We want humiliation. In our particular case, we wanted (well, I did) a shaven-headed Houston and Rioch to be paraded in chains in front of a baying crowd before the Stoke home game. We wanted them to read out blatantly-prepared statements admitting their guilt in allowing our beloved team to become such a shambles, before being thrown to the Ericsson-sponsored club leopard. Or was it just me?

Anyway, the sackings gave rise to an entertaining few weeks for the fans. The endless media speculation linking the likes of Gerry Francis and... er, well... Gerry Francis to the vacant post gave us something to discuss in the pub other than the weekly "who will play right-back today?" debate. Caretaker-manager John Hollins won the Ray Wilkins award for being a lovely bloke, but seemed to pick teams using some sort of lottery ball type random number generator. You could just see him in the dressing room at 2pm on a Saturday saying, "and today's midfield anchorman is..." (drum roll) "number 10, Kevin Gallen!" Unfortunately, though we chanted his name like never before, lauded the improvement in team spirit and cheered his instant demotion of Houston's Arsenal reserve signings, the fact that he had jelly in the part of his head where tactical nous is meant to be was all too evident.

With Gerry Francis ruled out of the running, it was left to Ray Harford to transform a team suffering from five years of mis-management into play-off hopefuls within a couple of months and with no money to spend. Somewhat naïvely, many of us actually believed he'd be able to do it.

Five years of mis-management... Bloody hell - I was trying to get through this without mentioning that bloody bleeding Richard bloody sodding Thompson and his bloody poxy family, who spent their time cheerfully dismantling our very promising Premier League team. But I can't. Still, at least they abandoned ship once we were relegated, otherwise who knows where we'd be now. Ooooooh, it makes my blood boil. Anyway, where was I? Oh yes, Ray Harford...

Some encouraging transfer dealings seemed to suggest that Harford had come to much the same conclusions as most fans about where our weaknesses lay - i.e. defence, midfield and attack. With Ray 'are you sure you only want a million for him?' Wilkins seemingly happy enough to take anyone we couldn't be bothered with down the road to Fulham, things looked to be moving the right way. Even the (inevitable) sale of Trevor Sinclair was greeted with no more than a shrug of the shoulders by most fans.

The arrival of Iain Dowie and Keith Rowland bought cautious nods of approval, and there was excitement at the prospect of seeing the talented Mark Kennedy - even if it was only on loan. And it was. Something wrong with a bloke who'd rather play in the Premiership than for QPR, I reckon, but never mind. Then there were the signings of Ian Baraclough and Tony Scully - both of whom looked promising. Booted through the out-door were Rufus 'who are you looking at?' Brevett and Matthew Brazier to Fulham, both to howls of indifference from most.

Unfortunately, the application of some tactical acumen seemed to unsettle many of the players, who responded by throwing their hands in the air and running around going "aaarrrggghhhh!" during matches. Well, that's how it appeared, anyway. The confused opposition would generally retain their composure enough to score once or twice. There were one or two exceptions when the team seemed to get the hang of things a bit - for example the 5-0 thrashing of Middlesbrough (just thought I'd mention it), but these instances were all too rare. In fact, there was only that one if memory serves.

Such was the level of faith being placed in our new manager that by February this year, with relegation a much more realistic proposition than promotion, there were still some (myself, shamefully, included) who were busy calculating the poor runs of form that would be required by Sheffield United, Birmingham, Wolves, Ipswich, etc etc, in order for us to make the play-offs. However, like all the best embryonic scientific ideas that have since been proved to be utter bloody rubbish, there was one simple error in the calculations on which this hypothesis was based - Rangers would be required to win at least three-quarters of their remaining games.

The low point of the season for me was the game at Stoke in March. At half-time, Rangers trailed to a wonderful Ian Dowie own goal and the players were heckled and booed from the pitch by the travelling fans. Things went from bad to worse to terrible, then onto catastrophic in the second-half, culminating in angry exchanges at the final whistle between QPR fans and the long-serving Simon Barker as he made his way to the tunnel. It was a bit too quiet on the bus back from Stoke after the game and it seemed that for many, the hitherto distant threat of relegation suddenly appeared very close indeed. *A Kick Up The R's* editor Dave Thomas, in a rare moment of humour, cheerfully suggested that maybe we might not make the play-offs after all. He has only just had the stitches out.

One week later, we arrived at Huddersfield with two signings who were to keep us in the division - Neil Ruddock on loan from Liverpool and some

some bloke called Vinny Jones. And my God, how our lightweight team cried out for a couple of big, scary, hard blokes. It might not have been pretty (although it wasn't actually as ugly as you might think), but it was effective. Vinny capped a commanding debut with a "Brazilian style wonder-goal" (his words, not mine) and Neil Ruddock proceeded, despite his blatant lack of fitness and pace, to highlight the gap in class between First Division strugglers and Premiership reserves.

Five draws later we went to Maine Road in need of at least a point for safety and despite falling behind after about 40 seconds, came away with a vital 2-2 draw. And what a game it was: end-to-end attacking play, comedy defending, fights in the tunnel (involving Vinny, surprisingly), a gun-wielding maniac taking pot shots from the roof of the Kippax, slapstick goalkeeping, fans tearing out clumps of their hair, screaming children, an attack by a swarm of killer bees and a truly remarkable own goal from Rangers' unofficial Player of the Season - Jamie Pollock of Manchester City. OK, I lied about the bees. And the gun-wielding maniac, actually. And while there probably were screaming children, I don't actually remember hearing any. There was definitely an own goal, though. And that meant that going into the final game of the season we were safe (barring an unlikely series of final-day scores, the like of which would have made Nick Leeson blush).

A season that had started with so much Scully (even though most fans realised it was a bit Trevor Sinclair), had gradually Barker-ed away into a grim relegation Ruddock. We finally managed to Karl Ready it by the skin of our teeth - but I don't think any of us still believe we are Premiership quality any more. And yes, I did try to think of a Rangers player's name to substitute for the word 'Premiership' in that last sentence. And no, I couldn't come up with one.

In Ray Harford, though, we have either got a manager who knows what he's doing or a manager who does a very good impression of a manager who knows what he's doing. The portents, if not wonderful, are quietly encouraging.

So, next season then, definitely. Promotion - no problem. We can't be stopped. We're on a roll. No, we really are this time. Honest.

A LARGE SCOTCH

Shrewsbury Town

Back in August there was optimism, with club and fans alike quietly confident of a successful season and a return to the Second Division.

New manager Jake King had been brought in from near neighbours Telford United, along with several players. A former club captain and member of our Championship winning side of '78-79, Jake was a popular choice as Fred Davies' replacement. It was also satisfying to deprive Telford of a man who after only around six months in charge was already being described as their best ever manager! The prospect of Town going up and Telford going down whetted the appetite

a large scotch
a large scotch
A LARGE SCOTCH
a large scotch
A LARGE SCOTCH
a large scotch
a large scotch
a large scotc
a large scotch

UNOFFICIAL SHREWSBURY TOWN FANZINE

YES, MR PROGRAMME EDITOR, WE CAN MAKE A MESS OF A PAGE AS WELL, BY USING FANCY FONTS & CRAP PICTURES.

ISSUE 20   ONLY 50p

for the first game of the season at home to Doncaster Rovers.

And it was a winning start, 2-1. Town had to hold on in the final minutes as Rovers (who looked quite dangerous) mounted a comeback, but it was three points and the opener we wanted. "Going up, going up, going up!" cried the Riverside faithful. Doncaster then went on to lose their next two homes games 8-0 and 5-0! Maybe we weren't quite as good as we thought...

Before the season started we all thought that defence would be our strong point but that we'd struggle to score at the other end. We couldn't have been more wrong as we managed to score three times against Brentford in the CCC and Cambridge in the league but let in five and four respectfully. In fact it was a bad start all round with only two wins in the first two months. There also seemed to be unrest in the ranks between players who had been signed under the previous manager and the new recruits. Those acquired by Fred Davies seemed to realise quite quickly that they would be on their way at the end of the season, or sooner if another club was interested. This affected their performances (when picked) and they appeared for the world as though they couldn't really be bothered.

Another problem was that most of the opposition had players that looked like something out of the *Land of the Giants*, while ours resembled

Snow White and the Seven Dwarfs. We were being blitzed in the air at corners and free kicks and we just didn't have enough height in the side to cope. Town tried to play neat passing football and usually beat anyone who looked to play the same way. It was the kick and rush merchants that we struggled against.

It was obvious that the club's main priority was to get a tall striker to partner talented newcomer Lee Steele up-front. We got our wish with the arrival of big Devon White from Notts County. Regarded as something of a big signing, because everyone had heard of him, Devon became an instant crowd hero. One of his first games for the club was at home to Rotherham, a truly memorable match - for all the wrong reasons.

In the opening minutes Devon went in for a cross along with Rotherham 'keeper Bobby Mimms. The 'challenge' left Mimms unconscious and out of the game with a suspected broken jaw. Devon escaped without even a booking and then went on to open the scoring. By now the Rotherham players were trying to kick their way out of trouble, and one member of each side was sent off for scuffling. Rotherham then had a further two red carded (and should have had at least two more) including the outfield goalkeeper who'd replaced Mimms, and then watched their third 'keeper of the day pick the ball out of net from the resulting penalty. Faced with eight men, Town made very hard work of finishing them off. The home crowd had already turned on our shot-shy players before depleted Rotherham scored a goal. Thankfully, it was the only one they managed.

Some better results followed this awful performance. A 3-2 win over bogey side Mansfield and a fantastic 4-1 win at Hull, our first away from home in over a year, made it easier to justify to workmates the many trips following a team who seldom won. But boy, you really *really* appreciate a victory when it finally arrives, though.

The Town followed this up with a good performance and a draw against Grimsby in the FAC. Down to ten men after having goalkeeper Benny Gall sent off, Town came from 1-0 down to earn a replay. Next came the match of the season, a 4-3 win over Macclesfield with Devon White scoring three goals and claiming, unbelievably, his first ever hat-trick.

After drawing 2-2 away to high-flying Exeter, we were starting to look towards the play-offs but first it was the cup replay at Grimsby. The referee for the match was the Premiership's Uriah Rennie, regarded as one of the best officials in the game. However, after harshly sending off our goalkeeper in the first match, he proceeded to send off two more in the replay - both very dubious decisions. To no-one's surprise Town lost the match 4-0. This was the turning point.

We lost four and drew one of the next five games before beating Cardiff 3-2. Suddenly Town fans were starting to look at the other end of the table. If Brighton and Doncaster put a run together, we thought, then there could be some serious trouble ahead. Our next match happened to be at Doncaster. A larger than average away support travelled north to witness an away banker. Everyone had thrashed Rovers, now it was our turn... It's hard to express the embarrassment, sadness and anger in the away end at the final whistle. We lost 1-0... Rovers were terrible and we were worse. An average women's Sunday League team could have beaten us both. It must go down as one of the lowest points in my time supporting Shrewsbury. The pessimists were already talking about the possibility of going out of the league, whereas a couple of months previously the talk had been about promotion.

More poor results followed before we had to travel to runaway leaders Notts County. We'd only won once in the last 12 games, while County were looking for their eleventh straight win. There could only be one winner - Town! Talking to some Notts County fans before the game, they were saying how Devon White would never play well against the club he loved, and how he would miss sitters on purpose. They were also telling us how many goals they were going to score. It was so satisfying when we took the lead and although White didn't score he did hit the post and had an excellent game. With the stadium clock well into the fourth minute of injury time we were already celebrating our second away win of the campaign, when heartbreak... County scored from an impossible angle. Town had played their hearts out and had deserved better. This result left us all wondering on the way home how we could play so well against the league leaders and so badly against the bottom club?

Although not getting three points was a big disappointment, it gave the players much-needed confidence and we went on to record some good victories, including a 4-1 win against fast-fading Peterborough. All of a sudden the relegation fears were banished and we were starting to look towards the play-offs again, which just shows you what a crap league we were in.

There were two more away wins at Rotherham and Swansea and a 3-0 home defeat of Darlington. Could we reach the play-offs? We were running out of games and had to rely on other teams to lose, but we hadn't given up hope.

The next match at Leyton Orient was vital. They needed to win to help their own push for promotion and had a bigger than average crowd cheering them on. Town played well but found themselves 2-0 down; we also had a player sent off. Then came the comeback of the century. Lee Steele had been promising all season but this was the match that really proved to us that he is a class striker. Almost single handily he scored two goals to bring us back on level terms. The Town fans went berserk! So imagine how we felt when Steele scored a winner with a couple of minutes to go. Now *that's* the reason I follow my team away from home!

Unfortunately, other results meant that our promotion dream was over, but we were still on a high and didn't really care. In our next game against Brighton, both teams had nothing to play for, although you wouldn't have thought so from the crowd reaction as we came from 1-0 down to win 2-1. We were on a roll - if only we'd had a better start at the outset.

Two thousand balloons added to the colourful finale and party atmosphere at the Meadow as the final curtain fell on our season. We 'blooded' several youngsters but Scunthorpe decided to play party poopers, winning 2-0. The disappointment of losing still didn't dent the enjoyment we'd got from the last few games. At long last it seemed that the club was going in the right direction. Well, it's fired my enthusiasm anyway, and next season can't come quick enough.

Source: The Ugly Inside

A SLICE OF KILNER PIE

Huddersfield Town

Played fourteen. Drew five. Lost nine. Five miserable points. And stranded. A further five points adrift of the second bottom team, still three more from Manchester City (*Manchester City* for f*ck's Sake). This was November, Horton had gone, Jacko had lost four of his first five and we'd given relegated Stoke a 16 point advantage.

Not an entirely idyllic start to the new campaign...

But the board had promised Jacko and Yorath money to spend so we brought in... Lee Richardson from Oldham and Barry Horne on a free from Birmingham reserves. Unbelievable! Tranmere had

Hi, it's Kevin Gray here, I'm going to need your best lawyer...no, it wasn't my fault but...

Moment of Impact: Gordon Watson's right leg takes the full weight of Kevin

THE INDEPENDENT TOWN REVIEW

Aldridge, City had Kinkladze, Pompey had half the bleeding Socceroos and we had Barry Horne, the ex-Welsh international. Well fire up the engine boys, we'll be clear of trouble by teatime.

But ha! What wizardry lay behind such scouting genius? Richardson (girl's haircut aside), a mastermind in the centre of midfield, and Horne? Fair enough, he's no gazelle, but if legends can be formed in just over seven months of sub-standard First Division football then this man is the king of them all. Barry bloody Horne. Oh Barry, Barry Horne... Barry, Barry, Barry Horne.

Our Student Union on a Saturday night would oft ring to the sound of his name. Rejoicing outside 'J.C's' on the picnic tables, whilst queuing for a burger at 'Mario's,' a John Smith's-fuelled celebration of his visionary passing and positional awareness, made all the more sweet by an away victory at Crewe, West Brom, Stoke or Reading that afternoon. The Horne man, a Welsh institution, now a Huddersfield Town legend firmly established in Loughborough University folklore.

With Baz around we always had a fighting chance, and to be fair whilst Jacko could never put out his strongest team, there were some pretty good ones, not least on the few occasions when he was able to field the centre-half trio of Dyson, Gray and big Andy Morrison. The only time that this clinical combination fell apart was at Middlesbrough, but Steve Jenkins was playing then as well.

To rate Jenkins as the worst international footballer I have ever seen may appear a little harsh, but then I witnessed the Cameroon friendly at Wembley before Christmas. And if I thought Sol Campbell was poor, Jenkins is comfortably more disorientated. Whereas the Spurs centre-half might struggle against Gianfranco Zola, Stevie would come a cropper with Ian Ormondroyd, such is his complete lack of positional awareness. Now I should let this go, but Jenkins is only spared the accolade of worst player ever in a Town shirt by Gary Barnett's flirtation in defence some years ago, and 'Skinny' was the slowest natural winger in the Football League. Imagine my delight then when Yorath straightened him out on the training field: "Welsh international? Yw mst by llaffyng et me, sonny jym!"

And that's the last time we saw him (rumour has it a bitter fist fight ensued, and knives were pulled from boot-bags, but that may be idle tabloid speculation).

Inheriting 'Skinny' Barnett's mantle of late has been Lee Makel. "He played in Norway with Blackburn" we were told. "So what? He's playing in our midfield now and he's f*cking useless."

Out went Makel.

By December things were looking up. We'd won a game for a start, which was always going to help. In truth we'd won quite a few and were on what constituted a 'roll'. So what does Jacko do? He replaces the tune the teams run out to prior to each home game with the music from *The Great Escape*. How does the team respond? We lose our first home game in two months. Masterful, Jackson.

If everyone has to have a blot on the copybook then that was his. An away win at West Brom followed straight after before table-toppers Middlesbrough rolled into town on Boxing Day. The now customary Bank Holiday full house saw us dominate large portions of the game. Subduing an ineffective Merson and all but marking Beck out of the game (the same defence had also shut out the probing Nigel Jemson of Oxford and the wizardry of Bury's Jimmy Quinn - 39 but still a handful). However it wasn't to be ours as Big Kev put into his own net. Nil-one. The band-wagoned 4,000 in the away end celebrated yet another undeserved victory. Arrogant t*ssers.

"...Jingle bells, jingle bells, jingle all the way, oh what fun, blah blah blah..." Yes we know. Dickheads.

"...Jingle bells, blah blah blah... Oh what fun it is to see the Town throw it away at home yet again when it seemed easier to put three or four in their net then one in ours off a corner... blah blah blah... don't you just love following a crap team etc etc"

Insanely jealous? Who - me?

Kev atoned for his little error two days later at the Pulse stadium, Bradford, putting in a sterling performance at the heart of the back four.

The Sh*tty fans were still a tad bitter about the big man putting Gordon Watson in hospital in the corresponding game last year. "Kevin Gray, Kevin Gray, W*nker! W*nker!" they all chanted with some gusto. Hey guys! What's a broken leg to your record signing between friends? We let you have Lee Sinnott back didn't we? "Where's your Watson gone?" and, "One leg! He's only got one leg!" echoed around the away end with equal passion. Tee-hee. Yet another Dolly wondergoal gave us a share of the points, with Kev clearing two goal-bound efforts off the line and generally playing a blinder. So the moral victory to us then.

By now a few more were beginning to believe in survival. We were clawing back ground on Manchester City (*Manchester City* for f*ck's sake! Were we ever *that* bad?) and Stoke by the week, but could never quite escape the drop zone. Like a damsel in distress in a Hanna-Barbera cartoon, we'd unlock one door of the baddie's castle, only to find the Hooded Claw waiting on the other side. In this case the shadowy 'Claw' figure was Blundell Park, bloody Maine Road (again) and the AutoWindscreen Shield, standing in line, shaking their heads and muttering, "Oh dear Town, cocked it all up again haven't you?" But with Jackson steering and Yorath the brake-man, our escape pod always looked capable of outrunning the rest.

However, by February the Second Division once more had a tight hold of our bell-bottomed trousers, and footballing outposts such as Chesterfield, Bournemouth, hell maybe even Macclesfield, were beckoning us down like a sinister Leslie Crowther. If only Town were playing for an automatic washing machine and Y-reg Austin Ambassador, the harsh reality suggested the price was entirely wrong. Merciless butcherings at Ipswich and Forest confounded misery; successive home defeats against Sunderland and Manchester more or less took the piss; soon my team were out of the audience and gliding down Crowther's stairs with an uncontrollable ease.

"Huddersfield Town - come on down!" My warped nightmares were getting worse.

And here my learned friends lies my great confession.

Tuesday March 3rd: Town 1-2 Manchester City.

For the first time in my comparably short footballing career I had given up hope. I knew no better when Town last went down in 1987, though I knew enough that impressionable young lads didn't support a team that won only six games in a season, and let more goals in than my own junior league side (ten-one? I doubt my dad would've stayed for the duration had Pannal Sports Under-9's put in a performance like that). But after this latest kick in the proverbials my optimism was spent, and belief all but gone. Hope hadn't so much sprung eternal as discarded the orange armbands and sunk. If HMS Huddersfield Town had a ruptured hull, I'd nicked the final lifejacket and jumped overboard. If my own child (if indeed I had one) dropped the baby Jesus in a school nativity play, I'd walked out in embarrassment before the three wise men had even got there.

Crimes of life don't come any more heinous than a man deserting his team, and my arse had well and truly twitched; I'd waited till nightfall and gone.

Daylight though and recovery. If the night had carried a storm and blown several big trees down, then successive away victories at Stoke and Reading cleared a couple off the road. A point at Bury and nearer, the delights of the modern game epitomised by engine failure on a grid-locked M66, limping into a garage at five to three and trying to change the God-damn oil in the driving rain. Nowhere to park, it was now twenty past three, we couldn't find our seats and the first action we saw was their centre forward diving into the mud for a penalty and a goal down. Our misery was confounded by the quite appalling standard of half-time catering (quick glance at the Colman's Guide... yep, they're below us too); no pies, no pasties, no sausage rolls, melting Mars Bars at 70p a throw.

Fortunately though, this anecdotal reflection mirrors our whole season; Richardson rescued the situation with a steaming volley and the supporters went home satisfied with the result, though not necessarily entertained. If many of the 3,500 who filled both ends of Gigg Lane were the hard-core, our faithful, then it will be interesting to see how many more join us behind the sticks in the new stand at Leeds Road. (Hmmm, a smoking ban in the upper tier. A curious decision. The cheapest seats in the ground intended to attract the working class fan, who is then told he cannot smoke. "Excuse me sir, can you put that out, it's obscuring my view." White elephant? Where?)

To be brutally honest it won't be lingering cigarette smoke that drives away the new breed of nineties fan. It'll be Steve bloody Jenkins or his donkey replacement or Stewart underachieving if he's still here, or his over-priced replacement if not. It'll be "we've sold Maskell, we sold Roberts and Booth and now we're selling bloody Stewart as well. I've had enough of this." It'll be 0-0 draws at home to Grimsby on a wet Tuesday night (why haven't we got any foreign flair? And can I have squad numberings and players' names on the back of the shirts?), an early and/or shock cup exit, or heaven forbid yet another home derby defeat. It'll be a promising start and fading away to obscurity; it'll be L**ds progressing in Europe but realistically not, it won't be another relegation dog-fight but probably will, and it'll only be a game after all.

It'll be everything we least expect with some crap football thrown in. And when we lose sight of domestic honours in September, expect tabloid revelations of bungs to health inspectors and food testers, stuffed brown envelopes postmarked Huddersfield arriving in Cambridge and the like. Our four man board and their insatiable appetite for success could herald sweeping changes in personnel. "Forget about a new full-back, that Colman's Guide reckoned our bacon rolls could do with some strengthening, and our tea is a little weak to boot. Sell Stewart, sell Dyson, in fact sod it, sell the whole bloody lot of them, and get me Ainsley Harriot!" Forget the Intertoto, we've got that 15th UEFA Cup place in the bag.

Good grief. Nine months of football for an away win at Maine Road and second place in the caterers' league table. And those were the highlights. Only Doncaster Rovers failed to win a league match before us, our reserve team went down, and bleeding Port Vale needed to win at our place to stay up and stuck four in without reply. Who says there is no pride left in the blue and white stripes?

What a bloody season. The Premiership ain't got nothing on us.

THE ABBEY RABBIT

Cambridge United

Just Another Season?

To be honest, mid-table obscurity was about the best that most United fans could have hoped for, given our by now ritual alarming collapse during the second half of the previous season. Our other ritual didn't exactly help our foreboding - summer book-balancing. Although this exercise netted us around a million quid, it saw arguably our three best players depart for the more opulent surroundings of the Premiersh*t, the Stadium of Light and, er... Watford. Given that the bank had kindly offered to reduce our overdraft facility, United fans were once again resigned to watching the manager rebuild the team with the usual motley crew of other sides' rejects...

issn 1355-1906

issue 49
nov/dec 1997

£1.00

the abbey rabbit

an alternative view of cambridge united fc

1987/88 - 10th anniversary season - 1997/98

inside this issue:

- rant - no wins since orient who's to blame?
- abbey returns - going nowhere at last!
- city boys - north of the river with graham daniels
- stuffing scum - ah those golden memories...
- lostboys - how to ruin a generation, twice
- media blues - how united took on the press and lost

and much, much more inside!

look at this!
90 minutes and the bloody seam's come un-stitched already!

replica kit... controversy rages!

However, Roy McFarland did appear to have attracted an above average group of cast-offs, which, coupled with our home-grown talents, had a few optimistic souls contemplating a play-off challenge at least. Their hopes were raised even further following the scavenging of the boardroom that liberated enough loose change stuffed behind the sofa to prise Martin Butler away from Walsall.

There were still a few gnawing doubts though: the reticence of Matty Joseph, to many *the* outstanding wing-back in the Third Division, to sign a new deal, and the subsequent reluctance of the manager to even consider picking him - despite his insistence at playing three at the back. Then there was the board's failure to stump up the cash for Walsall's Chris Marsh, despite him apparently turning down a move to Chesterfield, such was his desire to join us... And the darkening clouds from the north of the county, as Fat Barry and the Forces of Evil amassed the largest squad this side of the extras roster in *The Ten Commandments* as part of a general ploy to bankroll or bankrupt P*sh out of the division...

However, as the nation prepared to grieve, so the Amber Army celebrated as the team went top of the league following the clinical demolition of Leyton Ointment at Brisbane Road. The result was made all the sweeter by the opportunity to put one over ex-boss Tommy Taylor (again) and the increasing number of toilers that he'd attracted down the M11 at our expense.

The only blemishes on our early form were a couple of incidents that in hindsight would haunt us for the rest of the season. First, an opening day reverse at Scarborough, where despite out-playing the home side, a phrase incorporating the words 'cow's', 'arse' and 'banjo' springs to mind when describing our efforts in front of goal. The second concerned the Fizzy-Pop where, despite having the better of the Baggies, some incredulously dodgy refereeing put paid to any thoughts of a cup-run.

It would be tempting to suggest that as the first autumnal blasts swept across the Wembley of the Fens, so the second part of the prophecy was beginning to come true. Who were we trying to kid? With Di still fresh in the ground, Barnet, themselves smarting from a 5-1 thrashing at the hands of P*sh, were cast as sacrificial victims. Trouble was the Bees hadn't read the script and proceeded to give us a right old tonking. With the Abbey Kop heaping abuse on ex-scummer Clown Charlery, you can guess who opened the scoring...

Now there are certain incidents that occur at football matches that make you realise that it is after all only a game. One occurred in the following home encounter with Cardiff. Hanging-on for grim death to a 2-1 lead, our right-back Ben Chenery went in with his head where most people wouldn't. The pathetic sight of his body stretched out on the turf, coupled by the reactions of the other players and the sense of urgency being expressed by the club's doctor left many thinking the worst. Visibly shaken, the U's tried to hold out, but conceded a late equaliser - a day though where the result was purely secondary...

From then on it was downhill. By the beginning of November we were circling amongst the deadmen (with fulsome apologies to any Doncaster and Brighton fans who may be reading). We also discovered that contrary to popular belief in this the era of Bosman and freedom of contract, most 'free transfers' are - and let's not beat about the bush here - other clubs' rejects. And whilst there have been those who have grasped the nettle of a second (or third) chance, there have been more than a few that have seen United more as a respite on the downward spiral to oblivion...

Unfortunately, despite playing with five at the back (we were by now employing full-backs who needed a route map as soon as they approached the half-way line), the manager was proving rather reluctant in recalling the fans' favourite, Matty Joseph. There was a school of thought that sided with the manager - the argument being that if the player wouldn't sign a contract then he shouldn't be picked. This line of thought was shot down in flames when it was discovered that the *manager* had yet to agree a contract! With the club going 14 games without a win, a record on par with some of our less than halcyon times, the fact that the manager had somewhat forgotten to put pen to paper lead to a clamouring from certain quarters for his head.

Somewhat bizarrely we terminated this run with a 3-2 extra-time victory over Plymouth in the FA Cup, and this after being two down at half-time. This match will live long in the memory if only for a truly eccentric goal from

Trevor Benjamin. As the Plymouth goalkeeper and ex-Abbey favourite Jon Sheffield went to clear a ball in the box, he was somewhat distracted by six foot plus of brick shit-house bearing down on him at an extremely fast rate of knots. Now 'our' Jon has never quite been the same since he suffered a broken leg at the hands (or should that be feet?) of an overzealous forward, and has since that day been tied to his goal-line by a rather over-taut bungee... The result? 'Sheff' bottles it and weakly toe-pokes his clearance into Trev's looming bulk. The ball arced through the air into the net... We couldn't decide whether to cheer the goal or piss ourselves with laughter!

This all led rather nicely to a pretty juicy week at the start of December. P*sh, themselves riding high in the league (but hey, what did we care, we knew that they'd blow it), away, followed by a rather tasty-looking home cup tie against non-league neighbours, Stevenage. And so on a bitterly cold Tuesday, the Amber Army decamped to Cripple Sidings Lane - more in hope than expectation, it has to be said. For 70 minutes we more than held our own. In fact we made them look distinctly average (wags might suggest that we dragged them down to our level, for in truth, average is most definitely what we were). Then, in one of those bizarre tactical switches that often left us all exaspered, the U's decided to rest on their laurels... Off the hook, the scum pushed forward and scraped the win - we trooped off dejected. P*sh fans have to quickly learn how to count up to two - the number of times in the past decade that they've managed to beat us...

Last season, I berated the bane that is a lower division supporter's lot - abysmal and inconsistent refereeing. Our second cup tie of the season also hinged on a couple of highly dubious decisions from the man in black. Never mind the fact that we were awful, only salvaging a replay in the dying minutes. However, the talking point was the truly diabolical performance of a Mr Brian Coddington of Sheffield. Should you be purusing your matchday programme and note his name amongst the lists of officials be afraid... Be *very* afraid. First he managed to award the visitors a penalty that he alone amongst the 22 players and near 5,000 crowd saw. With United getting nowhere and Stevenage living up to their description of non-league cloggies, Mr Coddington, after 70 minutes of not affording our by now somewhat battered forward line any protection, decided to even-up the score by sending off one of their players after Big Trev had lost his footing. This was only a taste of things to come...

The replay at a packed Broadhall Way and United were cruising 1-0. Enter Mr Coddington, who in the space of a bizarre ten-minute spell managed to reduce our outfield contingency from 11 to nine. Despite bravely playing with three up for the entire second-half, sheer weight of numbers finally told - setting the scene for Stevenage's media spat with the Geordies... The only positive postscript was that it is with great credit that thanks not only to the U's bitterly dejected, but good natured, supporters, coupled with the sympathetic policing of Hertfordshire's finest and United's own stewards, that a potentially volatile situation was defused...

And that was the season over and it wasn't even Christmas! To his credit, McFarland knew this and used the second-half of the proceedings to forge a style of play for the new campaign. To our credit, for the most part, the fans were behind this move. We eventually abandoned the wing-back formation, a double-edged sword really, since although we were now generally tighter at the back, it meant that there was no place in the team for Fozzie - arguably the division's most cultured defender.

Now no-one in the Third Division could have failed to be moved by the plight of Doncaster Rovers, if only for the thought of 'there but for the grace of God'. Their visit to the Abbey saw them not only comprehensively out-play us for the first half, but go a goal up, which was greeted with wild applause by the Abbey faithful. Unfortunately, United turned into party-poopers by scoring twice in the second-half. However, Rovers will forever have a place in our hearts - if only for the fact that their following midweek game saw them pick up their first win away from home - against Scum at Cripple Sidings Lane.

Now the visit of Rovers had seen the *Rabbit* publicise the second 'Heart of Football' day, and our Friday night game against Lincoln (oh, the joys of Satellite TV) was to have seen a massive balloon release. Well, in a way it did, except it was a shame that the 1000-odd balloons that we'd organised to give away with the fanzine were, erm, 30 miles away. Still, the *Rabbit*, the balloons and around a dozen or so U's fans made the journey the following day down to Priestfield, where we joined fans from the length and breath of the country in lending our support to highlight the plight of both Doncaster and Brighton. Unfortunately, in a world increasingly gripped by the failed spectre of free-market economics, it is this author's fear that events such as those organised by supporters to highlight the ills of *our* game are going to become far more commonplace...

Given the air of gloom that surrounds this end of term report, it would be nice to end on an up-beat note. However, events at Ninian Park prevent even that wish. Already subdued by the moronic racist chanting from a section of the Cardiff crowd, United supporters were then gobsmacked to hear some friendly advice towards our players from one of *our* 'supporters' (although I hesitate to use the word). I'm as guilty as the next for not standing up and confronting said individual and his mates - (I'm not exactly photogenic - but I've kind of gotten attached to my looks!) - but the incident did at least awaken the public at large from their complacency. With the assistance of the 'Kick-It' and 'Show Racism the Red Card' campaigns, the *Rabbit* helped leaflet the next home game in an effort to raise awareness of the racism issue and hopefully this depressing incident will never occur again...

Still, roll on August 8th. The new season awaits and hope springs eternal... PLEASE!

THE ADAMS FAMILY

Wycombe Wanderers

It's an oft-mooted point that no matter how awful the reality of your club's season, at least on day one you're in the same situation as everybody else. True, it may not last more than a month, but at least that month glows with a certain joy until the rain sets in, flushing your heroes into soccer's sewer for another year at least.

A month did I say? Try 45 minutes - for that was all it took for the realisation to dawn that Wycombe's '97-98 season was unlikely to be radically different from the previous relegation-threatened crap-fest. Four-nil down to Wigan at half-time, heat-induced chef's arse, and being statistically the worst team in the Football League are cruelties beyond even those that Bernard Matthews inflicted on a nation of turkeys back in the eighties.

THE ADAMS FAMILY

THE FINAL ISSUE OF WYCOMBE'S NUMBER ONE FANZINE
ISSUE 32 APRIL 1998 - SORRY IT'S £1

BIGGEST EVER ISSUE

But to paraphrase the words of the song that Peter Mandelson once grooved to like an ecstasy-chomping mannequin, things could only get better, and they certainly did, with Wanderers storming up the charts to number three before finding reverse gear and familiar residence in the outskirts of relegation world.

It's fair to say that Vanessa Feltz is a prettier sight than Wycombe's league form of last season, but if that's the case then our general cup form was positively Fatima Whitbread, complete with a John Merrick of a performance in the FA Cup against Basingstoke. And being a cynical old wretch, I shall start the detail with this diabolical saga.

Of course, being a former non-league side, we are fully conversant with the odd shock result against the puffed-up ego-play of Football League sides, but even that was no preparation for losing after a replay to a side in the bottom three of the Ryman's Premier League.

After a rank showing at Adams Park earned a 2-2 draw, confidence had been high for the replay. Manager John Gregory sneered about Basingstoke having had their 15 minutes of fame, completely forgetting that under him and the previous joker Alan Smith, Wanderers' away form showed all the danger of a speeding milkfloat. And thus we travelled to Hampshire, performing so poorly that come extra time the team were without question hanging on for penalties. But if that in itself wasn't shameful enough, they conspired to cock that up too - thus ensuring that the traditional saviour of a poor season - the cup run - was no longer an option.

The real tragedy of this, though, was that no supporter really seemed overly bothered by the result. Indeed, the mood was one of resigned comedy on leaving the ground. At least, one thought, our motley collection of higher-league failures would be enduring a (medium) rare roasting from Gregory, and would at last realise that past associations count for precisely fuck-all in football. Therefore, when the team coach was spotted lurching along the A404, at the very least I expected to see a sober scene of repentant professionals...

Why am I still surprised that this humble landscape was in fact a picture of cards, joviality and waggish banter? Well clearly I've learned nothing about the modern professional, who takes vast sums of money for often hugely ineffective performances, whilst cribbing and moaning at any supporter who doesn't play the game and massage his fragile ego. And if Second Division professionals haven't got the sense to realise that a bit of humility is required after losing to an assortment of milkmen, posties and lollipop men (possibly), then that's their problem and not ours.

Of course there were brighter days, and none more so than in the matches when youth team manager Neil Smillie took over from Gregory, who left to perform a remarkable resuscitation act on the corpse formerly known as Aston Villa. There was utter joy after the 5-1 demolition of Plymouth that virtually secured our position for another season, and while the future will never exactly look bright at Wycombe - as long as we have a financial director who seems to take masochistic pride in telling all and sundry that there is NO money for transfers - Smillie's championing of hopefully hungry youth is the one prospect we have.

Utter joy however was one ingredient sadly missing when Wanderers lost 2-1 to local rivals Watford early in the season. This time though, it had nothing to do with the football (although a draw would've been nice), but the appalling scenes at Vicarage Road when Britain's newly-appointed 'Minister of Emotional Responses' Elton John took his seat the day after singing that dirge about 'England's Rose' at Grief-Fest '97™.

Now this is without doubt the wrong place to get involved in discussing you-know-who and the hysterics that followed, but by failing to rise up and salute the puffed-up, wig-bearing chairman of THE OPPOSITION, I feel I have an idea of what it's like to be a bigamist on *The Jerry Springer Show*. As Elton grinned and waved at the universal salivation, one became aware that if Wycombe dared to deny a Watford victory, Reggie would burst into yet more heartfelt tears and the nation would march to Adams Park with the sole purpose of burning it to the ground. It felt like we'd all paid twelve quid for the dubious honour of cheering up Elton. Still, She was The People's Princess and no doubt it's what She would have wanted.

For the first time ever, we at *TAF* had some success with our campaigns, none more so than when money-grubbing turncoat Mickey Bell returned to Adams Park with Bristol City. With tears dried and brows un-furrowed, it seems churlish to deny that the Bell-boy made the right move for his career, but every football fan must sometimes reserve the right to be a bloody-minded irrational madman, and it was with this in mind that we developed our own special welcome for Mickey.

Unfortunately (or should that be fortunately), our poster campaign for the occasion (head shots of Bell with either SHAME / JUDAS / CHARLATAN or MONEY GRABBER printed alongside), was heavily trailed in the local press, resulting in Safety Officer Frank Knowles sending out stewards to remove them in case they provoked a riot! And if that wasn't enough to qualify for over-reaction of the decade, the offending posters were handed over to Thames Valley Police as, ahem, 'evidence'! Rather predictably, the incitement to riot charges have failed to drop through the PO Box, although an irate Luton Town fan wrote to the local rag to suggest, in the light of grim events at the Gillingham v Fulham encounter, that our antics could have caused a risk to life; posing the question, what do they put in the water up in Bedfordshire?

Campaign number two saw *TAF* get right behind reserve 'keeper Brian Parkin, whose comical outings had been restricted to nil by the signing of Derby's Martin Taylor (who was often just as comical, but somehow managed to win the Player of the Year award). Taylor was suspended for the away trip to York City, and so an advert was published in the fanzine with the legend, 'It's not Darren Day, or Brian May, 'cos Saturday November 8th is BRIAN DAY'. Furthermore the advert implored the travelling public to wave clean sheets on the terraces to help Brian in his quest to keep one of these rare commodities. Naturally, we were just joshing (and space filling) and were shocked to the core on arriving at York to find a couple of sheets being waved around by some fine individuals with a lot more bottle than ourselves. Naturally, John Gregory got into a bit of a froth about it in the following Tuesday's paper, saying it was (yawn) "cruel and not the way to support a player." But was it worse than inflicting that Basingstoke show on us, Johnny? And should we really shed tears for a man who for two years received a handsome wage and a sponsored car despite being, shall we say, an utter goon?

And so to the future. Undoubtedly everyone in Division Two will be relishing the encounters with Joe Royle's 'Dogs of Shite'. Wanderers fans however will be awaiting another fixture with even keener anticipation - a meeting with those wretched dustbin dwellers Colchester United. The history between Wycombe and this weeping sore of a football team runs too deeply to explain fully here (an academic textbook might just do the job some day, and we're up for commissioning), but the hatred stems from the early nineties when Martin O'Neill was on his way to Deity status, and U's manager Roy McDoughnut was struggling with the complexities of decimal currency, which had only recently replaced bartering and fist-fighting in Essex as a means of trading. Whatever else happens, this is the game we dare not lose.

Finally, I'd like to close by mentioning that after six decent years, this fanzine will be no more for the new season, partly because the same joke looks a tad worn after 20 re-workings, and perhaps because the joy that was Wycombe has been partly discoloured by a surly, humourless, money-fixated beast that seems to think that a dopey mascot and some marketing chat is what football is all about. In fact, it's about winning and entertaining - and when that doesn't happen it's about ranting, moaning, debating and cursing. But perhaps most importantly, it's about caring enough to indulge in these activities. For it's my guess that when the inevitable meltdown comes, the 'pain in the arse' supporters and their money will be the only ones left.

Karel Poborsky finally finds something he's good at

Source: Another Vintage Liverpool Performance

ALL ABOARD THE WAGON TRAIN

Leyton Orient

"Blessed are those who expect nothing, for they shall not be disappointed." Not quite the Sermon on the Mount admittedly, but Barry Hearn's Season Of No Excuses could not have been further from that quotation if it had tried. Of *course* we expected something. We were fed spoonfuls of hype until we could swallow no more and were led to believe that the 11 brave soldiers who would step onto the delicious Brisbane Road turf on August 9th would bring unparalleled and unprecedented glory to this corner of London.

The signs were good. Dead wood was out, replaced with the young saplings of spring (don't blame me, the doctor gave me these tablets). In came £1/4m rated Dean Smith from Hereford, snapped up for a bargain £42,500, followed by Peterborough's Simon Clark (£20,000), made famous for having a cup of tea thrown at him by Barry Fry in the documentary, and on the eve of the season, our very own Lionheart in the form of free transfer Stuart 'psycho' Hicks. With last term's loan signings Paul Hyde and Carl Griffiths fully signed up and young winger Dave Morrison showing promise in the friendlies, everything looked (particularly through my own metaphorical glasses) rosy.

The warm-up games consisted of the usual defeats at the hands of non-league sides (Supporter of other club: "what do you mean, usual?") and two prestigious home friendlies against Arsenal and Spurs. Both drew capacity crowds and record gate receipts, and both were lost 1-0. Although there were high points, especially the kicking of David Ginola by most of our side and nearly scoring on a number of occasions against Arsenal (look, it was ten months ago, you can't expect me to remember everything).

So anyway, the season kicked off (what an appropriately used pun) with a home defeat against Cardiff City. Within four minutes Morrison was ruled out for the entire season with a terrible leg injury. The Coca-Cola Cup followed with a 4-2 aggregate mauling of Brighton, affectionately known as 'the scum' in E10 since their unprovoked attack on four of our players at the end of the

the orient fanzine that can see Wembley in the distance

ORIENT FANS STEAL ALL THE LIFEBOATS

SOUTHEND AND BRENTFORD GET THAT SINKING FEELING

OFFICIAL SPONSORS OF JASON HARRIS

ISSUE 13   50p   April 1998

previous season. This really was sweet, especially when followed up with a 1-0 win at their, sorry Gillingham's, ground the Saturday after. These games were interspersed with a loss at Scunthorpe where Steve Hodge played his one game for us and became the fourth international from the '86 World Cup squad to turn out in red after Shilton, Martin and Wilkins had done so in 1997.

We had some fun at Donny, winning 4-1 on a wet Tuesday evening. After going one down, Simon Clark headed a hat-trick and Super Carl Griffiths (Super is actually his legal first name) got the goals. Poor old Donny, they were so short of stewards that some enterprising O's donned the yellow coats and saw the game for free!

There followed an inconsistent run of form mainly due to a lack of goals from anyone except Griff, but the return to the side of Alex Inglethorpe in midfield helped to ease worries. Crowd favourite, and the man this fanzine got its wedge out to sponsor, Scott McGleish, was flogged to Barnet for £70k and replaced with Jason Harris (known as 'the Roadrunner' due to him being the fastest creature on the planet).

The undisputed highlight of the month, and possibly the season, was a 4-4 draw at Bolton's Reebok Stadium in the Coca-Cola Cup. It really was an amazing game and all 272 O's fans present will remember it for many a year. First, we thought we'd sing the whole 90 minutes without stopping. The players responded to the noise and took an early lead through, who else, but Mr C. Griff-meister. They equalised soon after but goals from Ingles and a magnificent 25-yard free kick from Joe Baker saw us go 3-2 up. Then they got a disputed penalty but a fourth from Mark 'only three more years till the testimonial' Warren levelled it up in the dying moments, much to the delight of his dad sitting amongst the away contingent. A small pause for thought here. A fellow away supporter, a friend who'd broken his ankle the week before while celebrating our equaliser at Swansea, was ejected after our third goal for dropping his crutch. Their stewards deemed that he was throwing it at Bolton fans, sitting at least 50 yards away. Football gone mad? Still, he can at least say he's seen us win at Bolton!

The dreaded FA Cup first round had us paired with Ryman League side Hendon. We crammed into their tiny ground and took the lead twice, only to be pegged back on both occasions. Boss Tommy Taylor and under-achieving players such as Naylor and Hanson took some serious abuse. We always knew we'd lose the replay; they had one attempt all night and scored with it. But Jimmy, as I always say, you've got to take your chances in this game. Quite.

A Tuesday away trip to Darlington (thanks, Mr fixture computer) marked the halfway point of the season. This was the worst O's performance I could remember; never had I seen a more inept side put so little effort in. Yet, more or less, it was the same side who'd already turned in some great performances and achieved creditable results. At this stage we had bugger all to show for our efforts. Sure our defence was pretty sound, Martin Ling was running the midfield and you could always rely on Carl for a goal or two, but there was no killer instinct, no cutting edge and sometimes there was no will to win.

Hearn was behind Taylor, but many suspected he was wielding a knife. In fact TT did a bit of his own wielding as Colin West, our hero of two years ago, was sent packing after nearly 50 goals for the club. With Griff's form he hadn't had a look-in since August and being the wrong side of 30, apparently had little future with us. The faithful could look back and salute his service to the club whilst admitting that it was time for both him and us to turn over a new leaf in our Orient books (I told you, it's these tablets).

Then came the return against Doncaster. How can an 8-0 win be crap? Never before have I seen such a poor side. OK we did play well but the fact that all our goals came within a 45-minute spell shows how many it could have been. However, 8-0 is just the sort of result Lord Barry looks for as he moves his express train of marketing and publicity onto the next stop. The next stop in this case happened to be Dean Court on a typical winter's evening for an AutoWindscreens second round tie. Needless to say, we fielded four fringe players and rested our key men for the promotion push. Result: 2-0, but at least it was free to get in - take note Baz. (Our last home game in the competition saw full price admission and an embarrassing attendance of 933 for a local derby).

The customary win over Brighton with two goals from Simmo was followed by a win at Rochdale and a 2-2 away at Exeter, a match overshadowed by a disgraceful challenge by Paul Williams on our 'keeper Hyde. He was ruled out for six months and to make things worse, they scored from the resulting loose ball. Simon Clark headed his fifth of the season with five minutes left to level it up, but this proved to be a bad move. You see, over the next couple of months our results just about kept us in with a sniff of the play-offs but our fate was sealed when the FA disciplinary committee, in its infinite wisdom, deducted three of our points for fielding ineligible players. What actually happened was that the then Secretary, Dave Burton, cleverly forgot to tell Tommy Taylor and Paul Clark that Clark, Hicks and Warren were all due to be suspended for the Exeter away game. When Clarky equalised in said game, some jobsworth from the Exeter press thought they'd see if they could disqualify the goal and hey presto, they struck gold. The local rags from the towns of our play-off rivals then joined in and, despite the players serving their suspensions anyway, we were said to have deliberately cheated.

It'll be funny the next time these small clubs want our help against the big boys and Hearn turns round and sticks two fingers up at them. So to the last game and we were on a hat-trick. The hat-trick of messing up everyone else's promotion push. We'd beaten Barnet, taken a point at Layer Road and now we had to send the 2,000 Torquay fans home crying in their Badger Juice.

Craig Maskell gave us the lead with a stunning volley from outside the box and Dean Smith got his fifth penalty and tenth goal in total (first O's defender since Kevin Hales to do so) to put us two up. I was especially happy when this goal went in as I'd boasted to my Premiership supporting friends that we'd have the highest scoring defender in the country (I didn't tell them he played midfield for half the year!). They got one back, but ha ha, we'd confined them to another year in the basement. Sorry Helen Chamberlain - does this mean you won't invite us back onto your show? We ended the season four points shy of the play-offs with a better goal difference and having scored more goals than Barnet, who scraped in. So, if only we'd conceded one less last minute goal and Burton had remembered to tell Taylor of the suspensions, we'd have been in the lottery. But supporting a team like Orient is full of 'if only's'...

Throughout the season we kept the nucleus of a very good side. Strong at the back (99 bookings testifies to this!), creative in midfield with Martin Ling orchestrating things (PFA team of the year) and powerful up front with Griff (22 goals - the Welsh cap is on the horizon). With Hydie back in goal and the excellent signing of Matthew Joseph to play at right back, our defensive unit will be complete once we add a left back (what about the Torquay geezer?).

Wim Walschaerts' midfield strength compliments Lingy's craft, and Dave Morrison will return. Add to that Alex Inglethorpe, Joe Baker, Kwame Ampadu and Paul Raynor to keep them on their toes and you have a good midfield. Maskell has been signed to play with Griff and meep-meep Harris provides good cover, as does Colin Simpson.

Perhaps the last few pieces of the Orient jigsaw are falling into place. Can we at last look forward with genuine optimism? Will I need to keep taking the tablets? Will we win the league? Will Elvis be found alive and well in the Main Enclosure? Will Baby Spice give me a massage? Let's hope the answers to all these questions, and more, are a resounding 'yes'!

AMBER NECTAR

Hull City

"That goal against Hull City? We'd forgotten what to do when we scored a goal."

That quote, surprise surprise, came from a Donny Rovers fan during an end of season TV documentary about the demise of the forlorn South Yorkshireman. The Tigers had finally arrived. After 94 years of trying, Hull City had reached rock bottom.

But when Donny beat us on their journey through hell in April, it was a far cry from the heady days of August when, without a ball of the new season having been kicked, it felt special to be a Hull City fan once again...

The Needler regime had finally been deposed, David Lloyd

8OP AMBER NECTAR

THE INDEPENDENT HULL CITY FANZINE #2

I was misquoted, y'see, what I said was 'the people of Hull are CARP - meaning they're akin to precious freshwater fish and a prize catch. Really. No, honest!'

LLOYD SETS THE RECORD STRAIGHT

and Tim Wilby had arrived with their mega-milllions and ambitious plans of sporting glory, Mark Hateley had replaced Dolan and the pre-season friendlies - which were watched by crowds twice last season's average - had suggested it *was* possible to turn donkeys into racehorses.

With every last ticket snapped up we sailed to Mansfield on the crest of a wave, eager to see the home side become lambs to the slaughter. But immediately, the bubble burst. The Stags scored twice and the Tigers were lucky to get nil. And we got nil in the next game, and the next, and the next... We were bottom of the league. But no-one was unduly worried; it was going to take time to sort things out with the take-over having only just happened, there were new players to be brought in, the dust needing to settle and all that.

Actually, the take-over seemed to take an age. Wilby had hoped to be in charge before the end of the previous term, but it all dragged on long enough for Fish and Dolan to give each and every out-of-contract player a one-year deal, despite the fact we'd just suffered the worst season in our entire history. It was a spiteful parting gift that was to tie Mark Hateley's hands for the whole campaign. Late in June, Wilby appeared like a pop star in front of a rapturous packed audience to tell of he and his partner

David Lloyd's sky-reaching plans for City and rugby neighbours Hull Sharks. We would be super teams playing in a brand new super stadium. City would have a big name manager with money to spend and we would be out of the Third Division first go.

But the I's weren't dotted and the T's not crossed, and as the players reported back for training they were greeted not by Wilby, but by former chairman Fish and his failure in command Dolan. 'HE'S BACK' was the headline as Dolan's chin filled nearly the whole of the front page of the local rag, but we only had another week to wait before the take-over was finally sealed and delivered. Out went Dolan and in came Atilla as Wilby delivered promise number one. From day one, Hateley signalled his intentions for City to play entertaining attacking football, and hurrah for that. It was wonderful in theory, but a shock to a team used to playing with nine across the back that they had to pass the ball to each other rather than boot it towards the halfway line.

Played four, won none, scored none, but at least some of the football was nice! To date Hateley's only new face was Scott Thompson who put the Scottish back into Scottish goalkeeper, though he was certainly not helped by the atrocious defence in front of him. The season kick-started with an extra-time win over Macclesfield in the Coca-Cola Cup, inspired by new face Glyn Hodges - yes *that* Glyn Hodges - who on his return from Honk Kong looked fat, lazy, and yet still a class above. Four days later came our first league win, but the Tigers had to score seven to make sure of victory as Swansea got four. It sounded a classic, but it was simply two shit defences - theirs unlocked at will by Hodges.

As Hodges hit the treatment table City failed to score again until a scrambled goal gave us a slender first leg lead over Premiership Crystal Palace in round two of the Coca-Cola. A day later City dropped a bombshell as they announced Tim Wilby had been relieved of his duties as chairman. It had been increasingly apparent that things behind the scenes were not as hunky-dory as we thought: ex-rugby league star Wilby had breezed into Hull giving everyone the impression he was a very rich man with unrivalled ambition. Ambitious yes, but a man with ideas above his station, as it later turned out he was in fact a caretaker on a council estate in London.

It was now evident that David Lloyd was pulling the strings. Wilby was just an agent acting on Lloyd's behalf, even though he seemed to have been given almost complete freedom to do as he wished at the helm of the club. Along with Hateley and his assistant Billy Kirkwood, Wilby had appointed a whole host of managing directors, commercial directors, executive directors, marketing managers... all of whom spent a couple of months at the club doing next to nothing before being despatched by Lloyd's henchman and new chief executive Mike Appleton.

The fact that weeks later Wilby would be found working in a bar in downtown Sydney illustrated exactly how happy Lloyd had been with the way his one-time partner had been running the club. How and why Wilby and Lloyd ever got together to take over our football club remains a mystery to this day.

Of all the new appointments only Hateley and Kirkwood remained and there was optimism that once Appleton had sorted out the mess left by Wilby, the duo would at last receive the backing they needed to get the Tigers out of Division Three. Two more league defeats came and went before the return leg at Selhurst where we lost again, 2-1 after extra time. However the Tigers had mauled the Eagles on away goals to set up a dream trip to Newcastle, thanks to our guardian angel in white - Steve Wilson - who by now had replaced Thompson in goal.

Then we signed David Rocastle - yes *that* David Rocastle - on loan from Chelsea in time for a home game with Scarborough, and he was immediately on the mark in a 3-0 win. Rocky was a class apart, and with new signing Matt Hocking and loanee Chris Bettney from Sheffield United shining bright, plus the possibility that Hodges and Hateley himself might one day return from injury, the new boss was beginning to build a side seemingly capable of going places.

So to Newcastle we went, with Gallowgate witnessing its largest travelling support in over 20 years. The Geordies in their wisdom decided to keep all Tigers fans on the coaches until after the game kicked off (and of course it wouldn't be the last time *that* particular club was to prove it no longer gives a shit about the fans). We did ourselves proud though, losing only 2-0, with injury-plagued Hateley making just his fourth - and last - start of the campaign, coming closest with a long range diving header.

Back in the league Rocastle came in for some very heavy treatment, notably at Barnet, Darlington and most savagely at Cardiff where the referee - I left my programme in a Cardiff night-club so I can't tell you his name - reinvented the word 'inept'.

The football was generally good, excellent at times when Hodges and Rocky were around, but wins were few and far between. No matter how many we scored, the opposition got just one more, apart from Shrewsbury who thrashed us 4-1 at home. Oh, and Hednesford who knocked us out of the FA Cup.

Rocastle, like Hodges, missed as many games as he played during his stay and the pair managed only one full game together. That came in a 3-1 thrashing of Colchester, and on the back of a 3-0 win over Donny (and almost a win at Hartlepool - Hateley waved his crutches angrily at the referee after the home team equalised three days into injury time). City looked set for a successful Christmas period and maybe a shot at the play-offs.

But we lost all our festive season games and the injured Rocastle went back to Chelsea. There was a brief high point at Millmoor where Hodges shrugged off his Christmas hangover (the most popular explanation as to why he missed the Boxing Day game) and masterfully orchestrated a near fight-back from 1-5 to 4-5, scoring twice and trampling several Rotherham players in his wake as the tried to unlace his boots.

At the turn of the year we were back in the bottom four, albeit with one of the best 'goals for' columns in the division. But Hodges was injured again and it was a month before we got another goal - on his return against Peterborough who we hammered 3-1. It was to be the Welsh wizard's last game before he moved to Nottingham Forest. What would we do without him? Lose was the answer, 1-0 at Lincoln and notoriously 2-0 at home to Rochdale.

There had been for some time an underlying feeling that things were far from right at the club. Apart from £20,000 for Hocking, Hateley didn't received a single penny to buy new players. Since Christmas the popular rumour was that Atilla had been banned from coaching the players in an effort to force his resignation. By all accounts, our players weren't even seeing a ball in training, as a fitness instructor from the rugby league club put them through their paces on the road and in the gym. This coincided with a period which saw City take just four points from 27.

The Rochdale game was a watershed. For once, Lloyd was at the game and even before the final whistle, supporters were saying the horror show was deliberately for his benefit, words that Lloyd himself was to echo in the post-match press conference. He called a meeting of the manager and players at which he told them exactly what he expected of them in terms of effort and fitness. Allegedly, one player offered to take charge of Lloyd's Davis Cup tennis team, if a fitness instructor could run a Football League team!

Whereas it hadn't been the showdown meeting everyone had expected, the air seemed to clear somewhat, though the next game was a 5-1 thrashing at Torquay. But there was a win round the corner - our first without either Rocastle or Hodges came at home against Scunthorpe to give us a healthy 13 point cushion over Doncaster and any worries of Conference football next year were allayed.

With loan player Steve Boyack teaming up with former Rangers mate Brian McGinty and inspirational skipper Warren Joyce in midfield, City were playing some decent football again, but the lack of power and know-how up front meant points were hard to come by. However, we were maintaining our cushion over the beleaguered Doncaster. Results were coincidental as we were all looking forward to next season when Hateley, who now appeared to have more of an understanding with Lloyd, could have a good clear-out and get together the team *he* wanted.

Then came April 4th. A win at Donny would confirm our safety, and over a thousand City fans turned out for a party. But you know the story: utter humiliation. Patience snapped and the players were left in no doubt as to the fans' feelings. It was just a shame David Lloyd wasn't there. We then took ten points form the last 15 to finish comfortably ahead in our mini-championships with the Rovers and Brighton. Another loan player David Brown from Manchester United teamed up with a revitalised and in-form Duane Darby to give us some presence in attack and some excellent football left us frustrated at what could have been.

On the other hand, it gave us some cause to look forward to next year. Hateley has released all but five of his players and is assembling his new squad. He has remained a popular figure with the majority on the terraces, and hopefully the time is coming when he can be properly judged. The trouble is David Lloyd, who gives the impression he never seems to know what he is doing. After investing some £3m in buying the club he has been more than reluctant in spending any more to try and make it successful. At first we thought Lloyd was the man who had what he takes. Now the feeling is he's bitten off more than he can chew.

A year ago the sleeping giant was stirring. It's a shame that since then though, he has never looked like waking up.

ANOTHER VIEW FROM THE TOWER

Blackpool

I've never seen the manager's office at Bloomfield Road, but I can only presume that for practical reasons it has a revolving door. In the past five seasons we've had four managers. The printers who produce the club's letterheads must be making a fortune! No sooner had the name 'Gary Megson' had a chance to dry on the club's note paper than he upped sticks and was off. The ginger whinger whose spectacular failure at Norwich had made him favourite for a career at McDonald's had been given a second chance by the Tangerines. In return, when he got the chance to pack his bucket and spade and head off down the M6 to Stockport, he was off.

**Blackpool FC Fanzine
Season 97/98 Issue 8** £1

So the annual managerial lottery got under way, and everyone from Terry Venables to Roy Race was linked with the job. Eventually, another rookie manager was chosen. Nigel Worthington, along with his number two, 'mad' Mick Hennigan, arrived at Bloomfield Road for a job he'd previously turned down. The new manager obviously had problems locating the club cheque book (which to this day I'm convinced is hidden under ex-chairman Owen Oyston's bunk while he's residing at Her Majesty's Pleasure) as new signings were few in number. The only 'name' to arrive at the club was Anton Rogan (wasn't he in *Fresh Fields* with Julia McKenzie?).

Blackpool never win their first game of the season; it's tradition. So 6,547 spectators needed artificial respiration and a long lie down after we beat those mad Hatters, Luton, on the opening day. Never mind; it wasn't long before we lost three games on the bounce and dropped 16 places in the space of 14 days. In a way, though, that remarkable fall from grace went largely unnoticed due to our 'Giant-killing' act in the Coca-Cola Cup. We're usually out of the aforementioned before most kids have gone back to school, but this year we were drawn against Manchester Pitiful. City at the time were going through one of their managerial crises (yeah I realise we could be talking about any time in the last 20 years here). After 240 minutes of football, it was all even, so City's expensive and experienced squad came up against 'Pool's cheap and cheerful team in a penalty shoot-out. It was like Arnold Schwarzenegger with his 52 barrel shotgun taking on John Wayne with his Colt 45. In the end though, it's not the size of your weapon that counts (ask John Bobbit), it's what you do with it. Sure enough, City's £3 million signing Lee Bradbury (stop sniggering at the back) launched the ball in to the night sky never to be seen again, leaving midfield maestro Mickey Mellon to slot the ball home for a fine Blackpool win. The next chapter of 'Pool's Coca-Cola Cup exploits is too painful to remember. Let's just say that Coventry must have given referee Mike Read the freedom of the town after he gifted them two unbelievable penalties (glad to see the tosser's given up refereeing and gone back to Albert Square though).

Mickey the Maestro headed off to Tranmere soon after that, and the idiot forgot to close the door behind him, allowing an escape route for James 'I'm so poor and hard done by I have to bleed my heart out to a national football magazine' Quinn (who went to West Brom) and the King of Bloomfield Road, Sir Tony 'there's only one...' Ellis, who made a shock move to Bury. Still, Nigel Worthington had the backing of the fans and when the Milltown Hillbillies from Burnley paid us a visit we were enjoying the start of our mid-table mediocrity. Chris Twaddle and his bunch of losers were bouncing nicely along the bottom of the table when they gifted us our annual three points, and six weeks later Gary 'P45' Peters brought over the lily-livered whites from Dungdale to deliver an early Xmas present for the Seasiders.

Thank heavens for Matthews and Mortenson. If it hadn't have been for them in 1953, Blackpool would still have the burden of having to win the FA Cup looming over them each year. As it is though, we've got our name on the cup and so we rarely attempt to get past the first round. After being knocked out by Hednesford Town in the previous campaign, we hoped to go one better by allowing Blyth Spartans a second round place. Things were going well at half time when we were 2-1 down, but the players obviously had a rush of blood and ended up winning 4-3. Still, four weeks later, we offered our scalp to Oldham Athletic who gratefully accepted, and that was the end of another cup run (well, cup dribble may be more appropriate). In the Windscreen Wipers Cup we enjoyed a spectacular 10-9 penalty shoot-out victory against York (our goalie scoring the winner), but obviously the whiff of fish in Grimsby proved too potent for the boys and we narrowly escaped having to go to Wembley when we were knocked out in the semi's.

By January, the balloons and streamers that decked out the Tangerine Club on New Year's Eve were given another airing as we celebrated our end of season party. We'd secured a mid-table position and nothing could budge us, our progress chart towards the end resembling that of a dying patient. That twelfth position in the league was ours and we weren't about to surrender it to anyone! With the departures of Mellon, Quinn and Ellis, Blackpool became a home for on-loan players. As if the Oyston family hadn't had enough trials, Bloomfield Road hosted its own version of a cross between *New Faces* and *Opportunity Knocks* as triallists and loanees alike filled our first 11 (personally I think it was a clever ploy to get us to buy the club programme, just so we knew who was playing). Fortunately, we hit the jackpot (one would hope more by judgement than luck) when local lad John Hills (who we'd let slip through our fingers by selling him once before) came on loan from Everton. Howard Kendall was obviously preoccupied the day we asked if we could buy him, as he remarkably let this gem of a player return to Blackpool. Greg Strong from Bolton soon became a fans' favourite, but had to return after three spells on loan (well let's face it, who'd want to play at the lovely new Reebok Stadium when you could come to Bombsite Road!). At the time of writing he's just been offered a three year deal and fingers are tightly crossed on the Fylde Coast.

The season ended with a whimper; a victory against Scumley at Turd Moor sadly not enough to send them in to oblivion and the end of season 'thriller' against Chesterfield just about summed it all up. In the annual Blackpool lottery to see who stayed and who went, Andy Preece and Dave Linighan were the remarkable losers, despite protest from the fans, as they were given a complimentary book of Pleasure Beach rides and shown the door. Sadly, Chris Malkin wasn't eligible for this year's lottery losers' draw but I'm looking forward to his balls being pulled out next May (even the donkeys on Blackpool beach say he gives them a bad name!).

Our goalkeeper Stevie Banks has once again won the *AVFTT* Player of the Year award, with bouquets going out to John Hills, Phil Clarkson and Andy Preece. The aforementioned Malkin received the 'George Michael (You've Blown It)' award.

Every year we ask the readers of *AVFTT* what they would like to happen at Bloomfield Road in the next 12 months and every year the answer comes back: "Can we have a new ground please?" Whyndyke Farm will hopefully be our new home, but at the moment there's more chance of Paul Gascoigne opening the Betty Ford clinic annual fête than *that* happening. Promotion is still an ambition, but with big-spending teams like Man City, Reading, Stoke and Fulham in the division next year, we're already resigned to the fact that a promotion play-off place is the most we can hope for.

Amazingly, the managerial merry-go-round continues to spin at Blackpool, with the news that Norwich have approached us to talk to Nigel Worthington. The tangerine faithful will be hoping that, for once, that revolving manager's door remains motionless over summer. See you at Maine Road!

ANOTHER VINTAGE LIVERPOOL PERFORMANCE

Liverpool

AFTER watching his '96-97 Championship plans wither and die with hardly a whimper, Evans' summer capture of Ince seemed to be the statement of intent that finally showed that this nice grey-haired old man was in fact more than a nice grey-haired old man. He'd finally cottoned on to what 40,000 others had been crying out for months and signed a midfielder that could tackle. Surely this was the beginning of the end of the Championship drought and the smarting Mancs were about to be reeled in.

Yet the very fact that one was more concerned with crappy Everton's relegation conundrum on the final day, than Liverpool's trip to Derby, showed that things had hardly turned out that way. By then, everything had gone for the Reds. Third place was secure, but it didn't matter.

ANOTHER VINTAGE LIVERPOOL PERFORMANCE Only £1

Sharper than Jamie's nose tweezers   Issue 7   October 1997

FA clamp down on elephant men

THE Football Association have shocked the nation by announcing new measures to rid the Premiership of ugly players.

The new rule is designed to make Premiership football a more saleable product on the European market.

In recent years English football's popularity on the continent has waned a little and the FA cite ugly players as one of the possible reasons.

The teams worst hit by the new laws will be Everton and Manchester United.

In order to escape huge fines, Everton are to give Neville Southall an early retirement.

The first to go for the Blues though will be Slaven Bilic. He invoked the extreme ugliness clause which means he must be sent on a free transfer.

Another player to be hit by a special clause is Andy Hinchcliffe. He contravenes new chin regulations and must leave the

Cont. pg Kvarme

Craig Short thinks Everton still have a Bearsdsley or eleven

I David James

The season began with obligation replacing the expectation of the year before, which in turn had replaced optimism, somewhere down the line. This Liverpool team has had the ability to do it for some time, but it was about damn well time they went out and did it.

Yet the all too familiar pattern of recent seasons soon resurfaced. It's hard to knock Ince, but if his arrival was supposed to banish the demons of inconsistency then it failed. Once again we had an eventful nine months but still finished without any of the trophies the journos have been saying we'd win for ages. It was the usual frustrating blend of sporadic brilliance interspersed with everything but. From mediocrity to skins v whites PE class incompetence.

It turned out to be the season of stunning McManaman strikes, the overdue putting to sleep of the 3-5-2 - but continuing defensive problems, farcical attempts to buy a foreign goalkeeper, star striker drug allegations, Barry Venison acquiring a normal dress sense... and an 11 Plus candidate called Michael Owen. Benefiting from the late start to the school term, Evans pitched the prodigy straight in at the Selhurst deep end and was rewarded with a goal. The kid never looked back; and it was just as well, for behind him 'stood' the incoherent body of people loosely termed as the 'Liverpool defence.' Bahh looked like he hadn't played for a year, Rob Jones *hadn't* played for a year, Bjornebye was crossing worse than the 16 stone fatso that plays left-back for the King's Head and Kvarme looked all at sea in a rearguard struggling to cling to the flotsam anyway. At least Mark Wright looked sound, but then a disastrous September and a struggling-to-put-one-foot-in-front-of-the-other performance at Southampton and his season ended there and then. He was last seen selling *The Big Issue* around Piccadilly Circus. His disappearance paved the way for Matteo to give the defence the kind of aerial dominance that only Ronnie Corbett could envy. It was four games in before we registered our first win.

That aside, things weren't that bad. But trying to play without a defence is like trying to get pissed at a bar only selling tomato juice. Injury meant that Robbie Fowler's season began late, but when he did return he was wearing that kind of haggard look that suggested he knew his efforts would be pointless in front of a defence leakier than a Home Office civil servant.

At least Ince was rubbing off some of his aggression on nice boy Jamie Redknapp. He returned to the side in November and promptly, glory be, won two tackles. It was the start of a metamorphosis that saw one of the best long-range passers in the game have his best season in a red shirt. Up front, Macca started the season on fire. A truly incredible goal against Celtic was followed barely week later by another of almost equal Maradonnaesque brilliance, a strike that condemned Villa to their third consecutive 3-0 Anfield hammering. Villa's £7m and supposedly reformed star striker was deeply overshadowed by the mazy dribbling of the spindly one, and the kid who had to be up early next morning for his paper round, that night.

Of course, it was all another flash in the pan, another Anfield false dawn. Just as it looked like things were about to pick up we lost 2-0 at Goodison. It's more than a joke when you can't beat the laughing stock of the Premiership. But the derby served as just a prelude to one of the most inept Liverpool performances seen in recent years. The Reds went out to Strasbourg in the second round of the UEFA Cup seemingly hell-bent on damage limitation. Yet going out to defend without a defence is like going into war unarmed. The resulting 3-0 rogering, by a definitely beatable side, made a mockery of the Beautiful Game. It was a complete disaster, a shambles - worse than David Mellor's haircut - and the daggers drawn for Evans were now sharper than ever... Justifiably so.

It was good to see the home leg won in some style 2-0, but glorious failure is supposed to be the domain of teams like Stevenage in the FA Cup. Owen went some way to lifting the gloom with his first senior hat trick against Grimsby in the sugary drink cup, but losing to Barnsley at home was just appalling. If there was any consolation it was that Everton had the only fans in the country not laughing at us. The Tykes' win sent them back to where they belonged, the bottom.

Another Macca super-strike beat the team that would go on to take the title. But losing a week later to the team that everyone thought would take the title, all but condemned us to the tags of nearly men for another season. With

4-4-2 now a permanent fixture and Evans struggling with his choice of midfield widemen - alternating left footed central men Berger and Leonhardsen on both right and left because he didn't know where to put Macca - showed a lack of tactical know-how. It was almost amazing then that 1997 should end with four straight wins, including the first of three within a month against Newcastle. Macca once again scored the kind of goal that makes you wonder why he always misses from six yards.

Yet barring those successes, the new year began just as inconsistently. Take for example our FA Cup 'run' this year. A tie against a Premiership club in the third round is a little unlucky, especially when it's Coventry - a team we traditionally struggle against. However, a home tie should have ensured our progress. Unfortunately, Anfield is no longer the feared fortress it once was. We can be as welcoming as the staff at TGI Friday's, dishing out three points to crap opposition as quickly as spiteful traffic policemen who nab careless drivers in speed traps. We defended like a bunch of amateurs after a night on the piss. Credit to Coventry but we were cack.

Then, as if by magic, our form picked up again. We eased the toothless Newcastle out of the fizzy pop cup and a great goal by Michael Owen settled the final part of the Magpie trilogy during the Anfield league encounter. Stunningly, we also beat Wimbledon at Anfield on this run, a feat rarer than finding a street vendor selling a Riedle T-shirt with the German's surname spelt correctly.

After beating Middlesbrough narrowly in the first leg of the CCC semi's, we had a Wembley final in our sights. There was no way we should have let the big spending First Division club back into the tie. But Liverpool rarely perform the way they are expected to and in a crazy first five minutes we lost the game. Once again we went out to defend a narrow lead with a team incapable of doing just that.

Virtually out of the title race, we tried to salvage a Champions League spot but that aim was all but dashed against Everton. We not only dropped two points, but Robbie Fowler picked up a freak injury keeping him out of the side until Christmas. Rumours have been circulated around Anfield that the Toxteth terror is not injured, but is in fact in drugs rehabilitation recovering from addiction. This will no doubt turn out to be complete bollocks even though Robbie is the sort who could fall in that trap. Whatever, we need his goals back. Even with Michael Owen there's still room for another 30 goals in our attack.

The quest for the Champions League was not helped either by Arsenal's resurgence or by our shambolic attempts to defend. From the home defeat against Southampton in early February, up to and including the 4-1 loss at Stamford Bridge, we conceded goals in 12 consecutive games. Not the form of major trophy winners! Half way through that run we finally completed the on-off transfer of Brad Friedel who took over from David James in goal. His introduction made little difference though, proving what many already knew, that it was the blokes in front of the 'keeper that were stopping our progress.

David James had become a scapegoat, and while he has to take a large share of the blame, even Superman between the sticks would have struggled to turn us into a title winning team.

More fun and games followed at Oakwell, when we took away a 3-2 win. After being shamed by them once, you'd think we'd have been up to prove the first game was simply a fluke. But no. We went a goal down but scrambled an equaliser before half time. Then Riedle scored a cracker to put us in the lead. Then, to stack the odds further in our favour, Barnsley decided they could take us on with less than the full 11. The Liverpool of old would simply have passed the game to death, making sure they couldn't nick anything back. Ah, those were the days. Needless to say, we couldn't string two passes together, they equalised, and our best tackle was when Ince wrestled an over frenetic Tyke fan to the ground. Luckily we came through with a late Macca winner, but why we always have to make hard work of an easy job is dumfounding.

The Gods' decided Liverpool could play with a brain again in the next game, and we needed it as we were at OT. As so often happens, we outplayed the Mancs on their own patch and little Mike displayed his unbelievable pace to make the score 1-1. Everyone knows that he then lost his head and got sent off, but to us he'd had the perfect game. There was a feeling that his dismissal cost us a win, but scoring at OT, nearly crippling one of their players and frightening Peter Schmeichel to death was a great performance in my book.

Inconsistency over the final weeks of the season meant that we had nothing to play for other than pride at Derby on the last day, and there's not a lot of that in the Liverpool players at present. No, at the death, our attention switched to the Bridge and Everton's morgue.

Gone are the days when we supported Everton as our second club. Gone are the days when we just didn't care about them. True, they are a complete joke, but they're a sick joke that most Liverpool fans want to see relegated. They are turning into flukey last day escapologists. They deserved the drop so badly this year that it was desperately sad to see them get away with it... Again.

What made it worse was that Barnsley and Bolton went down instead. Both had shown character and a commitment to the right type of football far beyond anything that Everton showed. Still worse, was the realisation that if we'd taken maximum points off Everton, they'd now be sporting the sponsor "Gone to One" on their shirts.

There's always next year I suppose.

BAMBER'S RIGHT FOOT

Torquay United

This game of football. What is it really all about? What is it that makes us put ourselves through all this time and time again? This cruel game tests my resolve, my commitment, my very being to the extremes of my capabilities as a football fan, and in particular as a passionate Torquay United fan. Fate deals me blow after blow and just as I think I can see a chink of light at the end of the seasonal tunnel, the flame is extinguished once more, plunging me back into the darkness and gloom of football's murky depths.

The pain of being stabbed through my embattled heart time after time is as searing now as it was the first time. I love my team, but seemingly they have another mistress... Misery.

Of course, it's true that footy fans the world-over supporting all the 'other' clubs out there are also subjected to these very same emotional tests at some time or another. But I'm not a supporter of those teams, I can only speak from my own, very personal experiences and traumas. Therefore may I meekly suggest that Torquay United fans have to deal with more than their fair share of angst and turmoil across the spectrum of football's highs and lows. Of course expectation plays a great part in the raising and lowering of a fan's desires and demands. To put this into perspective, you could say, and in fact I think many of us *did* say, that a mid-table finish would have been very welcome last season.. Not very ambitious I know, but when held up against the previous two, it would have been an indicator of better things to come.

No-one would or could have predicted what Torquay United were going to do, and it was with the usual trepidation that we filed out into the late summer sunshine to greet the dawning of a new season. It started well, got better and continued in much the same way... Incredible. The previous year we'd finished fourth bottom, behind relegated Hereford, Brighton and local Devon rivals Exeter City. The off-season had given us yet more reason for dismay with the likes of assistant chief coach Garry Nelson leaving for a plum job at the PFA and defender Jon Gittens being alienated from the club, looking unlikely to return.

To top it, chairman Mike Bateson decided that he'd had enough and promptly stepped down, handing the reins of power to a chap called Mervyn Benney. Bateson and his wife Sue retained ownership of the club, yet it was stated that Mr Benney had full control. However, few of us were convinced. "I'm my own man," stated Benney proudly. Yeh, and I'm a Chinaman.

His brief was to cut the overdraft in order to make the club a more viable proposition for prospective buyers... We're still waiting! Kev got on with his job and grabbed a few free transfers that were to prove masterstrokes of judgement, and Jon Gittens was somehow brought back to the club, possibly because he still had a year to run of a two-year contract. The season got underway.

We had a reasonably good start by any standards, let alone ours, and despite losing on the opening day during a tarmac-melting heatwave in Cheshire, where we were the esteemed first league guests of Macclesfield, experience told us something, and the hatching chickens were certainly not being counted just yet.

Doncaster, from early on, did tend to take the heat off the usual perennial strugglers, especially with Brighton seemingly so keen to keep them company. Doncaster's problems were all too public, and most people's money was on their slipping kicking and screaming into the Conference... Wise bet.

The entire season was scattered with memorable and unfamiliar incidents, which all added to the spice of the whole stew. The Coca-Cola Cup saw us defeat Bournemouth over two legs, to be rewarded with a plum tie against First Division Ipswich Town. Torquay held them 1-1 at Portman Road, only to capitulate 0-3 at home. But there was fun up ahead in the FA Cup.

October witnessed one of those unusual moments as Torquay United, 3-0 down at Boothferry Park in the 72nd minute, staged a magnificent, against-all-odds revival to draw 3-3. This illustrated a new spirit, fight and desire at the club.

So what was the reason for this turnaround in fortunes at Plainmoor? Well, this was largely due to new blood and the three Gs: Gibbs, Gurney and Gittens. Gibbs had arrived on a free transfer from Colchester after being released to make way for Scott Stamps... a player we'd sold to them; I'm sure even Colchester fans would agree that we got the better end of *that* bargain. Gurney had also been snapped up on a free from Bristol Rovers, and with Gibbs they gave us a whole new attacking option. Gittens was inspired and went on to become Player of the Year, despite having been sent home due to 'differences' the previous season. Another new freebie was Jamie Robinson from Carlisle. Okay, so his surname didn't begin with a G, but he was part of the new Torquay.

The FA Cup sent us to Luton where we witnessed a terrific rearguard action, topped with a spirited break and penalty converted by Paul Gibbs that sent us back down the M4 in raptures. The noise generated by the away supporters and their drums that day completely drowned out the pitiful efforts of the Luton crowd. Unfortunately, the Hatters' bitter rivals stung us in a replay at Vicarage Road in the next round. But it was still a magnificent performance and another noise triumph for the faithful at Watford.

The deal that brought loanee Jason Roberts to Plainmoor was, as usual, extremely suspect, with Wolves stumping up part of his wages and Torquay apparently making up the balance. That is, until a Players' Wages fund was launched that appealed to fans to dip into their own pockets once again so that Roberts could get paid. It got so bad that the club organised half-time collections in the crowd. You know the sort of thing: buckets and spare change. Now Roberts was worth every penny (literally), but I ask you, was this any way to run a professional football club?

Christmas served up the delights that are St James' Park (not the real one!), home of local rivals Exeter City. Earlier in the season they had come to Plainmoor and we'd played them off the park in one of the most keenly fought local derbies of recent years. However, it was they who scored the goals and took the points, after each side had had a player dispatched for an early bath. So, December 28th saw a typically cagey derby, with neither side wanting or daring to put a foot wrong, and in the end the two sides largely cancelled each other out. The 1-1 draw was played out in front of two equally cagey sets of fans, loath to sing or shout something that might get rammed down their throats later on.

We finished 1997 in tenth spot and the faithful braced themselves for the free-fall that the new year usually brings... Except that this time round, with a newly beefed-up front line to complement the pacey skills of Rodney Jack, Torquay started to settle into a rhythm. Having beaten Macclesfield at Plainmoor at the beginning of January, we then lost two on the trot against Colchester and Scarborough. But when Shrewsbury came to town, we duly dispatched them 3-0. This signalled the beginning of a record-breaking eight wins on the trot. A magnificent 24 points out of 24, which took us into March, and into the play-off frame. After being chasers for so long, we were finally up amongst the leaders, and how good it felt. Kevin Hodges was named Manager of the Month for February, we were second in the division and things were looking good.

It finally came to an end at home against Cambridge. But we picked ourselves up and over the remaining games we managed to keep in touch despite Jason Roberts being recalled to Wolves and then being farmed out to Bristol City, even though he wanted to return to us to complete his loan. This move probably cost us promotion, but hey, we'll never really know will we?

Torquay started to get nervous as the end of the season loomed into view, but at the end of March, and due in no small amount to other results, we were still holding on to that second place. April brought more angst as Rodney Jack gashed his knee in a freak training ground accident, and was sidelined for three games. Eight vital points were lost in his absence, and Torquay dropped a place to third. Going into the last game at Leyton Orient, we only needed a draw to gain automatic promotion for the first time in 32 years.

And so to Brisbane Road on a gloriously sunny May afternoon, where the assembled throng of Yellow and Blue had travelled to the capital to witness what they thought would be the crowning glory to a great season, and they had every reason to be confident.

Alas, it wasn't to be. Orient were two up at the break, and despite one of the most spirited and frantic attempts at a fight-back, Torquay just couldn't find that final finish. Andy McFarlane scrambled a goal to make it 2-1 but everything else seemed destined to go wide, high, short or whatever else. There's no doubt - it was as dramatic as it was heartbreaking. As late as the 96th minute, when captain Alex Watson sent a header crashing against the foot of the post, we were still in it, still fighting.

For us it was the suffering of the play-offs again, and as I sank to the pavement outside Brisbane Road, the tears flowed as I contemplated the cruel blows that this game can inflict on your soul. Well, I'd had enough, and to my shame I couldn't face any more disappointment. I was given a running commentary of the first leg at Scarborough by a personal stereo-wearing compatriot in the pub - an odd experience. Imagine my feelings when the Gulls swooped and stamped their authority on the tie, winning 3-1.

The return was a carnival. Rodney Jack put us 2-0 up within six minutes, Steve McCall, that now-departed wily midfielder, smacked in a world-class strike and a great run and finish from Paul Gibbs (also now departed), booked our place at Wembley. Their third appearance at the home of football in nine years.

Being forced to play the game on a Friday night meant that the two clubs lost out on a hatful of money. How did they expect the folks of Torquay to decamp to London on a normal working day? Moves are afoot by both towns' MPs to get the FA to look at the situation, and possibly offer some form of compensation. Don't hold your breath!

And so to the capital once more, only this time it took a great deal longer than usual courtesy of the coach from hell and some of the most bizarre navigational techniques ever known to man. Hence a late arrival and two rushed pints of lager was my re-introduction to the twin towers. The game itself... well... neither team imposed themselves on the game, but Colchester were promoted courtesy of a dreadful penalty decision, given when the ball struck the hand of Jon Gittens when he had absolutely no chance of avoiding it.

Congratulations to them and well done to our boys for a great season. But it didn't end there, as this summer has seen our management duo of Kevin Hodges and Steve McCall lured down to freshly-relegated local rivals Plymouth Argyle amid much bad feeling and acrimony. Paul Gibbs has joined them despite saying that he loved Torquay and never wanted to play against them! Really? John Gittens was effectively released from the club, without even being offered a deal to refuse or otherwise. The usual close season shambles.

Former promotion-winning captain Wes Saunders was unveiled as our new manager, and while Wes is a hero, we'll simply have to wait and see what kind of boss he shapes up to be. My worry is that if things turn sour, then the legend of Wes will be tainted, and his position in the folklore of Plainmoor will fade.

Even the World Cup had one last dig at me: hope, promise, crushing low, great high and then Argentinian robbery. Mind you, I'm addicted, and I know I'll keep taking the tablets, even though they're normally bitter pills to swallow.

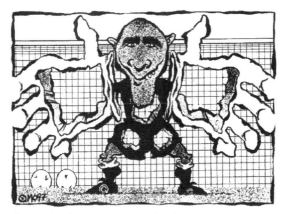

Source: Another Vintage Liverpool Performance

BEESOTTED

Brentford

Unfortunately, it is pretty hard to fully describe Brentford's season without using some very disturbing words - come to think of it, it's bloody impossible. 'Raped' and 'brutalised' are not often used in footballing terms, but in Brentford's case they are the only adjectives I can think of which adequately describe the way our club has been abused and neglected by a board which, in one short season, has guided our club from Second Division play-off finalists at Wembley to Third Division no-hopers at Halifax.

When David Webb switched from team manager to majority shareholder, few of even the most suspicious Brentford

cynics could have expected the body blows that were to follow. Admittedly, Webb had started to act in a strange manner in the lead up to his boardroom take-over, when our promotion push clearly became of secondary importance to him, but I suppose every hijacker's nine-to-five job suffers nearing the big day. But if the alarm bells weren't ringing amongst the Bees faithful prior to the boardroom take-over, the bizarre set of events that followed in the build-up to the new season got them wailing like air raid sirens.

The fact is that Webb sold virtually every player who could command a transfer fee, claiming a personal cut of 15% of all incoming monies in the process, then chose to officially step down as team manager two days before the opening day game at Millwall. A managerless team not surprisingly lost 3-0. Webb then appointed a replacement manager whose only previous honours in the game were winning the Welsh Cup while at Cardiff and guiding Torquay to the very foot of the Football League. At this point Webb decided to stop even coming to watch his team play. In a whole season he only saw Brentford play once. It was now becoming all too clear what his intentions were.

Every possible loophole in footballing law and every agreement Webb had made with the previous chairman were being stretched to the limits for his own personal financial gain. Nothing illegal was taking place, just a cunning and carefully planned raid on a football club outside the media glare, and to a large extent, outside of the public's interest. New facts were being unearthed every week in the *Middlesex Chronicle* as confused fans faced up to the dilemma of protesting at the matches or getting behind their struggling team. But in reality, Brentford Football Club never stood a chance of escaping relegation last season.

After a fortnight of speculation, when it became almost common knowledge that Micky Adams was about to become the new team manager, Eddie May and Clive Walker not surprisingly became the first scapegoats of the campaign and were duly sacked in November after being blamed for our poor league position. This would prove to be another managerial move that Adams would live to regret, as I'm sure if he'd been fully aware of the serious state of affairs at Griffin Park he wouldn't have touched the job with a barge pole. I suppose the fact that Webb refused to talk to Adams for the last three months of the season is all the proof you need of that really.

Micky Adams did put up a decent fight though, even if his playing style wasn't up to much. As they say, desperate times call for desperate measures, and believe me, at times Brentford were desperate. Experienced players like Warren Aspinall, Graham Hogg, Nigel Gleghorn and Glen Cockerall were drafted in to shore up our gaping defence and lightweight midfield, and for a short while at least, it did look like our new rent-a-team players may pull us clear of the drop zone. Unfortunately, the bubble burst again at Easter, with home defeats at the hands of our hated local rivals Fulham and to Wigan. Brentford failed to win their final home game of the season too, a six-pointer against Luton, and once more the advantage had been handed right back to our rivals as we had to depend on other club's results for survival. Oldham's superb ten-man fightback from 3-1 down against Burnley meant that our stay of execution was extended even further.

But yet another off-the-pitch twist helped cause uncertainty and speculation on the eve of the club's most desperate game for years. London's *Evening Standard* ran a story the night before the crucial game at Bristol Rovers, indicating that Micky Adams was about to be sacked and that Webb had sold his shares to Ron Noades who intended to become involved with team selections himself. A more appallingly, ill-timed story from a newspaper who ignores our club from one season to the next could not have been organised. So instead of an away terrace full of hyped up fans desperate to help their team win the vital three points, there was yet more confusion and disbelief at what was going on around us.

It is very easy to get carried away or get wrapped up in personal vendettas and churlish name-calling where football emotions run so high; that is why *Beesotted* has been very careful to only report fact when trying to inform the fans about what was really going on. But as focused as you try to be under these circumstances, certain details still make you sick from the pit of your stomach. A few examples:

For David Webb's £40,000 majority share-holding in the club (no, that's right, I did say £40,000, that's not a misprint) it is understood that Ron Noades has just paid the ex-Chelsea player in excess of £650,000. For Tony Swaisland and John Herting's £4,500 'investment' in a club they claimed to be life-long and die-hard supporters of, they are understood to have been paid around £125,000 each. For a man who was already a multi-millionaire and who had promised the Brentford supporters that he would never sell to anyone who didn't have the club's best interests at heart, ex-chairman Martin Lange offloaded it for peanuts to people who seemed only interested in their own financial fortunes. Lange has also recouped a massive chunk of his £1 million loan to the club in under a year, but in doing so has played a major part in strangling Brentford Football Club of its Second Division status.

The exact details in Lange's secret contracts and agreements with David Webb may always remain a secret, but the deals seemed to work very well for both men. Webb earned a fortune from a tiny club and Lange got all his loans back in an extremely short space of time. What we do know is that Webb was legitimately allowed to earn a salary of around £150,000 per year, plus 15% of all incoming transfer fees. I'll let you do the sums for yourself, but in just over a year Brentford sold Martin Grainger and Nicky Forster to Birmingham (£1.2m), Carl Asaba to Reading (£800,000), Marcus Bent to Crystal Palace (£350,000), plus Paul Smith, Barry Ashby and Brian Statham to Gillingham (£250,000). Hmmm, what's 15% of that little lot, plus £150,000 salary, plus £650,000 in take-over profits from Ron Noades? Quite a tidy little stash wouldn't you say from a relegation-bound club that was only averaging about 4,500 fans for a home game and were knocked out of the FA Cup in the first round? Is anyone out there still surprised that Brentford FC got relegated? Thought not.

So why hasn't the FA or Football League poured down on Webb and Co. like a ton of bricks and hauled them in to explain their actions, especially so soon after the Brighton fiasco? I suppose it's just a further example of the authority's neglect of their smaller, most vulnerable members and the media's current obsession with all things Premier. A couple of Newcastle suits were given more column inches than the Queen Mum will get (Gawd bless 'er), when and if she croaks, when they told an undercover reporter what anyone with half a brain knew already. Yet the plunder of Griffin Park hardly received more than couple of column inches. With so many football magazines filling our newsagent's bookshelves, and with so many sports pages in our newspapers, all detailing and fighting to find even the most trivial pieces of information about the game, it makes you wonder what the hell is going on when a serious situation like ours is unanimously ignored. Apart from *When Saturday Comes* and the tireless work of Jim Levack at the *Middlesex Chronicle*, nobody else seemed to give a monkey's chuff.

BIAS, Brentford's Independent Association of Supporters, was eventually set up to organise press releases and peaceful protests against the Webb regime, and to help educate a Brentford public who on the whole aren't traditionally at ease with direct confrontation with club officialdom. Without any sign of a struggle in the boardroom, or an outraged rival consortium waiting in the wings, BIAS knew that they could never win the battle with fan power alone;

all it could ever really do was to play its part in winning the war of words. That it did admirably and with good humour. All manner of sit-ins, red card protests and forecourt gatherings were organised. Along with a 25ft Admobile which drove to Webb's Essex home on February 14th with a caricature depicting Webb as a gangster partaking in our club's St.Valentines' Day Massacre on one side and a simple message asking "Who Ate All The Pi£s' on the other.

So as you can see, Brentford's season could not be described as a normal one by any stretch of the imagination. It was a desperate struggle both on and off the pitch from start to finish.

Although there were a lot of tears on the terrace at Bristol Rovers at 4.45, and a fair bit of sunburn too, on the whole I was surprised how philosophical the Brentford supporters were. But as we'd all had nine bitter months to prepare ourselves for the inevitable, I suppose in a strange sort of way our sadness and anger was tinged with a slight sense of relief too. As all true football fans know, when such a dark cloud hangs over a football club for as long as ours had, it is not usually just the rainwater that is washed down the gutter. The club underneath normally follows not far behind.

Now that Ron Noades has at last bought out Webb, hopefully the much needed rebuilding job can get underway. If the club can get back on track again and begin to move in the right direction, this could even be seen as a bright new start. But to be really honest, first and foremost, Brentford fans need to be convinced that Ron Noades is someone we can finally trust. That's not going to be an easy job for the ex-Palace chairman though, because after the traumas of the last couple of seasons, Bees fans are going to be a damn sight less gullible this time round. *Beesotted* will help make sure of that.

BERT TRAUTMAN'S HELMET

Manchester City

You'd have been pretty hard pushed to find anyone in Manchester last summer that didn't think City would be fighting to regain their Premiership spot... Little did we know! But then we *did* have Frank Clark in the manager's hot-seat. Clark had impressed the season before when, following a succession of managers, he had got the team playing some relatively good football whilst putting a few results together. All he had to do now was to build on those foundations with a few good signings. Instead of which, he bought a forward who, it quickly transpired, couldn't score to save his life and a defender we hardly needed, given that we already had

a team full of them on the club's overstocked books.

Yes indeed, welcome to Maine Road - home of the surreal.

Yet it wouldn't be fair to blame Lee Bradbury (aka Badbuy) and Tony Vaughan for the club's failings when so many others played their part.

Maine Road almost resembled the set of an Ealing Comedy at times last season as everybody blamed everybody else. The manager blamed the fans for having too high expectations and for scaring the players with their fervent home support, before blaming a 'Fifth Column' at work within the club as he made his way to the local job centre. The chairman appeared to be blaming the manager as well as certain players before he too went off to sign on. And the fans? Well, they blamed the manager, the players, the chairman, crap referees and, just out of habit, Alan Ball and Peter Swales.

Personally, I blamed Clark for our downfall. In my humble opinion he was a worse manager than Ball. At least Ball was operating against teams most of us have heard of, like Arsenal and Liverpool in the Premier League, as opposed to traditional nonentities like Bury and Stockport in the First Division. And yet how the mighty fall, for, perversely, we now find ourselves travelling past these local grounds and dreaming of seeing our team playing there. It certainly puts things into perspective when you're wishing for Gigg Lane and Edgeley Park rather than the increasingly fading memories of Highbury and

Anfield. Furthermore, a City win on either of those two local grounds next season would guarantee 'City Cup Giant Killer' headlines in the papers! That at least would be more than we'd managed last season.

The game at Bury resulted in a 1-1 draw whilst Stockport beat us 3-1. File these disasters alongside those at Ipswich (0-1), Birmingham (1-2 aet), Crewe (0-1) and it's little wonder that Clark was replaced by the rather more jovial Joe Royle. It's said that Clark received a £500,000 pay-off for his efforts and just to put that into perspective, the nation's best fans were hit with a hike in '98-99 season ticket prices. Only in football... Only in Manchester... And only at City! But roll on next season: Blackpool, Fulham, Macclesfield *et al.* I can hardly wait.

Source: King of the Kippax

BETTER RED THAN DEAD

Barnsley

From Despair to Where?

We came with hope in our minds, songs in our hearts, carrying the dreams and aspirations of every put-down, shut-down, so-called small club in the land on our shoulders. We came and we played until our legs were weary and tears ran down our cheeks. We came and we tried and we failed. But oh, what glorious failure. In failure we found hope. In defeat we could see the future. Down but not out, it was "Still Like Watching Brazil."

ISSUE NUMBER 2   ONWARDS AND UPWARDS   PRICE 50 PENCE

IT'S JUST LIKE WATCHING GRANGE HILL

BETTER RED THAN DEAD

BARNSLEY FOOTBALL CLUB FANZINE

Now we pass the brave new world of sanitised stadiums and lobotomised fans, Rupert Murdoch hype, pass the flame of hope and the poisoned chalice of regular smashings onto Charlton, the new first-years in the 'big school', who'll probably end up getting their head stuck down the bog a few times but who, let's hope, adjust quicker and last longer than we did.

The first time that Barnsley had competed at the highest level in over a 110 years of existence was a roller-coaster ride of frayed nerves and rapidly ageing bottoms, as fans and defenders alike leaked the brown slimy stuff from their nether orifices as soon as we were confronted with a half-decent striker. For much of a season, we found the leap from First Division to Premiership bigger and harder than a real big hard thing.

Running through the season, we had riots (well, if you can class a few kids and a couple of fat blokes running on the pitch as a riot), won at Anfield, defeated corporate luvvies (and the occasional footballer) Manure in the cup, witnessed the hard running of Ashley Ward, saw the emergence of Chris Morgan as a real star of both present and future, and revelled in the development of Adie Moses and David Watson into players of international class. Our supporters won friends but failed to influence people with a commitment and passion not normally associated with 'little Barnsley'. We also witnessed the antics of Gary 'Sodding' Willard, more of whom later, alligators.

Disappointments came in the performances of Georgi Hristov, bought (for a fee that probably cancelled the national debt of his native Macedonia) to score on the pitch. He rapidly became famous for, erm, 'banging them in' off it. First, in an interview with a Yugoslav journalist he allegedly said that Barnsley lassies were all slappers who drank too much, which as this came from a bloke the spit of Sam Dingle from *Emmerdale Farm* struck most people as a case of the pot calling the kettle a not-too-subtle shade of off-white. Then he was splish-splashed across the pages of the *Sunday Sport* as a local lass who sampled his goods complained of groin stains and a lack of action in the box, emotions that Reds fans could easily empathise with. Big Useless Eric Tinkler, a 'star' of Serie A, was also purchased for many several smackeroonies to little or no effect, and Dutch defender Arjan de Zeeuw, seen by fans as too good for the First Division, proved not quite good enough to mix it with the big boys.

Disappointment also came in the attitude of the club towards us supporters. Always a friendly place with friendly people, this was lost a little as the club seemed to get carried away with its new-found importance, and a wedge was driven between fans and the team they supported. Old faves like Shirley in the shop and her encyclopaedic knowledge of everyone and everything Barnsley were swept away. This new attitude was also seen in the refusal of the club shop to contribute to the Scarborough chairman's mad trek round the country looking for donations from all league clubs. To our shame we were one of the few refusniks. Criticism was not viewed too kindly and at various times pressure was put upon us fanzine types to shut our big gobs and toe the party line, resulting only in us shouting louder of course.

Relegation. The world's turned on its axis and we find ourselves back where we started from, with some lessons learned, a better team and hope still in our hearts. Relegation. There's no getting away from it; our first in over a quarter of a century, and, perhaps, felt all the more keenly because of it. Relegation. Just as the joy of promotion took an age to stick in our thick noggins, so does relegation.

Before the season started, opinion was divided about our chances of survival. There were those who thought we'd be down by Christmas and those who didn't think we'd last that long. In the end we were relegated on the penultimate Saturday of the season, having played some memorable games, been hammered a good few times and won many friends along the way.

The season ended as it began; with a home defeat. Against West Ham on that light, bright summer day, expectations and passions were running high, but not even the glory of an early Redfearn goal knocked in with his head, which had only previously been used for growing 'Desperate Dan' stubble on, could prevent the Hammers powering past us as the match went on. On the final Sunday, the weather and feelings were different for our relegation celebration against Moanchester United. The morning sun was washed away by the rain, just as our early season optimism had given sway to the despair of relegation. Although the Ora stand and the East stand gimmers, most of whom had been dead since dinosaurs roamed the earth and Eric Winstanley trotted around Oakwell, tried their best to raise the atmosphere, raise the roof and raise a smile, the overpowering emotion was sadness, however much we tried to hide it.

Disastrous early season form (which saw eight defeats out of the first ten games and the ball pinging its way into our net on a more frequent basis than Grant Mitchell gives Tiff 'backhanders' on *EastEnders*), and the warnings of Hansen, Lawrenson and others in the media that we were naïve and almost an embarrassment to the Premier League, seemed to be coming home to roost. Gradually we became more difficult to overcome, especially at home where we remained unbeaten from late November until we were beaten by Liverpool and Willard late in March. This coupled with a strong cup run that saw us dispose of three Premier League teams, including magnificent home wins over Manure and Totteringham, saw optimism pulsing through the veins of fans and players.

Then came the intervention of Gary Willard. In a mad, sad, insane display of refereeing that still defies belief or explanation, the season was turned on its head. A team that hadn't had a single player sent off in over a year suddenly turned into a cross between Leeds in the 70's and early vintage Wimbledon, at least in the eyes of Mister Willard. Three of our lot ended up taking their rubber duckies for an early bath as Liverpool finally broke our resistance and our hearts with a 90th minute goal after a stirring nine-man fight-back. From then on we were never the same team and our form in the run-in - seven defeats from ten games - almost matched our start as we were disrupted by suspension and a loss of belief in the fairness of life in the Premier League.

Talk was of conspiracy theories concocted by *Sky TV*, Lee Harvey Oswald, the CIA, the smoking man, the FA and the elite clubs to do the Reds down, get us relegated and keep Tottenham, Everton and Newkybrooncastle in the Premier. Although in the cold light of day it's hard to justify these feelings, the fact that we could even contemplate such thoughts is a comment on the Premier League and all it stands for. Set up out of the motivated self-interest of a few to make the rich richer and the poor poorer; not to raise standards, just to keep a bigger slice of the cake in fewer hands, it was easy to get carried away into believing the incompetence of one man was a more wide-reaching conspiracy.

What got us relegated was nad'vete 'early doors', as Big Fat Ron might say, and a lack of concentration at crucial moments coupled with a squad that lacked depth, particularly in midfield where we had too many peripheral figures who failed to make an impact. The saintly Danny Wilson made the mistakes that managers still learning their trade tend to make, particularly in the choice of some of our close season buys and also in sticking with some of the players who got us promoted a tad too long. Like Swindon and Bolton before us, we only started playing when about half the season was gone and we never really caught up (we were camped in the bottom three from late September onwards). Maybe part of the fault also lies with us, the fans, to an extent that early in the season it seemed that some of our players believed it really was 'just like watching

Brazil' and that they could play their football at the highest level without having shown the desire to battle for the right to show their skills. Perhaps we created false expectations and implanted false beliefs in our players who to a large extent were composed of journeymen and talented youngsters. The buggers believed their own publicity.

We didn't read all the rules; didn't realise that you aren't allowed to tackle 'England captain' Alan Shearer whilst he can kick several shades out of anybody he fancies, including his own team-mates like the unfortunate bookies' favourite Keith Gillespie. Didn't realise that 'sometime England captain' Paul Ince can moan and whine and kick and foul and get away with it all he likes. Didn't realise that big name players like Donkey Dublin will always get a penalty if they plop onto their backsides often enough. Didn't realise that it's one set of rules for the 'big clubs' and another for the like of us. Seems our defending wasn't the only thing that was naïve early doors, as these lessons were soon learned.

The media patronised us, tolerated us, buried us a hundred times, lost interest, praised us far too much and rarely got it right. So we got about what we expected there. Here's a *Better Red Than Dead* cut-out-and-keep quick guide to the season, as seen through tabloid eyes. Brave, battling, miners' strike, Dickie, brassed off, Barnsley chop, ey oop!, Parky, Arthur Scargill, cloth caps, Roland Barthes, proud tradition, 1912, whippets, more illustrious neighbours, naïve defending, shoestring budget, amongst the aristocracy, lumps of coal, radix malorum est cupiditas.

We will start next season as one of the favourites for promotion rather than relegation, which will bring its own pressures, but we have the players, the manager, the self-belief and the experience to rise again. Not the beginning of the end but the end of the beginning. We will be back, and Premiership II will have a different script to Premiership I.

BEYOND THE BOUNDARY

Oldham Athletic

The last time I was involved in a demonstration was over 20 years ago when I joined Anti-Nazi League marchers in London heading to Victoria Park for a rally and free gig by The Clash. Although there have been many causes since to which I have subscribed, I never felt motivated enough to get too involved. However, when the future and very existence of my football club was under threat, my allegiance to the cause could not be faulted. So on Easter Monday, having just watched Oldham go down 0-1 to Wycombe Wanderers at Boundary Park, I joined several hundred other Latics supporters in a pre-arranged post-match sit-in to protest at the way the club has been run down over the past five years.

No. 53
(February/March '98)

INSIDE: (YOU'RE) WELCOME TO THE
BATTYEDOME.
KIT SURVEY RESULT.
DOUG HODGSON IN THE
KITCHEN.
MEMORIES OF THE LATE 60's.
THE NIBS/LATICS CONNECTION.
MATCH REPORTS, LETTERS AND
MUCH, MUCH MORE.......

STOTT REVEALS HIS
CONTRIBUTION
TO LATICS PUSH
FOR PROMOTION

80p

Oldham Athletic have never been an attractive club, we all know that, but when our '15 minutes of fame' ended with relegation from the Premier League in '93-94 we still hoped that we'd be back up amongst the big boys soon. In the past we'd sold to survive like all other little clubs, but when Joe Royle managed against all the odds to bring together a side that could not only win things, but entertain at the same time, the notoriously sceptical Oldham public began to flock back down Sheepfoot Lane. All that was needed to keep us in the top flight were a few astute Royle signings, then we could look forward to years of success - perhaps even Europe was within our grasp.

But it all went horribly wrong. The side that had entertained the nation was slowly dismantled and finally torn apart. Attempts to plug the gaps with disillusioned journeymen, crocks and wasters added to the decline. Players were sold for millions, but peanuts were paid to replace them. Relegation to the First Division was temporary, we were told, but when Royle left the sinking ship and Graeme Sharp took charge, the Premier League began to look more and more distant. After another fruitless season, Sharp departed, blaming lack of ambition and a shortage of funds. Neil Warnock arrived with a proven track record of getting teams promoted from the lower reaches, but he was too late to stop yet another relegation. Two drops in four years; it was getting beyond a joke. By now the die-hards who were left were beginning to smell a rat. The money situation, or lack of it, meant Warnock's only signings were free transfers and players out of contract. We had to sell an asset, and by definition a good player, to buy.

Now, four years on from our brief sojourn in the Premier League, the club is flat broke, public relations are a nightmare, 65% of the supporter base has been lost and playing standards are woeful. They have been reduced to giving away Andrew Hughes, one of our brightest talents, to a club in the same division without allowing him to realise his true potential. As a blueprint for disaster, the Oldham experience could hardly be bettered. The club has made the catastrophic mistake of signing players on inflated salaries on their way down from bigger clubs, rather than looking at younger talents from the lower divisions, anxious to better themselves in a club with a progressive outlook.

However, despite all this, as the last of the Christmas decorations were being packed away, Athletic were still handily placed near the top of the tree, and a place in the play-offs was not beyond their reach. Several games later, and following a nose-dive of bungee-like proportions, the team were nearer Division Three. Warnock's stereotyped Route One method of play, which had been effective at home, was an absolute disaster away, producing only one win. In an effort to bring much-needed new players into the side, Warnock put our two main strikers up for sale.

Out of the blue, a consortium of local businessmen attempted to buy a controlling interest in the club, but were dismissed out of hand by local brewery and 48% major shareholders JW Lees. Given that Neil Warnock had been allowed to spend just £50,000 getting the club back to the First Division, supporters were understandably angry. Just who *were* these people who seemingly sat tight while the club self-destructed? Frustrated by weak explanations from the chairman and his board, 'Stop the Rot' was born, an alliance of like-minded supporters intent on showing their displeasure at the downward trend in the club's fortunes.

JW Lees were the obvious target. By their own admission they "took no active part in running the club." They weren't kidding. Nobody from the brewery had representation on the board; they didn't attend shareholders' meetings and never attended matches. STR decided to organise a boycott of all the brewery's pubs and products. Not easy, given that the Clayton Arms Supporters Club attached to the ground, a traditional meeting place and pre-match hostelry for many fans, was also brewery-owned. A mass leafleting campaign and valuable coverage in the local press produced a great result on the first day of the boycott. Local pubs reported increased custom and many supporters vowed never to drink Lees beer again. Even visiting Watford fans not only joined the boycott but erected a 'Lees Out' banner in their section of the ground.

Our PR and demonstrations continued for the visit of the *Sky* cameras and Bristol City. The national media got in on the act and more valuable publicity appeared in the *Times*, *Express on Sunday* and *Guardian*. *Radio 5 Live* and *Greater Manchester Radio* - where a regular Friday night football phone-in was completely taken over by Oldham supporters - also ran stories of the boycott. Despite all this, the brewery still refused to answer any of the many questions supporters posed. They did reveal that they had loaned Athletic £200,000 in January. However, the sale of Andrew Hughes to Notts County and top scorer Stuart Barlow to Wigan, close to transfer deadline day, turned out to be for repayment of the loan.

And so to Easter Monday. Almost four years to the day we'd played Man United at Old Trafford, a fact that wasn't lost on the many who stayed behind after the game. The demo had been panned to last 15 minutes, but 90 minutes later there were still several hundred supporters remaining. As chants of "We're here 'cos we love the club" echoed around the empty ground, I looked over to my right and spotted a middle aged female supporter close to tears. The people of Oldham are passionate about their cub, yet the faceless men who control the purse strings hold them in contempt. Our boycott is planned to continue into the coming season, so if you visit Boundary Park we hope you'll join us. You never know, it could be your club next.

ACCEPTING THE UNIVERSAL PRINCIPLE THAT ANYBODY CHOSEN TO BE THE NEXT BOSS AT MAINE ROAD HAS TO BE ABSOLUTELY PISSED, CHAIRMAN FRANCIS LEE PROCEEDS TO GET JOE AS GENIAL AS A NEWT BEFORE BREAKING THE NEWS TO HIM THAT HE'S LANDED THE HOTTEST MANAGEMENT JOB IN SOUTH MANCHESTER.

BLACK ARAB

Bristol Rovers

Hail O mighty Zork. Ruler of all Alpha Centauri !!

Yes boss. I'm back. I followed my instructions carefully. I infiltrated those primitive beings from planet Earth and got myself accepted as one of their kind. But I've come back to tell you that I have become a fully fledged Gashead. I've joined Ian Holloway's Gas Army and I'm off back to Earth as soon as I can get this bleeding spaceship fixed. The quartz crystal matter transposer's playing up again, and of course the repair shop "can't get the parts guv."

But you wanted my report on my stay on that strange little planet. Well here it is, though by the time you read it, I hope I'll have returned there - after all, the footie season starts in August. So sod you and your invasion plans, I'm off.

CITIZEN ERNIE TROTTER'S (E.T. for short) REPORT ON HIS VISIT TO EARTH. A SMALL PLANET ORBITING THE STAR SOL.

Landed August 12 Earth time next to a large building called 'The Wellington'. Disguised the spaceship as a black Ford Capri to avoid detection by the local populace. Right boss, here's my first complaint. You know all those highly paid 'researchers' we have to help us blend in with the locals on the planets we visit? Well, it's time you got some that know what they're doing. There I am in my 'Earthman' garb of bowler hat, pinstripe suit and umbrella. I entered this establishment called 'The Wellington' which turned out to he what Earth people call a 'pub' and everyone pissed themselves laughing at my strange attire. Next time you send some of our people to this planet, get them to wear a blue and white quartered shirt. Nearly everyone in this pub was wearing one. Oh, talking of pubs - the researchers are right about beer tasting foul, and lager tasting like woppit wee, but the stuff they call cider was better than our own Pan-galactic gargle blasters. Definitely the dog's bollocks.

I got into conversation with the locals and it seemed they were all going to watch Bristol Rovers, who apparently were the greatest football team the world has ever seen. Never having seen football before, I decided to join them.

This is where I encountered my first difficulty with currency. The jobsworth on the turnstiles refused to accept my Alpha Centaurian Fobble Beads, and I had to turn them into pound coins pretty damn quick.

Right. I'm watching this football thing, and it's really exciting. The object of the game as far as I could see was to kick any player not wearing the same colour shirt as you, and if a funny white round thing came your way you kicked that too, and if it happened to go between the white sticks and end up tangled in a net, it was called a 'goal', and if your team did it you went mad but if the other team did it you just shouted rude words. The Bristol Rovers fans, who call themselves 'Gasheads' worship a god called Barry Hayles. And as the game went on and I began to understand a little more of what went on, I could see why. When he got the ball no-one from the other side could get it away from him, and eventually he scored Bristol Rovers' goal. This started the 'Gasheads' singing a song about a girl called Irene. "Goodnight Irene, goodnight Irene, I'll see you in my dreams" they sang.

I enjoyed it so much I decided I would watch all Bristol Rovers' games. And it certainly proved an education for me. I now know that we are not the only 'visitors' to this planet. There are Asturians from the Andromeda galaxy here. They haven't even bothered to disguise themselves, and even appear on TV. They call themselves 'Teletubbies'. One has even started playing football. He calls himself Jamie Cureton.

Whilst we know these people are harmless, there is something much more worrying. Klingons have also infiltrated this planet and are currently engaged in a programme of disruption. This first came to my notice last November, when I went to Wigan to watch Rovers play, and the antics of referee Kevin Lynch raised my suspicions. Okay, so five red cards and nine yellow would have drawn anyone's attention, but in what was never a dirty game Mr Lynch seemed determined to send off the entire Bristol Rovers team. As the game went on, his actions became more desperate, the eyes more wild and staring as he struggled for excuses to send off Rovers players. I can only imagine that his FOURTH Rovers victim, Josh Low, was sent off for not fouling anyone, or for hiding on the wing, because that's all he ever does.

Having been alerted to the existence of Klingons on the planet I began to look for evidence of others. I soon found two more. One calls himself Scott Davidson, and has become chairman of Bristol City (1982) Ltd. He wears his disguise well as he appears to be a happy smiley human until something does not go his way. Then the façade slips, those same tell-tale eyes and wild stare as he throws a temper tantrum. As witnessed when he tried to persuade Bristol Rovers deity Barry Hayles to desert his worshippers for a mere £2 million and was told to get lost. Another Klingon is one they call Shaun Taylor, who has been playing in defence for Bristol City (1982) Ltd. This one is so brazen he doesn't even bother with a disguise. I'm surprised that no one else has noticed.

But back to matters in hand. Why did I report back so late when my mission on Earth was due to finish at the end of their year? Sorry, but once again due to football. Rovers had won two FA Cup games (against Gillingham after a replay, and against non-league Wisbech), something quite unprecedented for them. I had to stay for the outcome, and anyway by now I was really hooked. If they weren't winning 5-3 (Bournemouth) they were losing 0-4 (Grimsby). They eventually lost the cup game after a replay at Ipswich. But in the league, things were hotting up and Rovers were in with a chance of the play-offs. (I'm not going to explain, you just wouldn't understand how exciting they are). A 5-0 battering of Wigan (no Mr Lynch!) and a great win at Grimsby in the Easter snow set things up for 3,500 Gasheads to make the trip north to Blackpool wearing all sorts of strange attire, only to lose 1-0 totally against the run of play. But Blackpool and Bristol Rovers supporters proved there is hope for this planet by showing everyone the true spirit of football - shaking hands on the pitch after the game instead of fighting.

So it was all down to the last league game. Win it and Bristol Rovers were in the play-offs. With only six minutes of the game left, this looked extremely unlikely, with the score 1-1 and Rovers down to ten men. Then the god of Bristol Rovers fans decided to intervene. A cross from Matty Lockwood, and there was Lord Barrington of Hayles leaping to head a magnificent goal. So it's the play-offs then. I still couldn't go home despite those frantic messages on the vid-screen on the spaceship: 'E.T. phone home'.

First leg of the play-offs, and Rovers beat Northampton 3-1. But I got this funny feeling that someone had been meddling with fate; it should have been 6-1. I went to Northampton with the Rovers fans, but was feeling uneasy. Something strange was happening. I get the feeling that those idiot Simurians had been pissing around with the space/time continuum again. My fears were not unfounded. The Northampton team had been replaced by 11 Klingons who had obviously used their stun guns on the Rovers players before the game.

Rovers lost 3-0. No Wembley final. I was distraught. Now I'll have to return to Alpha Centauri and explain my long absence. Well sod that, I like it on Earth and I'm getting on very well with the young lady who ran onto the pitch against Brentford and removed her shirt, *and* she wasn't wearing a vest! I'm also working on a stun gun for opposition Klingons so that I can neutralise them next season.

Top scorers in Division Two this season. Will we be Champions next? Well we now own our own ground for the first time in 50 years (having just bought the Memorial Ground). They're putting a roof on the clubhouse terrace to keep the fans dry, and Gerry Francis is rumoured to be buying into the club. I'm using our secret Alpha Centauri mind controls on him to persuade him to do a management double act with Ian Holloway.

Manchester City... Stoke... Fulham... Notts County... Macclesfield. Huh! You've no chance against the mighty Gas!

THE BLUE EAGLE

Colchester United

Welcome to yet another tale of erratic and consistently inconsistent football that regular readers of *Survival Of The Fattest* will know *is* Colchester United. For once the end of the season came with a happy ending for the U's, but more of that later.

An opening day victory is always a good sign, Darlington being the unlucky visitors to Layer Road back in August, and no jokes about anyone having to come to Layer Road being unlucky please. We have to go there more than you do. But where was I? Oh yes, an opening day victory. Well after that, it was soon business as normal. The next few games saw an early exit from the League Cup, which

THE BLUE EAGLE

ISSUE 26

The Colchester United Fanzine
Written by Supporters for Supporters

"Pete Cawley complains after Revolutionary Hairgrowth Treatment fails!"

ALL FOR THE PRINCELY SUM OF
£1

included a lovely evening visit to Luton. The post-match highlight was the local lottery of walking back to our cars hoping that we were the lucky ones not to have had our windows smashed and radios nicked. Good idea though; wait until all the police are safely locked inside Kenilworth Road and then do your bit at boosting Halfords' audio sales! Our league form was equally erratic, going from fifth to 17th and back to fifth all by the end of September, a position which was to elude us again until the final weeks of the season.

Still, at that stage we all thought that the play-offs were where CUFC would finish up, as we always do (or very nearly, anyway), and not even the slow but gradual slide down towards the basement positions as Christmas approached dulled our optimism. That was until we remembered that traditionally it was after Christmas that things started going downhill, fast! Thank God for Doncaster Rovers.

Actually, that's not very fair. Donny had a real bad time, culminating in their departure for the Conference, and as a club, and a group of loyal supporters who've been there, we wouldn't wish that on anyone. The fact that they were sold down the river by those who are supposed to be the ones keeping a club going, well that must really hurt. Colchester United were the visitors at Belle Vue for the final game of the season, and to see the desperation of their fans was no fun. It's something that no true football supporter should wish on anyone, no matter which club they support (maybe even Wycombe!). Likewise the camaraderie seen between supporters of rival clubs in such circumstances is the sort of thing that makes English football worth being a part of, and the sort of thing that seems to go unreported in the media - funny, that!

Anyway, I digress. United fans also had to endure more than once, that wonderful quirk of the modern day game: the penalty shoot-out. Step forward the FA Cup first round. Two-two at Brentford's Griffin Park, 1-1 in the replay and lots of chewing of fingernails and looking the other way during the shoot-out. But for once the pens finished in our favour, 4-2. So on to round two at home to Conference new-boys Hereford, and, wait for it, a one-all draw. So it was off to Hereford on a cold Tuesday night in December. Did I say cold? I meant incredibly bloody bollock-freezing cold. Colder than Runcorn at an evening game. Colder than the New Den for an evening Autowotsit Trophy fixture with tornado-speed winds whistling through the stands. Colder than, well any other game I've ever been to.

A totally unmemorable event where no-one knew how long there was to go because that meant getting your hands out of your pockets to look at your watch! As 90 minutes approached, and yes it was a draw, there were those who happily admitted they would rather see a goal for Hereford than have to endure extra time. Not that extra time made any difference, as another 1-1 draw ensued and the dreaded penalties were needed. We lost this one though (5-4 for the stats freaks among you), and that rounded off a thoroughly poor evening just perfectly! Coupled with a hire car that had a special device fitted to ensure that the windscreen misted up every 15 seconds, it all made for a lovely trip back to Essex.

Of course our league form wasn't giving us anything to cheer about either, although a home win over obviously-going-to-be-Champions Notts County was a nice surprise. When we managed to throw away a 3-0 lead at Brighton, Hove and Gillingham Albion on Boxing Day, many thought it was all over. A view which was vocally shared with the assistant manager Steve 'I only play because I pick the team' Whitton, when the fanzine sponsored a match against Torquay in January. Unfortunately, we forgot that you shouldn't do that sort of thing when you sit in the main stand (have to keep that sort of thing in the terraces, old boy!), and managed to give the local papers their Monday headlines (cheers Derek!).

We'd like to think that our advice to the two Steves (Whitton and Wignall - the manager) spurred them on to great things, coupled with our editorial in the following issue of *TBE* that suggested that Wignall should market the rose-tinted glasses that allowed him to see the U's getting promotion. Whatever the cause of the amazing run that followed, we are happy at *TBE* Towers to admit that Wignall was right! From the home win against Mansfield on February 13th to the game against Hull on April 13th our record was spectacular: W9, D2 and L1. Promotion form in anyone's book. The mid-point of that run saw a wonderful 5-1 thumping of Macclesfield. We always get one great result every year, and so this is a good enough reason to mention our

7-1 crushing of Lincoln last season yet again! We were now fourth, just points away from automatic promotion.

The pressure got to the team though. Defeat at Chester on April 18th was followed by only a draw at home to Orient in the penultimate game. This meant that although we were pretty much assured of three points in the last game at Doncaster (and that was bloody close - just a 1-0 win), it was the play-offs for Colchester again. It's strange, because if you'd asked us if we'd have been happy with the play-offs at Christmas, you'd have had us all believing in Santa again! But when you were so close to automatic promotion, fourth spot suddenly wasn't the prize it should have been (*and* I missed out on my each-way bet at 12/1!).

And so the lottery it was. The first leg at Barnet was lost 1-0, so if we emulated our league 1-1 draw in the return, we'd be out, complaining that the play-offs were unfair and that we should have been promoted! As it happened, it was a nail-biting affair. We were 1-0 up from a twelfth minute penalty, then they equalised just before the break. Then a David Greene header ensured extra time, but we had to score or Barnet would go through on the away goal. Having never quite forgiven them for getting promoted over us in our first season in the Conference, it was sweet revenge when a David Gregory goal on 95 minutes put us into the play-off final against Torquay.

And so it was off to Wembley again, our third visit in six years, and the second in successive years. But it just didn't seem quite as glamorous as that first time back in the FA Trophy! Coupled with the move to a Friday night, which was admittedly much more of a problem for the Torquay fans than for us, it produced the lowest ever play-off gate at Wembley. But for once, fortune smiled on us in the game and the U's finished victorious thanks to a 22nd minute penalty. It may not have been the best ever game of footy, but I don't really care, now that it's over!

So, Colchester United in the Second Division, the first time we've ever been in a division with that title (think about it!) and once again the senior team in Essex. For once in my life I'm disappointed that I don't know many Southend supporters! I would also like to thank Hayden Jones from *Bamber's Right Foot*, the Torquay fanzine, for the note wishing us good luck in Division Two next season (it's that camaraderie again), even if he did think the penalty decision was dodgy... It never was!

Next year a whole new group of supporters can marvel at the wonder that is Layer Road. God knows what the Man City fans will make of it, but we don't really mind - we'll be moving to a new stadium soon, or so they keep telling us! Now, how do you get to Maine Road?

BOB LORD'S SAUSAGE

Burnley

King Waddle? 'King Awful!

If anyone's thinking of investing in a self-destruct button this summer, they'd be well advised to consult our chairman, Frank Teasdale. One year ago all looked rosy in the garden. Adrian Heath was settling in well and despite an anti-climactic finish to the '96-97 season we were all confident about a real promotion push. Inchy was lining up a few deals to fine-tune the squad and was about to offload a few of the hangers on. We couldn't possibly fail. That was until Teasdale withdrew the finance for the deals. Five days later Inchy was Everton's assistant manager and we were up shit creek.

So imagine our surprise

"The Meaty Burnley Fanzine With Only a Little Gristle"

Bob Lord's
SAUSAGE

October '97   Doom & Gloom Edition   Issue 2: £1

Ooops!

"Just give me the keys and I'll f*** off now"

when one Christopher Waddle appeared at the doorstep of Brunshaw Road a couple of weeks later with his big mate Glenn Roeder - you know, the one with the great record of management at Watford and Gillingham.

"We've been in this division for one day too long" they declared in unison. And then we heard all the usual guff about huge support, great stadium, Premiership potential, blah, blah, blah. Us fanzine addicts were in raptures. The possibilities for puns were endless. **Waddle Happen Next? Waddle He Do Now? Waddle It Take To Get Rid Of The Useless Bastard?** I even saw a woman wearing a tee shirt with **Waddle Stop Us Winning The League Now?** written on the back. Bet she feels a right berk now.

In hindsight, an opening day visit to Watford did bode ill for the season. By the time we'd lost our third consecutive away game by a single goal, the ecstasy of Waddle's appointment was turning to incredulity as we still hadn't managed a goal in over nine hours of league football. Everyone had their own theory as to why the onion bag wouldn't bulge. In truth, it was the fact that we were crap. The football was pretty, the defence was tight-ish and the strikers were working their arses off. Midfield on the other hand was on a long vacation. I envisage their return next season, though with the current personnel it may only be a cameo performance.

Our first Division Two goal was scored at York, and boy did we celebrate. Shame we got stuffed 3-1. A friend asked me afterwards if I thought we would still make the play-offs. The way we were playing, we wouldn't even have made the Third Division's.

Once we'd made our traditional second round exit from the Coca-Cola Cup (why do fanzine editors insist on calling it the *Fizzy Pop Cup* - as if it's a massively hilarious joke?) by getting hammered 4-0 at home to Stoke, yours truly had seen enough. The band of empty-headed 'Chris Waddle is God Whatever He Does' supporters were about to witness a dissenting view. On the spur of the moment I ditched the original cover for Issue 2 of the *Sausage* in favour of the one which you can see at the head of this article. It went down a storm in some quarters. In others the response was akin to a turd in a soup bowl. Some accused the fanzine of being anti-Waddle while others applauded us for being brave enough to comment honestly on the load of shite we were witnessing. The truth is that only three pages out of 40 openly criticised Waddle. It was me who was anti-Waddle, not the fanzine.

That didn't stop some people though. We achieved national infamy when the *Daily Mail* reporter, Richard Bott, visited Turf Moor in the absence of any Premiership games. He bought a copy and proceeded to make up quotes from the *Sausage* in his report. His new book, *Three Curries and a Shish Kebab*, allegedly contains the line "My name's Richard Bott and I'm a cunt."

The victory marked the beginning of a run of seven games without defeat. We even won away from home, but seeing as *everyone* won at Luton it didn't really count. On November 29th we won only our fourth game of the season, coming from behind to win 2-1 at home to Northampton. It was pretty insignificant really, apart from the fact that we'd actually won. The real talking point was that Waddle went on *Radio Lancashire* straight after and had a right pop at the fans. Apparently we had applauded the opposition's centre forward more than our own. Which isn't all that surprising when our leading goalscorer, Andy Cooke, was sat on his arse wearing number 12. Lee Howey was favoured up front, despite the fact that he was horribly out of form. And a defender! Among the horseshite that came forth were comments that "This isn't a big club anymore" and "I don't give a shit; once the fans start shouting for me to go, I'll go." Strong words indeed. Did he really mean it? We were soon to find out.

The season was proving to be a nightmare. Waddle was now complaining about lack of funds, but he knew we were skint when he took the job. He spent a million quid at the outset but frittered it away on three bags of shit, namely Lee Howey, Mark Ford and Michael Williams. In fairness, Williams came on a free transfer from Sheffield Wednesday and immediately proved his worth - nothing! My God, this fellow is the worst footballer I have ever clapped eyes on. He couldn't pass, tackle, head or shoot. He couldn't even stand up! So his presence was sorely missed post-Christmas (yeah, and Kenny Dalglish oozes charisma!).

Unfortunately for us, Waddle believed that the previous season's top scorer Paul Barnes was the reason for our poor league position. Talk about addressing the symptoms and not the cause. Barnes was sacrificed in favour of Andy Payton, who himself had been sacrificed from his hometown club 14 years previously. When you look at Payton's record since returning to Burnley you'd be tempted to say that Waddle's judgement was spot on. You'd be wrong. The upturn in form was down to one man: Glen Little. Half way through the season Waddle and Roeder appeared at a Supporters' Club meeting to answer questions from the floor. When asked about Little, Roeder replied "Glen Little isn't fit to lace Chris Waddle's boots." Shortly after, a £100,000 deal was struck with Notts County to take him to Meadow Lane. Thank the Lord that Sam Allardyce couldn't raise the funds. Little eventually won a place in the side, and his inspirational performances just about kept us in touch with the other relegation candidates above us. Four months after winning his place, Little was the subject of a £400,000 bid from Stockport. Needless to say Waddle turned it down. From bag of shit to bag of tricks, the lanky winger saved us. Make no mistake about it. Meanwhile, Andy Payton was scoring goals like they were going out of fashion. And nearly all of them were important - especially during the run-in.

We embarked on another seven game unbeaten run and, despite demolishing York 7-2, the highlight was a 3-2 victory at Deepdale. Neil Moore's 94th minute winner was a joy to behold, not because it was spectacular, but rather because it secured our second away win and, for once, we'd had an ounce of luck.

Then just as we heaved ourselves out of the bottom four, defeat after defeat followed and we were sinking fast. I'd resigned myself to relegation by the end of March. We were playing so badly and losing so convincingly that the journey planner to Torquay had already been consulted.

The run-in to season's end promised to be like a wake. That it didn't turn out like that is still proving difficult to believe. Every time we lost, we went and won the next game. We lost against Millwall, Wigan and Bournemouth and disposed of Grimsby, Fulham, Bristol City and Northampton (shame on the Cobblers for surrendering six points to us). Finally, it all came down to the last game. For ourselves and Plymouth Argyle this was on a par with the Liverpool - Arsenal Championship decider of 1989. If we didn't win, we would be relegated and Plymouth would stay up. We also needed Brentford to fail to win at Bristol Rovers.

Almost 19,000 turned up at the Turf to witness the occasion. Andy Cooke gave us an early lead with a header and helped settle the nerves. But news was filtering through that Bristol Rovers were down to ten men. As if to compound the despondency, Plymouth equalised. I couldn't handle it. I couldn't handle the five pints I'd sunk before hand either. So when Cookey headed in the winner I was having a leak. It was the perfect metaphor for the season - a piss-take! Brentford lost and went down with Plymouth. We danced on the pitch and patted each other on the back for a job well done. After all, we had done *our* bit this season.

For the supporters of Plymouth I have genuine sympathy. I apologise for the heartbreak and wish you a speedy return. To the supporters of the rest of the division I bid you all a big 'Fuck Off'. For nine months we've been taunted with relegation chants and that God-awful "Cheer up Chrissy Waddle" song. My indignation was never stronger than when I saw a group of Bournemouth fans goading us with relegation gestures and fake mirth. I was genuinely gutted for those supporters 18 months previously when it looked like they were about to lose their club. I won't be wishing them all the best for next year, that's for sure. And then there was the Carlisle débâcle. After their 2-1 victory at Brunton Park they spat in our faces, kicked and punched us and wished us a happy time in Division Three. Yeah, the last laugh was on us, you bunch of neo-Scottish thugs. Enjoy Division Three, it's where you deserve to be.

Waddle has gone and he's taken Roeder with him. He's also taken his paranoia and his trite clichés. In the end, everyone else was to blame for Burnley's position except himself. He accused the local press and the local radio stations of stirring up trouble and, latterly, wouldn't even do interviews for *Granada*. He regularly moaned about the mindless speculation and tittle-tattle in the papers, but what the hell were they supposed to do when he treated them with contempt?

We all welcomed Chris Waddle with open arms. The fans couldn't have been more supportive at the start. After all, he was the man we wanted. We could forgive his Italia '90 penalty miss. We could even forgive him his horrendous mullet haircut. We are so desperate for any crumb of success that we would have forgiven his pants media profile - if we could have had the compensation of a winning side out on the pitch. The fact that it all ended so acrimoniously was entirely his own fault. His commitment to Burnley Football was never 100 per cent. Before the crucial clash at home to Grimsby, was Waddle agonising over team selection and injuries? No, he was sat next to John Motson at Old Trafford commentating on Man U's game against Liverpool. It also transpires that he had signed a contract to commentate on the World Cup for the BBC. So while the rest of Division Two were going to be re-building their squads, Waddle would have been passing judgement on Denilson and Ronaldo. Hardly time spent profitably.

Most of us have this romantic notion that football should be played on the deck - accurate and creative. Because all we want is to be entertained, right? Wrong, wrong, wrong. What we really want is to see the ball hit the onion bag more times than the opposition. Whether it's route one or Clough-esque passing - it's all about goals. Waddle's problem was that he wouldn't compromise his principles, even if that meant Third Division football.

News filters through that we've just appointed Stan Ternent as our new Messiah. Will he lead us to the Promised Land of Division One? Whatever happens, his philosophy is for direct football, not the pretty stuff. And if that means scoring more goals than we concede then there will be no complaints from me.

BRIAN MOORE'S HEAD

Gillingham

It is impossible to write any review of Gillingham's season without first making mention of the events of March 28th. The warm glow of a vital win over Fulham was quickly extinguished by the news of the death of Fulham fan Matthew Fox outside the ground. It was difficult to comprehend how such a thing could have happened at Priestfield, and it was not made any easier to handle by the inflammatory and inaccurate reporting by the media. As time has passed, and it has emerged that the victim was not exactly an innocent bystander, it still feels like there is a stain on our club that will never disappear. We have continued to feel the backlash, with

dawn raids on the homes of both Gillingham and Fulham supporters (which were not, according to the police, connected with Matthew Fox's death - but of course, as I'm sure we're all well aware of the dastardly reputation of both club's fans). It will take a long time for the wounds to heal, and I'm sure there will be those who will be looking to start a war when the clubs meet again. But despite what the media may have claimed, there was no history of bad feeling between the clubs before the death of Matthew Fox, and true supporters should come to the fore and ensure that there will be none afterwards.

'97-98 was a season of ups and down. Gillingham were involved variously in a promotion battle and a relegation fight. We were sometimes entertaining, other times as dull as ditch water. The stars of the season were undoubtedly Ade Akinbiyi and Paul Smith. Akinbiyi, playing his first full season of league football, showed a devastating turn of pace and an eye for goal (if I can lapse into programme speak for a moment) and was too hot for most Second Division defences to handle. Smith, a summer acquisition from Brentford, was the epitome of ever-present consistency in midfield, and pipped the aforementioned Akinbiyi by one vote in the Player of the Year poll (I can exclusively reveal that it would have been the other way around if my mate and I had got around to voting!). Also mentioned in despatches are central defenders Barry Ashby (signed from Brentford - whose fans seemed to be getting a bit miffed that we keep nicking their best players - all I can say to them is Nicky Forster - they'll know what I mean) and Guy Butters, who had the misfortune to break both his leg and his cheekbone (although not necessarily in that order) but still finished second top scorer and the most reliable penalty taker we've had in years. Meanwhile, young Jim Corbett dazzled on the wing as the season drew to a close.

On the debit side, last season's top scorer Iffy Onuora failed to impress, and was flogged to Swindon in March, scored on his debut at QPR then broke his cheekbone after colliding with the ref in a later game, and last year's Player of the Year Andy Hessenthaler divided his time equally between whinging, diving and crab impersonations (not to mention following up last season's dozen bookings with another ten this time around). We also failed to find an adequate replacement in goal for Big Fat Jim Stannard (who played about half the games, while various loaners, none of them - bar Mike Pollin - any better than the rotund one, appeared in the rest). New signings Neil Masters, Brian Statham and Mark Patterson proved to be either injury-prone or crap (and in some cases both). A special mention here for Statham, who managed to get himself sent off twice in his first seven appearances for the club including his return to his old lot, Brentford (again!), where he unaccountably decided that jumping up and down on one of his former team-mates was a sensible thing to do. The referee, unsurprisingly, failed to agree, handing Brentford a penalty and Statham an early bath.

In the final analysis Gillingham failed to make the play-offs because they didn't score enough goals, simple as that. Of course, when you miss the boat by that narrow a margin there is bound to be a lively debate about where it all went wrong (many are still arguing about the '78-79 season, when we missed promotion by a single point). There is a body of opinion which suggests that our failure to grab a play-off spot was all down to chairman Paul Scally, who failed to come up with the cash to allow a deadline day signing or two.

Mind you, there is a faction at Priestfield that blames Scally for everything, from the price of the tea to global warming, and they probably won't be satisfied until we've won the Premiership, FA Cup and Champions' League (in the same season, mark you). These people are missing the point. First, panic buys on deadline day very rarely work, and second, Gillingham actually blew their season away during the months of November and December.

At the end of October we were third in the table with 24 points from 14 games. Between November 1st and Boxing Day we took just four points from ten games, were knocked out of the FA Cup by Bristol Rovers and lost at home to Third Division Peterborough in the AutoWindscreens Shield. And by the turn of the year we'd slipped to 17th. I've thought long and hard about this, and bearing in mind all the facts and figures, can come to but one conclusion: the team were kidnapped by aliens and then replaced by extraterrestrial doppelgangers identical in every respect bar one - they couldn't play football to save their lives. When you compare the rest of the season to those dreadful two months it's really the only explanation. Some of the performances we witnessed defied logic, reason and the laws of mathematics. Points were tossed away by virtue of late goals against Millwall (two in the last seven minutes), Blackpool (last minute) and, most unbelievably of all Southend, against whom we contrived to turn a 1-0 win into a 2-1 defeat by conceding goals in the 91st and 94th minutes, thus handing the Shrimpers their first Priestfield victory since dinosaurs ruled the earth. The run culminated at Dean Court when Gillingham ruined everyone's Christmas for the second year running by losing 4-0. Mercifully, the sinister alien experiment was concluded as the new year began, and the real team were returned to their rightful places (with their collective memories suitably adjusted, obviously) to carry on where they'd left off. A nine match unbeaten run lifted us back into the play-off race, and the form of the previous two months appeared all the more inexplicable as the Gills romped to victories at promotion-bound Watford and Bristol City on consecutive Saturdays (the former made all the more memorable by the live *Sky* coverage allowing the watching nation to view Gillingham at their best, outplaying the home side from start to finish).

The unbeaten run ended disappointingly at Wycombe, and the last two months of the season were to prove equally frustrating. Poor form away from home was largely negated by a run of six straight home wins, but it seemed that every time we climbed into the play-off zone we would immediately shoot ourselves in the foot and slide back out again. We had numerous chances to consolidate a top six berth but continually failed to do so. Fortunately the other contenders were all falling over themselves (or in Fulham's case, their wallets) to do the same. Clearly it was going to go to the wire.

We travelled to struggling Plymouth on the penultimate Saturday, knowing we needed a win to keep up the pressure. What followed was one of the worst games of the season, but everyone who was there will claim it was brilliant. Eighty-nine minutes of tedium and frustration ended with Paul Smith scuffing a shot into the bottom corner. Ironically, having moments earlier been frantically trying to raise the team from their torpor by urging them to throw everyone forward, we spent the whole of injury time urging them to pull everyone back in blanket defence. The final whistle sounded to joyous scenes on the away end, whilst the Plymouth players and fans looked on in stunned disbelief as if unable to comprehend the fact that they'd just been all but relegated by a spawny injury-time goal. The task was now clear - a win at home to Wigan would put us in the play-offs; anything else would leave us at the mercy of others. A 0-0 stalemate saw us fall at the final hurdle. The injury ravaged team had given their all, but in the end they just didn't have anything left in the tank. Of course, that didn't make the failure any easier to take, nor did the thought that three of the four teams that made it would be suffering the same disappointment as us in the following weeks.

Next year is not going to be any easier. We have been joined by the likes of Stoke and Man City, whilst there are several teams with multi-million pound transfer budgets, of whom Fulham are but one. The Gills meanwhile have lost top scorer Ade Akinbiyi (to Bristol City for £1.2 million - plus a 40% sell-on clause, so hopefully he'll score 30 goals by Christmas and they'll be compelled to sell him to Liverpool for umpteen squillion quid) and outstanding 17-year-old Jim Corbett to Blackburn for £1 million (watch out for him in the next few years). Neither will be easy to replace, but hopefully Tony Pulis will spend wisely (presuming he himself hasn't been snapped up by a bigger club by the time you read this - it's going to happen sooner or later) and mould a side that will challenge once again. Fingers crossed and remember - keep watching the skies.

Source: Seaside Saga

BUILD A BONFIRE

Brighton & Hove Albion

"Move along please - nothing to see here..." says PC Beard to the throngs of Brighton fans.

Brighton followers have had the most traumatic few years in their entire history. It's been well documented within the media, and world-wide support has been phenomenal, probably because it could easily happen to your team next. Things can only get better, we tell ourselves - mainly because we daren't think about life without our football team. No matter who you support, I pray you don't have to go through the nightmare that Albion fans have endured. The latest season can be summed up as the same-old same-old.

uild a **ONFIRE**

A Football Fanzine For Brighton

BHA vs DONCASTER
26.01.97

THE FIGHT TO SURVIVE

ISSUE 3   *Feb '98*
SURVIVING THE MONEYMEN!
10% donation to BHA. Keep the faith!

£1

It started with our home of nearly 100 years being demolished to make way for warehouse stores; the Goldstone having been sold by our then chairman, Bill Archer. At this stage we'd resigned ourselves to travelling to our rivals Portsmouth to watch home games, a path that could only lead to bankruptcy. How long could we survive on gates of just a few hundred with no other income, and what sort of welcome would we receive from the Pompey faithful? Increasingly it looked like an asset-stripping exercise as the club appeared to be wound down.

But there was a glimmer of hope in the form of Dick Knight. Ad-man and fan of over 30 years, he had thrown his hat into the 'possible purchaser' ring towards the end of the '96-97 season. Unfortunately the intransigent Mr Archer wasn't looking for a buyer... Stalemate. Only after increasingly bitter protests did the FA decide to help and requested that all parties go to the independent mediators CEDR. Even then it was a case of Knight wanting 100% or nothing, with Archer refusing to sell up. These tensions continued throughout the close season. It was an interminable summer of watching and waiting, not even knowing if we would be allowed to continue in the Football League. Not being able to do anything, just having to wait is unbelievably frustrating. From a cultural aspect it was 'our' club but it soon hits home how little 'we' matter in the financial circles now running football.

During this time it was announced that we would be playing our home games in Gillingham... a mere 150-mile round trip. There were also going to be restrictions on the Brighton fans within the ground too, segregating them from our despised chief executive David Bellotti. The downward spiral looked set to continue, when, after seemingly years of non-movement, Dick Knight finally wrested control of 49.5% of Brighton. He was now officially chairman; a fellow football fan led our board and we could finally say good riddance to our main protagonist... Joy, joy, unconfined joy.

The nomadic season started with the high point of the year, a 'friendly' against long-time rivals Crystal Palace. We played them off the park and felt that prospects were looking good for a mid-table position. This despite the disappearance of our traditional blue and white stripes, replaced by a kit cloned from Wigan, Torquay, Lincoln etc... Sacrilege! Long live the stripes. We also had an encouraging pre-season tour of the West Country playing against the likes of Tiverton. That was when Brighton's young teenage prospect John Westcott was introduced to the first team. Steve Gritt was always encouraging him, building his confidence, and he continues to learn and can still get better. Look out for him.

So with confidence high, a mostly fit squad and despite having to play every game away from home, we went into August boldly and brashly. Who could stop us or keep us down? No-one!

The loss away to Swansea on the first day of the season and the nine further games without a win brought us thumping back to reality. Nothing had really changed. To make matters worse, it seemed that referees hated us (it's not as if we all get that feeling, is it?). And just because of some little protests in the previous year or two, the police had us marked down as category C fans (trouble makers in old money). Then came the resentment, not on our part, but rather in the shape of Leyton Orient fans. They hated us. They were even considering us as their new rivals. You could trace the enmity back to last season and the ruck at the Goldstone. On that occasion one or two of our more hot-headed brethren had tried to, shall we say, interrupt proceedings after Scott Marshall had made some rather provocative hand gestures to a full and emotionally-charged North Stand. How they screamed to have us kicked out of the league. And all because we were/are/always considered a BIG team and they are always going to be Brighton wannabes. The trouble was that they kept beating us. It was very *very* annoying losing to teams like Orient.

Mind you, we never did shake the losing habit finishing with just 35 league goals and a mere 35 points. Guaranteed relegation figures in any other year except for the misfortunes of Doncaster Rovers. Apart from the Donny and us, all of the other teams in Division Three were very much of a muchness. The only difference was either a commitment to compete and win or a manager with the tactical awareness to out-psyche the opposition. We were found out on both counts!

At one point, cash was tighter than a scouser's perm and we had to release our main money earners, who just happened to be our most experienced players. This wasn't going to help our performances, although it did help us stay financially afloat. The strategy then appeared to be to fill the gaps with cheap bodies - no one of any standard you understand but enough to keep us ahead of 92nd position. Thanks to these shrewd dealings and a new marketing manager who knew what he was doing, we are still in business now and looking forward to bringing the team back to Brighton.

On the playing front (yes, there was even some football played) the season was full of Swansea and Orient-type games. In the league we had limited highlights: beating then leaders Peterborough away 2-1, over Christmas. This after playing Colchester at the Priestfield on Boxing Day, being 3-0 down at half time and then coming back to draw 4-4. It was more exciting than Sunderland vs Charlton! The fans that left at half time and went back to the pub missed a true Christmas cracker.

Other wins are now listed in full - Rochdale, Doncaster, Scunthorpe (twice), Chester and the previously mentioned Peterborough. Six wins out of 44 league games, 48 if you include first round exits in all cup competitions. We couldn't even win the Sussex Cup! Not good enough for ANY team, professional or otherwise. These stats were the undoing of messiah Steve Gritt who was sacked by Dick Knight. Sure, he'd pulled off the miracle of '96-97, but we were back in big trouble THIS year, and no manager could survive in his job with such poor results. The players have a lot to answer for, undoubtedly, but Gritt's tactics weren't up to the job.

Then Brian Horton joined us as manager. Re-joined us to be correct, as he'd captained the Albion during the most successful period in our history. 'Nobby' soon showed his passion for the game and has recently confirmed that he will continue to reshape Brighton into a winning force again. It won't be easy though, by any stretch of the imagination. Even under his control, Brighton still only registered two out of their six wins. He now knows just how hard it is for any manager to do well at this level with little money.

Brian Horton has openly said that he appreciates the fans of the Albion. They are constantly striving to raise funds and 2,500 regulars have streamed out of Brighton every fortnight to make the Gillingham trek. But next season, with the team back in Brighton, there's every indication that we'll pack our temporary home with 6,000 per game. The potential to rise again is still there.

Finally, here's a quip from our esteemed manager that sums up the Albion perfectly. After yet another defeat he turned to one of his players and asked how long they'd been throwing away leads and then losing. "Four years" was the honest reply.

CHELSEA INDEPENDENT

Chelsea

The more things change, the more they stay the same.

No, I could never quite grasp that either - until this season. A Chelsea cup double and the sight of a Chelsea captain lifting the FA Cup on *Grandstand's* opening credits show how much things have changed. But we beat Tottenham, so no change there.

But to be honest it's been a strange season. Following up the cup win was always going to be tight, but holding our own against Manchester United in the Charity Shield and then being unlucky to only draw up at Old Trafford got the season off to a good start.

However, the atmosphere at games was awful all season - as was

Does my head look big in this?

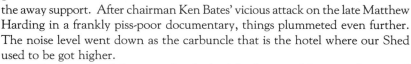

Coca-Cola success goes to Luca's head

the away support. After chairman Ken Bates' vicious attack on the late Matthew Harding in a frankly piss-poor documentary, things plummeted even further. The noise level went down as the carbuncle that is the hotel where our Shed used to be got higher.

I'm not one of these people who hark back to a golden age of restricted views, rivers of urine and police charges but I can't help but feel a tinge of regret that a lot of the fun and noise has gone from football. How much of this is down to the changing profile of match-goers I don't know. But in certain parts of Stamford Bridge each tackle, pass or shot is greeted with a rustle of paper and then, after a moment's pause, a whispered chorus of "Lebeouf."

This phenomenon started at the Bridge during the last year and a half of Hoddle's reign, where we began to play attractive football and occasionally looked unbeatable, and it continued with Gullit's tenure. Many of the first 'nouveau' fans now have season tickets. I have no problem with that; I want as many people to enjoy football - and Chelsea in particular - as possible. But do you really have to sit behind me, braying "carefree, whomsoever you may be" in your overly loud and grating middle class accents?

Supporting Chelsea now appears to be more of a test of how badly you're prepared to be treated. Whilst the catering has improved no end, it's still galling to see that a slice of processed cheese can add 50p to the price of a burger. And when Coors sponsored us we at least got a 'premium' lager for our £2.40. Now it's Fosters. I mean, *really*. Who in their right mind would drink that rubbish?

And then there's all this Chelsea Village nonsense. This is the holding company for Chelsea Football Club, and although it trades heavily on the club's recent success it doesn't appear to give too much back. Rumours fly about the club being invoiced for mineral water by Chelsea Village catering and that many of the CFC products in the new megastore - which is bigger than Man Utd's - make money for Chelsea Village Merchandising, not the club.

What's basically happened is that a new company with a range of interests has begun using Chelsea as a springboard. If it all goes wrong there's always the *Sky TV* money, or, failing that, a large piece of real estate in central London known affectionately as Stamford Bridge to flog. I for one think that sucks. The cost of season tickets - and match tickets in general - is getting prohibitive. Plus, if you're like me, you're sure to spend a fair bit in the pub, all of which is making football an expensive day out. People are picking and choosing their games more than ever. Yet when some people complained at the 40 per cent price hike for the '98-99 season others were heard to say "we'll still buy our tickets - *we're* loyal!"

But back to the football. We saw some poor performances, although there were some highlights such as thumping Spurs 6-1 at Three Point Lane and beating a reasonably impressive Derby 4-0 at home. It was always going to be difficult to top the previous season, although a few more years of mediocre performances with cup wins at the end would suit me fine.

Stockholm was absolutely brilliant. Despite all the talk of violence - and the Swedish press were apparently predicting rampaging hordes of fans and open warfare in the old town, Gamla Stan - the Swedes were friendly and welcoming. There was no trouble, despite 2,000 Chelsea fans sleeping rough the night before the game. During the day of the match, the pub we drank in had Stuttgart and Chelsea fans mixing happily and singing long and loud. By mid-afternoon we even had them singing "Ten men went to mow."

Never have I seen so many drunk people looking so happy. The next day was spent greeting people with wide grins. To top it, we even saw the King of Sweden, although sadly he wasn't riding a bike or carrying a basket of flowers. Apparently he was holding a diplomatic reception. My argument that I should be let in, as I was an ambassador for England (which is what we were always told on school trips abroad), cut little ice. Instead I had to settle for a stroll through the old town and picking up a couple of souvenirs.

In many ways it was different to the previous cup wins. The FA Cup was sheer elation, one of the best days of my life. The Coca-Cola was a good day, but a little disappointing. We couldn't even gather around the ground to welcome the team or have a beer in the Shed bar, as the hordes of tough-looking security guards kept ordinary folk at a distance.

But I'm glad I didn't miss Stockholm: if you get the chance, watch your team win a European trophy. I highly recommend it. You'll even enjoy the hangover.

Mind you, the FA Cup win hangover had continued most of the season for some players, most notably Zola. He never looked fully fit, although the cup winner was a cracker and he did grab a hat-trick against Derby in a good display. Even their fans gave him a standing ovation when he was taken off towards the end.

One player who impressed when given a chance was Tore Andre Flo, a summer signing from Tromso of Norway. For such a big, ungainly lump he's remarkably quick and has good control, which is a bit of a novelty at Chelsea when you remember all the hours we spent watching Tony Cascarino plod along upfront.

A hat-trick against Tottenham is always going to endear a player to the Chelsea faithful, but over the course of the season he scored some important goals - including a brace during an impressive display in Seville against Real Betis. Sadly, by the time you read this he'll have probably moved on, falling foul of the over-rated, over-paid, over the hill buying system.

Don't get me wrong; I'm delighted to see big names play for us, but then I was delighted when we signed Mal Donaghy. To make a consistent challenge for the Championship I can't help but feel that we need to go about things in a different way. There is a big difference between having the likes of Shearer, Beckham, Ince or Adams and the players we've signed.

Star names alone don't guarantee success, as Newcastle have found out. You need a solid base on which they can perform. We haven't got that yet, as was proved against Arsenal (repeatedly), Liverpool and Manchester United. And that's the difference.

THE CIDER'ED

Bristol City

Forget Massive Attack, forget Portishead and forget Roni Size. Despite what you may have heard it is actually Bristol City FC and, more precisely, The Wurzels who have been most influential in our region's rise to musical credibility. It was the lyrical genius of the latter, certainly the world's favourite West Country bumpkins, that provided the audio accompaniment to the Robins' return to the First Division after an absence of three seasons, and that was aurally savoured by away fans from as far afield as Carlisle and Plymouth.

The Wurzels released their hit single, *One for the Bristol City*, in 1977, after City's promotion to the First Division proper. Throughout '97-98, as we sang along to *Drink Up Thee Cider*, the belief that we could once again stake a claim for top-flight football emerged. We may have escaped only from the Second Division, but down 'ere in 'Brizzle' such an ascent is being viewed as incipient of an unrelenting surge to Premiership football. Or as the hoe-wielding musicians more eloquently put it, *Now they're in the groove / Pretty soon they'll prove the finest in the land.*

However, cider-guzzling and tractor-driving are overshadowed in Bristolians' affections by City, so it's only right to move from our raucous farming chums and look at footballing affairs. A cliché it may be but at the end of the season the league table doesn't lie. However, to conclude from the gap between City and Watford and the rest of the division that '97-98 has been a walk in Ashton Park would be untrue. A few instances of footballing excellence - best illustrated by an exquisite 4-1 victory over Grimsby - have been surrounded by many matches of truly Second Division quality and, at times, we started to worry that a 16 point gap from the play-offs in mid-January just wouldn't be enough.

This is strong testament to the pervasive Fortress Ashton belief, passed lovingly from father to son, that Bristol City are one of the dozing Gargantuans of the English game; and such a mentality saw the level of expectation at the season's start hopelessly accentuated. Because almost a million pounds had been spent in the summer. Because we'd flirted with play-off success in '96-97. And because, above all else, the manager was a former Gashead, it really was a case of automatic promotion come May 2nd or a vicious lynching, involving whips and tomatoes, of everyone involved in running the club.

Therefore, only the most naïve of supporters were at all surprised when premature calls for the detachment of John Ward's head started after the 2-0 defeat at Gillingham on 4th October. For the record, the manager survived the abusive barrage, head in place, and we finished the season promoted as the Second Division's second highest goalscorers, with more wins than any other team, having kept 16 clean sheets, and with the second best defensive record in the division. Moreover, the players followed the match at Priestfield with 15 unbeaten league games, of which 13 saw us take three points, with eight wins in succession. When we lost 1-0 at Fulham, on 28th December, the dissenters had miraculously subsumed themselves into the more patient majority, forgetting of what they had been complaining, and JW was hailed as the Messiah to lead us to the mercantile land that is Rupert Murdoch's Premiership.

However, it is slightly unfair to criticise those who expressed their dissatisfaction without considering the context of their complaints. Until 70 minutes through the York fixture, two weeks after the Gillingham débâcle, Ward had chosen to play with what had become a generally defensive 5-3-2 formation. Without erratically skilful play from Barbadian hair-changer Greg Goodridge, without a central defender who could genuinely play the *libero* role, and with the productive Tinnion-Bell left-sided partnership removed, many matches became cautious performances from players who seemed as uncomfortable with the system as the fans.

That calls for the sacking of Ward coincided with the loudest cries for the reintroduction of 4-4-2 was unsurprising and it is to his credit that he changed things during the fixture against the Minstermen. In an apparent capitulation to fan opinion he responded as desired when chants of "*Bring on the Goodridge*" reached a crescendo. The superb run of results that launched City from 19th position on 4th October to second place on 1st November, and left us in an automatic promotion position until the season's end, was due to the formation change and therefore the influence of the re-selected Barbados captain Goodridge and the repositioned Brian Tinnion - who arguably had his best season for the club.

Without giving an unfair reflection of us cider'eds, it is worth considering that Tinnion, the inspiration behind many of our 25 victories, and disputably the player of the season, was almost hounded out of the club by (again) a minority of supporters during 1994-5. Survival of his stint as the whipping-boy simply underlined his character and it is not an exaggeration to say that of the players who have represented City in the past ten years, few have shown more pride in the club than 'the Tinman'. This was reflected by the disappointment of many, when during the promotion run-in, and in Shaun Taylor's absence, Gary Owers - rarely the inspirational figure that local journalists would have fans believe and already placed on the transfer list - was chosen as captain above the man who celebrates every corner with a clenched-fisted "come on!"

Epitomised best by his role in the consecutive 4-1 home wins over Millwall and Grimsby, the form of Tinnion was partly due to Mickey Bell, his eventual left flank partner and a £175,000 tribunal steal from Wycombe. It has been a peculiarity of City teams in the past few seasons that the left-back role has been filled superbly: this year we had Mickey, last year Darren Barnard (now of Barnsley and Wales) and previously Martin Scott. As a result, the difficult task of filling the hallowed position was, at the start of the season, thrust upon Mickey by the magical thrusting fairy. He performed the job magnificently, scoring match-winning goals on six occasions in the process.

Aside from his overall contribution, Bell was also indirectly responsible for one of the season's most amusing events. At Ashton Gate, against Wycombe, the away fans wittily tried to target him with "*Judas*" chants. However, in their torrents of vitriol they neglected to realise that lookalike Jim Brennan was actually playing in the position that the penalty taker supreme held at Adams Park, with Mickey playing further upfield. In several humorous instances the bemused Canadian under-21 international was labelled a traitor. Sadly for Jim this led to a haircut. Unable to cope with living in the shadow of his teammate he quickly opted for the distinctive Graeme Le Saux look.

However, the level of influence Mickey had over the campaign was slightly worrying. Whilst few would deny the dominance we showed in home games with Chesterfield, Preston and Oldham, and away at York, it was disconcerting that the only difference between the teams proved to be Bell's penalties. It is, quite simply, imperative that we do not squander chances with such regularity at the higher level. However, with the late-May purchase of Ade Akinbiyi from Gillingham for a club record fee of £1.2m, to fill the void left by Shaun Goater, goalscoring worries have been allayed and few fear that we will experience again the sort of net-finding difficulties that caused our 1995 relegation.

The irony of having to replace Shaun Goater with Akinbiyi has been lost on no-one. Whereas the former Gillingham striker has joined a club that will play the likes of Wolves, Bolton and Birmingham next season, 'Billy' will entertain, among others, Colchester and Lincoln. To clarify matters, Shaun departed on transfer deadline day with the claim "I want to play at a higher level" still resonating in the ears of supporters. His move up in the world, of course, took him to Manchester City - a club battling to avoid relegation from the division to which we would be promoted just 15 days later. With money obviously being the key factor in Goater's move, it was not surprising that many cider'eds took enormous delight in seeing Joe Royle's side relegated on the last day of the season. City players joining in chants of "Goater's going to Macclesfield" on College Green, before a civic reception to celebrate promotion, demonstrated the general feeling. Good riddance? Most think so.

Having highlighted just a few memories of a great season, there remains much to say but space allows only cursory reference to some important points.

The impact of youth-team product Tommy Doherty after his introduction against Gillingham was massive and the words 'future England international' are being whispered quite seriously in these parts. Equally, the influence of ex-trainee Louis Carey has been immense and he should prove a mainstay in the team next season. Alongside the outstanding Shaun Taylor, now approaching his 63rd birthday, Louis has been phenomenal at the heart of a solid backline and is testament to Ward's tactical astuteness; the move there from right-back reinvigorated his game.

Moreover, JW's guile in the transfer market has been revelationary: Adam Locke, a free from Colchester, has been a major factor in our success whilst Colin Cramb, equally, looks an excellent prospect. The former Doncaster star proved an immediate favourite with the Ashton Gate crowd simply by putting absolutely everything into his game: he looks like he cares. His tenacity - best highlighted by a penalty won against Blackpool when he effectively forced the defender into a foul - complements pace and strength, and has been important in securing his popularity over Steve Torpey, euphemistically described by some as an archetypal English centre-forward. More importantly, though, Cramby continues our 'Scottish psychopath' striker tradition after Joe Jordan and Ian Baird.

Of the games themselves, three victories over the amusingly poor Gas stand out, while the 4-1 away defeat of Brentford proved particularly satisfying after the heartache suffered there in last season's play-offs. The Coke Cup victory over Leeds, which made us the best team in the world (Wardy concluded we were better than World Club Champions Juventus because they'd lost to Manchester United, beaten themselves by Leeds), was a highlight. The atmosphere at Burnley will be long remembered after our promotion a day earlier thanks to Grimsby's draw at Wycombe. The tension of the last day at Preston, which saw us fail to take the Championship, was palpable, especially with Teletext displaying the Watford score in executive boxes behind the away terrace. And finally, of course, the two 1-1 draws with Watford will endure in the minds of supporters.

In fact, it's impossible to separate the greater part of this season from the battle with Watford for the Championship. There has been a great deal of 'good humoured banter' among rival fans in a fight that, at times, was turning after each fixture, and that must be attributed largely to the long-standing friendship between Ward and Graham Taylor. The Easter Monday Ashton Gate fixture against the Hornets was long billed as the 'Championship decider' but the final result, a 1-1 draw that gave Watford promotion a couple of days after we'd secured it ourselves, failed to open a gap for either team. Perhaps, considering the Second Division-high crowd of 19,141 that served to emphasise that both teams have the resources necessary to re-establish themselves in the upper echelons of English football, the draw was the fairest result. In every respect the two clubs have matched each other throughout the season, and surpassed everybody else.

Indeed, only at the season's climax did our turnip-managed rivals take the title, City's defeat at Preston contrasting with Watford's triumph over Fulham. However, few left Deepdale with real complaints - all that counted was promotion. So, after three years in the Second Division wilderness we're back, the fans expectant and the board, led by Scott Davidson, ready to deliver. As The Wurzels would surely say, it's now not long before the higher divisions will once again... *hear the sound as we shout / Ooh ar ooh ar.*

Source: *Stand Up*

THE CITY GENT

Bradford City

Well, after consulting widely and taking all things into account, *City Gent* would say the season could be summed up as follows: IT WAS ALRIGHT.

Right, that's done then, but it leaves us several words short of the article length that the good editors of this book suggest. So to fill up at least some of this space we are going to make some awards (again). These are the work of the usual suspects, who gathered together to mull over the season whilst enjoying a few pints in the Old Bank one evening. So if you disagree with anything or are mortally offended by our more acerbic comments, you are wasting your time writing to *City Gent* to complain. Anyway here we go:

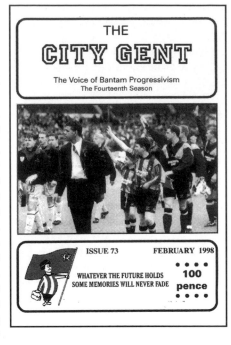

How wrong can you be award - Goes to those nice Crewe fans who came to Valley Parade early in the season and complemented City on their skilful attacking football. They added that they didn't think their team would survive in Division One (we still call it Division Two but we'll try and not cause confusion) if they had to play "teams as good as City every week." (They finished above us, mid-table in the league.)

Heroic away journey award - Goes to the ~~lunatics~~, sorry loyal fans, who went midweek (with overnight stay) to see Bradford City Reserves play Carlisle Reserves at Gretna (City's first competitive match on Scottish soil). During the match we were playing good football but losing when Paul Jewell (assistant manager at the time) turned to one of our fans and asked, "Can you believe we are losing this?" "Yes," replied the fan. Given the size of our squad and the quality of players we regularly had turning out for the reserves, those of us who watch these games expected a successful season. We were wrong.

Curious nickname award - City fans have always had a rather strange attitude to giving players nicknames. Some clubs seem to have one for every player, even though this is often of the Chazza or Bigsy type (Edhino, I am sure, would be called Eddie at some clubs but remains Edhino to us). We on the other hand tend to have fewer, but try for stranger or more confusing ones

(Sean McCarthy was always Scud even when we were moaning about him being sold). Hence it was with great delight that we heard one announcer mispronounce John Dyer as John Drier, so we promptly renamed him 'Spin'.

Arseholes of the season award - Tough competition for this one. David Mellor was obviously suggested for all the bollocks he talked about the sacking of Chris Kamara. However, as the man is such an arsehole all of the time anyway, his nomination was ruled out. Next up were the TB fans still gloating about that thug Kevin Grey breaking Gordon Watson's leg (the same ones were usually responsible for the racist chanting about Chris Kamara). Popular as their selection would have been, they were clearly overtaken by the excrement from West Bromwich Albion who thought it oh so clever to sing songs about the Bradford fire. Filth as you are, we hope you never have to go through anything like it. I'm sure the majority of decent Baggies would disown you. Definite winners.

Player most likely to be abused by opposition fans - Edhino.

Player least likely to understand the abuse by opposition fans - Edhino. (Well, unless they've arsed themselves to learn Portuguese.)

Low point of the season - Again, much competition for this award. Getting stuffed at home by Sunderland and the pathetic performances away at Bury and Crewe all received nominations. However, due to the sad old buggers who predominated at this get-together, the defeat by Park Avenue in the Bradford Centenary match just won. The City team contained many first team regulars, and the other players were mainly squad players who could expect first team appearances, but we still lost. On top of that the night was bloody freezing and Geoffrey managed to lose the half-time penalty shoot-out against the Avenue chairman. (Mind you, the goalkeeper was an ex-Avenue player so we're a bit suspicious about the outcome.)

High point of the season - Ignoring suggestions for "that booze up in Manchester before the cup," "the curry in Nawaabs after Portsmouth" and similar, the nomination for actually going top of the league for a short period *was* going to win. (Some of us have still got the *Telegraph and Argus* posters 'Super City Go Top'.) That was until friends returning with drinks pointed out the Cup Final win over L**ds United should get the award. Okay, it was the Northern Intermediate Cup, but a win over L**ds is a win over L**ds. And Gareth Grant got a hat-trick. Winner all the way.

Favourite chant - When we played Stoke City, their lot were having a stop out protest, not coming into the ground until ten minutes after kick off or something. However, as the ground filled up with Stoke followers - before kick off - a jolly chant of "We can see you sneaking in" broke out in sections of the Bradford crowd. (According to some Stoke fans they were 'too big for Division One' in seasons past. I wonder if they'll be far, far too big for Division Two. It is curious how many fans think their club is 'too big for Division One'. They think they have a divine right to a Premiership berth just because they inhabited the First Division back in the seventies or eighties. Look, it's about the playing ability of your current squad! Sorry, a digression, but it does get up our noses).

However, our top chant is Bradford City's answer to the constant crap we're subjected to from the United east of Pudsey and the Cottonopolis capitalists - "There's only one United and that's a chocolate biscuit!"

Away chant of the season - The curious chanting of "We're the best behaved supporters in the land" by Charlton fans definitely gets a special mention. But the clear winner comes courtesy of one of the frequent mispronunciations of a player's name over the tannoy. This time it happened at the pre-season friendly against Newcastle United and resulted in lengthy chanting by the Geordies of "There's only one Penis."

License to lurk - The *City Gent* photographer for looming up behind Alan Ball during a TV interview after Portsmouth had just escaped relegation at Valley Parade. Many City fans weren't too mortified to lose at home in the last game and so condemn Manchester City to the drop. Indeed, many even joined in with the Portsmouth celebrations with chants of "Are you watching Manchester?" This dislike seems to stem from Manchester City's appointment of Joe Royle. For some curious reason a number of Bradford fans think Joe Royle accepted the post as our manager after Kamara's sacking and was the 'big name' we'd been promised. Supposedly he reneged on this when approached by the "bigger, higher paid, higher profile" post at Maine Road. All nonsense no doubt. I'm sure Joe Royle is not a money-grabbing, traitorous egotist.

Player of the year – With the *City Gent* poll as yet uncounted, goalkeeper Gary Walsh seems to have won the club's award and various others. A good choice as he saved points (and face) for us on more than one occasion.

City Gent **curry guide experience of the season** - The All You Can Eat Sunday buffet at Nawaabs on Manor Row for £8.95. Top quality food, and boy, could we eat a lot.

Corn dolly football quote of the season - "You can't play a centre half in defence."

Corn dolly non-football quote of the year - "Now the weather's getting warmer I'm thinking of shaving my head off."

Best new demand of the Bradford City Liberation Front - The Chairman's un-Bantamlike campaign to remove Mellor as head of the Football Task Force to end. Mellor should be taken out and shot like the cringing white gnat establishment lickspittle deserves.

Best old demand of the Bradford City Liberation Front - No referees or assistants at Valley Parade. All decisions to be made by popular will of the Kop.

CLAP YOUR HANDS, STAMP YOUR FEET

Watford

Champions! Who would have thought it after our wretched finish to the previous season? And it was all so easy. Our first success in years and our first piece of proper silverware in 20. And here a similarity begins, as '77-78 was the first season we were managed by Graham Taylor. Who says lightning doesn't strike twice?

I must confess that I had my doubts when GT had had enough of working behind the scenes - and doubting GT is almost a hanging offence at Vicarage Road! He hadn't managed at this level for 19 years, and the previous term, despite Kenny Jackett's sterling effort, had been appalling. Still, as

Clap Your Hands Stamp Your Feet!
No.45   August 1997   £1

WATFORD VISIT THE SUMMER SALES AT LONG LAST!!!

And if either of you mention fruit I'll bang your heads together

Still padding out the pages with the same old crap!!!

soon as GT moseyed on back into the hot-seat, you knew there would be money to spend and within days Jason Lee arrived from Forest. At long last - a tall striker with some ability. A few weeks passed and then Peter Kennedy, Dai Thomas, Chris Day and Micah Hyde all joined up within a matter of days. The money GT had been promised hadn't even been touched, thanks to the selling of Kevin Miller to Palace and Kevin Phillips to Sunderland. Oh, and some Irish buffoon left under the Bosman ruling with "nothing to prove." Wolves this coming season will have the press featuring heavily on GT's return. "Sod that" will be Watford fans' reply. It'll be a perfect opportunity to abuse David Connolly who 'went to Feyenoord and won f-all'.

So the season was set and Chris Twaddle's Burnley were the first visitors to The Vic. A five-figure crowd and a comprehensive 1-0 win sent the Watford fans home happy. Twaddle seemed to be impressed by his team's performance, insisting that they deserved a draw. Well, in my book, to earn a draw once the opposition have scored, you should at least cross the half-way line and force the opposition 'keeper to touch the ball. More of him later...

I hate Spurs. No; I *detest* Spurs. It was a Watford victory at White Hart Lane in November 1982 that started the long-ball rumpus (and led to all of Taylor's teams being accused of playing that way). So I was not best pleased while driving home from work, when I found out we had signed 'Rocket' Ronnie Rosenthal, albeit on a free transfer. However, it took an absolute bullet on his debut at Swindon to change all that. I was going to say it was a rocket but that would have been too obvious.

The first away game was at Carlisle. Fortunately it was a Saturday, but if you'd suffered the journey I did, you too would've wished it was a Tuesday night. Being stuck on a coach for hours on a Saturday in August with the temperature in the eighties is not pleasant at the best of times, but to be with no toilet, no video and no air conditioning, made it almost unbearable. It was a good job we won with a Johnno special to seal the victory.

The good times were back! We were winning games far more comfortably than the scores suggested, and unlike the previous season, everyone was getting in on the act. Keith Millen even managed to score with a bicycle kick against his former club Brentford, in front of their fans just to make it doubly sweet. September ended and we were top. Superb!

October 4th 1997. A normal day for most. Not if you support Watford. Local derbies are always special, particularly as Watford hadn't won one for ten years. Normally it was us going into the game with a list of injuries running into double figures, but this time it was L***n's turn. Just 59 minutes later, the game was effectively over. We were 4-0 up - and it would have been more if the referee had awarded us the most blatant penalty of the season. Mind you, there would have been a riot if he had, as the home fans were not best pleased with the carnage going on in front of them. We spent most of the second half wondering how to get out alive. Within days, the celebratory T-shirts were out and the video wasn't too far behind. When you've waited ten years for something to happen, you just go with the flow...

We started to pull well clear of the pack, with only Bristol City on our heels, and by Christmas we were through the 50 point barrier. It would take a miracle for us not to go up. We hit our first dodgy spell and actually lost an away game at Burnley, which prompted Twaddle to say that as they'd won 2-0 and only lost 1-0 at Watford, if it was Europe they would have won on aggregate. What a twat! Maybe that defeat was the kick in the proverbials we needed, as we won the next three games. End of January, 64 points in the bag, 19 points clear of third. Promotion by the middle of March was a possibility, until *Sky* decided to put the kibosh on us. Why are we always so abysmal when broadcast live at home?

From the Gillingham game right through to Easter we only won two more, and *they* were lucky! Nervousness turned to alarm as Bristol City overtook us at the top. "Don't panic" was the cry from GT - but it's hard not to look at the worst case scenario when you've only won two out of 12 and you've struggled to hold onto leads.

We needn't have worried. After five months unused, Jason Lee's scoring boots were taken out of the locker and dusted off. His winner against Wrexham may have taken a massive deflection, but come the final whistle, Watford were almost home and dry, and everyone celebrated. At least I *think* that was what Keith Millen and Tommy Mooney were doing when the final whistle went (and in public too!).

The next match was optimistically labelled 'The Title Decider'. Jason Lee put the Hornets one up, only for City to equalise within minutes. One-all the final score and although no title had been decided, we were promoted. Somehow, the celebrations were mooted; it was a bit of an anti-climax. But there was still that title to go for... Bristol were faltering, but we could only draw with Grimsby (tip for punters: it is written in stone that when we play Grimsby you can bet on at least one 0-0 during the season). Two to play, and even all six points wouldn't guarantee us the honours. First up were Bournemouth, and a chance for Steve Palmer to don the 'keeper's jersey and go one step nearer the record of starting in every shirt number during the season. Despite a hatful of chances we could only win 2-1. So it was all down to the last Saturday, where Bristol City were at Preston and we were at Fulham. News soon filtered through that City were losing... The pressure was off! Gifton Noel-Williams gave Watford the lead, Fulham equalised but then up popped Jason Lee to score the winner, and 20 minutes later Watford were THE CHAMPIONS. Party time!!

Despite our poor run-in we still managed to finish 18 points clear of third, and though we didn't know it at the time, we were promoted in the middle of March! And in a surreal finish to the season, not many fans got to see the trophy actually presented to the players. Sure, we saw the trophy been paraded around town on an open-top bus, but I'd have much rather been sitting in the Vicarage Road End, watching Robert Page walk up, shake the hand of a Nationwide dignitary, receive the trophy and lift it in front of the adoring faithful. Maybe it will happen at the start of the season, but I doubt it. But who cares. To quote Freddie Mercury and Queen *WE ARE THE CHAMPIONS*. It will be in the record books - and no-one can take it away from us.

It really was a remarkable season. I wonder what it would have been like if we'd had a Kevin Phillips in our team; a natural goal-scorer. We had a run of just two wins in 12, yet still finished as far ahead of the pack as when the run started. And GT was in profit with his transfers. Supporters even found time to argue over what the team should run out to. Maybe *Z-Cars* will return. But at the end of the day, the mission was accomplished and promotion was achieved. It won't be easy back in Division One and there will need to be investment in the side, but after two years of hell I am so glad to be going back to Vale Park and not Sincil Bank.

The final words should go to Chris Twaddle (the real reason why we lost the shoot-out in Italia '90 - we were still in with a chance until he belted the ball over). When we thrashed Burnley at the outset, Twaddle commented that "we'll see where both teams are at the end of the season." Well, Chris, I don't want to disappoint so... I make it 19 places, 36 points and trophy winners by outright and aggregate victory. Stick *that* up your fat arse!!

COCK-A-DOODLE-DOO

Tottenham Hotspur

This was a season of many contrasts. The lack of team spirit throughout the club almost proved disastrous. Yet, somewhat ironically, it was Ginola and Klinsmann, neither of whom were entirely comfortable at the club, who eventually saved us from the ignominy of relegation.

And the lack of fight evident on the pitch for much of Tottenham's season provided a stark contrast to the combative nature of the relationship between the club and its fans. At a time when football proved it had never been more popular, the club strove to ensure it was never more unpopular with its followers.

Pre-season, events did not bode well. Our best player, Teddy Sheringham, was sold to Manchester United for a knock-down price following a row with Alan Sugar in which Ted had dared to say what every Tottenham fan knew - that the club had limited ambitions. Critical supporters were labelled "idiots, morons, and big-mouths" by our charming chairman, and a *CaDD* writer received a 15 minute tirade on the phone from Sugar himself. The club slammed critics for not having the facts, but resolutely refused to shed any light on what was going on. Daniel Sugar even threatened to "run away" at the new kit launch when pressed on the Sheringham sale.

A high-profile chase for Middlesbrough's Juninho followed. Many thought this simply a PR ploy, finding it hard to believe the man who raged against silly prices (unless he was charging them) and invented Carlos Kickaball would sanction an £11m bid for a Brazilian. More likely it was just a doomed pursuit of the impossible. Sugar had abused foreigners, abused Middlesbrough over the Barmby sale, and stated publicly that Spurs couldn't compete with the big boys. It was no surprise when Juninho opted for Atletico Madrid. We did eventually recruit Les Ferdinand and David Ginola from Newcastle, and although most fans were reasonably pleased, the impression remained that the players were signed because Newcastle were having a clear-out rather than because they fitted Gerry's master plan.

Our first game, inevitably, was United at home, and Sheringham got a hostile reception from supporters who'd regarded him as a hero just months before. Some saw this as depressing evidence that the crowd was taking on the bitter and twisted personality of its chairman; much the same way as pets develop their owner's characteristics. But we all still enjoyed Ted's penalty miss, and Sol Campbell's upfront reaction cemented his standing as a Spurs favourite.

The last laugh was United's though, as they beat us 2-0. Defeats at West Ham and a drubbing at Leicester followed. At Highbury the usual gruelling contest between swashbuckling football and a dull but effective use of the offside trap took place. But this time it was Arsenal buckling their swash and Spurs who left the pitch to the refrain of "Boring, Boring." And during a shameful performance against mighty Carlisle a new Tottenham anthem was heard: "We're shit, and we're sick of it." On top of everything else our legendary injury problem was worse than ever, although, of course, this wasn't the fault of the club physios. The pattern for the season was set.

At *Cock-a-Doodle-Doo* we were able to monitor the club's contempt for its supporters through readers' letters detailing their correspondence with the always charming Claude Littner, chief executive and Sugar's right-hand-man. Any supporter who dared to voice any criticism at all could expect something like the following in reply (and this is a direct quote from a real letter): *Your comments regarding the injury situation display a high degree of ignorance and downright stupidity. Newspapers make ridiculous statements and comments, and some gullible fans such as yourself just believe the garbage.* That's customer care, Tottenham-style.

As the season wore on, contact with the fanzines was banned, and our supply of pictures - provided by an agency that relied on access to the club for the bulk of its work - dried up at around the same time. The two things could not, of course, be related, as TH plc's commitment to the free market is well known. Despite all this, I found myself strangely in agreement with Sugar on one thing. While Gerry Francis seemed dead in the water, getting another manager in mid-season would be both difficult and possibly counter-productive. And anyway, the problem was more than just an increasingly clueless manager with no confidence in the transfer market.

Despite Sugar for once showing some loyalty and regard for someone, Gerry fell on his sword as the year drew to a close. His replacement Christian Gross was an unknown quantity for most of us, but his "I came on the tube" stunt, while derided by the national press, did go down well. Let's face it, it was about the first time the club had indicated it even understood the concept of positive PR in years. Nevertheless, it was just a stunt and things weren't improving on or off the pitch. Sugar, already on record as saying Les Ferdinand was a waste of money, now informed us that Gross was in charge because he was "the only idiot available." Relegation was now being discussed openly when the news that Klinsmann was coming back broke. Surely now we'd stay up?

However, first came a game against Fulham in the third round of the cup; a match with worrying giant-killing potential. As it happened, Spurs ran out easy if unconvincing winners, but the tie did mark a turning point in the mood of the home support. The overbearing attitude of the stewards and police had been causing some annoyance for a while, with standing up and singing (or in one case to let someone out to the toilet!) frowned upon, although not in the away end. At the Fulham game, stewards confiscated a replica FA Cup cut-out. This prompted a 15 minute protest which involved the entire East and South stands singing "Give him back his FA Cup," and then "When the stewards went up to nick the FA Cup we were there" and most controversially "I'd rather be a Gooner than a steward!" Eventually they shamefacedly returned the trophy, prompting much celebration and singing of "Ee-ay-adio we won the cup."

This was far more entertaining than anything that had been served up on the pitch for weeks. But while the crowd's performance was to improve, the team's did not. Initially Klinsmann didn't look the player he was and it soon became clear that he and Gross didn't see eye-to-eye on tactics; well, the coach was making some very odd decisions. One prime example was replacing a forward with a defender in our fourth round tie with Barnsley, thus letting them back into a game we had been winning easily. The replay brought yet another midweek humiliation up North. The referee was a disgrace but so were Spurs, and Barnsley would have won even without the help of the man in black... Time to 'concentrate on the league'.

Despite an encouragingly hard-fought win against West Ham, in which Jurgen finally scored his first goal for us and bonkers old Harry Redknapp engaged in a scrap on the pitch, relegation was looming ever larger. Of the players, only Ginola, who was - with respect to L'Oreal - head and shoulders above the rest, emerged with any real credit. Sol Campbell was showing the strain of trying to organise Tottenham's shambolic defence, Berti was encouraging only in glimpses and Ruel Fox was just plain dreadful. But at least Klinsmann was starting to look sharp, even though he wasn't getting the service, and Walker coped reasonably in the circumstances.

As the season wore on Klinsmann and Gross seemed continually at each other's throats over tactics. But Gross was in a difficult position. The atmosphere at the club meant every individual had to prove themselves rather than function as part of a team. And Gross was also under pressure to show who was in charge. He slapped down Klinsmann when it was revealed that the player had apparently been lured back with the promise of some input into team affairs. He also forbade David Pleat, installed as director of football when Francis resigned, from getting involved in any coaching.

Then there was *that* contract with Klinsmann that stated he could not be dropped under any circumstances. Any lingering respect for Sugar, sparked by his recapture of the player he had once so publicly fallen out with, was dissipated when news of this nonsensical clause came out. Suspicions about Jurgen's motives grew too.

Each match was now vital and our run-in just happened to contain a few six pointers. But in a season where we never won two games on the trot, the final weeks were always going to be a tense affair. Despite good wins at home over Bolton and away at a poor Palace side, we didn't seem to be able to claw ourselves to safety under our own steam. Joy in the pub after a win always seemed short-lived as results went against us. Deeper in trouble, we faced the prospect of having to rely on other teams for survival.

With one weekend to go, the drop was still possible. We returned to Selhurst Park to face Wimbledon; always tricky customers. It turned out to be the outing of the season. Tottenham fans unrestricted by the oppressive stewarding at White Hart Lane swamped the ground. Huge flags were passed over heads, loud choruses of every song in the repertoire were belted out and the celebrations got wilder and wilder as Spurs blew the Dons away with a stunning second half display. Klinsmann scored four of our six goals, prompting mass love-ins as he ran to the crowd, and visitors to London Bridge station were treated to the sight and sound of several hundred Spurs fans whistling the theme to *The Great Escape* as they marched through. Arsenal made us safe the next day by thrashing Everton.

Despite a predictably lacklustre performance against Southampton in a meaningless final game, we took encouragement from the fact that when Gross could choose his first choice eleven, the side appeared assured and adventurous. Things look more positive for the new season, although we still have to strengthen the defence and install some creative edge in midfield. And there were some other positive signs as well. A surprise victory away at Blackburn and a Ginola-inspired and wonder-goal capped 3-3 draw at home to Liverpool was the best match seen at White Hart Lane for ages.

However, with season tickets up 20% and concessions for kids and pensioners withdrawn in most parts of the ground, fans will be hoping for much better performances on the pitch. Perhaps we'll then have the chance to properly show our support off it.

COME IN NUMBER 7, YOUR TIME IS UP

Bristol City

As August 9th drew nearer, our confidence and optimism grew - nothing less than a play-off final victory at Wembley would do. We had looked good pre-season, especially in a 1-1 draw against Liverpool, when Michael Owen looked lively too. In fact, our campaign was not overly different from his: a slow quiet start, a sharp burst with mountains of goals and a few uneasy spells; but on the whole, excellent. But only three days away from the start, we were dealt a cruel blow. Last year's Player of the Year Darren Barnard joined Premiership 'giants' Barnsley for £750,000, less than a month after signing a new three year contract

for us. One of the pre-season signings Sean Dyche, a cup hero last year with Chesterfield, arrived for £275,00, and kept physio Buster Footman company for the majority of the season. He managed only nine token appearances before retiring hurt. He scored though... but sadly no one told him that we change ends at half time down South, and he duly opened his account for Preston.

It was a strange start to the season; some shaky performances at home which nevertheless resulted in comfortable victories, whilst away, we struggled to get a single point. In late August we had our second leg of the Bristol League Cup derby. After a 0-0 draw at Ashton Gate it was down to the rugby ground. City supporters were transported to and from the match in an eight-strong bus convoy from Ashton Gate to the Memorial Ground, otherwise no entry to the match. We sped through Bristol city centre at great speed, bringing a halt to early evening traffic. To see the St. James' roundabout, Broadmead and M32 brought to a stand-still for us was a sight never to be forgotten.

Poor performances against Fulham and Wrexham were to be the build-up to our league cup match, an away trip to Elland Road. Sixteen hundred City supporters made the journey and made up a sizeable chunk of a very poor crowd of just over 8,500. Perhaps Leeds fans only turn out to see Manchester United... Despite the large vocal support, City failed to rise to the occasion and lost 3-1. Our hopes for the return leg were all but dashed.

After our lacklustre and predictable 1-1 draw with Bournemouth, some supporters were obviously disgusted: the final whistle was met with a chorus of boos and jeers. The following week, letters and calls flooded into the local papers and radio stations. We were not happy, and something had to be done. A return to 4-4-2 would be a start. This wasn't the City we knew and loved; they were poor, played long-ball and there was no exciting attacking play. Ultimately, there were no wingers as Junior Bent had joined Blackpool the previous month and Greg Goodridge hadn't been seen since he had arrived back late from pre-season training from his native Barbados. But he was recalled for the following match against an under-strength Luton Town side, three of whom were making their league debuts. We managed to win at a canter.

Then, after an unexpected 2-1 victory against Leeds in the cup, early October saw the low point of the season. As one supporter put it, "That's it - our season's over." And after the 2-0 defeat at Gillingham you wouldn't have found many who'd have disagreed. Another fan was so incensed that during the second half he charged from his place on the terrace to confront the manager. Meeting substitute Mark Shail, he demanded to see Ward immediately and get an explanation. Shail's response was "He's a bit busy at the moment, mate." The angry fan stormed back to his place on the terrace, demanding to see Ward after the game, then. (Six months later, the same man was seen leading the promotion party at Burnley with the chant "Johnny Ward - we're proud to sing that name." How things change!) After the Gillingham defeat the table showed that City were in a sorry state: Nineteenth, whilst Rovers were second. We had just three league wins and only one point away from home (and *that* had been won on the opening day).

What happened next was quite remarkable, and totally unpredicted: thirteen league wins out of 15! We'd zoomed up the table to the comfort of second position, 16 points clear in the promotion zone, and within spitting distance of Watford. During this time though, we did lose to Bournemouth in the FA Cup at Dean Court. It was to be the first of three defeats against them, *all* at the dreaded seaside resort. As well as that, we had 'the big one' at Watford, billed as the title decider. Nearly 4,500 City fans made the trip with both sides all but guaranteed promotion. We played out a predictable 1-1 draw.

The first game of 1998 resulted in our fourth victory over Millwall in little over three months - God, they must have been sick of the sight of us! They managed only one goal against us compared to the eight we put past them. But our purple patch was soon to end... We should have predicted it: two visits to Dean Court in the ten days following the shield defeat. I elected to boycott our third visit in eight weeks to the South Coast and it proved to be a wise decision. We lost 1-0. Blackpool away stunned us all (and by the way, how come when we go to Bloomfield Road it is always on a Tuesday night in February, while Rovers seem to get them for their last away game of the season in April or May?). We were 2-1 up with two minutes to go before the ball fell to Junior Bent, a City player for seven years and veteran of nearly 250 games for the Robins, infamous for his wayward shooting and lack of ability to find the target. But not this time! All of 25 yards out, he lobbed 'keeper Keith Welch with a perfect chip which nestled in the bottom corner to earn Blackpool a share of the spoils. Git!

Derby day arrived in March, 11 days since City had last played. We had been scheduled to play at Oldham the previous Friday live on *Sky*, when despite 400 or so City fans having made it most of the way there, the match was controversially postponed at 5.30. Both Oldham and *Sky* were heavily criticised, but still no apology for our wasted journey has been forthcoming. The fourth and last derby of the season was once again conducted without any incidents between rival supporters (after the last league derby hit the headlines for the wrong reasons 15 months ago). We duly beat the Gas for the third time, and the Rovers taunt of "will you ever beat the Gas?" which rang around when Rovers were at Trumpton was now changed to "will you ever beat the reds?"

As transfer deadline approached, Ashton Gate was a hive of activity. Top-scorer Shaun Goater left for relegation-bound Manchester City for £400,000 - or as he put it "an ambitious move to further my career and to fulfil my desire to play in the top flight." !! Meanwhile, Sean McCarthy and Jason Roberts both arrived on loan (the latter appearing in just one match before leaving to play for his country). Grenada - that is Wycombe - was possibly our most important match of the season. We were now only ten points clear of Grimsby who had two games in hand. But City overcame their big test and won 2-1 and then managed to win the next two games to virtually clinch promotion.

Grimsby kindly handed automatic promotion to us on a plate by failing to win either of their two games in midweek, so on Easter Saturday, 3,000 City fans enjoyed the promotion party at Burnley. 'The Big One' provided another bore-draw as nearly 20,000 packed into Ashton Gate to watch us share a goal apiece with Watford. The main talking point wasn't the match, though. Forty eight hours earlier, the England Monarchs American football team had played on the pitch. The word 'Monarchs' was clearly visible emblazoned across both penalty areas, despite failed attempts by the ground staff to disguise them in green paint, as were the pitch markings and end zone markings and numberings. It was a disgrace, not only to the club, but also to groundsman Steve Drew who the previous week had been voted Groundsman of the Year for our division.

The rest of the season was a bit of an anti-climax, but we were still in pole position for our last match at Preston. Of course, we went up there expecting the Championship, but we lost and it went to Watford instead. (By the way, the date was the Second of May, interestingly the *exact* same date on which eight years earlier we'd blown the Championship after losing 3-0 at the Gas, giving rise to Hazel Potter's Rovers' fanzine). But let's not forget that '97-98 was *our* season: apart from promotion we did the hat-trick over the Gas!

COMMUNITY SERVICE

AFC Bournemouth

I am a Hollywood director; a sucker for the sentimental back street, small town, tear-jerking blockbuster. And I have an idea...

Early summer of 1997 a town's beloved is saved, finally, from the grim reapers of receivership, apathy and black horse bankers. A French film star, Franck Rolling, arrives on horseback and is swiftly joined in the back bar of the last chance saloon by the up-and-coming matinee idol Edward Howe. Fresh from his starring role as Danny in a West End musical comes Jonah the Greaser shooting from both hips, and heading in from the wings it's the film's maverick star Hissing Jason Brissett.

community SERVICE

The fanzine of AFC Bournemouth
Community Club - Issue 1

YOUNG SCORES AGAIN

INSIDE YOUNG SCORCHES SHEARER - CHAIRMAN'S GM - ABSOLUTE ROTTERS
COCKNEY CHERRIES - ANTI SAINTS STUFF - DEANO'S COURT JOURNALS

£1

And the action is non-stop, explosive, and, to the cheers of moral crusaders nationwide, fun for all the family. And it ends as all such stories are meant to end: victory in a Wembley final and promotion to Never-Ever-Land.

Trouble is, I'm not actually a Hollywood director. I am not even particularly renowned as an ideas man. And I can only tell it how it was, much as I might have wished for a fairytale ending. Wembley victories remain, for the supporters of Bournemouth and Boscombe Athletic Community Football Club, as elusive as a snog off Posh Spice. Division One, the Premiership's drop-out club? Never-Ever-Land.

We commenced '97-98 as Europe's first community owned football club. I could explain what this means, though as it is, as yet, more of a philosophical thing I'll leave the philosophers amongst you to philosophise. Suffice to say it meant a new boardroom of frankly bloody decent directors and no more money than we had previously been used to.

Expectations were uncertain. Critics of the new structure offered long odds on lasting out the season. After all, what chance was there for a club with a dilapidated stadium, a board run by a thirty-something city slicker, no white knight backers, and the pre-season signings consisting of a French chef and a Martin O'Neill reject, both on frees?

But Dean Court had the decorators in, a former youth team player was limbering up for his starring role, the nucleus of the previous year's mid-table hangers remained, and Chef Rolling was (almost) to prove to be the icing on the cake. All we wanted was the first match at home and we could all celebrate in style. True to form the fixture computer fluffed its lines and gave us Northampton Town away. A neat ground surrounded by cinemas and chain restaurants, a sunny day and a decent turn-out of Cherry revellers all pointed to a one to none reverse. But lo, no. We won.

Funny month, August. A month when most of us are trying to stretch out our meagre holiday entitlement and patching roofs for the winter deluge. There wasn't to be a great deal of patching for the Cherries who closed the month on top of, rather than in the pie. The summer's final match, a home victory against Blackpool, was described with such unbridled enthusiasm by the local *Echo's* reporter that even the hardened cynics amongst us believed we were in Rio watching Brazil. For Rivilino read Rawlinson. Ronaldo? Pah! Anyone can knock a ball around an airport; you want to try a winter's night, cheered on by 124 travellers and friends in Wigan, mate.

A home defeat at the hands of the Grimesby Towners was followed, for me at least, with a train journey back to London with a Fishhead. And the fact that the Fishhead said nothing the whole journey but merely sat and smirked was, by some distance, the most provocative act by any opposition supporter last season. At the time I consoled myself with the knowledge that Grimesby weren't that much and it wasn't as if they'd beaten us in a Wembley final.

Whilst we contented ourselves with the passing blend of football that Mel Machin had been cultivating over the previous two seasons, a lack of finishing power became evident about four games in. Now there is no doubting that defensively Mel is a gifted manager. As each new forward or attack minded midfielder joined the club, so they were transformed into defensive kingpins. There were occasions when I'm sure I identified a 7-2-1 formation. But Mel did try. Graeme Moanlinson, a bit of a teenage wonderkid, was initially signed on loan. Trouble was, he was more intent on volleying torrents of verbal abuse than he was the ball. A Norwegian superstar, 'a powerhouse of a player' was mooted and then there was, albeit fleetingly, talk of a signing that would 'knock our socks off'. When a Romanian flavour was added to rumours I awaited Hagi's arrival. Jimmy Quinn then promised to join - definitely and without fail. But he was offered another 20 notes, 'round the back, under the headlights, and we'll keep it from the taxman' by the Fryster and stayed put for the people of Peterborough.

In the spirit of openness the board had taken to taking to the stage, well the raised platform at the far end of the Supporters' Club, to update the baying throngs once a fortnight or so. With the natives restless for reinforcements there were rumours of boardroom discussion about new forwards. Ken Dando, one of the board's more public figureheads, was dispatched stage left and allegedly told to say nothing about new players for fear of raising expectations. Unfortunately, the occasion got to Ken who duly announced the imminent signing of two forwards both with proven goalscoring pedigrees. This proved to be, as you might expect from a Dandyman, a fanciful suggestion.

One new forward eventually arrived in the shape of Christer Warren, a Southampton reserve. Christer's lack of pedigree should, in hindsight, have been accepted as an indicator of his likely goalscoring return. Warren was described by chairman Trevor as 'swift and with better technique' than one Steve Jones, the greaser supreme and latterday hero. Unfortunately the Jones boy was then signed on loan and Trevor's comparative analysis was found wanting. Four goals in five games awoke Charlton Athletic who quickly recalled him for the bench.

By this time we'd been dismissed from the FA Cup, thanks to the bane of every football fan, the dubious referee's decision. Prior to the cup tie in question, Neil Young, football superstar and rock dinosaur, had, thrillingly for a Neil Young banner-waver like myself, broken his goalscoring duck with two fabulous strikes. Those with obscured (or just plainly biased) views insisted they were mis-hit deflections. Mind you these are the same people that still protest that Maradona handled in 1986. Turning back to the cup tie and following a spell of sustained pressure, Horse the Younger killed the ball dead from a goal kick, hip swivelled his way past several (maybe even 11) hapless challenges before firing in a half volley from all of 35 yards. I would have granted Young the freedom of the Borough, and thrown in a knighthood and Cadbury's Curly Wurly for good measure. The statisticians? They cold-heartedly recorded 'offside'.

An away trip with first class rail tickets, Marks and Spencers sandwiches and a triple pack of Walnut Whips (between two of us!) saw us land in Cleethorpes, home of the Grimesby Towners. On this occasion the Fishhead couldn't travel with us, although we did arrange for a post match 'well played and hard luck' session with the father of the Grimey one. At half time we were one up and anticipating the after-match gloating to come over Fishhead the Elder. But the history books recorded a late home recovery and odd goal victory. Still, I took heart at the time; after all it wasn't as if we'd been beaten in a Wembley final.

And then a funny thing happened. A Wembley final beckoned. It was only to be a Shield Final but it was a final nevertheless. In truth I think we must have danced with the devil to get there. A first round bye, a home tie in every round and the first leg of the Southern Final away. The away leg was hurdled as if Sally Gunnell were our middle name. The home leg was a desperate affair. Despite Goalmeister Young's swerving strike (I say it takes true genius to swerve a ball through 90 degrees - doubting Thomases say it takes a deflection), Walsall's French Lieutenants looked like they had rewritten the script and provided us with yet another big gate defeat. Despite living in the digital age, the clock continued its analogue countdown. And then time stood still, Franck Rolling left his berth at the back and notched the vital strike.

Fortunately it was to be Grimseby in the Final. After all, what was the likelihood of losing to the same team three times running? The cameras rolled and were quick to swoon over the youthful matinee idol. But whilst Edward perspired the Chef and Hissing Briss were overlooked, dramatically and undeservedly, for a fading B movie actor (Mark Stein) and Swifter Christer. Steve Jones had remained a Valiant and could only sit and watch on, with Brylcream glistening. Grimesby did it again and it rained on the way home.

But we'd never been to Wembley before and, even in defeat, there is something to be said for the small fry getting to swim in the big-time ocean. My prediction of a Bournemouth turnout of 20,000 was slightly over half right, as close to 36,000 made the journey. And looking around at the time it seemed that everyone had come with a flag, rosette or egg mayonnaise sandwich. Yet, in a funny way, I didn't feel as though I belonged. Belonging, to me, is a Tuesday night 300-mile round trip to a bleak midwinter goalless draw at home to York. Belonging didn't mean that you had to know the names of those you stood or sat with, but it did mean knowing their faces and sharing around the half-time toffees. Wembley was the brief flirtation with the supermodel but it could never really match catching the last bus home with your girlfriend and a bag of chips. Of course, had we won, then I may well have stuck it out with Claudia.

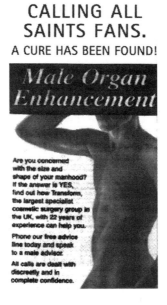

CURIOUS BLUE

Chelsea

Walking past the low-light brass seafaring lanterns, columns draped with fishermen's nets and porthole displays in the walls, we're led to our table. I choose the terrine des langoustines with foie gras and leeks as a starter, while my companion opts for the mussels steamed in cider. We reassure ourselves that, while not quite Arkle's, the top-notch Irish restaurant of the Chelsea Village, Fishnets is nevertheless a destination for 'seafood aficionados, stylish couples and discerning business lunchers', and at least we don't have to mingle with the oiks eating 'pub grub' in The Shed sports bar. For my main course I select the John Dory roasted in shallots while my...

oh, I'm sorry, you wanted to talk about football?

Get with it, daddio. Football's only a small part of the scene at New Chelsea, dontcha know? We got hotels, we got house wines, we got travel agents, megastores, celeb supporters, extortion, bordellos, workhouses for the poor and needy - we got a goddam theme park on the go here, and you want to talk football?

Okay, I'll tell you about football. It's been a funny old year.

You know that feeling when you can't remember the last time you got yourself laid (and if you're the sort of person who buys a book like this, you probably do), and like a Labour government, you've forgotten what it was like? Then, one day, you suddenly find yourself in with a shout, and you know you're in, and the joys of all things carnal are just around the corner? Only it turns out she was just a pissed-up Teessider who'd already gone down on you before the big day, and the excitement lasted all of 43 seconds, and the whole thing ends up a bit of an anti-climax? Well that's what it was like at Chelsea a year ago, when we got our leg over with a proper cup for the first time since decimal currency.

A season on and we've won two more cups with possibly our best squad ever, finished in our highest-ever Premiership position, Stamford Bridge is sold out for just about every game and we're continuing to strengthen the squad for a realistic challenge on the title. Yet there's still something rotten in the state of Chelsea. More than ever there's an overwhelming stench of greed and exploitation about the place, complemented by a plain old-fashioned nastiness from the man at the top.

Like it or not, we're the epitome of trendy New Football. I don't want to mythologise some pre-*Sky*, pre-Gazza's tears golden age, but things were so much simpler once. Supporting Chelsea used to *mean* something - it used to confer an identity, even if that identity was one of long-suffering stoicism and a rueful acceptance of under- achievement. For many of us that was easier to live with than the fact that now we're relatively successful, we're being fleeced as mercilessly as market forces will allow.

We've always been an expensive team to support, but this season it has become absurd. Last summer, those of us who couldn't afford the £450 for the cheapest season ticket began, as usual, by forking out £30 for club membership and the privilege of being able to buy tickets, without discount, for home games, plus a lovely Christmas card and a free (crikey!) fixture list. We were also informed of a new 'loyalty points' scheme, whereby those attending home matches would accrue points that would allow them a chance to get tickets for any semi-finals or Wembley appearances. This seemed like a reasonable idea, but was mysteriously never mentioned again until we actually got to Wembley, when the club announced, without apology, that they were dropping that particular plan. Unfortunate for those who had braved rainy Coca-Cola midweek winter slogs, comforted only by the knowledge that they were clocking up Cup Final points. Ho-hum.

The club also bought its own travel agency this season. Very handy with a string of European ties coming up, especially when the only way the club will sell you tickets for games abroad is through an official package with Chelsea Worldwide Travel Ltd. (Actually in contravention of a European Court ruling, but since when has some pesky foreigners' law mattered a jot to Ken Bates?) Fine if, for the Bratislava game for example, you were willing to pay a minimum of £115 for two 24-hour coach trips with no overnight stop, seeing nothing of Europe but a car park on some Czech industrial estate. Unfortunate for the rest of us, who either had to travel independently on the off-chance of getting a ticket, or had to try to work out what the hell was going on through the fuzz of *Channel 5*. So it goes.

Ken Bates is a strange man. At times it seems as though his goal in life is to exact bitter vengeance on a cruel world that's done him wrong. October saw the anniversary of the death of Matthew Harding, a man loved by Chelsea fans and genuinely admired by football supporters across the country. Bates' response was bizarre. He decided that "the silent minority" (?!) of Chelsea fans didn't like Harding, that they saw through his rabble-rousing and his man-of-the-people posturing. In fact Bates announced that Harding had been nothing less than an evil man, on a mission to destroy the holy work of Chelsea Village. Harding was never a saint, but Bates' slagging of his dead rival, apart from the barbaric insensitivity it showed towards Harding's family, also displayed his contempt for the fans who admired him. Nothing new there, then.

But there was to be another, more consequential clash of egos at Chelsea before the season was done. Amid all the revelations and recriminations of a few days in February - the PR manoeuvrings, those gross and 'netto' figures, the clandestine 'Laudrup Meeting', our insight into the floor plan of the managing director's office, the whole sorry shebang - a tragic drama was revealed in the sacking of Ruud Gullit. The real story isn't in the dirty mechanisms of Gullit's ousting, it's about the inevitable fall of a flawed hero, with Gullit as the bemused Caesar, toppled on the forum steps.

Gullit's appointment as player-manager brought an unprecedented glow of success to Chelsea, attracting big-name players and raising our profile to that of real contenders. We knew all about those Dutch dressing room bust-ups and the arrogance of the man, with his constant irritating references to how great things were at Milan and Sampdoria. But he was charismatic, articulate and likeable, and we happily swept our doubts under the carpet. Some of us even forgave him for that horrible 'tache he sported in his pomp.

Gullit's ego was part of the package. The studied cool inspired respect, the squad rotation brought results and a proper trophy, and for a while all was looking rosy at Chelsea. But an unhealthy myth was building around the man. Surrounded by the likes of fawning Harry Harris and so many two-bit pundits, unquestioningly acknowledging him as an icon of New Football, Gullit began to believe that myth. There are only so many times a man can hear himself described as a genius before he starts to believe he really is beyond the mortal. The flatterers, with all their 'we are not worthy' hosannas, ultimately aided his downfall, for there is only room for a single Omnipotent One at Stamford Bridge, and our white-bearded god is a jealous god.

So Ruudi had left the building, and the real shock was that Vialli was installed as his replacement, with a contract as manager that extended beyond the end of the season. Vialli is a charming, popular and intelligent man, and while it could be argued that his appointment was a safe crowd-pleaser, he remains a 'name' player with the charisma to attract other names.

Although it at times seemed like a bit of a sideshow to the politics, I think it's time to talk about football now.

A handful of games can summarise Chelsea's season. By the end of November we'd had a pretty good start and were nestled nicely in the top five. The defence had looked traditionally shaky but scoring goals didn't seem to be a problem. After a dodgy first month or two, Ed De Goey was starting to look sound, Frank Leboeuf was playing some blinders and Wise and Di Matteo were consistently sharp in midfield. Derby came to London on a run of form that had taken them up to sixth in the table, playing exciting football and scoring freely. This was going to be a test.

We murdered them. With one of the most fluid and powerful team performances I've ever seen Chelsea produce, including a Zola hat-trick, we stuffed them 4-0, and that could have been doubled. After the third goal of the rout, "We're gonna win the league" rose up in the Harding and Shed Ends with a conviction we'd never heard before. Everything looked possible.

By the new year it was business as usual. Following the chastening thrashing by Man U in the cup and a League Cup semi-final first leg at Highbury where we were flattered by a 2-1 defeat, we had to go back to Arsenal again for a league game. By this point the team had lost the plot. We had to endure a toothless, aimless display, with the Clock End's humiliating "One man went to laugh, went to laugh at Chelsea" ringing in our ears as we went down 2-0. Amazingly, we were still second in the league, but if we continued like this we were going nowhere. Gullit was gone within the week.

Vialli's first game in charge was the second leg of the semi. Fired-up, powerful and direct, Chelsea stormed it 3-1, with a 30-yard screamer from Di Matteo that has to be one of the goals of a lifetime. It was a grand night, and all the sweeter for finally getting one over on the Arse.

The feverish passion of that night could never last, though, and by the end of February, and a string of league defeats, the Championship challenge was realistically over. Instead we focussed on another Wembley date with Middlesbrough, and the Cup-Winners Cup.

The two cup campaigns were strange. It was only confirmed at the semi-final stage that the League Cup winners would qualify for Europe, so the early rounds had a pointless air about them, played out by half-arsed squad selections in a half-full ground. Likewise in Europe, where apart from that snowy night in 'the land of the troll', there was nothing to get excited about opposition-wise until the quarter finals in March. After going down 1-0 in Vicenza in the semi first-leg, back at Stamford Bridge it needed a brilliant comeback from two-down on aggregate, with three stunning goals from Poyet, Zola and a classic Mark Hughes volley to round it off. It was one of the most exciting games I've ever seen, and I think it's fit to be called a 'glory, glory night'.

So the season ended with that night in Stockholm (or in my case with trusty *Channel 5*), and another '70s millstone shrugged off. So far this summer we've signed Laudrup, Casiraghi, Ferrer and Desailly, and we've got a good batch of young players coming through (I fancy Mark Nicholls and Jon Harley in particular to go far). On the pitch things are looking good.

But the football, she is coming home with a season ticket price rise of over 50%, a corporate hotel stunting an undersized Shed End, a £70 bill for home programmes alone, a range of Chelsea Village wines and a souvenir leather-bound, silver-embossed book, 'a must for every true supporter' at £600. If we are priced-out, and gates do fall, Bates says "we will know that unlike the board, the fans are not ambitious." It's that hyped-up myth of New Football that forces long-time supporters into that blind 'loyalty whatever the cost' corner, resentful of the 'new fans', and no more so than at Chelsea. It's a myth that disenfranchises people like you and me, and that only bulges the coffers of people like Ken Bates.

So I'm choking on my foie gras, while Santa Palmer-Tomkinson (yes, her sister, I shit you not) is selling silver Perrier bottle sleeves for £200 a chuck in the hotel, and in the background I can hear the greasy voice of that slimeball Mellor telling us how smashing this footy lark is. If this is heaven I'm bailin' out.

DERANGED FERRET

Lincoln City

Can you remember what you were doing on May 2nd 1988? If you are a Lincoln City supporter the memories remain - a packed Sincil Bank to watch the Imps regain Football League status and a party well into the night. Fast forward ten years to May 2nd 1998 - a packed Sincil Bank to watch the Imps attempt to gain promotion to Division Two. But unlike '88, our fate was not in our own hands. In one of football's great ironies, the other team in the race was Torquay, the same club that by virtue of an injury-time equaliser had condemned us to the GMVC all those years ago. An awful first half v Brighton at Sincil Bank was softened by the news that Torquay

DERANGED

SEASON 97/98 ISSUE 5

A LINCOLN CITY FANZINE

BARRY AND JASON IMPLEMENT
FOOTBALL TASK FORCE POLICY

'LET'S KICK RACISM OUT OF FOOTBALL'

FERRET £1

were two down at Leyton Orient. Within 15 minutes of the restart the Imps were two up, the tension lifted and the party began... But hold on, a man with a radio shouts "Torquay have pulled a goal back," and a draw was good enough for them. Then Brighton pulled a goal back in injury time but it was too little too late for them. Our part of the job done, Imps fans swarmed onto the pitch. Four minutes remained at Brisbane Road. At the death Torquay hit a post but couldn't score... "Lincoln's going up, we're going up, we're going up" echoed around Sincil Bank and the party began.

The final Division Three table shows Lincoln in third place and automatically promoted. But the man who laid the foundations for promotion wasn't around to see the job completed. John Beck, reviled by many, including a fair proportion of Lincoln fans, had been relieved of picking the team in March and dismissed shortly afterwards for, as chairman John Reames put it, "three serious breaches of discipline." One was fairly well documented as Beck was alleged to have assaulted a YTS player earlier in the season. Another was for taking time off after a game but the third breach remains unexplained. A war of words began with Beck claiming that a hidden agenda was being pursued. He reckoned that his taking two days off work was being used as a get out by the club so that they didn't have to honour a compensation clause in his contract. He vowed to take legal action and the outcome of that is awaited with interest.

Whilst the club stated that results were not behind Beck's sacking, the on-field performances had not been particularly good to watch. An 18 match unbeaten run had taken us to the top of the table by the end of November, but it was built using Beck's beloved long ball game, a solid defence and a host of one goal wins. It wasn't pretty to watch and the Lincoln crowds disproved the theory that fans will watch anything as long as the team is doing well. Cracks appeared when first Gainsborough Trinity footballed us to death in the FA Cup but lost in a replay, and then Emley were only denied victory at the first attempt by a 99th minute City equaliser. In the replay they came from two down with 15 minutes left to deprive us of a third round trip to West Ham. The first "Beck Out" chants were heard at Peterborough as Fatty Fry's men thumped us 5-1 to end our unbeaten League run.

By the end of January, City had slipped as low as tenth in the table before a gradual recovery took place. Our chairman meanwhile had gone on holiday to Australia for six weeks, just like most dedicated supporters do in the middle of the season! He returned in time to witness a drab and boring draw with Swansea, at which the crowd vented its anger at our style of play. "Beck Out" was no longer being shouted by a few but by the majority. The next day, Beck, perhaps unwisely, boasted that the club couldn't afford to sack him. Well perhaps they couldn't, but they did all the same!

Chairman Reames then insulted our intelligence by claiming in the press that a new experienced manager would be appointed and an announcement made within a few days. When a few days later nothing was heard from the club, he wondered where the story had come from that an announcement was imminent! Instead, Shane Westley assisted by Phil Stant and Keith Oakes were put in charge, and they began encouragingly with three straight wins. By the end of March, City were back up to sixth.

April began with a City player being called up for international duty! Dean Walling flew out to the Caribbean and played two games for St Kitts and Nevis and thus joined a very select bunch of players who've been capped whilst at Sinny Bank. Whilst away he missed the most controversial match of the season, away at Macclesfield.

Whilst Moss Rose meets all the criteria for entry to the League it still leaves a lot to be desired. Playing there when it was raining heavily didn't help the mood, nor did the antics of the home 'keeper in the first half when he twice appeared to direct abusive comments at two of Lincoln's black players. Then at half time the Macclesfield mascot came up to us and made obscene and provocative gestures. To see Roary the Lion being escorted off the pitch by the Police was one of the funniest moments I've ever seen at a football match, but the fact remains that his actions could have caused serious trouble. As it was, trouble erupted on the pitch. City 'keeper Barry Richardson kicked a Macclesfield player as he was on the ground. Virtually every player piled in and the punches flew. When calm was restored, referee Lomas initially was going to restart play with a free kick to Lincoln but after consulting both linesmen sent off Richardson and Macclesfield's Sedgemoor. The loss of our 'keeper proved the costlier as Macc scored the only goal in the final minutes. After the game Richardson claimed he flipped because of the racial abuse his teammates were getting from the Macclesfield players. Not surprisingly the claim was denied but given the antics of their 'keeper in the first half... Subsequently the FA charged three City players (Richardson, Barnett and Thorpe) for their part in the fracas.

The visit of Peterborough was a win or bust game. In a reversal of the first match, City destroyed Posh, going three up at half time and starting chants of "Fry out." It seems that our friends from down the A15 match our dislike of a man, who in our GMVC days said he was going to bet his house on Barnet getting promotion rather than Lincoln. A hard-fought win over Exeter meant we went into the last two games of the season still in the hunt for automatic promotion but strangely not even assured of a play-off spot.

Six hundred City fans travelled north to Darlington for our penultimate game. An early lead was cancelled out and then we fell behind. But despite Beck's departure the work ethic remained and with two minutes of stoppage time showing, Dennis Bailey (the one who scored *that* hat-trick at Old Trafford for QPR) slotted home an equaliser with virtually the last kick of the game. The point was priceless. It meant a confirmed play-off spot and the chance of automatic promotion; which is where we began....

When John Beck took over at Sincil Bank in 1995 the club were perhaps on the slippery slope back into the GMVC. He promised us survival and achieved that aim. He said we would need a season to rebuild and consolidate. Last year we only missed the play-offs on the last day. He said we would reach the play-offs in '97-98. The team that he built exceeded that. That he wasn't around to take the plaudits shouldn't detract from what he achieved at Sincil Bank. He saved our football club, turned it around and made us proud. Our slogan ten years ago on returning to the Football League was 'onward and upward'. It has taken us until now to move on. Hopefully in *SOTF5* we can relate how Lincoln City will have moved up still further.

EXCEEDINGLY GOOD PIES

Rochdale

Twelve months ago I wrote that I *didn't* want to be talking about Dale having extended their unbroken membership of the Basement Division by yet another year. Unfortunately, that scenario has been played out and now many of the Spotland faithful are finding it hard to see when this depressing run will, if ever, end.

On his appointment in the summer of '96, Graham Barrow was seen as the manager to lead us into the Promised Land of Division Two. So far, he and his teams have failed to deliver, so we can still look forward to more trips to Exeter, Hartlepool, Scunthorpe and Darlington in the new campaign. Indeed, one prominent Dale fan has claimed that his car is on autopilot when it comes to finding the route to our away fixtures!

THE ALTERNATIVE VOICE OF ROCHDALE A.F.C.

EXCEEDINGLY GOOD PIES

EVEN THE DALE BALL-BOYS AND BALL-GIRLS ARE ANXIOUS TO KNOW WHICH IDIOT IS INSIDE DESMOND!

Issue 24, November 1997   No rip-off £3.50 here, Dale **£1**

Barrow's main failing, which surfaced in a major way last season, was picking his favourites instead of the best available team. Positions were often shuffled to accommodate Mark Bailey, Mark Leonard and Andy Farrell, who were quite simply not good enough, whilst more skilful performers were played out of position or not at all. But the boss wasn't slow to defend his selections. He was once heard to say that Farrell and Leonard were the two players that opposition managers always mentioned over an after-match drink. Well they would, wouldn't they? You'd just made it easier for them by playing these two in our side! But wait a minute, didn't Farrell pick up a Player of the Year award from one of the breweries that supplies Spotland? Ah yes, but scurrilous rumourmongers alleged that Graham Barrow made that selection himself, and if that was the case the 'gong' winner could only ever have come from one of three!

Unfortunately, Barrow doesn't like criticism of his favourites and resorted to rebuffing fans during first team and reserve matches. This led to confrontations between supporters as opinions differed and tempers boiled over. It seems that the more optimistic and mild followers appreciate that others have an opinion but would rather they didn't voice it. Surely a contradiction there!

All these negative vibes stemmed from watching a struggling team in what was a very poor division. And the one thing, more than any other, that really frustrated the fans was paying good money to witness performances with little fight and effort. Obviously if Dale were playing well the fans would be happy, but when we were having a hard time of it, the least we expected for our support was a bit of honest sweat and toil.

Most of this fighting spirit was lacking away from home, or if we went a goal behind in cup games. Dale picked up just ten away points last season, with six of those coming at Doncaster and Hull! Contrast this with the home form and it is easy to see why supporters were on short fuses. Dale won 15 (yes, fifteen) games at Spotland, collecting a record number of home points in the process. It was the biggest number of home victories since our only promotion season of '68-69 and included impressive wins against promoted Macclesfield and three of the play-off contenders. Fortunately we scored the first goal in each of those matches or it could have been a different tale. In two seasons under Barrow's management we have won just twice when conceding the first goal and the most recent of those games was in September 1996! All that the boss can give as an explanation is "We need more devilment," or "We keep shooting ourselves in the foot!"

In spite of the doom and gloom on the pitch, off the field, events have been much more positive. Our 16-year-old reserve 'keeper Stephen Bywater has joined West Ham in what could become a very lucrative deal, but not as much as the widely reported £3 million. The new Pearl Street stand opened in October and looks splendid - surely one of the best new facilities in Division Three football.

The club's commercial department gained new staff last summer (both ex-*EGP* editors) and they have increased membership of the weekly draw to its highest ever level, around 13,000 members, as well as introducing some excellent merchandise into the shop. In addition, the Matchday Programme was voted fourth best in the Third Division, although considering most of it was compiled by past and present members of the *EGP* team this comes as no surprise!

Towards the end of the season Dale turned in their usual crop of good displays, which unfortunately conned the manager into announcing a very small release list. Let's hope though that my pessimistic outlook is totally wrong and Dale can make some quality progress next year. We shall see...

EXILED!

AFC Bournemouth

From Dean Court To Wembley

I know that football can be a 'funny old game', as someone once said, and that the fortunes of football clubs change from year to year. But I think I can safely say that the turn-round from the situation at Dean Court just 12 months ago, when we were all but dead, is as remarkable a change as you'll ever see... Anywhere.

So let's look back at the season, which has seen many notable 'firsts' for AFC Bournemouth. Having survived just two months before, it was wonderful to see AFC Bournemouth walk out at Northampton's Sixfields Stadium as Europe's first community-owned

EXILED

SOUVENIR EDITION OF EXILED
COVERS THE 1998 AUTO WINDSHIELDS
TROPHY FINAL
AFC BOURNEMOUTH V GRIMSBY TOWN
19th APRIL 1998

WEMBLEY SPECIAL

club still very much alive and kicking. In many respects the fact we were even there was quite an achievement, but to win 2-0 with a couple of quality strikes from Vincent and Fletcher just summed up the new fighting spirit.

Despite the Coca-Cola Cup defeat against Torquay, we managed to hit top spot for the first time since the '86-87 Championship season, after home wins against Wigan and Blackpool. But that's as good as it got, as we never really came close with a fourth place our next best on October 18th following a 2-1 Dean Court victory over high-spending Kevin Keegan's Fulham. This period also saw us pick up an excellent win against Preston North End away, as debut-boy Christer Warren bagged his first goal for the Cherries. But these were the only victories in an eight-match spell that included four draws. The next few didn't improve things much either as we managed to draw three and give Plymouth their annual three points in a rain-drenched 0-3 drubbing. Oh well, the management may change but mid-table has been our historical home.

Then it was the first FA Cup fixture under our new status: a first round encounter with Essex-based Heybridge Swifts of the Ryman League. I have to admit that they gave a good account of themselves (like they do), but ultimately lost out to goals from Robbo (2) and a superb strike from Beardsmore (why can't he score 'simple' goals?). Two wins (Southend and Carlisle the victims) brought us a much anticipated (don't forget the extra £75,000 as well - thank you) Sunday game live on *Sky Sports* against Bristol City in the FA Cup. The match had all the excitement a neutral could have wished for, as far as football was concerned. As for my nerves, they were certainly tested - just as well given events later in the season! Almost straight from the kick-off Bournemouth dominated the game and gained a well-deserved single own-goal advantage. The turning point in the game was an injury to Beardsmore that forced his substitution and allowed City to totally dominate the centre of the park. Chance after chance came and went for City. But in the end a combination of inept finishing and World Class 'keeping from Man of the Match Jimmy Glass, meant that a wonder-strike from John O'Neill and a neat turn and finish from Steve Fletcher sealed a memorable win. And a place in round three for the first time in years.

Back in the league, two defeats just before Christmas showed up an embarrassing lack of 'something extra' up front and prompted Machin into action. Enter the mercurial hero Steve Jones from the depths of the Charlton Reserves. His impact was immediate as we slammed FOUR past a shell-shocked Gillingham and Jonah scored two. Okay, the Gills were down to ten men (Pennock showing he's been totally converted to the Tony 'that's never my elbow embedded in Jonah's face' Pulis' way of things). It was a fine performance nonetheless. For the Bournemouth faithful, there was another present to behold with amazement - A NEIL YOUNG GOAL!!!!!!!!!!!!!!!!!!!!!!!!!!!! Having lulled us into a false sense of security (two wayward, corner flag, south end type misses), he finally produced the strike we'd all been waiting for. The celebrations fell short of the much vaunted strip performance of Neil Young worshipper Jerry Tosswell - and thank goodness for that!

Next up was a trip to our dear friends at Bristol Rovers where hardly a moment goes by without something happening. That day was to be no exception. Despite taking the lead (through Jonah) we managed to totally give it away in unbridled festive fashion as we sunk to an incredible 3-5 reverse. Comments on the match have had to be omitted for fear of upsetting those of a sensitive nature!

Having played Bye in the first round of the AWS, we started 1998 against the mighty Leyton Orient in round two. Goals from Fletch and Robbo secured passage to round three - little did we know...

Of the two games against Northampton Town, I saw little evidence to suggest they were play-off material, especially as AFCB managed to score five past the Cobblers this season to round off a fine double. Just to prove what a strange world it is, their manager even suggested that they were the better side. Please - if that's the case, then I'll put money on Roy Garner to win Miss World!

Defeat against Huddersfield (FAC3) was hard to take, especially as we had a perfectly good goal disallowed for reasons known only to the ref and linesman. With Jonah back at the Valley, our lack of firepower helped Blackpool and Oldham keep easy clean sheets. Thankfully it was just a blip as six of the next seven ended in victory. A second Dean Court encounter with Bristol City was billed (by them) as a chance to gain revenge for their earlier cup exit.

Needless to say they were sent packing again, this time thanks to a stunning strike from Vincent. Fletcher consigned Bristol City to their THIRD Dean Court defeat of the season, prompting requests of "can we play you every week?" The City fans didn't look too impressed. But let's face it - they should know better. I can only assume they are relieved about promotion, if only to avoid the mighty Reds next season. Two Warren strikes (remember him?) secured victory at Saltergate, which was good preparation for the AWS Southern Area Semi-Final against Luton. In another tense night of football the tie swung in both directions. Franck Rolling saved everyone from the possibility of extra-time and 'goalden goals,' with a timely strike with just minutes left.

Defeat at Grimsby was followed by disaster at Fulham. Not that we were complaining about Robbo's super strike to seal a superb victory, rather we were worried by Keegan's comments, heaping praise on Bournemouth... And we were right to be concerned as we proceeded to drop stupid points against Preston, Wrexham, relegation-bound Plymouth, Brentford and Southend (another 3-5 - less said the better).

Away from the league, results were much better in the AWS. Against Walsall on a damp Tuesday evening for the Southern Area Final (First Leg), AFC Bournemouth excelled themselves - beyond anything I could have imagined - on a ground where league points are rare for us. 'AWS Hero' Franck Rolling settled nerves with a close range headed goal to send the large away support absolutely bananas. Then to cap it all, Beardsmore (on his return) scored an absolute beauty from distance to seal victory on the night. All done and dusted, we thought. The second leg was as exciting for the Walsall fans as the first leg was for us! Do we enjoy making life difficult for ourselves? The two goal lead was swiped away from us but mercifully victory was secured as an own-goal and 'AWS Hero' (now god-like figure) Rolling guided us home 4-3 on aggregate.

"WEMBLEY, WEMBLEY, WE'RE THE FAMOUS AFC BOURNEMOUTH AND WE'RE GOING TO WEMBLEY..." A dream come true. Twelve months ago we'd have been pleased with a day trip to Wigan (no disrespect to the quality of Springfield - of course).

So April 19th rolled around after weeks of anticipation/panic - what a day to savour. Well over 30,000 people (some even genuine fans!) turned out to support AFC Bournemouth as they took to the finest footballing stage in the land for the AWS Final v Grimsby Town. To see the team walk out on the hallowed turf certainly choked me, as I'm sure it did many others. The excitement and anticipation of taking the Trophy home was heightened when John Bailey (my Man of the Match) capped his superb performance with an opportunist goal - what a moment. Unfortunately, it wasn't to be as the Mariners clinched victory by one of those 'Goalden Goals'. Gutted or what? Many said the game didn't matter, but when we lost we were all desperately disappointed. We'd have loved to have won this competition properly at Wembley, because it would have certainly beat winning the competition at Boothferry Park, like the last time against Hull.

With Wembley out of the system, the league season finished on a positive note with a five out of eight games winning streak. AFC Bournemouth completed the season ninth on 66 points. It's worth pointing out that this was our highest placing and points tally for six years which proves that the club *is* moving in the right direction. Machin may have his doubters, but every year since his return the final points tally has gone up. As for the top ten finish... Well, it's nice to back in the leading pack again.

On the playing front I've been impressed with many of the first team, but Howe and Bailey stand out. Bailey for his commitment and Eddie for breaking into, and holding onto, his first team place. And now of course he's played his way into the England U-21 squad. Certainly justified, if the overwhelming majority vote he polled in the *Exile's* Player of the Season award is anything to go by.

Next season, Division Two will be huge, especially with Notts County, Stoke City and Manchester City joining other residents like Fulham and Burnley. But we're quietly confident that the Bournemouth revolution will not be derailed and another great year awaits us.

Time, as ever, will be our judge.

Source: Ferry 'Cross the Wensum

FERRY 'CROSS THE WENSUM

Norwich City

Did *anyone* get what they wanted? That's the question City fans are asking themselves after season '97-98. The board didn't get the 16,000 average crowd they asked for; the supporters didn't get the promotion we longed for; and Mike Walker certainly didn't get to see out the third year of his contract. Even Ipswich fans, no doubt loving all of this, didn't get what they wanted - outplayed and outfought by little Charlton (well done on the sending off, Danny Mills; shame you're still an arrogant fucker who's going to be the laughing stock of the Premiership in '98-99). Ohhh, how we chuckled!

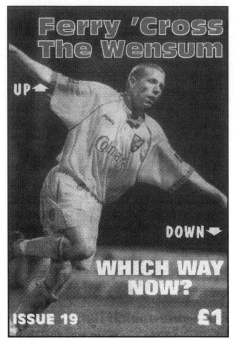

Pre-season should have given us a bit of an indication as to how the year was going to go. Although we managed to keep all our young 'stars' (with the exception of Andy Johnson, but there was nothing the club could do about that), the only team we managed to beat before the campaign begun was Hibs reserves behind closed doors. Bear in mind that we also played Dumbarton, St Mirren and Greenock Morton when you think about that statistic! Arsenal also gave us the thrashing of a lifetime, a result that saw many Norfolk people putting their wads on a Gunners' Championship, and many expensive holidays being taken this summer with the winnings!

So the season started - and finished - in August. We lost the first three matches, amazingly finally getting our first points at the Stadium of Shite (Joke! It's actually very nice compared to all the other new grounds springing up) in Sunderland where we were the first team to beat them. Actually, we managed to double Sunderland in the end but despite that I would still say they were the best side we faced; I really cannot believe that they are still in our division while a pile of crap like Middlesbrough have gone up. Anyway, back to our own pile of crap who continued in the same inconsistent ways as the previous season, beating Ipswich one week (lurverly!) then losing to Tranmere the next, winning against both Forest and Sunderland in the same week then losing to Crewe.

Motivation had to be the problem, and this is probably in the end what cost Walker his job.

We spent the last third of the season worrying about relegation; a ridiculous situation for us to be in, considering that players of the calibre of Bellamy, Forbes, Llewellyn, Coote and Kenton were now coming through and playing as well for the first team as they had for the youth team only a year before. Unfortunately, and not for the first time at City, it was the older players who were not pulling their weight. Players on big fat contracts signed when we were relatively wealthy and in the Premier League contributed very little to our campaign, and then had the gall to moan when they were released at the end of the season. You weren't worth it boys; you'd been liabilities for over two years and NCFC can't afford any more of *those* after Chase. (Yes, we're still going on about him, no, we haven't forgotten, and no, we will never forgive).

As for Mike Walker, well, virtually everyone was very patient with him all season. He had the undoubted support of the vast majority, right up to when he was sac.. sorry, left by mutual consent. There were one or two dissenting voices, mainly from the type of people who only go to football because they know they can have a go at someone without the worry that he might come and get them back! There were just a couple of occasions when the crowd as a whole had a go. The first was in the opening half at home to Birmingham, just two weeks after the most painful day of our lives (Ipswich Tahn 5 City 0) when we went two down just before half-time - a game in which we were very unlucky in the end to only draw 3-3. The second came at home to Bradford during the height of relegation fever when we had failed to win a game for 12 matches. Interestingly though, on both occasions the furthest the crowd went was to sing "Walker, sort it out." Also, the team started playing infinitely better after this (relatively mild) abuse was aimed at them.

In fact, after that Bradford game, there was a poll carried out by the *Evening News*. I wondered whether it might go against Walker - although most people wouldn't do the dirty in public on our greatest ever manager, would they vote against him secretly? But no, the verdict was a two-thirds majority for him to stay, and as far as we were all concerned, that was that, end of story; Walker would get his third term. However after two successive 5-0 home wins, albeit sandwiched by another terrible away defeat (this time at soon-to-be-relegated Stoke) and escape from demotion clinched, the board announced that Mike Walker had left the club by 'mutual consent'.

Of course, we all know what that usually means and this was no exception. He was pushed big style. When the odious Roger Mumby (trade? Public relations!!) and company begged Walker to come back, he did so on the understanding that three years would be needed to start turning things round. The majority of supporters thought he deserved to see out his contract and there was no warning that the 'mutual parting of company' was in the offing. Indeed, just three days earlier, Mike and Mumby had sat together at a Supporters Forum discussing plans for season '98-99!

There was fury in the papers where suddenly it appeared that far more than two-thirds were pro-Walker. The fact that the bloke's wife had died during the season, the truly terrible injury problems we had to put up with all year and the lack of money made available to plug the resulting gaps were all used as reasons to back Mike up, but to no avail; the decision had been made and it was final. I had hoped that because of the way the split had been made, in a very cynical and clinical way, someone had already been lined up to take over the managerial 'luke-warm seat' (well, we're not *that* big a club, despite what we may like to think!). Unfortunately, it's now six weeks after the event and we still don't have a manager. Many names have been mentioned, a Steve Bruce/ Bryan Hamilton dream team seems favourite at the moment, but people keep dropping out because of the apparent shambolic way the appointment process is being run. So much for us hoping the board knew exactly what they were doing and were going to be devastatingly decisive!

Anyway, there was still one more game to go after Walker left, away at Reading for the final match ever to be played at the dump that was Elm Park. Over 3,000 City supporters for some reason decided to forgo their Sunday dinners and turn up for this totally meaningless mismatch. Reading were already relegated, and it showed, while we were playing for, well, nothing really. Pride certainly doesn't come into it with Norwich City players, but whatever we were playing for it worked 'cos we ended the season on a high note, another Bellamy goal giving us a 1-0 win where really we should have won by many more.

So that was it, season '97-98 was over and not a lot had changed. We're still heavily in debt, the new manager will have very little, if anything, to spend without selling Darren Eadie and we'll still have to travel to and laugh at the pig sty that is Portman Road and its inhabitants. On the other hand we might have a fantastic new go-ahead managerial team in charge, the conveyor belt of class players from the youth team looks likely to continue now we've been awarded 'academy' status from the FA and we look like we could be flogging 10,000 season tickets for the new season. The future's bright, the future's... yellow?

FLY ME TO THE MOON

Middlesbrough

This was the season that everyone wanted to get out of the way as quickly as possible. It was the means to an end season; close your eyes, replace style with guile and wake up in the Premier. That was the gist of things at any rate, but above all it was a massive gamble. The fans surfaced at last from the most emotionally debilitating campaign of all. The heartbreak of defeats in two cups and last match relegation at Leeds had left their mark, and that was to be Nationwide football with a team shorn of its jewel, Juninho. But amazingly the wayward Emerson was still with us. And breezing into town Riverside Dogs style was Ravanelli who put pen to

paper to shoot us back up to the top flight. The fans were magnificent; they invested in the future by breaking all previous season ticket records and selling out 28,500 seats from a total of 30,500, just leaving a bare minimum for away fans. And then came the big signing, and what an ambitious move: Paul Merson, after arguably his best ever season, was spirited away from the Arsenal squad system and handed the responsibility of digging us out of a hole.

The first game was a real shock to the system. While we were still mentally in the Premiership, Charlton Athletic were valiantly tearing us apart with an exhibition of the smash and grab Nationwide pressing game. Only a last-ditch Italian job by Festa and Ravanelli saved us from an embarrassing first game home defeat. Lesson heeded but not learned.

Next came a couple of weeks of trauma as Stoke came, saw and defeated us. Ravanelli had seen enough, he wanted out. The feeling was mutual. He upped sticks, taking the entire contents of his club owned house, kitchen sink and all (well, almost), to the south of France where he would live happily ever after. Not! Middlesbrough looked to youth and Danish streaky striker Mikkel Beck came out of the silver shadows and forged a fairly lucrative partnership with born-again Paul Merson. Old hand Andy Townsend was brought in to steady the ship in midfield, where amazingly the wayward son Emerson was still there and beginning to sparkle. Cartwheel goal celebrations were performed by teenage wing-whiz-kid Anthony Ormerod as he scored his debut goal and Middlesbrough found their feet. Still-floundering Sunderland were beaten twice, Emerson's volley lighting up the Stadium of...

Progress was never steady; victories at Oxford, Norwich, Swindon and Bury were accompanied by setbacks. One-nil up on *Sky Super Sunday* at home to Sheffield United and then the Dean and Dane show took over. Bowled over in the pot of Molineux gold by Robbie Keane, and then acutely embarrassed at Maine Road 0-2, the worst ever early Christmas surprise. Still, we had shot down many of the early season front-runners and Paul Merson's rehabilitation was so complete he even earned himself an England squad recall.

It was then that the Emerson show samba'd its way into the tabloids again. Eternally linked with Benfica and Tenerife, Middlesbrough had drafted in hair-alike cousin Fabio to placate him. Fabio turned in a spectacular debut, earning the terrace accolade of a rededication of Juninho's own song. Fabio never played again. Crazy! Both Brazilians jetted to Brazil for Christmas, Emerson having argued his way into a very timely suspension. He was never to return, shifting his festive partying to the sunshine isle of Tenerife and another relegation dogfight. Without the spark and strength of Emerson, Middlesbrough and Merson were never the same. It now really was back to the grindstone. Forget flare - just get us to the Premiership at all cost.

Anyway, for the first time in anyone's memory Middlesbrough didn't suffer a festive free-fall. As well as further league success stories we marched on in both the Coca-Cola and FA Cups. Victories against Barnet, Sunderland and an extra time nerve jangler against Bolton sneaked us into the quarter final of our favourite trophy. Wouldn't you know it was super Craig Hignett who scored his second successive last-gasp winner at Elm Park? It was a controversial goal but Festa lost his vest after his perfectly good winner was disallowed only minutes earlier. Next came a shocker at the usually happy Valley where Charlton stormed us off the pitch 3-0. Afterwards when someone asked Bryan Robson about substitutions he admitted he might easily have substituted the entire side. We were dire and Charlton were frightening. A warning shot!

In the FA Cup fourth round, Paul Merson advised Tony Adams not to make his comeback against us because our pitch was in such a state. He didn't heed the advice and Arsenal looked every inch the Championship force as they cruised to victory. We hadn't fielded a full side; clearly we were learning a few lessons from last season, but what did this say about the future of the FA Cup? Worrying. Oh, and *Match of the Day* cameras caught Paul Merson pulling a goal back against his old club. Who else?

Then it was back into semi final mode again, but with all due respect to Stockport and Chesterfield, a two-leg tie with Liverpool surely looks a far more difficult prospect on paper. No one expected any kind of result at Anfield, even most of the away fans just hoped we could keep the tie alive. But these days Boro have a cup tradition, and what a performance they gave. With McManaman being marked off the pitch by young Steve Baker, Townsend, Higgy and Mustoe tore into the Liverpool centre, Merson slammed us 1-0 up from Hignett's threaded pass. The Liverpool fightback was thwarted by the rock of Nigel Pearson, whose Man of the Match performance had big Ron Atkinson purring on *ITV*. In the end we lost 2-1 but we held our heads up proudly leaving the new Anfield Road end. Stoke City saw the last Middlesbrough action for prodigal son, striker Jaime Moreno. The Boy from Bolivia scored a crucial goal at the Britannia but returned Stateside, disappointed at his lack of opportunities.

But Middlesbrough had other irons in the fire. Remembering last season's Coca-Cola semi duel, Bryan Robson swooped for the very promising Alun Armstrong, and that was not all. An on/off saga finally ended favourably as 33-year-old forward Marco Branca signed for a little over a million pounds from Inter Milan. "We'll go up now that we have signed Marco," promised his good mate, Boro centre back Luca Festa.

So to the second leg of the Coca-Cola semi and Robson pulled a fast one over Roy Evans, immediately slipping Branca into the starting line up. What a dramatic start to a game: in a whirlwind opening five minutes Middlesbrough had hit Liverpool for two. A Merson penalty from Beck's run and a Branca finish to a Merson through ball were just too much for Paul Ince and Co.. The atmosphere was electric; the game seemed to stretch on forever as Middlesbrough gallantly held on. A third major cup final in two years; suddenly all the suffering seemed worthwhile. What a night! But things got better, because our next visitors were local rivals Sunderland, Nationwide form horses and now sprinting towards the Premiership in front of 40,000 in their fortress of Light. We murdered them. Marco Branca was the kiddo again, scoring a brace, and Alun Armstrong also marked his debut with a goal. In February things were so very, very good. Promotion and a Cup Final, this *would* be a special season after all.

Beware the Ides of March. The final game of February had been another Boro victory, 1-0 over Crewe, but our Aussie 'keeper Mark Schwarzer had been injured, along with, unfortunately, last season's FA Cup final 'keeper young Ben Roberts. The number one shirt would be in the hands of veteran journeyman Ooh-Andy Dibble. Oh dear. We went to Forest on the crest of a wave and they destroyed us 4-0. The midweek recovery at QPR was even worse: 0-5 and a red card for mild-mannered Andy Townsend. Disasterful. What went wrong and how to immediately remedy it? Snap up Marlon 'penalty king' Beresford from Burnley and sling out the bloated Dibble. Nigel Pearson would only play if his fitness level allowed and unfortunately Michael Thomas still had a couple of games to lumber through during his loan spell. Never mind; the month would get worse, much worse.

There were a couple of bright spots in this six weeks of woe. We needed to score six against Swindon to return to the top of the league and thanks to three doubles from Branca, Armstrong and Maddison we achieved it. The bookies' hearts were broken by a spectacular overhead kick from our man Marco.

Then came the Coca-Cola Cup Final, a dream return ticket to Wembley and an early chance for revenge against Chelsea. We made the most sensational pre-final signing of all, when Paul 'Gazza' Gascoigne returned to the North-East to join his chum Bryan Robson. It was another wonderful day but it turned so very, very sour. We held out for 90 minutes but new Colombian international striker Hamilton Ricard spurned our best chances. "He was nervous, we've not seen the best of him yet," chairman Steve Gibson informed us. The 2-0 extra time defeat left the fans heartbroken, it was so traumatic to lose again within the Twin Towers of WemBOROley that many Boro fans swore they could not face returning for a possible play-off final. We'd better go up by the direct route then. Anyway we had Gazza now!

Things quickly got worse. Hamilton Ricard almost snatched a point from the jaws of defeat but he fired wide of an open goal in injury time at the Hawthorns. At the final whistle he was left on the ground in tears. Then to Bramall Lane where the normally outstanding Schwarzer made a blunder and we were 1-0 down. Branca had been dropped and refused to take any further part, while poor Ricard had the nightmare of his life. Playing in front of the team that had almost bought him, and hundreds of thousands of disbelieving *Sky* viewers, he missed a season's worth of near open goals. He wasn't alone; Merson missed a penalty but later pledged his future to the team. This was it; we were finished, it was the play-offs for sure and how on earth could we hope to compete with formsters Ipswich and Charlton?

Before the Sheffield United game I'd been contacted by *Radio Five* who asked me whether I would do an interview (at 7.15am) about Gazza and the Boro, "but only if you lose," they added. I agreed: we wouldn't lose! Oh dear! Does this tell you something about the mentality of the media and their dubious agenda i.e. Gazza signs, is an instant disaster for Boro, big story, blah, blah... Disgraceful!

There was only one thing to do now, namely win the last six games, a feat way beyond us all season. Meanwhile Sunderland would have to drop points, but at the very least we would go into the play-offs in form. And what a run it turned out to be. Everything altered at Easter. On Good Friday, Sunderland squandered a home lead over QPR and were pegged back to 2-2. I saw one of our coaches, the legendary Gordon McQueen, that night and he was unable to contain himself with delight. "At last we've got some luck," he roared. It was just the break we needed. The following day we hammered Bury 4-0, Ricard finally scored and Branca blasted our only hat-trick of the campaign. On Easter Monday we hung on for a hard fought 1-0 victory at Reading while Sunderland dropped two points at West Brom.

What followed was three weeks of incredible tension; Sunderland still had to go to Ipswich and the season was on a knife-edge. There was the bruising battle with Man City, Schwarzer's phenomenal one-man show at Vale Park and then the joy of that Sunderland defeat at Ipswich. We stumbled against Wolves, but Ricard's equaliser was crucial, leaving our fate in our hands for the last game against Oxford.

So here we were, right down to the wire. Branca was injured but Armstrong had postponed a back operation to lead the line and Craig Hignett was given a recall to make one last telling contribution before leaving the Boro. At half-time it was 0-0 and elsewhere, Sunderland were ahead. Nerves were at shredding point. Merson seemed to be trying to carry the whole weight of our hopes on his shoulders; perhaps that penalty miss at Bramall Lane was still preying on his conscience. "Robson shouldn't have changed the team again," was the desperate shout from my left, "Armstrong shouldn't be playing." But within minutes of the restart Merson had split the Oxford defence and Armstrong coolly slotted us infront... Ecstasy! Hignett and Merson then combined to provide Armstrong with a tap-in. Jubilation! Higgy placed a third and hammered in a fourth. "Stand up if you're on the P*ss" chants reigned all around the ground. Oxford pulled a consolation back and their fans joined in the marvellous scenes of celebration. It was a remarkable coincidence but 30-years before, we had needed to win our last match to gain promotion. The score that day: 4-1; the opposition: Oxford United (including a certain Ron Atkinson in the line-up).

So, back in the Premiership again. I wonder if we can have a nice steady season of consolidation this time around. Not a chance! The Boro have got helter-skelter syndrome in their genes. There's never a dull moment being a Middlesbrough fan.

FOLLOW THE YELLOW BRICK ROAD

Mansfield Town

The Stags' centenary ended with the lads finishing just above mid-table, which is where this season would rate in the grand scheme of things of the previous 99. Somewhere in the low sixties would be about right I think. Here is the best and worst of it.

The Good Times: A trip to Sincil Bank early September gave us our first away win. A goal apiece for close season signings Steve Whitehall (a pearler of a curler and his first league goal for us) and Lyseden Christie saw the travelling Yellows victorious in this early local derby. Scarborough at home in November was also a memorable

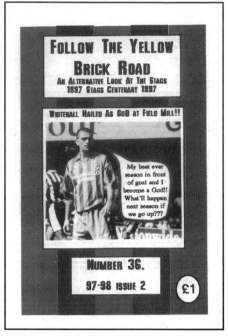

game. Deep into injury time it was 2-2 then the referee gave us a penalty (which we eventually put away). The Stags were chuffed with a fortunate 3-2 win, Scarborough were somewhat miffed about it and scuffles broke out in the tunnel at full-time, with both teams being subsequently reported to the FA. A rare Steve Harper hat-trick against Darlington in a 4-0 win was down firstly to the Darlo player who was marking him for most of the first half before getting himself sent off, and then to the Darlo manager for kindly deciding not to move anyone across to mark him. Exeter City and Peterborough were already on the slide when we stole away with all six points within a week and helped our play-off ambitions along the way. The spanner we threw into Barnet's own play-off hopes turned out to be no more than a minor set-back for them, but the sight of former Stags player Lee Howarth receiving his early bath chit from the ref made the trip south worthwhile.

All Square: Mid-table with 11 games to go, and then going every one of those games unbeaten - you'd think it would put us into a play-off place, wouldn't you? Not us. Seven of them ended in draws, with 2-2 a popular score (Scarborough, Rotherham, Orient, Torquay and Hartlepool all shared four goals with us). And earlier in the season we'd thrashed Doncaster at home with just a 1-1 to show for it. Despite Donkey Rovers showing their early lack of promise, we just couldn't seem to put the ball away.

The Bad Times: The absolutely, completely worst game of the lot was the trip to Cambridge. Although we only lost 2-0, in all honesty we were bloody crap beyond all belief. The highlight of the game (for us anyway) was when it started snowing and the ref brought on an orange ball. Second place goes to another disaster which occurred on a cold Tuesday night in February when Cardiff thrashed us 4-1. Oh, and missing a first minute penalty at Notts County must rate in there somewhere, too!

A Cup Run? No chance. The Coke Cup: A first leg hat-trick by Lyseden Christie helped us to a 4-2 home win against Stockport. But last year's semi-finalists did us in the return leg. Losing 5-3 (but 7-6 up on aggregate) the game entered into injury time. Within the space of a minute, we'd collapsed and conceded two goals and went out, by the odd goal in 15! The FA Cup took us up to Oldham. The huge travelling army of blue and yellow roared around Boundary Park (and a few local pubs) and became the proverbial twelfth man, helping the other eleven to a 1-1 draw and a replay. Sadly, however, victory wasn't forthcoming and a quick exit from the World's greatest cup competition came about courtesy of a 1-0 defeat. The AutoWindscreen Shield: This provided our best cup run. A first round bye paired us with Wrexham in round two, which ended 1-0 to us. A Tuesday night trip to Preston in the quarter-final sorely tested us (the fans, that is!). To say the game was poor would be an understatement: we just looked as though we didn't care about a potential Wembley outing and a single goal saw our cup hopes dashed for yet another year.

Player Of The Season: Steve Whitehall. After years at Rochdale, and with him scoring in almost every game he played against us, he made the move south, forming a partnership with Christie. They soon set about banging the goals in, although we had to wait a month before Steve finally found the back of the net. He soon overhauled Christie's total and set about climbing up the top-scorer table. His total of 26 (leaving him just one short of 100 league goals) was only bettered by Jonesy at Notts County getting a pair on the season's last day.

Loan Player Of The Season: Paul Gibson. A goalie from down the pecking order at Manchester United came to help us out when regular man Ian Bowling was struck down with injury. Some excellent performances endeared him to the crowd in his three month spell at Field Mill, which was sadly cut short with an injury. Can we have him back, Mr Ferguson, please?

Couldn't Organise A Piss-up In A Brewery: The home game against table-topping local rivals Notts County must go down as the worst organised football match in Stags' history. Despite the fact that County were clear of the pack, they were always going to bring a big crowd to Field Mill. The ground (whose current capacity of around 6,500 seems an insult to the late seventies when 10,000 + regularly turned up with room to spare) was packed to the rafters. Notts County were said to be bringing around 3,000 up the A60, and they were allocated half of the ground, which meant that we Stags' fans had to give up one of our stands. And since the so-called 'powers that be' had decided not to make this an all-ticket game, it was a case of first come, first served. Some season ticket holders couldn't even get in because the ground was full to capacity. Stags and Notts fans mingled outside when the gates were shut demanding admission; then some enterprising Stags broke down a gate to the North Stand and rushed onto the terraces. Now, I've been in the North Stand when there were 16,000 crammed into Field Mill and still had room to move around, so when they shut the gates at around 2.30pm with its supposed current capacity of around 800 reached, you could see why those outside looking in were a bit miffed with all that space going spare. The game itself was effectively lost when the red mist rolled over the eyes of Christie and he head-butted a Notts defender. The remaining ten men did their best but went down 2-0.

The Chairman: Keith Haslam. The bloke in charge of the above débâcle was already under pressure from the fans. He was (and still is) due up in court on an insurance charge and is under pressure from the league to resign his place on the League Committee. Luckily (for him), after this latest balls-up, the Stags had a run of four away games and so a bit of the heat died down. Determined not to make the same mistake again, he announced that the game against then high-flying Peterborough would be all ticket. "Get your tickets now - none available on the day," ran the story in the local press for weeks before the game. But in the meantime, a wheel had fallen off the Posh wagon and they were slipping down the table. And so come game day at the end of March, the Posh were out of a play-off space and with two days to spare, and less than half of the tickets sold, the club announced that you could pay at the turnstiles. Well, thanks a bleeding bunch! Not a word of apology for all the inconvenience of having to go down to Field Mill to get a ticket or braving the queues on matchdays. The season ended with half-time and full-time pitch protests against the chairman.

Chant Of The Season: Aimed at our chairman with reference to his court case, and sung to the tune of *Three Lions*: "He's going down! He's going down! He's going, Haslam's going down!"

Player Power: For the last two months, the Stags players didn't get paid. The PFA stepped in, while the chairman put it down to bank errors. Yeah, right! When it happened a second time, the players took the law into their own hands, blocking the chairman's car so that he couldn't leave and demanding a meeting and their money. He eventually coughed up the readies. When our new goalscoring terrace hero says in public that he'd be better off moving to a club that will stump up the cash on time, there has to be something seriously wrong.

Redevelopment: Finally, work is to begin on rebuilding Field Mill. All being well, three new stands will grace the ground by the Millennium and the capacity will be back up to around 11,000. Mr Haslam went around saying that work would definitely start after the last game of the season. Just one small problem with this - the fact that we didn't actually own the ground had a slight bearing on the construction. But three weeks later, this minor setback was sorted out and hopefully work will begin within the month.

So as you can see, it's been a memorable season, although mainly for the wrong reasons. The bad points off the pitch have tipped the balance from those on it. With the start of the Stag's second century just around the corner, let's hope it's better than the end of the last one.

BARRY FRY DECIDING WHICH CLUB TO RUIN NEXT.

Source: Deranged Ferret

THE GOONER

Arsenal

When Man United beat Chelsea back in February to stretch their lead to 11 points, the considered wisdom was that United had all but put the ribbons on the Premiership trophy. One bookmaker in Manchester even took the unprecedented step of paying out on a United title triumph. Was this a £50,000 gamble? Not a bit of it, thought Mr White, no one else could touch United. Do the bookies ever get it wrong?

A clutch of continental signings had arrived at Highbury over the summer. Prominent amongst these was Marc Overmars, the Dutch international winger from Ajax.

Gilles Grimandi and Emmanuel Petit, fresh from Monaco's title winning team, joined for a combined fee of five million with Petit negotiating with Tottenham before cheekily borrowing the money for a cab to N5 to sign for Arsenal. Luis Boa Morte, Chris Wreh (George Weah's cousin) and Alberto Mendez, a complete unknown from FC Feucht, a German Fifth Division team, were also added. Arsenal's chances were, though, largely written off, with both fans and neutrals alike feeling that second place in the League and a cup win would constitute a more than adequate return from the expected 'transitional' season. It proved to be anything but.

However, the early signs had been promising. Bergkamp's form at the start was sublime and he won the award for Player of the Month both in August - when he became the first man in the 25 year history of the Goal of the Month competition to sweep the board - and in September. His hat-trick at Leicester, described by Alan Hansen as the finest he had ever seen, and his two goals in the 5-0 drubbing of Barnsley made it 11 goals from 11 appearances for the Dutchman.

For Ian Wright, though, the early part of the season revolved entirely around when, and not if, he would break the all-time goal scoring record set by Cliff Bastin. Three goals in the first two games left him needing just one to equal the record. The tension clearly affected him and it was not until four games later at home to Bolton that he finally achieved the magical mark. In true Ian Wright style he almost blew his celebrations by revealing a '179 Just Done it' T-shirt after scoring his record-equalling 178th goal. Happily for Wright, though, just four minutes later he tapped in from a yard for surely his easiest ever goal, confirming his place in the Arsenal hall of fame.

The bookies established Arsenal as favourites for the title but in truth the only game of the first ten against a team in the top half was Chelsea, and that result was only secured with a Nigel Winterburn blockbuster three minutes from time. Scoreless draws with Palace and Villa brought suspensions for Bergkamp and Petit respectively before Derby blew us away at Pride Park. A classic 3-2 victory against United at Highbury (thanks Platty!) was followed by a defeat at a Ron Atkinson-inspired Wednesday and McManaman's winner at Highbury for Liverpool saw us slip to fifth. Ian Wright's winner at Newcastle said more about their shortcomings than our abilities - and then disaster struck.

The 3-1 home defeat by Blackburn marked the worst performance since the arrival of Wenger. The team looked shaky and out of sorts and Adams in particular looked way off the pace. Wrighty's acrimonious 'exchange of views' with supporters in Avenell Road did little to help confidence. With the Gunners now in sixth position, a European place looked doubtful, and not even the most ardent fan believed that we could still win the title. During a fraught team meeting, the defence complained that they were being overstretched by the lack of midfield cover. As a result, Wenger detailed more defensive duties to Petit and Vieira and this tactic was to prove a masterstroke in the Premiership campaign.

Marc Overmars scored both goals in a 2-1 win over Leeds in mid-January and from this point on his form was exceptional. Port Vale were disposed of on penalties following a turgid draw at home in the FA Cup. The following round saw an almost perfect result with a 2-1 win at Middlesbrough - Merse scoring for the Teesiders. The momentum was beginning to build and the team was starting to put together some impressive performances. Southampton were brushed aside at Highbury, as were Chelsea, with both goals coming from talented youngster Stephen Hughes. Such is the depth of talent at Highbury that even a five-year contract may not be enough to keep him. Giles Grimandi's exquisite volley did for relegation candidates Palace - a fine result given that eight first choice players were missing. A goalless draw at Upton Park at the start of March saw us 11 points adrift and seemingly contenders for little more than second place.

The mood after West Ham was really one of enforced resignation. If we won our remaining 12 games we could still be Champions but with a trio of tough away games to come, including a visit to Old Trafford, we had to win at Wimbledon to stand any chance. The previous attempt to stage this game had ended in floodlight failure, and this time a discarded shopping bag, thought to be a bomb, delayed the game again. When it finally kicked off, Chris Wreh's fine strike after 21 minutes was enough to win it but it was only thanks to an awesome second half defensive display by the young Austrian 'keeper Manninger that kept us in it. That win in many ways restored the belief that the title was there to be taken, and the celebrations of fans and players alike reflected this. With United losing to Sheffield Wednesday it meant that a win at Old Trafford would see us just six points behind with three games in hand.

Marc Overmars' 81st minute winner capped a Man of the Match performance to beat United for the second time in a season and suddenly everyone began to believe us. Alex Ferguson pointed out in typically gracious fashion that we still had to win the games in hand but these two wins had changed everything - the belief was back. We knew we could be Champions. After all, the last time we beat United home and away was in 1991.

A home win against Sheffield Wednesday courtesy of Bergkamp was cancelled out by United winning at home against Wimbledon thanks to two off-side goals. But his red card against West Ham in the FA Cup quarter final for some TV-captured elbow work meant that he would be absent for the next three games, and with Wright still recovering, the very inexperienced partnership of Wreh and Anelka would lead our attack away at Bolton. We needn't have worried as another inspired team performance and brilliant goal from Chris Wreh gave us all three points. In surely the best week of his career, Wreh again struck the solitary goal in the semi final against Wolves, a game more memorable for the thousands of fans that missed the kick-off than the action on the pitch. With Bergkamp still suspended and Wright struggling to be fit Anelka and Wreh again led the line in the Cup Final rehearsal against Newcastle. Two fine goals from Anelka and a 30-yard Goal of the Month screamer from Vieira sealed the points, making it five straight wins in the league. Two days later, Arsenal's quick fire start in the game at Ewood Park saw us 3-0 up in 15 minutes and 4-0 up before half time. The level of performance blew away any remaining doubts. We were watching the Champions and we all knew it.

Of course, there were still plenty of games to negotiate but with three home games in the next four, surely the title was ours for the taking. Together with a 5-0 win against Wimbledon, including a long-awaited goal from Emmanuel Petit, and United being held at home by Newcastle we went top for the first time since the middle of October. An away win at Barnsley, all but condemning them to First Division football, meant that home wins against Derby and Everton would seal the title for the first time in seven years. Petit's vital strike against the Rams brought us to the brink of the title but the celebrations were tempered by a hamstring injury to Bergkamp which looked likely to keep him out of the run-in and possibly the Cup Final. But we didn't miss him as we cruised to a 4-0 win and the title against Everton, an own goal from Bilic settling the crowd's nerves. Goals on either side of half time by Overmars finished the game as a contest before Steve Bould's delicate chip (yes, that's *delicate* chip) put Adams clean through with a minute on the clock. The skipper chested the ball down before firing home with great aplomb. The perfect finish to an unforgettable day.

With the Championship secured, the team took a collective foot off the accelerator and lost their remaining two league games before stepping out at

Wembley to face Newcastle in the FA Cup final. Twenty-five thousand red and white cards made an impressive façade during *Abide With Me* and before long the team were matching the off-field performance with Marc Overmars' sixteenth goal of an excellent campaign setting us on our way. Dabizas and Shearer hit bar and post respectively in a four minute spell before Anelka's control and pace from a ball over the top by Parlour took him clear of Howey to score with a low shot to past the stranded 'keeper. Two-nil and game over - the Double double was ours.

"We have won more than the FA Cup, we have won the Double. It is a remarkable achievement," said Arsene Wenger afterwards and you have to agree with him. The run that the team put together was unbelievable, with the renowned Arsenal spirit playing a vital role. The team effort was matched only by the quality of the football - something that numerous column inches reflected. This double perhaps was not as dramatic as the last, but images of Ray Kennedy's goal winning the league at White Hart Lane and Charlie George prostrate on the turf are hard to match. Coming out of Wembley, my Dad called me and just said "Twenty seven years I've waited for that." I never thought I'd see it in my lifetime but I have, and it was a privilege to be there. Arsene knows.

TOTTANIC

Starring
KATE WINSNOTHING
and
**LEONARDO DI
TROPHYCABINETSEMPTY**

GRORTY DICK

West Bromwich Albion

"...Home of lost causes, and forsaken beliefs, and unpopular names, and impossible loyalties..." MATTHEW ARNOLD talking about Oxford University, 1822-1888

"I hope his drawers drop down and catch fire..." GLYNIS WRIGHT talking about Ray Harford circa Christmas 1997...

When I was doing 'O levels, round about the time Jeff Astle played (well) as opposed to singing (badly), a fiendish torture frequently inflicted on me by sadistic teachers (who must surely have trained with the Spanish Inquisition) was to have me write the dreaded 'Compare And Contrast' essay. For those who have been spared such horrors, let me explain. You are given the

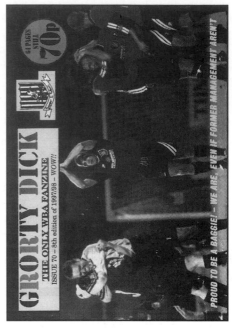

names of two books (or species, or chemical compounds) and asked to wax lyrical on their relative merits (or otherwise) for four sides of A4 or so. A tedious exercise, and yet, when it comes to write a definitive supporter-summary of season '97-98 for this weighty tome, I find myself doing much the same thing, essentially, comparing and contrasting the loyalty, or otherwise, to the club of key Albion performers this term...

Hughsie. A flame-haired lad who, 12 months ago, was essentially one of us; a hopeless case, Albionwise. Oh sure, a Conference striker with Kidderminster, but when not performing for them he was a Brummie Road regular at the Shrine. His long-overdue signing by The Disingenuous One was greeted rapturously by all and sundry - how long had we been advising Buckley of the lad's talents - how long had we been met with outright hostility or worse by fish-features? His outings in pre-season friendlies looked promising. His inevitable apotheosis came in our second away game of the season, versus Crewe Alex. Albion were in arrears, and, seemingly dead, dead, dead. Enter Hughsie, as sub...

Remember the film, *When Saturday Comes?* Just like Sean Bean, Hughsie scored a brace, both from seemingly non-existent chances, very late on. He was one of our own, getting to wear the coveted blue and white shirt, being our saviour in our hour of need... Which was why, when he scored the first,

Hughsie dived into the crowd - and was why, when he scored the winner, the crowd dived onto Hughsie! We're looking towards 20 goals or better from the lad next term - Wulves, you have been warned...

And what about our veteran '93-94 promotion goal-machine Bob Taylor? At the time of writing, his Albion future's uncertain. Influential opinion within the club evidently thinks he's past his 'sell-by date' vis-f-vis this division, consequently it's highly likely he'll be elsewhere next term. Shame. Like Hughsie, he cares. About the club, about the supporters. Even about former players fallen on hard times - as far as I'm aware, Bob's only one of two current players to visit Alzheimer's Disease-plagued former manager Ronnie Allen in his nursing home. In any case, is our man that discardable? Did quite a creditable job during his two loan spells with then-Premiership Bolton; any supposed 'has-been' that can stick one past a) Peter Schmeichel and b) The Claret And Spew can't be all that bad, can he? I'm currently hearing rumblings in the press that the door to negotiations isn't quite so firmly padlocked as it was; I do hope someone's seen sense...

That's loyalty for you. The antithesis is Ray Harford. Our former leader who left us for a handful of silver to subsequently flirt with relegation, courtesy of a supposedly more ambitious club ensconsced in The Smoke. What made the parting all the more hurtful was the fact that just once, just this once, at the time of his yuletide leaving we seemed to genuinely look the Premiership part. Victories over Wulves (thanks, Keith Curle!), Bury, away (magical day, that, thanks to a hat-trick from the Cheating Canadian), and Port Vale (at long last) had seen us placed firmly in the promotion driving seat come December. Then came the bombshell, following which came that precipitous decline, somewhat reminiscent of comparatively recent Albion doings aka Alan Buckley. Reverses against Sunderland (ouch! - that bloody music would contravene the Geneva Convention if forcibly played to POW's in time of war), the 4-0 FA Cup humiliation at Villa Park; Huddersfield, Reading, Crewe... It reads like a litany. Crash, bang, tinkle - down the table we went. Did we really flatter to deceive that heady first segment of the season? Was it Harford's departure that precipitated our subsequent decline? When polled, a third of this fanzine's readership thought so. Another third blamed our finest themselves. They may have a point. Read on...

It's not only managers that can do the dirty on clubs. Players show a quite remarkable talent for doing similar, especially when overly-loquacious agents are involved. Schmuck-features Eric Hall and a certain diminutive overly-greedy Canadian entitled Paul Peschisolido are a case in point, though the hand (or financial brain) of a certain Ms Brady in this affair should not entirely be discounted. Reckoned Fulham would be in the Premiership before us, did we then? Nice idea Paul, shame about the play-offs...

Andy Hunt. Another case where Mammon reared his huge, huge head, and a Baggie, duly mesmerised, bowed beneath his feet. Yes, Andy, on your day, your striking talents reach the boundaries of Premiership status. You have the capability to become a member of that charmed circle - should you put your mind to it. You don't achieve the giddy heights by time and time again failing to put away chances my ginger cat would have slotted in without difficulty - then Peschisolido-fashion attempting to hold the club to ransom for vastly increased wage demands. The big time demands a level of commitment directly proportionate to the immense salaries offered at that level. You're out of contract, Andy, the Bosman's talking, but Premiership clubs are most definitely not...

Compare and contrast... Hughes with Pesch, Taylor with Hunt, Harford with... DENIS SMITH? Well, our ex-Oxfordian, being an ex-Stokie, certainly isn't short of a word or three. Since his arrival at the Shrine, he's attended more supporters' club functions than any of his predecessors did within their entire Albion career, and what's more, through passion, hard work and sheer force of personality, he's succeeded in winning over an initially pretty hostile Baggie audience. It helps, coming over as totally honest, of course; but Denis has 'told it like it is'. He hasn't promised to change the world overnight, unlike some we've had. Where he's perceived shortcomings in certain players, he's told us so, sometimes in terms that can only be described as 'forthright'.

Great to relate towards the fag end of last season, he put the confidence back into the players, who were greatly aggrieved at Harford's sudden departure. Consequently, a worrying haemorrhage of points was stemmed before it gave rise to problems at the wrong end of the table. Buys? Matt Carbon, from Derby County - a real diamond. What was Jim Smith thinking of in letting him go? Mr Quinn, Mr van Blerk - experienced players well-immune from barracking. This culminated in a superb mini-run of results, most notable of these being that superb 4-2 over the Blades at their own foundry, not to mention the 2-1 home win over Boro', Gazza and all. Didn't like Sean Flynn's close attentions one little bit, did we, Paul?

Oh, yes, finally - one personal milestone for me. While Mr Smith was putting his feet under the metaphorical Albion table, I finally clocked up my thousandth Albion first team game as a spectator - the culmination of a journey which commenced when I was ten and would have arrived sooner but for the intervention of shift work. Welcome to the elite world of the 'seriously sad' Baggie, Mrs Wright... Sad, yes. Mad? Maybe. But, tell you what... I don't regret any of it, ever. And will you be saying the same thing two score years into the future Mr Harford, Mr 'P', Mr Hunt?...

HANGING ON THE TELEPHONE

Huddersfield Town

Anyone giving the final Division One table no more than a cursory glance might suppose that Huddersfield Town fans had had little to shout about. But that would be to overlook a truly remarkable recovery, which had Town supporters singing *The Great Escape* as early as December. An escape no one thought possible, given the horrendous opening two months under Brian Horton's managership.

The '97-98 season was Brian Horton's third and ultimately last in charge of Huddersfield Town. During his tenure, the bright new dawn, promised after Neil Warnock's side had secured promotion to Division One, slowly but surely disintegrated before our

eyes. Yet if you listened to the very credible-sounding Mr Horton, everything could be explained away as either bad luck or bad play (but obviously never bad management).

At the end of last year many amongst us had asked what more he had to offer. We'd just witnessed a season typified by lacklustre displays, devoid of ideas and passion, from a side that survived relegation by a whisker but ultimately appeared unwilling or unable to perform as the manager wished.

A total of zero signings in the summer filled no-one with anything other than a sense of forbidding, and having personally witnessed the most shambolic display from any Huddersfield Town side I could remember in a pre-season defeat at Conference side Halifax, I was foremost amongst those predicting disaster.

I was joined on the doom and gloom trip by everyone else who made the journey to Oxford for the league opener, as Town crashed to defeat without managing a single shot in the entire 90 minutes. Horton maintained after the match that it was far too early to judge, and that we certainly didn't need a large striker as so many of us were suggesting. And after all, he knew best. Another eight games and still without a win, a clue or a prayer, the board finally did the necessary and dispensed with Horton. He'd become too intense, too involved and too uptight to make the right tactical decisions at key moments in the game, and was unable to achieve anything more from a set of players who appeared to have lost all respect for him.

Two days later the appointment of Peter Jackson as manager and Terry Yorath as coach fuelled optimism and doubt in equal measure. Optimism that the most passionate Town player of recent times could bring back some of his unquenchable spirit and that a coach, of some standing, could actually orchestrate a revival. The doubt persisted whether the squad had the talent to deliver.

The latter emotion seemed well-founded as the first five games under the new regime highlighted all the team's frailties and vices, leaving us with no wins and only five points with 14 games gone.

It was always going to take something special to get us underway, and Stoke City provided the push. The manner of our victory brought pure joy as Town's third goal was rolled into an empty net, with the Stoke 'keeper still in our penalty area following his poor man's Peter Schmeichel impression at a last minute corner. From that win, a steady, unspectacular, but highly committed and professional escape act saw Town ultimately survive at the expense of Reading, Stoke and Manchester 'we're too big a club for Division One' City. Helped in no small measure by some astute signings; none better than Wayne Allison, the big target man Horton had said we didn't need.

Recognising that coach Terry Yorath was a major, if not *the* major, influence on our survival, the only concern was that he was slowly but surely converting the side into a Wales XI. A team including Jenkins, Browning, Horne and Phillips appeared to testify to this. Speculation was rife about behind the scenes planning and future team selection, should Yorath assume total control. Come ten to three on a Saturday, and Terry might be giving last minute instructions:

Yorath: "Right Boyos, Jacko's finding it a bit hard being understood around here lately, so I'm going to go through today's team. Right then, in goal Max Boyce... no excuses today Max!"

(from the shower area) "Baa, Baa"

Yorath: "No.11, shut them sheep up! Back four... Steve Jenkins, Shirley Bassey, Harry Secombe and Neil Kinnock on the left"

Jacko: "Does Jenkins *have* to play, Tel?"

Yorath: "He's Welsh, boss"

"Baa, Baa!"

Yorath: "No.11, shut them sheep up. Right where was I? Oh yeah... midfield: Tom Jones, Ruth Madoc, Windsor Davies and Gareth Edwards. Remember Tom, in the air when we are away, but on the green, green grass at home"

"Baa, Baa!!"

Yorath: "No.11 - shut them f***ing sheep up"

Jacko: "Are you sure Jenkins *has* to play?"

Yorath: "I've told you boss, he's Welsh!"

"Baa, Baa!!!"

Yorath: "No.11, shut them sheep up... Now! Up front today: No.9 Richard Burton; stay on your feet today Richard, what the hell are you after - an Oscar? Finally, No.11, Anthony Hopkins."

"Baa, Baa!!!!"

Yorath: "Subs today... Ewe, Ewe and Ewe. Right boyos, get out there and get f***ing stuck in!"

Jacko: "Tel, about Jenkins..."

Yorath: "He's Welsh, boss"

Jacko: "Yeah, but Terry..."

Yorath: "He's *Welsh*, boss"

Jacko: "He's shite, Terry"

Yorath: "They're *all* shite, boss"

Jacko: "They're all Welsh, Terry"

"Baa, Baa!!!!!"

Yorath: "No.11 - will you *silence them lambs?!*"

THE HANGING SHEEP

Leeds United

"Things," as the song goes, "can only get better." So after watching the necessary and yet depressing catalogue of nil-nil'ers the season before, an improvement was more than a must. Had the committed been made to endure more of the same, then committed is what we surely would have been...

Graham's philosophy of not spending any more than he had to was in evidence yet again as he recruited David Robertson, Bruno Ribeiro, Jimmy Floyd Hasselbaink and David Hopkin for a combined fee of as £6.5m - not bad in today's terms. Bruno and Jimmy have effectively quadrupled their values. The jury is still out on the other two.

THE HANGING SHEEP

Issue No. 48
Jan/Feb 1998

He's here, he's there
he's every f*****g
where Harry Kewell.
Except Leeds?

Inside;
Billy Bremner tribute,
Ground Rules, The view
from the cheap seats,
celebrity Leeds fans etc etc
etc....

£1

the independent Leeds fanzine

The early season defeat of Manchester United was overshadowed by seven hours of violence around the city centre and ground. Wanted posters and dawn raids followed as the number of arrests around the stadium rocketed to a near 20-year high. It can be no coincidence that a change of Football Intelligence Officer has been the catalyst for numerous violent incidents this season. Whilst the new 'regime' work out their game plan, the hoolies are taking advantage.

Although the number of arrests would suggest that hooliganism is rapidly becoming popular amongst our support once again, it is worth noting that a large percentage were for nothing more than drunkenness and other petty 'offences' such as two-fingering the ref. The police were obviously doing their part in trying to bump up the number of exclusion orders issued prior to the old Coupe du Monde. All very well, but the clever yobbos don't get arrested for such trivial matters - if at all.

If last time around was notorious for bore draws, then the exact opposite can be said of this season. Leeds produced some great football at times, but perhaps more importantly it was the work rate that impressed from a team willing to put the effort in - Rod Wallace excepted of course. He's decided to cash in on the Bosman ruling. So much for loyalty eh, Rodney? The fans had stuck by him and under George Graham he'd flourished on the pitch rather than floundered on the bench as had been the case during Wilkinson's last days in charge. Good riddance to yet another footballing mercenary...

Notable matches included the televised 4-3 victory at Blackburn, a 4-1 demolition of Newcastle, a 4-3 victory against Derby (after being 3-0 down), another four goal haul at home to Blackburn and the humiliating 5-0 drubbing of Derby in their own back yard. All good stuff under Mr Graham, so was there a down-side? We're talking about Leeds here. Of course there bloody was.

Yet again our abysmal record in the domestic cups came back to haunt us. Shitty Reading dumped us out of the Coca-Cola Cup 3-2, whilst crappy Wolves turned us over 1-0 in the FA Cup. No surprises there then.

If our cup form (a contradiction in terms there) resulted in the usual humiliation, at least our push towards the top five never really faltered all year. A few hiccups cannot detract from a very encouraging first season under Stroller. The squad, whilst capable of beating anyone on their day, is still three or four quality players away from challenging any higher up the league. Only time will see if the powers that be are willing to part with any decent amounts of cash.

Our first foray into the big spending world of Premiership players ended with some guy from Bolton preferring to go Villa rather than come to Leeds. Although to he honest I'm not so sure that I could care less about a guy who was to cost £4.5m and £20,000 a week in wages, especially when you consider that he was the kingpin of the midfield of a team that went sliding back into mediocrity once again.

Caspian, or Leeds Sporting as they now prefer to be known, tied up the buying back of the ground off Leeds City Council, a cash/share deal of some £11.4m securing the freehold on Elland Rd. The proposed ice hockey and sporting arena has been put on the back burner for another 12 months, apparently due to residents' concerns.

Call me cynical if you want, but I would have thought that when the council agreed to sell the ground, the topic of planning permission for the new sporting arena would have no doubt cropped up. I'm sure a gentleman's agreement would have been sorted out over a few G&Ts. You know the sort of thing: "We'll buy the ground back and give you some lovely Leeds Sporting shares to make even more money when the new venue is up and running, and all you have to do is give us one of those super planning consent orders, Mr Councillor..' nudge, nudge, wink, wink.

Then again I could be completely wrong in my understanding of how big business works in the all new care-about-the-environment-and-people nineties. Another rumour is that Leeds Sporting simply haven't got the cash. That would certainly explain why Leeds spent less than Crystal Palace in transfers, with only Graham's astute buying disguising that fact.

Just how long he can sustain such a situation is anyone's guess and as Manchester United, Arsenal, Liverpool and Chelsea continue to chuck ever-increasing amounts of cash at new recruits, Leeds' chance of challenging any higher than a top six European spot looks doomed. Managerial experience might count for a lot, but money positively screams in football these days.

The penchant that top flight managers seem to have for overseas players has started to cause more than a few problems, not least of all at Leeds. Graham found himself continually at odds with the Australian and African FAs respectively - both associations guilty of pulling rank and removing both Lucas Radebe and Harry Kewell from the fray for long periods of time, their numerous and irritating absences coinciding with the dips in United's form. It's great to have internationals in your side, but not when their continued absence jeopardises the club's chances of domestic and the now impending European honours.

As football continues to ride the crest of a wave, the club decided to reward the loyalty of the fans (average gates went up by some 8.1%), by hiking ticket prices by up to 22%. The lowest adult matchday ticket will cost £20 for an 'ordinary' match, the most expensive costing a mere £30. Such blatant profiteering on the back of a reasonably successful season cannot be explained away with glib excuses about what so-and-so charge elsewhere. The fans are being taken for a ride and would be well advised to think carefully when spending their money. Similarly I afforded myself a wry smile when the chairmen collectively kicked *Sky*'s pay per view idea into touch, our own chairman Peter Ridsdale stating that they needed to "look after the fans." Pretty patronising when you consider that he and his cohorts have whacked up season ticket prices by up to four times inflation.

Leeds Sporting have been at the forefront of the pay per view idea from the start, with more than the odd rumour that Leeds United TV will be the first single club channel to spring up in a year or two. You can be assured that if Premiership chairmen turned down *Sky*'s megabucks offer, then it has nothing to do with looking after the fans or concern over the eroding of the traditional Saturday Fixture list - Nosireebob, it's because they'll have something else up their Rolex-wearing wrists which will mean that they'll be coining even more cash in themselves.

From a fanzine point of view, our next issue will be both our 50th and tenth anniversary edition all rolled into one. Just how much longer we'll keep churning fresh copies out is unsure, but with football demanding ever increasing amounts of money from the hard-pressed fans, we as fanzine producers are worrying less and less about tight deadlines and more and more about value for money. Having said all that, I'm sure that the club will put together the most affordable travel package possible for those supporters wishing to follow the Whites in the UEFA Cup this season...

THE HATCHET

Bury

If City Is A Sleeping Giant, Is Bury A Midget On Steroids?

Following Bury's meteoric rise from Division Three to Division One in the previous two seasons, it was inevitable that '97-98 would prove just a bit more problematic for the heroes in white. Suddenly we were little fish in a rather big pond - and we hadn't even looked particularly large when we were in the little pond! Although we had been promoted as Champions, our average crowd had been no more than 4,500 and we were told there was no real money to spend on team-building. Our friends in the media were having a field day - how on earth could 'a club like Bury' cope with the likes of Forest, Wolves and Manchester City? Jim White writing in *The Guardian* thought he had it sussed when he said that Bury, Stockport and Crewe found themselves "elevated so high the surprise is they are not suffering nosebleeds." Predictably, we were once again installed as odds-on favourites for the drop.

But here at Bury we are well used to being the underdogs. And so while critics flinched and pundits sneered, The Shakers rolled up their sleeves, got stuck in and proceeded with the time honoured task of putting the skids under anyone who dared to think of Bury as three easy points. Well most of the time, anyway.

Our first season back in 'the top half' of football for 29 years got off to a very satisfactory start. In September, Gigg Lane was packed to the rafters to see Bury hold Manchester City to a 1-1 draw in what was the ground's first ever live televised match. As November started we moved up to our highest position (7th) after inflicting a comprehensive 2-0 defeat on eventual Champions Nottingham Forest. Then it all went pear-shaped. Four days later struggling Portsmouth beat us 2-0 at Gigg Lane and within days, still short of cash, Bury sold leading scorer and brightest prospect David Johnson to Ipswich in a deal worth a million pounds. Bury went on to endure a very bleak mid-winter slump, going 14 league games without a win.

By February we were in bottom place and the Johnson deal, accepted in November as inevitable, was starting to look like one of the worst bits of business in the club's history (and believe me, there have been many). In truth, though, we hadn't been playing particularly badly, and with a bit of luck some of us thought we might just be able to pull things around...

On Valentine's Day, Bury dispersed the gathering gloom in unforgettable fashion at Maine Road, when Shakers hero (and boyhood blues fan) Paul Butler scored the only goal in a typical 'blood and thunder' derby match. The contrasting effect this game had on the two clubs involved was dramatic. For many City fans this was the last straw - one even ran onto the pitch and, to cheers from fans of Bury and City alike, ripped up his season ticket! Chairman Francis Lee didn't last much longer. Perhaps he should have concentrated on his primary business interest - manufacturing toilet paper in Bolton (enough said).

For Bury, however, the Maine Road result was a turning point, and set the scene for the run-in. Gritty, hard-fought home wins and a roller-coaster set of away results - the highlights of which were the 3-1 destruction of Birmingham and the final day win at QPR - eventually ensured Bury's survival.

The most worrying development came after the season finished. Manager Stan Ternent and assistant Sam Ellis have just been lured away to Second Division Burnley. Ternent was, without any doubt, Bury's most successful manager since the war - the Boer war! Stan's close links to Burnley in the past, and the fact that he and Ellis worked at Gigg Lane without contracts, meant that losing them had an air of inevitability about it. It can be a depressing thought to consider that your manager moved down a division in order to advance his career, but this is nothing new for us.

It's not clear at the time of writing who will take over, but let's finish on a few optimistic notes.

Whoever comes in will find a club that last season enjoyed a 50% increase in home support - yes, we're well over 6,000 now! Another year like that and we'll be into five figures! Also, we know how to get behind our team. I know one Man Yernighted season ticket holder who says the atmosphere in our South Stand makes Old Trafford sound like a morgue. And, speaking of the team, we've got players who will sweat blood for the cause. As long as they don't all piss off to join Stan at Burnley, of course!

On the whole, then, an exhilarating, nail-biting struggle of a season, made enjoyable by the fact that we stayed up - and, for the third year running, proved that what the media knows about football in general - and Bury FC in particular - could be written on the back of a stamp!

HEAVEN ELEVEN

Reading

The Bookie is Never Wrong

66/1 for the Championship, favourites to be relegated - what were these so-called experts on? Hadn't they heard of our £800,000 proven striker? Hadn't they ever sat in a London taxi and listened to the cabbie yapping on about a dream to manage a Nationwide Endsleigh League Division One club? Obviously not. Enter Terry Bullivant and Carl Asaba.

These two in my view can add the following points to their CV's :-

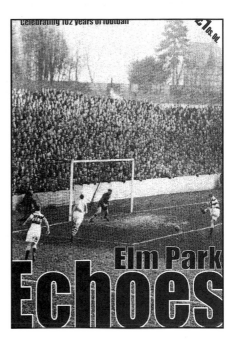

1 Most money spent by any Royals boss - £2.5m
2 38 players used in season
3 Lost most games in one season
4 Worst ever goal difference
5 First time club ever finished bottom
6 Most games in a season without scoring
7 Most games lost by more than three goals - 14 in all
8 Club captain never appeared in a Royals shirt throughout
9 Equalled best ever run in League Cup
10 Best run in FA Cup for 63 years

I put the last two in just to get me in a more positive frame of mind to complete this review. It's probably a bit harsh pointing any of the blame towards Asaba, owing to the complete lack of service he got throughout and the obvious scarcity of coaching skills he received. However, Bullivant was way out of his depth and the sharks should have got him earlier. In a nut-shell, Bullivant got appointed ahead of Wilkins, Lee, Sanchez, Rioch etc... Immediate reaction from the fans was that the chairman had gone for a cheap option. However, optimistic as us lot down here are, we dreamed of a 'master stroke' being pulled off! Sadly though, the writing was on the wall a few games into the new campaign when we lost 6-0 at Prenton Park (five down at half time). Results like this were something we would have to get used to as the season progressed, and talk of relegation started late autumn.

Nevertheless, the chairman persevered with his appointments, seemingly unaware of the club's downward spiral into Division Two.

By spring, the fans had had enough. Against (then) fellow strugglers Port Vale, taking her cue from the referee's whistle signalling another shambolic home defeat, a lone female leapt over the advertising boards and planted her rear smack in the middle of the pitch. The inevitable happened and hundreds followed suit, with cries of "Bullivant Out" ringing around the ground. In contrast though, a crowd of real young'uns (who for some unknown reason were right behind him - letting their youthful enthusiasm get the better of them!) stayed on the terraces trying to rally up support for the chirpy Cockney. This didn't go down too well and a few punches were thrown. It's a sad state of affairs when you start rucking amongst yourselves - but that's how it happened. As usual, the chairman gave the manager his 'vote of confidence' which, as we all know, meant he was for the chop.

Ten days later away at Oxford, Reading fans turned up in huge numbers. Whether it was to have a go at our rivals or to increase the pressure on Bullivant - who knows? Either way, both were achieved. After the final whistle, whilst some of the Reading lot were having running battles around the Manor Ground, a few others lay down in front of the players' coach and refused to budge. This just p*ssed Bullivant off even more and a day later he was a gonner. He says 'resigned', we say 'pushed'.

So there we had it. A £37m, 25,000 all-seater stadium waiting for the beginning of the coming season, and there we were: managerless, clueless and propping up the table. Then unexpectedly, just as total depression was setting in for the most ardently loyal fan, an announcement was made: Tommy Burns to join Royals. We'd been along this road earlier in the summer when Burns turned us down at the last moment to go to Newcastle - but this time it was for real. The only slight hitch was it was 24 hours to transfer deadline day, we had ten fit players and were due to play Ipswich (a) on the Saturday. Not a problem for Tommy - he signed seven players in one day, a number he reckons he could've doubled if time had allowed.

So off we set to Portman Road - a new manager, half a new team and 1,700 followers.

Excitement wasn't the word, and the anticipation of Burns' success was reflected in the Reading fans, who gave vocal encouragement to such an extreme that it totally shut the Suffolk folk up. Even when we were a goal behind and down to nine players (having had Legg and Bernal sent off), the away support just got louder and louder. After the game (which did finish 1-0) many an Ipswich fan commented on the tremendous backing we'd given, even in the wake of potential defeat. An outsider could easily have thought we were a team pushing for promotion rather than the poor sods propping up the rest.

Tommy Burns could do no wrong. He made the effort of inviting all the fans to the ground whereupon he endeavoured to speak in depth about his plans for the future of the club. Reading needed this, as the previous two management regimes had total disregard for the supporters and their feelings. Tommy was a breath of fresh air and although he had picked up some of Dalglish's incomprehensible language, we knew what he was on about just by his facial expressions. Okay, a few weeks later Forest sent us down to the realms of Division Two... But in all honesty, yeah, it was tragic to see us relegated and even more sad to see our final ever league game at Elm Park after 102 years end in defeat to a Bellamy goal against Norwich, but the future looks more than promising. Burns has been given the task of an immediate return to Division One and by all accounts seems to have been given the freedom to spend his way out of the division. Reading will line up away at Wrexham for the first game with the majority of Scotland's squad for Japan/Korea in 2002. Pat Bonner has also been taken aboard and his experience should be well appreciated. Every club's fans have dreams of their heroes gaining promotion - but there is a buzz in this town that makes me think we'll definitely go up. I could be made to eat my words but somehow I have this little hunch that this is our year.

Now it's off to the bookies again - after all, they can't *always* be right...

Footnote: To commemorate Reading's final game at Elm Park, fanzines *Heaven Eleven*, *TTB*, *Elm Park Disease* and *The Whiff* joined forces to produce a 68-page special (*Elm Park Echoes*). It contained fans' memories of the ground and an introduction by Tommy Burns, which was pretty good since he'd only been there 5 weeks out of the 102 years!

Source: In Dublin's Fair City

HEROES AND VILLAINS

Aston Villa

It was all going to be so easy. A blistering hot day at Filbert Street was to be the portend of things to come, Stan and Dwight would be banging the goals in and our defence would hold steady, just like it always did. Four games and four defeats later it was time for a radical rethink. Unfortunately there wasn't one and the Villa struggled for the next six months.

Sometimes they looked good, as when hammering Spurs at Christmas with the help of a couple of goals from Stan the Occasional Man, but too often they were unimaginative, unambitious and just plain uninterested.

However, the UEFA Cup was another matter entirely.

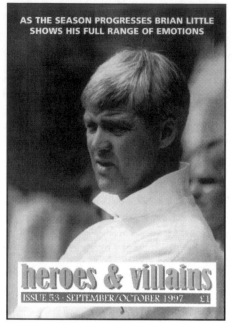

AS THE SEASON PROGRESSES BRIAN LITTLE SHOWS HIS FULL RANGE OF EMOTIONS

heroes & villains

ISSUE 53 · SEPTEMBER/OCTOBER 1997   £1

Round one sent us to Bordeaux, a great place to hang out for a few days in beautiful weather with friendly locals and a local produce they were keen to show to its best effect. Nil-nil over there, 1-0 in extra time over here. Round two will go down in history: Bilbao, we'd heard, was English-friendly, and Newcastle had enjoyed themselves here a couple of years ago. The reception we got beggared belief. It was likened at the time to being invited into a massive party and we were treated as honoured guests rather than football supporters. The festivities went on long into the next day and the return to Villa Park saw the West Midlands Constabulary carousing with the Basques, a million bye-laws broken and their supporters getting applauded out of the ground. *The Evening Mail*, normally the Voice of Over-Reaction, called for Bilbao and Birmingham to be made twin cities. Football should always be like this. No, *life* should always be like this. Steua Bucharest was an anti-climax but a battling performance saw Villa, two down at one point over there, pull a goal back and into the quarter final for the first time in 20 years, thanks to a comfortable 2-0 victory at Villa Park.

And so back to the league. There had been rumblings of discontent in the ranks all season. Dwight Yorke, the nicest man in football, was reputed to be unhappy. Savo Milosevic wanted out. Club captain Gareth Southgate was openly questioning the club's ambitions. Sasa Curcic was virtually on strike.

Stan Collymore was making up for his appalling performances by giving every newspaper in the country a page-worth of stories a week. Supporters were beginning to lose patience. Nemesis came at Ewood Park on January 17th.

Losing 5-0 was but a fraction of the story. All through the game supporters had been venting their frustrations with ever-increasing anger. Brian Little refused to change the team round, the players had no passion, what chances we had were missed. With seconds remaining Savo missed another, and something, somewhere snapped. Supporters finally lost patience, he gestured back at them, and one or two tried to get onto the pitch. The next few days were filled with many people calling for his head, with others leaping to his defence and saying the fans were wrong. Funny, that. No matter what happens there are always some supporters who blame their own rather than the inadequacies of the team.

Milosevic had been caught on camera spitting on the floor and making a similar gesture towards the crowd. He tried to justify this by claiming, spuriously, that he recognised people who had been running him down all season. Hmmm. He was transfer-listed, the Villa beat Albion 4-0 in the FA Cup fourth round the following Saturday and a fragile peace was restored. Villa lost to Coventry in the fifth round, the first time they'd ever beaten us at Villa Park (we couldn't give a toss about Coventry, but the laughably hysterical reaction from their supporters almost made defeat worthwhile) and the cease-fire was over.

By now it was getting to be more interesting watching the crowd than the match. Milosevic came back against Manchester United and several supporters walked out in protest. He was booed at the start of the game and applauded at the end. We lost. Next game, Wimbledon away. Big Fat Ron once got his cards after a defeat here, and that's how it proved for Little Grey Brian, after a game when supporters actually came to blows over the 'Milosevic Question'. Little's inevitable departure was a source of sadness for those of us who can remember him as a great player and wanted him desperately to be a great manager. But a trophy and two top five places in three years aren't enough anymore, and the arrival of the high-profile name who would surely replace the introspective Little was eagerly awaited. Venables, Gullit, Robson; all were in the running. And so came John Gregory from high-flying Wycombe Wanderers.

His reign got off to a good start with a 2-1 victory against Liverpool, courtesy of a winner from Stan Collymore. It would be nice to think that the team gave their best performance of the season due to an attack of conscience over the way they had behaved under Little. Nice, but naïve.

And so to the UEFA Cup again. One-nil in Madrid, one down at half-time at Villa Park. There came a thunderous fight-back to level on aggregate, but the final push just wasn't there and out went the Villa on away goals, for the third time in a row. Unlucky, but we missed three good chances in the away leg and you can't do that at this level.

So back to the league, and the couple of wins needed to stay up. No problem. Nine wins in 11 matches (the two defeats were, naturally, at home to Bolton and Barnsley) and a last day win over Arsenal left us with a chance of Europe. Blackburn's 89th minute winner meant a final seventh place, itself an achievement considering the dramas of the previous nine months, but then came Chelsea's Cup-Winners Cup victory that put the Villa back into Europe. No club in history can ever have had such a dramatic turn-around so quickly.

Alan Thomson knew a good thing when he saw one, and has joined from Bolton. Then just to round it all off, Stan Collymore did his bit for Anglo-Swedish relations by dragging Ulrika, and the name of Aston Villa, through the Parisian dirt. A squalid end to a sometimes squalid, but ultimately (just about) successful season.

Source: Sky Blue Army

HEY BIG SPENDER

Derby County

It's been an extremely memorable season for supporters of Derby County. We finished as the ninth most successful club in the country during only our second season in the Premiership, while threatening, for six months, to make a coveted UEFA Cup qualification spot our own. It was our first term in a new stadium, watching our first signings from AC Milan, Fiorentina and Buckingham Palace (Queen Lizzie made just one appearance - perhaps she didn't impress at her trial). And of course, there was the Wanchope factor. My problem is that I find this all very difficult to recall without prompting, so I'll take a browse through the results' page of the final programme of the season.

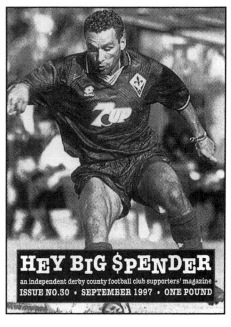

HEY BIG $PENDER
an independent derby county football club supporters' magazine
ISSUE NO.30 • SEPTEMBER 1997 • ONE POUND

Ah yes, that last game, a crushing 1-0 victory over Liverpool reserves (whose fans showed far more interest in the outcome of a game played at Goodison Park for some reason) does linger in the memory. You see, my brother-in-law and I had no fanzines to sell before kick-off. So, having been free to stay in a city centre pub until 3.40, imbibe in the odd half, as you do, and then take the free bus to Pride Park in a drunken haze, we whipped the North Stand into a frenzy of vocal support worthy of a Cup Final before eventually celebrating Paulo Wanchope's fluky winner with the kind of jig that wouldn't have looked out of place on finals' night of *Come Dancing* at Blackpool Winter Gardens. All this before partaking in an altogether completely image-shattering display of male bonding which started with a hug and finished with us disappearing over two rows of seats - backwards - ending up in the missionary position on the laps of several disgruntled 'family types' a couple of rows nearer the pitch. Memorable because we still have the bruises and embarrassing flashbacks to remind us. Of course, on the terraces it wouldn't have mattered a jot.

So why does our first season in a luxury new state of the art stadium leave so few unprompted memories for me? Well, there's one simple answer to that question, and for me it's the main reason why Pride Park is such an improvement over the Baseball Ground (this and the fact that you can actually see the pitch from the seats)... LAGER is back on the menu at the refreshment kiosks. Not a spot of 'trouble' have I seen at Pride Park in this, its first year, yet I'm sure the majority of the 30,000-ish average attendees have been mostly in a state of part or total inebriation at the majority of fixtures. If this is the future of football - superb views of a perfect pitch sporting a Rams side composed almost entirely of full internationals stuffing some of the biggest clubs in the country in front of great atmospheres and plenty of booze - then I'm all for it. Ah, but the cost, I hear you saying to yourself. At £20 a game, £40-odd for the obligatory replica shirt and £2 for a relatively piss-weak pint, how does the average Joe afford it? Well, they don't, do they - not indefinitely at least.

And that's why, this summer, I will stop being a dedicated fanzine editor and holder of a season ticket for the past five years. Having seen every home game during that time, and most before that for the previous ten years, and visited virtually every ground in the country, taking in most pre-season friendlies, as well as over 50% of all away games, I will become one of those part-time supporters who is forced by personal circumstances and the aforementioned imaginative pricing policy of my beloved club to 'pick and choose the odd game'. So I'll probably get to Southampton, Wimbledon, Charlton and perhaps Leeds. Great... As Keith Loring, Derby County's chief executive explained during our February interview with him, "I don't feel guilty taking money off fans if they know they're going to see the benefits on the pitch because the money's for Jim to buy players like Eranio and Baiano." They're the honest facts I suppose.

So for me, no more 2-0 up at half time against the then Champions-elect, singing "We're gonna win the league" in the concourses at half time. No more marvelling at the Bald Eagle's inexpensive collection of mostly unknowns, which have been modelled into a team capable of producing the closest thing to total football I'll ever experience, including the safest pair of hands I've ever seen at the club, those of Mart Poom. There'll be little opportunity to witness the industry of the ever-improving Lee Carsley, Darryl Powell and Jacob Laursen, the silky skills of Stefano Eranio (when he's not being inexplicably sent off), the work-rate and technical perfection of Gabrielle Batistuta's old mucker Ciccio Baiano or the comically talented and hugely entertaining Paulo Wanchope. And that's not forgetting the old warhorses who've more than done their bit this term: Robin Van der Laan, Dean Yates, Chris Powell and Igor Stimac. Or the still improving Gary Rowett, Dean Sturridge and Christian Dailly, and the youngsters who have started to force their way into first team plans: Marc Bridge-Wilkinson, Rob Kozluk, Rory Delap, Deon Burton and Steve Elliott. Only Paul Simpson (now at Wolves), Jonathan Hunt, Mauricio Solis, Russell Hoult, Paul Trollope (at Fulham) and Ron Willems could look back and say that they'd had disappointing seasons, and that's because they were either sold or hardly given a sniff of first team action. Even new signing Lars Bohinen had a cracking game against Liverpool on the last day of the season.

In fact when you look at that lot, it's a sign of how far we've come. Especially when you consider that last season's star player Aljosa Asanovic was allowed to leave mid-season for Napoli because he was struggling to get a game. The same can be said of Ashley Ward who almost helped saved Barnsley from the drop.

True too that I'll miss the ecstasies and agonies of being a full-time Rams supporter. It really is only Derby who can hammer Arsenal 3-0, Blackburn 3-1, Sheffield Wednesday 5-2 and 3-0, Southampton 4-0, 3-0 and 2-0 and West Ham 2-0, then throw away a 3-1 lead at Reebok Stadium with ten to go, get beaten by Barnsley and only take one point off Crystal Palace. As soon as pundits and press noticed that the Eagles were perhaps headed for a whole season without a home win, Derby fans were shaking their heads in droves, proclaiming that we'd be the club to oblige. And what about Manchester United? We hammered them 2-0, for 45 minutes at least, with Paulo re-living his wonder goal of last season in the first half and us sarcastically saying "We're scared now!" as the out of form Andy Cole came on in the second half... He naturally got the equaliser a minute or two later.

What I certainly won't miss will be the humiliations (usually live on *Sky*) such as 0-5 at home to Leeds (back in the pub with 35 minutes to go). Or 0-4 at home to Leicester with hundreds standing about in the concourses below the stands after just 15 minutes dazed and confused, in zombie-like stupors mouthing "I can't watch any more" to no-one in particular. Oh, and the almighty embarrassment that was the floodlight failure.

But before I sign off as a true full-time supporter there are a couple of things I want to put straight:

- The funereal "Oh Andy Cole, Andy Cole" chant heard at Old Trafford during the latter part of the season was stolen from us. It should go "Oh Ba-ai-no, Ba-ai-no." If you're gonna sing songs like the Italian supporters, at least sing 'em about Italian players.

- We were 250-1 for the title for '97-98. No one thought we could win it, obviously, but we finished ninth - three places, six points and seven goals better off than the previous year. Next season's early odds see us tipped for relegation (100-1 for the title) - only ahead of Wimbledon and Sheffield Wednesday (at 150-1) and below such luminaries as Spurs, Everton, Newcastle, Middlesbrough and F****t. Damn, I won't get to see us stuff that shite next season either. Are bookies mad or what?

- Alan Hansen, the peoples' pundit, who became Paulo's greatest fan during the season, actually took the piss out him several times on *Match of the Day* just prior to the Costa Rican's flurry of goalscoring activity at the end of September. The jock then changed his mind. Alan, we don't forget.

- Talking of *Match of the Day*, we are still the very last fixture to appear on their goals round up at about half past midnight. Even when the press started dubbing us "the entertainers" we still only featured when we were playing Manchester United, Arsenal or Chelsea as the main match. The

BBC ignored us when we won two Championships in the seventies - a leopard never changes its spots.

- Sorry to the couple in Row R whose laps we ended up on just after Paulo's winner against Liverpool.

Now I've taken the time to trawl through the high and lowlights of '97-98, that comfortable plastic seat at the very back of the North Stand is starting to look tempting again already, regardless of Premiership-land's inability to grasp the concepts of the cost of living and inflation-matched price rises.

Barcelona in the big pre-season friendly at Pride Park, eh? Then there's the thought of Jim's bargain purchases in the summer sales; I'd not considered that, had I? And Deon Burton's heroes welcome back from a glorious campaign, when he's earned the Golden Boot as the Reggae Boyz' star striker at France '98. And it still works out cheaper than subscribing to *Sky* anyway! And what else is there to do on a Saturday afternoon / Sunday tea-time / Monday night after all?

I'll see you there next season then!

HIGHBURY HIGH

Arsenal

In the end, it was all a drunken haze. If Gazza can wreck his England career with a few beers and a chicken kebab, then most Arsenal fans will have blown their chances of even a kickaround in the park. My kidneys still hurt and my liver has slapped in a transplant request, but I still can't get the smile off my face. I know that *Survival of the Fattest* readers are seasoned fanzine buyers, used to wry, self-deprecating humour, so I'm afraid you'll have to excuse my celebratory, self-satisfied tome. But I'm sure you won't begrudge my happiness - after all, we *did* stop United.

I would, at this point, like to thank Manchester United. Not

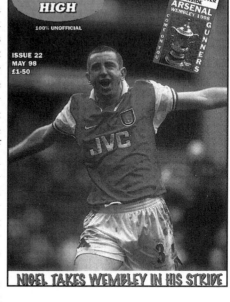

for the title - Arsenal won that through their endeavours, but I would like to thank them for making our away trips so pleasurable. When a team is chasing a Championship, it whips the opposition fans into a frenzied, seething mass, desperate to put the glory boys in their place. In these circumstances, the walk back to the car after taking three points can be a daunting prospect. In fact, as Arsenal closed in on the title, the travelling Gooners were greeted in Northern towns as though we were allied troops liberating occupied territory.

I don't know how United managed to get so unpopular, but it certainly meant we enjoyed ourselves. The Barnsley fans, in particular, were magnificent, serenading supporters' coaches with chants of "Champions." And this after a crucial home defeat which virtually sealed their relegation fate. Of course, I am under no illusion that Arsenal are suddenly popular. But it was nice to be treated as the good guys for a change.

In the end, the team was playing so well we were beginning to feel invincible. The defence was rock-solid, Petit and Vieira ruled the middle of the park, Overmars scared the life out of opposing right-backs, whilst Parlour worked tirelessly on the other flank, and up front we could even cope with the loss of Bergkamp and Wright. This may sound arrogant, but now Arsenal have thrown down the gauntlet, the effect will be a general improvement amongst the top teams. Ferguson will lose his complacency and splash out some of United's fortune, and Chelsea have already invested in internationals such Laudrup and Desailly. I really believe that English clubs will now start to make their mark on the European competitions as a result.

If invincible was the feeling at the end of the season, that certainly wasn't how we felt during the Christmas period. 'Vulnerable' would be the polite adjective, but that wasn't the term most Arsenal fans were using. To most pundits the Championship was already over by the New Year, and even as late as March, a Manchester bookie was confident enough to pay out on United winning the title. In other words, it was a roller-coaster season for Arsenal, and not even the most fanatical would have dreamed about the Double in January.

It was a season that can be neatly divided into four sections, so let me take you through each phase of Arsenal '97-98. The Four Seasons...

1) The Indian Summer (August - October '97)

Is Bergkamp the best Arsenal player ever? That was the question on everyone's lips as we basked in the early autumn sunshine outside The Highbury Barn pub. There wasn't much point talking about the game we'd just witnessed, because for all intents and purposes it was more like a training session. Admittedly, Barnsley had yet to adjust to the Premiership, but the gulf in class was as wide as the Grand Canyon. And anyway, Barnsley were just the latest victims of the awesome attacking machine. 'Collective Skinning' was the term *Highbury High's* Eddy Pratt used to describe the way Arsenal laid siege to opponents' goals. Only Tottenham had managed a zero in the 'goals against' column, and even then the woodwork had saved them four times.

So back to that question: is Bergkamp the best ever? Back then we had no doubts. Carling Player of the Month twice in succession; a first ever clean sweep in BBC1's Goal of the Month. There was nothing defenders could do to stop him. Tug his shirt or kick him and he simply got better - ask Francis Benali. The Player of the Year was already sewn up. Watch out Ronaldo, Dennis is after your FIFA title.

If Dennis was our best ever player, then Ian Wright is our greatest ever goalscorer, and I'm sure Cliff Bastin would never have dreamed of such a celebration. Avenell Road filled with adoring worshippers as Ian Wright performed *The Full Monty* after the Bolton game. It wasn't to be the last time that Wrighty's appearance at the dressing room window would make the headlines, but on this occasion Wrighty could do no wrong. He even celebrated the record too early, revealing a Nike 'Just Done It' T-Shirt after his first goal. No matter; on this form there would soon be more. Highbury soon erupted into a frenzy of congratulations when he tapped in the crucial goal, and David Seaman sprinted the length of the pitch to join in the celebrations.

The midfield and attack remained unchanged during this period and started to really gel, with the front three piling up an incredible 24 goals in the first ten games. The defence was more generous than usual, conceding wasteful points at Everton and Leicester, and there was a lingering worry that we picking up a few too many yellow cards. But we didn't really care. This was a team that was steamrollering all in its path and simply couldn't stop scoring. All we really needed to do was cut out the sloppy goals conceded and we would be on our way.

2) The Season of Illwill (October- December '97)

The second longest night of the year - Dec 22nd, and all the darker without floodlights. Even darker were the moods in The Railway Telegraph, Thornton Heath after the abandoned Wimbledon game:

"OK, answer me this question: which Arsenal player would get into Manchester United's first team?" the disgruntled Arsenal fan demanded from the unseasonably gloomy gathering.

"Bergkamp... just about"

"Vieira?"

"No, they've got Butt"

"Cole's better than Wright. Adams is finished. Overmars is good, but is he better than Giggs? Schmeichel and Seaman - no contest, Seaman's lost it."

And so it continued. Ah, the fickle football fans.

It was at Selhurst Park back in October against Palace where it all started to go wrong. Bergkamp lost his temper again, but this time the outlet for his anger damaged us: another yellow card and a five-match ban. Overmars missed the first of three matches through injury, and we failed to score a single goal in any of them. It got worse the week after, a sterile 0-0 at home to Villa, enlivened only by Durkin sending off Petit (for violent conduct! If Petit had really had a violent motive, dwarf Durkin would have certainly known about it). Right or wrong, that was Manu out for four games. The settled side that had created so much was dismantling before our eyes, and it finally fell apart at Derby where Wanchope punished Wright's penalty miss.

A glorious home win against United only papered over the cracks. Grimandi gifted Big Ron the points at Hillsborough whilst Wright argued with the fans. Liverpool won at Highbury and we never even look like scoring. Wright finally hit the net at Newcastle, but then came the nadir that was Blackburn - the most undisciplined performance from an Arsenal team I can remember. Collectively we were awful, but the chief culprits were Wright, who lost all semblance of control, and Adams, who totally neglected his defensive duties.

The club stood at a crossroads after the Blackburn game, and no-one really knew which direction we were going take. It seemed quite feasible that we would descend into chaos. Yellow card fever was rife, questions were asked about the ageing defence, and there were even malicious rumours that there was an Anglo-French divide that was destroying the spirit within the club. Happily, these fears would prove to be unfounded, and Wenger brought it back from the abyss, but at the time we weren't so sure.

What went wrong in the final months of 1997? The statistics tell the story. In the first ten games, Bergkamp, Overmars and Wright scored 24 goals. In the next ten matches, they scored a combined total of two. Yes, we beat

United, but we had turned into an ordinary team that occasionally lifted itself for the big game (Southampton always beat United, but rarely get above mid-table).

Only the ever-dependable Parlour could really hold his head high, whilst at the back Adams put in some of the worst performances of his career; so bad in fact that he verged on quitting the game. Thankfully, we now realise that he had become a shadow of himself through injury, rather than a terminal loss of form, but the thought that our ever-reliable captain was so vulnerable was a real cause for concern.

So, three wins out of ten games - goodbye Championship.

3) Putting up the Barricades (January - March '98)

In the new year, the team dug in and began to grind out some results. It wasn't always pretty, especially against Port Vale in the cup. That tie remained goalless until extra-time in the replay, and was ultimately decided on penalties.

In the league, almost unnoticed, an unbeaten run began, even if the team were hardly impressive. At Coventry, a goal apiece for Bergkamp and Anelka gave us a lead so undeserved that all the away fans could do was laugh at the absurdity of it all, until Dublin finally settled the score.

The date of the Coventry game, January 17th, is worth noting. The next time Arsenal would concede another league goal would be April 11th - almost three months later. It was clear we were struggling to score without the prolific partnership of Bergkamp and Wright, so the team apparently decided they would simply protect, with their lives, those they did score. Adams and Keown limbered up for the fight, the French legionnaires Petit and Vieira built a human barricade in the middle, and a baby-faced Austrian 'keeper called Alex Manninger stepped in for the injured Seaman and acrobatically stopped everything that came his way.

It was back at Selhurst again in March when the team and the crowd realised just how much the spirit and determination had returned. Christopher Wreh, seemingly the least effective Wenger buy, scored the crucial goal (echoes of Martin Hayes in '89) in the first half, and Wimbledon launched their unique battering ram assault. Arsenal closed ranks and declared they would not pass. Another clean sheet: one-nil to the Arsenal. The jubilation on the players' faces spoke volumes.

For the first time all season we felt absolutely sure we would no longer throw away a lead, even if the next game was against the Champions on their own patch. Another 1-0 and the shouts and screams of delight from the Arsenal corner echoed round the otherwise silent Old Trafford. The jubilation continued four days later, when an FA Cup semi-final place was booked after another penalty shoot-out nail-biter at Upton Park, on a night made even more tense after the red mist (and card) descended on Bergkamp again.

4) The final flourish (March - May '98)

After all the graft, tension and defensive determination, the confidence surged through the team, and the goals started to rattle in. Difficult fixtures such as Blackburn, Wimbledon and Newcastle became exhibition pieces. The pace of Overmars, Anelka and Bergkamp struck fear into defenders' hearts whilst Vieira and Petit pressed further forward, peppering the opposition goal with long-range cannon-ball shots. The season ended (ignoring the two game hangover after the title was won) as it began, with a swaggering Arsenal keeping the Carling Opta boys busy with their 'shots on goal' statistics. When Adams blasted home Bould's through ball, just minutes before lifting the trophy, the final nail was driven in the 'Boring Boring Arsenal' coffin.

It was a remarkable season, illuminated by double Player of the Year, Dennis Bergkamp, but the awards could have gone to any of the first-team players. Everyone played a crucial part - a high accolade for any team, and in particular a tribute to Arsene Wenger. Thanks for everything Arsene.

Oh yes, there was also the small matter of the FA Cup. I'm afraid my memory is a bit blurred on this one, but I'm told I had a good time! From the magnificent sea of 25,000 red and white cards during Abide With Me (organised by *Highbury High*, *The Gooner* and David Dein, Clare Tomlinson and John Hazell from Arsenal) to the victory parade next day, it was all a bit too much to take in.

I need a summer rest from football - except that there is the small matter of France '98!

Source: The Gooner

THE HOLY TRINITY

Aston Villa

"... Brian Little, who is undoubtedly one of the best managers around. With Stan on board, and fortune pointing towards a good season, just watch us go in '97-98."

Prophetic words indeed, scribbled by yours truly in last year's edition of SOTF. I expect that the call from the BBC offering me a position of football analyst will be a bit longer in coming.

"Just watch us go...", and 'go' we certainly did - straight to the bottom of the Premiership after four straight defeats. The worst start in our 124 year history. Fortunately, three straight wins in the league and a solid 0-0 draw in Bordeaux meant that we quickly recovered. Villa had climbed back up to ninth in the table, and we were favourites to progress in the UEFA Cup.

The Holy Trinity

Issue 16   September / October 1997   £1.00

Brian's Make or Break Promise

" We Will Achieve Success This Season "

AN ASTON VILLA FANZINE

No-one was fooled by this run of victories, though. The team's performances had been just as poor as in the opening four games, and over the next couple of weeks the trend continued. Villa supporters had to endure home defeats to Chelsea and Wimbledon, an unconvincing draw against an abysmal Sheffield Wednesday, our - now annual - 0-3 thumping at Anfield, and scraping a last minute equaliser against a Crystal Palace side that had not won at home. Just for good measure, our interest in the League Cup - a competition in which we usually do quite well - was ended at the first hurdle with another 0-3 reverse, this time at Upton Park.

At the end of November, Villa were languishing in fourteenth position, with an early exit from one cup competition already registered. Stan Collymore, our record £7 million signing, had scored just one goal in 17 games. Even top scorer Yorke had only notched a measly five goals - and he was obviously unhappy at being asked to play a deeper role.

The saving grace of the season was obviously the team's performance in Europe. Whilst we looked second best to almost every other team in the Premiership, we met, matched and beat three very good sides en route to the UEFA Cup quarter final. Certainly, and sadly too, it seemed that there were quite a few players in our squad who were only intent on performing at their best in this competition. The three pre-Christmas ties also handed Villa's travelling army with some varied places to visit.

First stop was Bordeaux, and only a few days after being drenched in Barnsley's excuse for a football stadium, it was T-shirt and shorts weather in sunny France. Around 2,000 of us made the trip, mainly because it was easy to get to, and also because not many realistically expected us to progress any further. Bordeaux were probably the most technically gifted side that we faced in the competition, and Savo Milosevic's extra-time goal in the return leg rounded off an impressive victory for the Villans.

Next stop was Bilbao in the heart of the Basque country (don't call them Spanish!!) for a match against Atletico. It is difficult to write about the experiences of the few days spent in the city without using a mass of clichéd superlatives, so please bear with me. Quite simply, Villa's trip to Bilbao was the most amazing, unforgettable experience I have ever had as a football supporter. The people of Bilbao were extremely warm and friendly, and many of us received gifts such as hats, scarves, wine, and even champagne. Inside the ground, the visiting Villans were given a standing ovation from the hosts at the end of the game. Then the fun really started, as after-game parties began in the bars around the stadium, and the visiting Brummies were made more than welcome. The two sets of fans sang the night (and the following morning) away. The West Midlands branch of the Athletic Bilbao Supporters Club had been well and truly initiated. It is fair to say that many Villa fans will be returning to the San Mames, even if Villa never play there again. Oh, by the way, we won the tie 2-1 at Villa Park.

The third round destination couldn't have been more different as we were posted beyond the Iron Curtain to Bucharest, the capital of Romania, to face Steaua - the army team. The scenery was grim, the weather was terrible, the locals weren't friendly and the police and army presence on every street corner meant that you were constantly looking over your shoulder. On the plus side, the food and beer were cheap, and the women were unbelievably attractive. At the game, the pitch was dreadful, and the crowd was hostile. Two goals within a few minutes of each other in the first half suggested that Bucharest would be the end of the European road for the Lions. However, a much improved second half display - including a rare European away goal - set us up to complete the job at Villa Park. At least we had one thing to smile about over the Christmas period.

Comfortable home league wins against Coventry and Spurs also cheered the Villa faithful, but underneath the grins the fans still remained unconvinced. Spurs were terrible, and we always do well against the Sky Blues - otherwise, it was business as usual. After a narrow defeat at Manchester United, manager Little unbelievably declared, "I'm glad that one is over with." At our next game, Villa Park's lowest league crowd of the season witnessed an uninspiring 1-1 draw with Southampton.

New year, new hope - well at least for the first two days of 1998 when we didn't play any football. The FA Cup third round saw another pitiful performance, a 2-2 draw at lowly Portsmouth. The replay was hardly awe-inspiring either, Villa scraping through with a 1-0 win. In between these two encounters, a late equaliser rescued another point - this time at home to Leicester. Things were looking bleak, but they were about to get much, much worse.

Brian Little was a very popular manager due to the success that he had brought in his first full season, and mainly because he was also one of our greatest ever players. Therefore, it was very difficult for the majority of supporters to criticise him or call for his head. However, after a string of inept performances, the Villa faithful could take no more. Ewood Park was the setting as we surrendered to a 0-5 humiliation. An excellent away following had given tremendous support for the first hour of the game, but when the fourth and fifth goals went in, they turned, with chants of "You're not fit to wear the shirt," and, "Are you watching Brian Little?" (He did not use any substitutes in this match - obviously sufficiently pleased with what was on the pitch).

He escaped a lot of criticism after the match though, due to the actions of Savo Milosevic. After missing an open goal, with Villa already 0-5 down, there were heated exchanges between a group of Villa fans and the Serb, ending with Milosevic spitting on the ground and staring out this group of fans. Over the next few days, media coverage from Villa Park focused on whether Savo would ever don the claret and blue again. It could be said, though, that the true culprit for the day's failure got off very lightly indeed. This incident only acted to prolong the agony. Three successive home defeats - including one against Coventry City in the FA Cup (their first ever win at Villa Park) were followed by a defeat at Selhurst Park against the Wombles. We were in 15th position and falling. It was all too much for Brian; with the greatest dignity he admitted his mistakes and that he was unable to turn things around and subsequently resigned.

Twenty four hours later, and we were faced with another shock. After reading about the likes of Gullit, Robson and Venables in the morning papers, the new boss was to be... John Gregory. The appointment was a worry. Gregory had no experience of top flight management (apart from a short stint in the backroom staff at the start of Little's reign); surely he wouldn't be able to stop a team that was destined for the Nationwide. He wasn't recognised as a big name in the sport; surely he wouldn't be able to attract the big names on the playing front. Instead of preparing to face York City with Wycombe, he would now be plotting the downfall of Atletico Madrid in a European quarter final; surely the gap was too great to bridge. No-one blamed Gregory for the appointment though, (given the opportunity, anyone would have done the same). Most of the criticism was directed towards our esteemed chairman Ellis for what seemed to be another cost-cutting exercise.

In the end, we need not have worried. Despite going out of the UEFA Cup to Atletico Madrid (only on away goals after a thrilling win at Villa Park), we witnessed a dramatic turnaround in the league form as the team won nine out of their last 11 games. Amazingly, the only two defeats were at home to relegation certainties Barnsley and Bolton. The team was buzzing again, and was producing the football of which we all knew it was capable. In fact, I would say that our first half display against Sheffield Wednesday in May was our best 45 minutes' performance since the opening day of the '95-96 season when we put three past Manchester United.

This story even has a happy ending. Victory over Champions Arsenal in the very last match ensured European qualification for the third year in succession. Our run of form at the end of the campaign certainly helped to erase the doubts over Gregory's appointment. In fact, his actions in the first few weeks of the summer (beating off several other clubs for the signing of the excellent Alan Thompson, and his hard line with contract rebels) has only served to enhance his quickly growing reputation. There certainly is a sense of optimism again about the new season - but this time there won't be any predictions from *these* quarters!

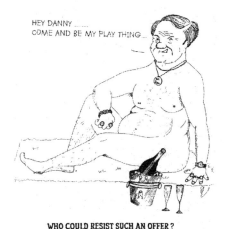

HEY DANNY ....
COME AND BE MY PLAY THING....

WHO COULD RESIST SUCH AN OFFER ?

Source: Better Red Than Dead

IN DUBLIN'S FAIR CITY

Coventry City

So yet again the Sky Blues found themselves embroiled in a last day relegation battle where events elsewhere were as important as success on the field. Still, it made a refreshing change to be a spectator at someone else's end of season constipation-curing conflagration. No doubt Everton were inspired by Coventry's long history of previous final minute escapes and they managed to rise to the occasion. But what of our season? Well, in the words of the great Wee man himself: "it was an utter disgrace".

This infamous quote was part of Gordon Strachan's post-match analysis of the Sky Blues v Arsenal fixture. He was not a happy man after seeing his team outplay the future Champions for 90 minutes. So where did the problem lie? Well, let's hear him explain in his own words:

> *In Dublin's Fair City*
> (elephant droppings)
> THE UNOFFICIAL FANZINE OF COVENTRY CITY F.C.

As the bookings pile up, Strachan sacks the team psychologist

DARREN HUCKERBY
exclusive interview

ISSUE
14
JANUARY 1998
£1

"*We had skill, character, chances. We had good players on the pitch. And what do we get? A referee who spoils it for everyone. It was an absolute disgrace. We hammered them; make no mistake about that, we hammered them. Ever since I said something about David Elleray and referees we have had nothing from referees at this club and it's gone beyond a joke - an absolute joke.*"

So there you have it. We were better than the double-winning Premier League Champions and but for some biased refereeing decisions we would rightfully be leading England's challenge in next season's Champions' League.

Other commentators adopted a less conspiracy theorist line of argument for our ultimate lack of success trophy-wise. They pointed to our table-topping position in the bookings league with the inevitable suspensions and team disruption created by the many enforced omissions. Players missed huge chunks of the season due to indiscipline. At one stage, Gordon and his boys were such regular visitors at League disciplinary hearings that the FA were considering supplying us with our own private waiting room. Noel Whelan didn't even require the intervention of a referee to be sidelined. He missed the first half of the season due to an injury sustained in a fight with a high street shop window after a few Lucozades in a local night club.

So what sort of season was it? Well, let's play a quick game of Word association football. What do you think of when I say ...

    'Newcastle'?   *Shearer*

    'Man Utd'?   *Glory-hunting Southern fans*

    'Liverpool'?   *Perms and Spice boys*

    'Coventry'?   *??*

Go on, you said "relegation battle" or "Houdini," or something along those lines, didn't you? Well, take a quick look at the final table and see if you can find us. Higher... higher... higher... Look - there we are, just outside an UEFA Cup place. Not bad for relegation favourites. So what happened? Simply, Gordon has transformed the side he inherited from Fat Ron from perennial relegation strugglers into a decent looking team capable, on their day, of beating anyone (suspensions permitting).

The campaign started, as they always do, with hopes higher than expectations. This was the year when in the movie world *Titanic* swept all before it. Some foresaw this as an omen for our long-heralded ultimate relegation, but Captain Fat Ron had gone to sink Sheffield Wednesday, leaving Gordon in sole command of HMS Coventry. It was to be a happy transformation as new faces were blended in with varying degrees of success.

Gordon has bought widely and wisely. The bargain basements of Scandinavia were plundered in Viking fashion and some real gems unearthed. Roland Nilsson had played in England before and he has brought a maturity and confidence to the defence. Magnus Hedman has proven a worthy successor to the peerless Oggy. Martin Johansen and Trond Egil Soltvedt have battled to get a place in the side; Soltvedt succeeding and producing some solid, workmanlike displays; wisely choosing to save his best performances for the win at Villa Park.

Other new faces failed to shine so brightly. Laser Lightbourne got his first chance on a stormy winter's evening at Blackpool but he was blinded by all the bright lights; later blaming his glaring misses on the Blackpool crowd shining laser torches in his eyes. Sadly he failed to live up to expectations and left us without scoring a goal, though happily he enjoyed better success at Stoke, despite their ultimate relegation.

Gary McAllister's season came to a tragically premature end as injury ruled him out from Christmas onwards and foiled his World Cup aspirations. Meanwhile our scouts were still active and managed the deal of the century when George Boateng was snapped up from Feyenoord for small change. Viorel Moldovan appeared for a club record £3.5 million; quite a lot to pay for a substitute, but he rose to the main occasion, scoring the winning goal at Villa Park in the FA Cup. An historic goal as it marked the first win at Villa's den for Coventry against our greatest rivals. It would be greedy to ask him to top such an achievement. Sadly our cup run petered out at the quarter final stage in a penalty shoot-out at Sheffield United. With Newcastle awaiting in the semi's it was a real case of 'what might have been'.

Our talismanic striker, defender and part-time skipper Dion Dublin started the season with a hat-trick against Chelsea, and not only did he win

England recognition and a nomination for PFA Player of the Season, he even won a share of the Golden Boot award, despite spending part of the campaign deputising as a centre-back for absent colleagues. Of all his achievements, perhaps the most remarkable is that he ended the season still wearing sky blue, despite countless offers from many (ahem) bigger clubs. His striking partner Darren Huckerby dazzled all, often even himself, with his mazy runs and candidates for Goal of the Season. Darren is apparently known at the club as Forrest Gump because of his articulacy and the fact that he spurned a move to Old Trafford. He and Forrest would also appear to use the same barber, but I digress.

However the sum of the season lies way beyond the combination of these sparkly parts. While we have fretted over the attempts to poach Dion, Darren, Telfer, Breen etc, to such a point that an appeal to The World Wide Fund for Nature looked necessary, the real men we need to hold onto share a carroty colouring. Thus, ginger-topped Gordon Strachan and Dutch master George Boateng have performed wonders and have both been instrumental in the rise of this titanic side. So, as far as Coventry City are concerned, the Sky Blue's future is bright; the future is orange.

As a post-script I thought you might like to share a bit of off-the-field news. Don't fret about the absolute arse the French made over this summer's World Cup arrangements. What else could we expect from a country whose leading tourist attraction is a huge electricity pylon with an overpriced gift shop half way up? A country whose citizens choose to squat over a foul smelling hole in the ground, surrounded by decades-old faeces, and then poke the result of their straining down the hole with their bare toes rather than sit on a mahogany seat on a porcelain bowl reading the back page of their daily paper?

The good news is that things will be much better organised for the 2006 tournament where the cream of the World's footballing nations can look forward to displaying their talents on a disused gasworks on the northern outskirts of Coventry. You see, we have plans afoot to build a £60 million stadium that will be the best in the country. With a retractable roof and retractable pitch it is due to become an integral part of England's (ultimately doomed - the Germans will win on penalties) bid to host the tournament in 2006. When you have stopped laughing at the fact that we can't even fill a 20,000 seater stadium in the heart of the city I would advise you to take a look at the plans (they are on the CCFC website). The City Council have already given their approval and building will soon commence. You see, our chairman Bryan Richardson has big plans for our little club. So far he's had a Midas touch and even sceptical Coventrians, still smarting at their filly for believing John Sillett in 1988 when he proclaimed we would win the league, are beginning to share his dream.

So when you're after a ticket for the England v Malta World Cup Quarter-Final to be played at Coventry in 2006 - just remember where you read about it first.

IT'S THE HOPE I CAN'T STAND

Sunderland

If you don't know how Sunderland's season ended, there can only be one reason for it. You were obviously holidaying on the planet Zog during the last week of May. If some folk really are still scratching their heads, let me refresh your memories. Charlton four, Sunderland four after extra time, Charlton won by seven penalties to Sunderland's six. Still not spark any memories? John Saddler of the *Sun* wrote that it was the best ever game he had witnessed at Wembley, and others said it was the best game to be staged at the National Stadium since the 'Matthews' FA Cup final of 1953 (that's 45 years). Not that *that* is any consolation to a Sunderland fan.

Of course, the game *was* memorable. I'm sure the (very) few impartials inside the stadium and *Sky's* viewing neutrals had a ball; but to me it was two hours of the worst kind of hell. Typical Sunderland, to give you so much hope only to scotch it at the very last. Typical bloody Sunderland, to be ahead three times (yes *three*) and to throw each away. Typical Sunderland, to be leading with only five minutes of normal time remaining when our goalie went AWOL and tried for a corner-ball that was nowhere near him; and typical Sunderland, to concede a goal by a player (Richard Rufus) that had never scored before. Ever! Typical Sunderland, to match Charlton penalty for penalty, keeping the agony going until the seventh kick. Typical Sunderland, to concede a hat-trick to a home-town boy; and typical for Sunderland's missed penalty to be taken by Michael Gray, a player who has red and white blood pumping through his veins. Also typical was the reaction of the fans to Michael's miss. Seconds after Illic gathered Gray's, it has to be said, weak shot, cries of "there's only one Michael Gray" roared around Wembley. Typical Sunderland, to be good losers again. It really *is* the hope we can't stand.

But we all could have predicted this. It just wouldn't be Sunderland to have a boring end to the season. Only twice in the last 20 years have the club's efforts resulted in mid-table safety. All the others have seen Sunderland engaged in a battle to either beat off relegation or avoid promotion, with the result that the club has changed leagues eight times in that period.

Sunderland's fans have never had it easy. Maybe that's why the Wembley defeat was taken with such honourable stoicism and why the feeling persists that next season we will walk the league. Bring on Crystal Palace, Bolton and Barnsley, we say. In our free-scoring mode we can beat any team in this league. This is where something is going a bit odd on Wearside at the moment. As a group of fans, we are strangely optimistic about next season. We lost in the best match Wembley has seen by a measly penalty shoot-out. By a team that hadn't beaten us under the normal rules of the game over three and a half matches during the season. Beaten by a team that finished the regular league season two points below us. Had we won one single, measly, miserable, meagre point we would have been promoted automatically and Middlesbrough would have been consigned to the play-offs. Imagine Gazza missing a penalty at Wembley? Now there's a thought.

That Wembley game mirrored our season as a whole. One-nil down in the 20th minute, the lads played pretty poorly in the first half generally and Charlton deserved their lead. Our start to the league was equally mediocre, losing three out of our first four games. We were still suffering the hangover of relegation from the Premiership and Peter Reid had made a couple of underwhelming signings during the summer. Lee Clark was the kind of player we wanted, and the fans started to gain heart when he joined the club. But others of Clark's calibre were conspicuous by their absence. 'Obscurity' was the watchword gleefully bandied about on Wearside during the summer of 1997. "Kevin who?" was the reaction of most journalists to the arrival of a little known striker from Watford. Then Jody Craddock (can he cook a good pie?), a lanky centre-half from Cambridge, came aboard. Add to that Chris Makin from France, and that was about it.

Things improved a bit with three successive wins. Then disaster struck and many fans finally lost patience with Reid, as did this fanzine, calling for him to resign. On the first Saturday of October, Sunderland were handed a 4-0 drubbing at relegation-bound Reading. Reid was playing his usual stubborn game of sticking old war-horse Kevin Ball in a very defensive-minded midfield and continued to leave the sparky, but no less hard, Alex Rae on the bench.

Our major problem during the doomed Premiership campaign was our inability to score goals. Four players (Ball included) led the scoring charts with four goals, and this problem didn't seem to be going away. The fans were crying out for Reid to buy a striker. Sunderland continued to be linked to various journey-hit-men, as well as the occasional thoroughbred, but the constant refrain coming from the manager's office was "he's no better than what we have at the club already." This was starting to take on the mantle of a weary, sick kind of joke with the fans. Reid is stubborn, no doubt about it. He won't be rushed into buying and certainly won't pay what he regards as "silly money" for a player. The problem is that his definition of 'silly' is what others consider to be the market price.

After the Reading game, Reid had a remarkable stroke of luck. Andy Melville, almost single-handedly blamed for the Reading defeat, was dropped. Hello, Jody Craddock. That game also resulted in a few injuries. Kevin Ball needed a rest. Welcome Alex Rae. Richard Ord's back played up, forcing Reid to switch Darren Williams to centre half. Also, Niall Quinn was back from an early season injury and started to play regularly. With the acquisition of Nicky Summerbee (swapped with Craig Russell) from Manchester City, Reid started to field the side that most fans had been begging and praying for for ages. Martin Scott's injuries led to Reid fielding a new combination of full/wing backs in Darren Holloway and Micky Gray. The average age of the back four fell to 20, an advantage during mid-season, but a statistic which would come back to haunt the team later in the campaign. The midfield was taking on a worryingly creative look, with Alex Rae linking up with Lee Clark, and Nicky Summerbee on the right and Scotland B international Allan 'magic' Johnston on the left wing. Up front were the mighty Quinn and super Kevin Phillips. This was the start of a 23-match unbeaten run that saw us take second place by the end of March. But four wasted points over an awful Easter and defeat at Ipswich in the penultimate match of the season saw us surrender second spot to Middlesbrough. And that led us onto *that* game against Charlton.

The writing was on the wall from the very beginning. We'd played catch-up, after a bad start, for most of the season, only for slip-ups to cost us dear at the death. In the play-off final the lead was continually being traded, just as we'd done with Boro in the closing months. As one team slipped, the other failed to take advantage. But just as the games ran out, Boro were lucky to be where it mattered. Defensive slip-ups cost us dear at Wembley too, the third goal particularly. Mind you, our defensive performances had begun to wobble alarmingly. Two late goals conceded to QPR and a late goal at West Brom cost us those four points over Easter.

Some say Craddock was never quite as solid when he came back from injury at (ironically) Charlton. Rae was harshly sent off in the same game and never regained his place to Kevin Ball. Why? At Wembley, when the penalties ran out, Charlton were the lucky side not to have missed a kick. It's all down to chance. What if Mickey Gray decided to take his kick further down the roster? Then, maybe a Charlton player would have missed and we would be in the Premiership. There are so many what-ifs. What if we'd held out against QPR and West Brom? What if Alex Rae hadn't been sent off at Charlton? What if Jody Craddock hadn't been injured? What if Michael Gray hadn't got himself sent off at West Brom? What if Peter Reid had consigned Kevin Ball to the bench when Rae was eligible to play again? What if we'd signed Ronaldo? If my Grandma had wheels she'd be a bus. The long and the short of it is that none of the 'ifs' happened and we can speculate till the cows come home as to what might have been. What we do know is that we are favourites to win the First Division next season and there's no reason why we shouldn't. Except, of course, if Reid plays Kevin Ball in goal. But that, as he would say, is football.

JACKANORY

Swansea City

It was an annoying and frustrating season in many ways but one Swans fans will never forget. It ended up being the second worst season in our history thanks to inept performances on the pitch matched by similar feats off it. The scene for a turbulent season was set in the summer, as chaos reigned in the weeks leading up to the first game. The on-off take-over saga by windscreen replacement company Silver Shield from Doug "I saved you once, what more do you want" Sharpe was not the ideal preparation for Jan Molby and his team. Players left in their droves, thanks to insulting contract

A Swansea City Fanzine

Jackanory

Issue Eight   Apr/May 1998   50p

Cork Lines Up Pre-Season Tour Of Ireland

Inside : Tribute to Robbie James, An Interview with Tony Cottey, Paul Raynor, Mouthful Of Lead, Snatched from the Cradley, Wandering Stars, 97/98 Supporters Poll, T-Shirt Corner, Beer and Footy plus lots more.....

offers, and were replaced by inexperienced but promising League of Wales signings. Still, the ever-faithful supporters turned up hoping that this season would be the one in which we finally left the dungeon behind.

Promises of promotion, the Premiership and a new stadium seemed as far away as ever as the Swans slumped to seven defeats in the first ten matches. This led to the dismissal of the popular Jan Molby, in a move for which the new board still hasn't been forgiven. The players had let the manager down but many were young and inexperienced and Molby knew that the answer lay with the signing of a few experienced pros. The board refused to back him. This difference of opinion between chairman Steve Hamer, and Molby meant one of them had to go, and since Hamer had only just installed his favourite tipple in the boardroom it had to be, sadly, the big Dane. That led the way for one of the most farcical episodes in the club's history. It was like something out of *Mr Benn*.

"Hello Mr Adams" said the shopkeeper, "What'll it be today then? Spaceman's outfit?"

"No" replied Mr Adams, "I'm tired of floating in space, being a clown and slaying dragons. I want something more challenging, something more exciting."

The shopkeeper paused for a moment then suddenly remembered the large guy with the Scouse/Danish accent who had been in earlier that day. "I know. I've got just the thing for you," he said. "It came in this morning. It might be a bit large on you but it should be okay."

And with this the shopkeeper handed Mr Adams a Le Coq Sportif tracksuit with the initials JM emblazoned on the side. Mr Adams entered the changing room, took off his hat and was suddenly transformed into the manager of Swansea City FC. He walked through the door and into a world of lower league football, hidden agendas and a windscreen replacement business.

"Hello, I'm Mr Adams" explained the new arrival on the training pitch.

"Thank God you're here," said a relieved Alan Curtis, "we need as much help as we can get at the moment. The team is full of kids. We need experience." Ahh, experience, thought Mr Adams, and with this thought in his mind he sped off to meet the chairman.

Mr Adams arrived at the club and was greeted when getting out of his car by the local and national media. A scarf was hurled in his direction. "Hold it above your head" cried an *Evening Post* reporter. "Any comment?" enquired a *Sky Sports* reporter. Mr Adams duly obliged and then headed for the boardroom wondering just how big a spotlight it was he'd walked into.

"Mr Hamer, we need experienced pros," he told the chairman. "Let me have some money to go spending."

"You can't have any," said Mr Hamer, "Look here's a brick, go smash a few windscreens. That should generate enough money."

I've got to get out of here, thought Mr Adams and, as if by magic, the shopkeeper appeared and said "Quick - come through here," and with this advice Mr Adams walked through the door of the manager's office and ended up back in the shop's changing room.

As he walked back along Festive Road he reflected to himself what a lucky escape he'd had. Just then a bald-headed bloke appeared and asked him for directions to the nearest costume shop. Mr Adams reached into his pocket, pulled out the Swansea City scarf and gave it to the bloke and wished him luck. He'd need it thought Mr Adams. What an adventure!
THE END.

Of course that baldie turned out to be Alan Cork. Not the North Bank's immediate choice of replacement to continue the footballing philosophy brought in by Molby, but whoever stepped into Jan's boots would, apart from tripping over themselves, have had their work cut out. Cork's past haunted him in some respects and the thought of the Swans playing a physical game accompanied by the airborne approach didn't exactly have the punters flocking to the Vetch. Fortunately for Corky a trip to Cardiff loomed large, the perfect opportunity to put the smile back on the faces of all Swans fans. Thankfully, the team delivered the goods.

The Swans won 1-0 thanks to a Keith Walker pile-driver in what the *Guardian* newspaper described as the "Ugly Rumble in the Basement." Frank Keating, their reporter (a questionable description of his occupation), described the travelling Jacks in the away end as a "thousand or so yobbish taunting supporters" and elsewhere in his drivel he us called "oafs"! Keating had obviously missed the failed attempt by Cardiff fans to invade the pitch when he bent over to pick up his white stick to smack his yelping guide dog!

Then, just when you thought the good ship Swansea City might be heading for calmer waters, the Chester City home game was postponed. A team of suits from the council visited the Vetch to give it a safety certificate but declined to hand over the 'playing permit' because the back-up generator wasn't working (the new 50p apparently wasn't to blame) and this needed to be fixed in case of an emergency. They also said that there was too much rubbish down the Vetch (a comment - I think - on the rubble behind the North Bank and not the playing staff).

These comic capers had us shaking our heads in disbelief, but the news that the City of Swansea had lost two of its greatest ambassadors stunned, shocked and saddened Swans fans the world over. This was the season we lost Ivor Allchurch MBE and Robbie James. Ivor, 67, the 'Golden Boy' of Welsh football, died at his home in Swansea. He was one of the most gifted footballers Wales has ever produced. An old fashioned inside-forward whose technique, vision and passing skills were exceptional. His pace and dribbling skills often left a trail of floored opposing players in his wake. He was capped 68 times by Wales. Robbie, 40, died playing the game he loved so much. The former Welsh international had made his debut for the Swans a month after his 17th birthday and played in every division under John Toshack's Super Swans. Robbie had cunning and awareness second to none; his brain worked at twice the speed of ordinary mortals. He had no fear of flying boots, no fear of the consequences and he had one of the most lethal shots the game has ever witnessed, ripping them in from all distances. He was a gladiator. Throw him in the pit and he'd fight for the shirt. He was capped 47 times by Wales.

Pride and passion. It was something the two late greats had in bundles, but what of the present squad. Did they know what it meant to wear the white shirt of Swansea City? Cork may not have known it when he took over the hot-seat but he certainly did after a couple of months in charge, especially after fan demonstrations. He tried to instil into the players what it meant to play for the Swans but some took it too far and indiscipline set in. Appleby threw more punches than Naseem Hamed in his effort to get back to the changing room to make the half-time cups of tea and Tony Bird proved to one and all at Cambridge United that mud sticks, especially to linesmen!

Results were poor and so apparently was the food at the Vetch which was condemned by Colman's in their football food report. They went into the away end against Macclesfield and were confronted by small brown slimy objects, but beyond the away fans were dodgy pasties. This came as quite a surprise to many Swans fans as the batch of contaminated savouries had been designated for the home game against Cardiff City!

As the season drew to a close we thought it couldn't get any more bizarre but it did. Someone invited Uri Geller down the Vetch! Was this a cheap way of fixing the clock above the Centre Stand, those in the North Bank asked themselves? Or had he come to hypnotise us into buying season tickets in the summer! Who knows? And after he bent a few spoons in the centre circle, who cared?

Well there you have it. A season with little joy and jubilation, but plenty of despair and despondency. At least some things never change. We still finished above Cardiff City!

JANUARY 3, '88

Portsmouth

When I wrote a review of Pompey's '95-96 season for this very book it was along the lines of 'poor season... might have gone down... last day trip to Yorkshire... won... stayed up... hope it never happens again'.

Well, apart from changing a few players and opposition names, it was pretty much the same again. Yet it was different.

In some ways this year's miss wasn't as near. Early in the second half on the final day we were 2-0 up at Bradford, knowing a win was enough whether Man City won 1-0, 100-0, or 5-2 for that matter (shame, eh?). So there was no nail-biting as we went into the last ten minutes knowing one goal either

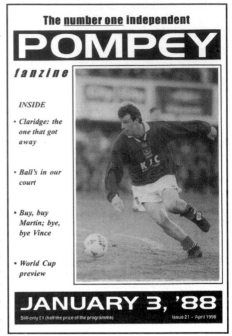

The **number one** independent

POMPEY

fanzine

INSIDE

- *Claridge: the one that got away*

- *Ball's in our court*

- *Buy, buy Martin; bye, bye Vince*

- *World Cup preview*

JANUARY 3, '88

Still only £1 (half the price of the programme)   Issue 21 - April 1998

against us or for another team at another ground could condemn us, as had been the case at Huddersfield in '96.

But in other ways, we went closer to the drop this year than last time. For in mid-February we found ourselves with a mere 24 points - six less than our nearest rivals and seven short of the safety of 21st place. That was three weeks after Alan Ball, villain to some club's fans, hero to ours, had returned to our manager's office to try to save us from a fate that Terry Fenwick and Terry Venables had seemingly condemned us to.

The damage done by Fenwick on the pitch was roughly equivalent to that done off it by Venables. The latter walked away with about £500,000 for a season and a half's 'work' - which, if the work he put in was anything to go by, must have meant his hourly rate was about £2 million. The former walked away with 500,000 "we want Fenwick out" chants ringing in his ears - though, never one to take a hint (nor lots of them), he refused to jump and had to be pushed.

When Ballie arrived ten days later it was to a tumultuous reception. Others - Man City, Stoke, Exeter, for example - scoffed when we hailed our messiah and began to celebrate First Division salvation and, in truth, he took a while to sort things out and turn relegation form into survival form. It was on a cold, grey afternoon at Crewe that things started to happen, despite a suicidal second half defensive show that saw us lose 3-1. A section of the long-suffering fans started singing and dancing as if we'd just secured the Championship and a new tone was set.

If there has been a more spine-tingling atmosphere at Fratton Park than the one created three days later, on a blustery Tuesday night, when just 8,611 turned up to see bottom placed Pompey play mediocre Stockport, then I'd have loved to have been there. Remarkable as it may seem, this was the match when our fans decided that the only way to save the team was to make a noise. A loud noise. A non-stop noise. "Alan Ball's... Blue and White Army... Alan Ball's... Blue and White Army," they sang. And sang. And sang. Louder when Stockport attacked. Longer when the final whistle loomed. And it worked. We won 1-0. Oh, and the only goal was scored by the other piece in the jigsaw that Ball's return had helped complete - another 'old boy' hero, Steve Claridge.

The turn-around had begun and it wasn't about to end there. The fans remained in good voice as Ball's boys beat Reading, West Brom, Stockport and Swindon to reach mid-March out of the bottom three. But Pompey being Pompey, they didn't follow the hard bit (getting out of the drop zone) by doing the easy bit (staying out). They lost a few more games and gave themselves more hard work to do. The slump went on a bit too long for people to remain confident or even defiant. So with two games left we had to win them both and rely on one or two others to drop some points. Everything went our way on the penultimate weekend, as we bludgeoned Huddersfield 3-0 and heard how the tale of two Cities, Stoke and Manchester, was one of dropped points. That left us knowing victory at Bradford would be enough, barring some bizarre sequence of occurrences that involved something like John Rudge scoring eight goals for Port Vale, Neil Apsin sprouting a full head of hair and Mick Mills having a penalty saved for Stoke.

So for the second time in three years, the prospect of yet another season in the same division - we are now its longest serving team by several years - didn't stop scenes of wild joy marking the final whistle. When the tickertape had settled, joy became mere optimism; optimism that next season will be more fun and more comfortable. (We thought '97-98 would be good, as you'll know if you read our review in SOTF3. Still, can't be right all the time.) We have Alan Ball at the helm and we should, by the time the season begins, have replaced hearts who are not in the club with some whose are (selling Simpson and Hall and buying Claridge would be a good start). We also have a fan base that's fully behind the management - something we never really had while El Tel and Hell Tel were here.

What we do still lack is widespread support for the chairman. Martin Gregory, against all odds and various take-over bids, is still ensconced despite having put the club up for sale more than three years ago. Some (me included) think he's currently our best bet. The only alternatives have been unproven speculators who might or might not have been able to put money where their not inconsiderably sized mouths were. And at least, under him, we still have a football club that's no lower down the leagues than when his family bought it from their predecessors exactly a decade ago. But other fans believe him to be hanging on only to try to get as much money for the club as he can, as if it were a second-hand car. They have protested long and loud but he has remained unmoved.

To say the season overall was anything better than one in which regular defeats - some of them humiliating - and boardroom battles were the order of the day would be to look at it through royal blue-tinted spectacles. You can't lose at home to Reading and forget it easily. I mean, honestly. *Reading.* And it was 2-0.

There were highlights. Well, at least higher-lights. At the end of August we were in the top six and our multi-national strike force, Swede Svensson and Aussie Aloisi, threatened to work well together - then international call-ups meant they only played about three more games together. And at the turn of the year, we almost knocked Villa out of the FA Cup. Two-one up with minutes to go. Who do you think won the replay?

And though it was born out of desperation, our little run of five wins in six in February and March was memorable stuff, no more so than when we outplayed West Brom at The Hawthorns. A month later, though it was a day on which we lost, our trip to Sunderland's Stadium of Light (mental note: must remember not to worry too much about giving away penalties when we play there this season...) was memorable, for the surroundings if not the match, though that wasn't bad either. You have to hand it to Sunderland, they've shown the way forward for new stadiums (some say stadia, but that's almost as poncey as the name of Sunderland's, so I'll avoid it). When we went, there was an orchestra, ear-blowing sound system and ballerinas. And it actually worked well. Mind you, I thought Bradford's majorette girls were pretty good too.

Other highlights? Not really, but such a joyous end to the season means it will forever sit fondly in people's memories.

As for '98-99, we're already looking forward to it. Being anticipated especially keenly is Crystal Palace's visit to Fratton, which presumably will bring Venables back for the first time since his bitter departure. And who'd bet against him giving his old mate Fenwick a job at Selhurst? That would be too good. Not that we're bitter or anything, we just want those two to fail dismally for the rest of their careers. Like they did with us. Altogether now: 'Alan Ball's... Blue and White Army..'

KEEGAN WAS CRAP REALLY

Doncaster Rovers

The final league table shows Doncaster Rovers FC firmly adrift at the bottom of the table. We deserve to be there. We have been without doubt the worst team in the Football League. We have set a number of records on the way, which include the longest run from the start of the season without a win and the most league defeats.

And you only have to scratch beneath the surface to find many reasons why the Rovers have become the worst team in league history. Richardson and Dinard (an off-shore company popularly thought to be owned by Richardson) own a majority stake in Doncaster Rovers. Belle Vue, the Rovers home, has recently

AN INDEPENDENT VOICE FOR ROVERS FANS

become prime land with the racecourse on one side and the new retail park on the other. However, the council that leases it to the Rovers owns Belle Vue. The land is also covered by a restriction of use meaning that only sports can be played on it. Asda, which has a store behind the away end, is very keen to buy the land and therefore a change of use from the council is required. But the council have stated on a number of occasions that they will not deal with Ken Richardson, and therefore the sale of Belle Vue, and the subsequent building of a new stadium, will not happen under the present owners. This explains Richardson's asking price of nearly £4 million, which for a club deeply in debt, with small crowds, and now not even in the league, is extremely steep.

The seeds of this sorry and sad tale were actually planted the season before when it was revealed that manager Kerry Dixon wasn't picking the team. It wasn't long before Kerry decided he'd had enough, and left with his dignity intact. Unrest, among what must rank as the most patient fans in the world, was now growing out of control. Individual and mass pitch invasions were becoming commonplace. They remained peaceful, despite the best efforts of certain people in recommending an alternative approach.

The playing squad has been systematically run-down, with seasoned pros like Dean Williams, Jim Dobbin and Ian Gore being mistreated and then freed. Darren Moore (Bradford), Colin Cramb (Bristol C) and Jon Schofield

(Mansfield) were sold before the first ball was kicked. That was the heart ripped out of our team. They were at first replaced by genuine non-league players from clubs like Curzton Ashton, Hyde and Workop. No disrespect to the clubs mentioned, but these guys were way beneath league standard. The epitome of the non-league imports was goalkeeper David Smith - acquired from Sunday league football - who turned out against Brighton. It transpired that he was Weaver's neighbour and is affectionately remembered as our Tellytubby 'keeper. Weaver tried to explain away Smith's poor performance by saying that he'd had been threatened as he ran out at the start. The fact that the poor lad was nearly 20 stone, couldn't jump and was plainly well out of his depth was plainly beyond the grasp of Weaver.

Towards the end of the season the club reduced the amount of professionals at the club to just a handful and turned instead to the youth team. Although results didn't improve the performances definitely did. The kids showed pride in wearing the red shirt of Doncaster Rovers and appeared eager to turn out for us.

The Brighton game at the beginning of October was the catalyst for much of what has happened since. What Brighton brought to Belle Vue that day was experience, ideas and most importantly organisation: stickers, balloons and the most troublesome crowd seen at Belle Vue since the hooligan days of the eighties were all in evidence that day. On police advice, Weaver and Richardson left Belle Vue at half time. Two games later, Richardson stated that he was having nothing more to do with the Rovers and has not been seen since.

The Supporters Club, who had been badly mistreated by the Richardsons for a number of years, finally took a key role against those in charge. An independent group called 'Save the Rovers' also came to prominence at the beginning of the season. These two groups helped to organise much of the on-going protests.

Despite not winning until December 2nd (thank you Chester), we were warmed by the fact that Ken Richardson was to be tried at Sheffield Crown Court in January 1998 for conspiracy to commit arson on the Belle Vue main stand. As usual, British justice being the best in the world, the trial was postponed and is now scheduled for 1999.

The rest of the on-field action was more a test of endurance. As Richardson left he put Mark Weaver in full control. Weaver had never played or managed a professional football team, although he used to sell things for Stockport County. During the entire nine months we managed to beat four teams: Chester, Shrewsbury, Peterborough (A) and Hull. How any of their managers stayed in jobs after that is anyone's guess. Things got so bad that we recorded our (and indeed the league's) lowest-ever crowd of just 739 against Barnet. We've been so bad this year that even Scunthorpe managed to beat us at Belle Vue. Now *that* is abysmal!

With Richardson and Weaver at the helm, many of the people of Doncaster, already resenting the payment of £8-10 to watch the worst football in the league, refused to turn up in numbers. The *Doncaster Star* and its reporter Steve Hossack, gave a voice to Weaver and printed almost word for word whatever he wanted. This, understandably, infuriated the Rovers fans and you can be sure that the *Star* is not on best-seller list with the Belle Vue faithful. Indeed Mr Hossack threatened to sue *KWCR* after we published some rather libellous statements about him and his paper. Although we shouldn't have printed them, and we did print a retraction, it was what everyone was, and still is, thinking.

During the season we have been labelled as mindless idiots, threatened with private security firms and had ID cards touted as a way of making us behave and keep quiet while our football club is murdered. The FA, Football League and the Football Task Force have done absolutely nothing. There were reportedly three consortia waiting to buy the Rovers. The price kept going up and up. The year before, the FA had stepped in and brokered a deal between Archer and Knight at Brighton. Despite repeated pleas they have ignored the situation at Belle Vue. The FA are no doubt glad to see the back of us. After all, we are a small club which even under good owners would struggle to make it to the lofty heights of the Premiership. That's all football's about these days, isn't it?

We are still no closer to being sold. Rumours are rife, some so far-fetched that they're unbelievable. We're being linked with hosts of different people and clubs, with groundshares and mergers. And of course total oblivion can't be ruled out. A mystery Irish consortium are constantly at the forefront of these rumours, probably due to the fact that no one will disclose their identities. Anton Johnson and his consortium, which have been trying to buy Rovers for nearly two years, are by far the fans favourites.

So as the final curtain is drawn on our league status we still find ourselves in limbo: no closer to being bought and just a little closer to going out of existence. So to all those of you that have had poor seasons count your blessings. To all of the fans of Newcastle, so angry with Hall and Sheppard, get a life! You didn't have even a *tenth* of our problems. To all the Barnsley and Bolton fans left crying when your teams were relegated, grow up; they'll still be there next year. Doncaster Rovers FC look like slipping away. Unlike Newcastle and Brighton we have no famous fans to help our cause. No one will mourn the death of our club. Our ramshackle ground will be demolished and replaced by an Asda. You won't miss us. Be honest - how many of you pine for Gateshead, Barrow and Accrington Stanley? Well, *I'll* miss us and I'm bloody angry about what's happened!

KICKER CONSPIRACY

Burnley

That a season of initial high promise was such a near disaster shouldn't have been such a surprise. We beat Stoke, West Brom and others in the race to appoint Waddle, then spent the rest of the season rubbing our eyes in disbelief at the miserable fare on offer. Although Waddle's World Cup credentials are well known, few bothered to dig deeper than Glen Roeder's England coaching appointment. Had track records at Watford and Gillingham been brought into the equation then we would have been better prepared for the shambles to unfold.

The season kicked off on a baking August afternoon's visit to champions-in-waiting Watford.

Kicker Conspiracy
(A BURNLEY FANZINE)

Is there a penalty clause in the contract?

I ****ing hope not!!

Scorchio!!

INCHY WADDLES OUT -
- WADDLE INCHES IN

Produced by the HUDDERSFIELD CLARETS
Volume 2
Issue No 1 : August 1997

Fans! Remember!!
Price cut of 2.5% in real terms.
Still only £1

What was optimistically adjudged a competent performance ended in a 0-1 defeat. Waddle had spent considerably to bring the new faces of Mark Ford, Lee Howey, Steve Blatherwick and freebie boys Chris Woods and Mike Williams. All had played Premiership football so great things were expected. A Roeder-esque emphasis on defence, with three centre backs and Howie as captain was adopted. Unfortunately the downside to this meant that established players were initially dropped then played out of position when recalled. Cooke started the season under suspension and no matter how our strikers were shuffled we couldn't find the cutting edge which had made us second highest scorers the previous term. At our first home game Waddle himself chose to play a defensive role against Gillingham and could thank some generous refereeing decisions, no doubt inspired by his reputation, that Akinbiyi et al didn't make mincemeat of us. This 0-0 set the tone for the rest of the ensuing binary sequence, 0-1 (Southend a), 0-0 (Bristol Rovers h), 0-1 (Chesterfield a), 0-0 (Oldham h). By this time we were in the brown and smelly, bottom, with a miserly three points from six games and null goals.

We had a modicum of success in squeaking past a very clogmanlike Lincoln City in the Coke thingy. True, we were playing textbookishly correct tactical formations but players were scared to be venturesome. Nobody got round the back and hit the bye line. As posters advertised 'Men In Black - Now Showing', we were left screaming, "Men In the Box - There's Nowt

Showing." Barnes lacked confidence and support, but it was he who struck our first goal away to his old colleagues, York City, to put us 1-0 ahead. Glen Roeder's ears must have been burning on account of the pro-Harrison chants but he ignored the hints, kept him on the bench, we stopped playing football and were swamped 3-1. It got worse with a 0-4 (h) defeat to Stoke on the eve of a holiday departure.

Wads and Roeds, seemingly gripped by their messianic billing, were determined to grab the squad by their ears and give them a good shaking. Left out in the cold were Andy Cooke (about to have his most prolific goalscoring season), Gerry Harrison (earlier personal differences with Roeder from Watford days), Marco Gentile (Premiership pedigree according to Ruud Gullit and the son of an Italian World Cup player but a man marker "not likely to fit in"), Paul Smith (who was being watched by Aston Villa), Damien Matthew and Nigel Gleghorn. It was surprising that the supporters' patience with Waddle lasted as long as it did. A home draw against pub crawler Kurt Nogan's latest staging post, Preston, and a last minute defeat to co-strugglers Brentford were the only sources of holiday disharmony.

Then Creaney arrived on loan from Man City. The pie chomper duly made goal scoring look like falling off a log. A brace against Wycombe and two more in our first home win (3-1 v Carlisle) heralded our first ascent from the bowels of the Nationwide number two. A seven game unbeaten run, with wins against Walsall (h) and Luton (a) meant at last we had a functioning strike force. Though much was said about a permanent signing, Burnley came nowhere near agreeing personal terms. Thirteen points out of 27 + eight goals from nine games = no reasonable contract offer from Burnley + a hurried recall by a struggling Man City embarrassed at how good he was looking.

Significantly, Burnley's first win was witnessed by the Dutch contingent of Breda fans - hello Paul, Guus, Richard, Jurgen, Moleen and Paul. By this time we were running out of lucky talismans and superstitious rituals. Heroic morning swims of up to 80 lengths only produced two home wins. Working hours became less football-friendly, Waddle started messing up team selections (again), Lyres was sold to Preston and the Longside lost patience with Howie. A downturn in results coincided with Creaney's departure. Three successive defeats including an embarrassing home 0-3 FA Cup howler against Rotherham brought the ending of the honeymoon period. As the teams were announced for the Northampton home game, boos that Lee (no I'm not Chrissie's brother-in-law) Howie was preferred to Andy Cooke and cheers for the return of old favourite Big Bad Johnnie Gayle stung Waddle. Even when we overturned a 0-1 deficit he shunned the goal celebrations by sulking and mard-arseing his way back to the halfway line. A couple of hours later came an astonishing attack over the *Radio Lancs* airwaves, alleging that the fans had given them "dogs' abuse." After this, disaffection with Waddle prevailed. Renderings of "Chrissie Waddle's Claret and Blue Army" petered out as did Wads' interest in performing to even half decent (leave alone World class) standards.

Another source of discontent was the board's lack of interest in securing investment. Out of both cups and with gates sliding below the 10,000 necessary for loan repayments, a loss-making season was inevitable. With no sponsors for either of the two new stands, the loss of the Endsleigh deal and the spectre of relegation hanging heavy, supporters were becoming annoyed at the board's inertia. C.I.S.A. became pro-active in opening up channels of communication and briefing fans, media and investors. By Christmas they had given the lie to the board's contentions that there were no willing investors - since May they had been stonewalling an offer from a New York based tycoon - and the duly briefed shareholders gave them a rough ride at the Boxing Day AGM.

Back on the pitch, Clarets were back in a tailspin. A 1-3 defeat at Bristol City was scant reward for a venturesome display. A feeble 0-2 home defeat to the pie eaters (Wigan) was down to some indifferent keeping by Marlon and a 0-1 *Sky* defeat to a rather poor Fulham showed just how down on our luck we were then. It had even got so bad that a 0-0 draw at home to Chesterfield was a relief. The next away defeat at Gillingham (0-2) proved auspicious not because Chris Waddle found he was as unpopular with Burnley fans as Glen Roeder was with Gillingham's, but because of how quickly Glen Little's 20 minute sub appearance made him Man of the Match.

This guy had undoubted talent but hadn't sufficiently harnessed it to be an automatic selection. Earlier in the season he had gone AWOL back to London but now, like Cooke and Harrison, had forced himself into the reckoning and was set to show Messrs Waddle and Roeder a thing or two. How Glen Roeder was to regret saying, "Glen Little isn't fit to lace the boots of Chris Waddle" at a supporters meeting and how much pleasure supporters would have recalling this is now local folklore. Anecdotal undercurrents from meetings not just with players but a variety of football media pundits circulated, attesting to a shambolic approach in training, coaching and match preparations.

A 2-0 home win against runaway leaders Watford was our best home performance. It was fast and frenetic but we outclassed them with a typical pre-suspension brace from Cookie. At last Wads showed a touch of managerial astuteness in swapping an out of touch Barnes for Huddersfield's out of favour Andy Payton. His 13 goals from 24 starts were essential to our eventual survival. Signings of Henderson and Robertson added a bit of strength to the squad but it was the boys who had been cold-shouldered earlier - Glen Little, Andy Cooke and Gerry Harrison - who did the most. Seven wins out of nine got us upwardly mobile (leaguewise) and through to the AWS northern finals. Notts County (2-0), York City (7-2) and Carlisle United (4-1) just couldn't live with us at Turf Moor. We looked rocky in twice coming from behind against Burnley old boys PNE (Parkinson, Nogan, Eyres), but who's looking a gift horse three points like that in the mouth?

Could it last? No. Our old friend Dame Fortune had a few more wet fish slaps about the face in store for us as she explained, "Sorry old bean, but runaway success isn't for the likes of you. Firstly you've got to understand the principle of feast and famine. Here, let me show you..." Wrexham (h) 1-2 (a fitting reward for fielding seven central defenders), Brentford (h) 1-1, Carlisle

(a) 1-2 (some hairy moments getting out), Walsall (a) 0-0 (goodbye Marlon, hello £400k), Luton (h) 1-1, Millwall (a) 0-1 and we continued getting sucked deeper into the relegation swamp. Typically a creditable AWS northern final draw (1-1) at fishy Grimsby was followed by a 0-2 home reversal which was the cue for more discontent and anti-Teasdale demonstrations.

"Sack the board" is sometimes a bit of a knee-jerk reaction to a bad run, but here at Turf Moor it's thoroughly deserved. The board hadn't just blanked Ingleby's offers, they declared in favour of a mystery bidder (later Peter Shackleton) who was long on promises about what he could achieve with money (that wasn't his) but short on credibility and any visible backers. Chairman Teasdale had failed to acknowledge any form of communication from supporters, media and willing investors for so long that his pariah status was an accepted fact of life. Local radio recorded a 307:1 poll in favour of an Ingleby take-over which the board should have heeded. Instead they recommended the £12 million Shackleton deal backed by 'Swiss banking interests' offering a £1 million 'gift' which never materialised. Very fishy indeed.

By now we were some points adrift at the foot. Even I was having difficulty convincing other fans that the cycle of feast and famine could yet work in our favour. No doubt having witnessed the do or die commitment of local boy Andy Payton who was always scoring, getting injured then needing to be subbed, Wads signed another local, John Mullin, who hadn't cracked it at the Stadium of Light. It worked, we had the lions' share of play against Grimsby to run out 2-1 winners. Next we held onto an early goal by Andy Payton at Northampton to record our only double. Blackpool scabbed a 2-1 win at Turf Moor courtesy of some dodgy reffing decisions and we had another clash against league leaders, Bristol City. John Ward, their manager, was given a heartfelt ovation from both sets of supporters before collecting his Manager of the Month award. Another hard-fought encounter was decided by Payton's opportunism, even though he took no further part. We were still bottom cos all the other strugglers, like us, were making a good fist of it. Luton had pulled clear, Carlisle were just beginning to wobble after looking safe and everybody except Southend seemed to be garnering useful points.

Easter Monday took us to a place famous for its pies, pier, Northern Soul, mintballs and of late The Verve. Unfortunately Wigan's Springfield Park shows no sign of Whelan's wad and remains the very quintessence of a 'Shit Ground No Fans' patched-up bomb site. Backed by a noisy away contingent, Burnley played like men inspired by Orwell's observations on *The Road To Wigan Pier* or "Like a cat in a bag; waiting to drown; this time we're going down." Nil-two down at half time, a Glen Little goal started a fight-back. Roeder aided the cause by subbing Payton. We eventually succumbed to the Wiganites, 5-1.

Fulham, despite outplaying us for long stretches, were outgunned by Cooke and Payton. Strange that - a club dripping with money should be sponsored by GMB but that's one of life's little ironies (just like Paul Moody trying to be harder and cleverer than Harrison). Two places from safety but with one game in hand meant all sorts of statistics and scenarios were bandied around, but basically one safety place was available to either Brentford, Plymouth or ourselves. We desperately needed an away win to make our extra game count. Dean Court rates as a happy hunting ground but Bournemouth were cock-a-hoop after their Wembley day out. The ref didn't spoil things for them either. He ignored Glass' obvious trip on Cooke when he came second, in his own penalty area, to a through ball. So incensed was the commentating Phil Parkes he had to apologise on air for suggesting Burnley fans might form a visiting lynch mob if they found out his address. The refused penalty cost us dearly; instead of taking a 1-0 lead we surrendered the initiative, losing 1-2. Oldham (a) failed to appreciate how much this game meant to the Claret army; over 5,000 Clarets travelled and hundreds were locked outside. An early opening Andy Cooke goal sent the travelling support into short-lived delirium - the equaliser taking a mere minute. But Burnley were at their attacking best and two more rapier attacks yielded sublime finishes from Weller and Little. This was us 3-1 up at half time. Oldham went down to ten men when a defender was red-carded for a foul on Cooke. We should have cruised it but the rain came down, we panicked like frightened rabbits, kept giving the ball away, brought on a defender and were twice caught out for not knowing how to defend. One point taken meant we'd missed the chance to pull out of the bottom four. With just one game to go it was understandable that most fans felt about the same as when we lost 1-5 at Wigan.

The *Kicker Conspiracy* team had an exec box for the relegation decider against Plymouth. Like the Titanic's passengers gathered around the brass band, at least we could go down in style. Waddle's learning curve had cost us dear. Most fans thought it was they who picked the successful team by calling for reinstatement of favourites and conducting public debates through media outlets. The board's inability to come to terms with their business responsibilities had alienated many. Still, 21,000 (unofficial figure) turned up in what was an emotional encounter for both sets of supporters. First blood however went to Brentford with the news that Bristol Rovers were down to ten men. Then it was our turn and Turf Moor erupted when a trademark Little/Cooke manoeuvre brought the breakthrough we'd long threatened. News of Bristol Rovers going 1-0 up against Brentford reinforced our position. Then Keith's dad got in the way of my mental directives when we were defending a tricky situation, 1-1 and Plymouth had nicked the 20th 'safe' place off us. I told Keith's dad to be more careful next time he went to the toilet. The pre-match beers meant it was soon my turn. After carefully picking a way through legs and closing the door I turned round. Just in time too. Matthew, who had been anonymous, put in a useful ball to Cooke, who'd worked a bit of space and biffed a header into the onion bag for 2-1.

The second half was a formality. Plymouth didn't look too dangerous but fingernails disappeared, the butterflies intensified and some were unable to watch. Bristol Rovers scored a second and despite the seven minutes' difference we knew we'd done it at the final whistle. That was the survival taken care of. If we're going to prosper the board is the next place for setting improvement targets.

KING OF THE KIPPAX

Manchester City

'96-97 ended with City in their lowest-ever final league position, 14th in the real Second Division. However, since we'd been in the bottom few when Frank Clark arrived just after Christmas we were not going to complain too loudly.

Frank had turned the team round within a few weeks. The goals started to flow at the right end, and the defensive cock-ups were reduced at the other. Gio was performing some wonderful stuff, Nicky Summerbee was beginning to play more like his dad than his mum, and Uwe rediscovered the purpose of the wood and netting structures situated at each end of the pitch. Therefore '97-98 promised a challenge for promotion, and although Forest, Boro and Sunderland stood in our way, a place in the play-offs was a realistic target.

Pre-season went well and ended with a 3-0 win at Burnley where Lee Bradbury, our record signing at £3 million, scored twice on his debut. But when the real thing started everything went pear-shaped, yet again.

The arrival of Bradbury caused Frank a few headaches. I believe Bradbury was bought to replace Rosler, who at the time was interesting a couple of Premiership clubs. Unfortunately for Frank it never got past the interest stage. He had to play our record signing *and* Rosler, who was the only player who seemed capable of scoring. This was a bit of a problem because they were too similar and couldn't play in the same team.

Frank also had a problem working out what to do with Nicky Summerbee. For some reason, Clark wouldn't apply the tactics that had previously forced our climb to safety: allowing Summerbee to feed Rosler from the wing. Instead, he kept one of them on the bench for much of the time. He also tinkered with the midfield, and in time-honoured tradition he played a central defender at left back. After four league games we were without a win and also out of the League Cup courtesy of a penalty shoot-out disaster against Blackpool.

Then we went silly and won at Forest, ending their unbeaten run and enabling us to play party-poopers for once. In the next game we drew at Bury where David Morley scored our equaliser in a very impressive debut, and Tony Scully had a great second half on the left wing. Wouldn't you know it? Both were dropped for the next home game, a defeat by Norwich. This result may not appear too unusual, but Norwich hadn't won at Maine Road for over 30 years! We could usually rely on them to provide us with four points, even in a bad season.

One week later it was all smiles again as Swindon headed back to Wiltshire after a 6-0 stuffing. But our happiness was short-lived as injury-ravaged Ipswich beat us 1-0 in the first of four consecutive defeats in which we failed to score a single goal. A loss at home to rock-bottom Huddersfield came ten years to the day that we beat them 10-1, and *Sky* marked the anniversary by providing their couch potato bastard customers the chance to see just how bad we really were.

Words can't describe how bad our first half performance was at Stockport. I'll just say that we were extremely lucky to be *only* 3-0 down at the break. Under normal circumstances, this level of performance would have been rewarded with a chorus of "What the fuck is going on?" However, as this question has never received a satisfactory answer, at Edgeley Park it was replaced with "You're not fit to wear the shirt" and "You're only here for the money."

Harsh? Not to those who attended most of our games. And as you probably know, there were thousands who turned up every week to watch City home and away. Some of the most loyal fans in the history of the game had earned the right to chant these apparent insults. The club has been taking the piss (and our money) for over two decades and we've got nothing to show for it. Twenty eight thousand on average for home games in our worst-ever season. 'Football daft' in the North East? Yeah, anybody can support a winning team...

The media have also ignored our magnificent support. Tens of thousands watching a crap team is a zero-interest story as far as they are concerned. But fans acting like dickheads on Cup Final day, or turning up to make inane comments whenever *Sky* are in town is considered far more interesting.

Opposing fans, particularly those of Sheffield United and Wolves, sympathised with our plight and told us horror stories about life in the real Third Division. They seemed genuinely concerned. In fact, at times it seemed that everybody in the country - with the exception of our players, coaching staff and directors - wanted us to survive. When rival supporters offer sympathy instead of taking the piss you know you are in big trouble.

Off the pitch, things were going just as badly. Gio Kinkladze wrote off his Ferrari and picked up 34 stitches in his back. As the jokers quipped, he went round three drivers and hit the post. According to rumours he was racing with Summerbee, but the club denied it of course. It was even rumoured that City pushed for a prosecution; well we needed all the points we could get. Summerbee's involvement may be unconfirmed, but he was soon on his way to Sunderland in a swap deal for Craig Russell (a striker/winger - depending on which paper you read - who Clark played at left back! To be fair to Frank, he actually tried to play him as a left wing-back, but he wasn't one of those either).

An own goal from the unlucky Kit Symons gave Wolves a victory at Maine Road, and then we lost at Birmingham in yet another joke game. Georgian Murtaz Shelia gave us the lead in the 88th minute of his debut. Three minutes into injury time the home side drew level and *five minutes later* they scored their winner. Does Steve Bruce attract referees with duff watches?

The festive season did nothing to end the topsy-turvy nature of our season, as a great win against Boro (spoilt only by the antics of their dickhead supporters) was followed by a defeat at Gresty Road on Boxing Day. Only the Football League computer could arrange for the team with the smallest allocation of tickets for visiting fans to play host to the team with the largest travelling support on Boxing Day. I got there early to try to get a ticket from a tout but ended up watching the first half through a narrow gap in the gate, and listening to the second half on the radio as I drove home.

1997 ended with a home defeat at the hands of Nottingham Forest. We should have launched an inquiry into the pitiful performance that led to Forest being 3-0 up inside an hour. Instead, the club took heart from our two goal fight-back and the injury time chance that could have led to an equaliser. Needless to say, they completely overlooked that fact that Forest switched off at 3-0 up. Without recognising there was problem, they never had a chance of finding a solution

1998 couldn't be any worse. Could it? After Bradford were dumped out of the cup, and Portsmouth were crushed 3-0 at Fratton Park, we thought that maybe things were looking up after all. Oh, the innocence of optimism...

Nicky Summerbee, Niall Quinn and Peter Reid returned to Maine Road and left with three points. West Ham knocked us out the cup, although Rosler did miss a potentially match-winning penalty with the score at 1-1, and Charlton scored an injury-time equaliser to deny us a much-needed league win. Kit Symons' personal nightmare looked to be over after he headed us in front against the Londoners with a few minutes remaining, but then his hashed clearance led to their equaliser and normal service was resumed.

But changes were afoot. The home defeat by Bury had unexpected consequences. After the game a major shareholder called a local radio phone-in and had a go at club chairman Francis Lee. A few days later Lee acted and sacked Frank Clark, and within hours Joe Royle was appointed as club saviour. Clark received limited sympathy as his team selections, tactics and substitutions had been perplexing fans all season. When we lost he didn't know what to do about it, and on the odd occasion when we won, he didn't know how it had happened so he couldn't repeat it.

Royle had about three months to save us. He had the support of both the board and the crowd, who could still remember him as a player at Maine Road. He started at home against Ipswich, and after an early goal gave us hope, two late goals saw the points wander off in the direction of East Anglia. Despite this, the start of the Royle era will probably be remembered for a bizarre sequence of substitutions. Lee Crooks replaced Richard Edghill at half time. On 66 minutes, Crooks was replaced by Paul Beesley, and eight minutes later Beesley himself was replaced by Lee Bradbury. None of the substituted players appeared injured. Joe Royle had become the latest victim of the Maine Road Madness!

While Royle strengthened the team by buying Jamie Pollock, Shaun Goater and Richard Jobson, he weakened it significantly by refusing to play Kinkladze. The most skilful player in the Nationwide League was injured, sulking, dropped or "not in the right frame of mind." He also brought ex-Blue Ian Bishop back to Maine Road. Bishop's earlier spell at Maine Road had lasted less than 12 months, but he was still loved by the fans. Unfortunately seven years is a long time for a footballer.

Time is no kinder to ex-professional footballers, and Francis Henry Lee, once of Manchester City and England, resigned as chairman following increased pressure from fans and fellow board members. David Bernstein, a lifetime fan and alleged financial wizard replaced him.

With five games remaining we were just above the drop zone. Easter, as the cliché goes, would be critical.

Tickets for the final game of the season at Stoke went on sale on Easter Saturday, so we nipped in to Maine Road on the way to Wolverhampton. The Wolves fans wished us luck and their players didn't seem to want to chase a play-off place, so it all seemed so easy when Jamie Pollock put us ahead. But the prospect of three points was too much for our goalkeeper Martin Margetson. A harmless corner went straight into his hands, before popping out, through his legs and over the line.

I'd have settled for relegation there and then, as that incident summed up the present pathetic shambles that was Manchester City FC. Kevin Horlock smashed a free kick into the top corner to regain the lead, but five minutes from time we needlessly conceded a free kick and the game finished 2-2. On the face of it a draw at Wolves was a reasonable result, but when you lose at home to Bury, Huddersfield, Port Vale, Stoke and Oxford you have to win the tricky away games to compensate.

Two games later Birmingham pulled the broken watch stunt again by winning in injury time at Maine Road. Boro away on a Friday night was another wasted holiday as we lost 1-0 despite playing against ten men for 45 minutes. With two games remaining our fate was still in our own hands. If we won both we'd be safe. Gio returned for the visit of QPR and scored in the first minute. If only Royle had played him earlier? Rangers weren't safe themselves but they didn't seem that interested, so we decided to give them a hand. Margetson dropped the first bollock by picking up a back pass and allowing an opponent to take the ball out of his hands and roll it to ex-City man Mike Sheron. Shez *never* missed open goals from five yards out, and he wasn't about to start.

Then the great workhorse Jamie Pollock scored one of the most ridiculous own goals ever witnessed at Maine Road. He ran 20 yards to break up an attack, battling for the ball and hoofing it high into the sky. He continued running in an attempt to be first to the falling ball as it re-entered the Earth's atmosphere just above our penalty area. His looped header back to Margetson was perfectly placed at chest height in the centre of the goal. Unfortunately, Martin had come for the ball, and it floated softly over his head and into the net. The fans had been asked for 90 minutes of concentrated support, and they gave it. The players were not even prepared to give a few minutes' concentration and commitment. It might seem that Martin Margetson cocked things up too often, but he can't take all the blame. After all, how can a goalkeeper be expected to play with confidence and enthusiasm when the manager has already told him he'll be on his way at the end of the season? Which school of management did Joe Royle attend?

The final day of the season saw our first visit to the Britannia Stadium, the shiny new home of Stoke City. The inmates gave the visiting supporters the sort of reception that an American president might expect in Iraq. Minimal space for visiting fans' cars and an ambush at every turn could easily have been avoided if the stupid bastards who designed the stadium had turned the huge areas of wasteland surrounding the ground into parking.

City sold their allocation almost immediately and many Blues travelled the short distance to Stoke to buy tickets in the home sections. The first fights broke out about half an hour before kick-off but the trouble was almost under control by half time. It erupted again after the match but, according to the stewards, it goes off after every home game and the police and security staff have no intention of doing anything about it.

What about the game, you ask. Well, various combinations of results could have seen us to safety as long as either Port Vale or Portsmouth, both with tricky-looking away games, didn't win. The rest, as they say, is history. A thumping 5-2 victory proved pointless as Vale and Pompey both took maximum advantage from opponents who just rolled over and died.

Obviously a last day shafting was preferable to being out-shouted again had we visited them next season. Bradford were also happy to avoid future games at Maine Road as they've lost on their last four visits, and Huddersfield reckoned the loss of one huge set of gate receipts was a tiny price to pay for relegating the team that beat them 10-1.

In the end we went down with a goal difference of minus one, which is almost unheard of. We'd managed a few decent wins, but the almost constant stream of narrow defeats took their toll. As for our home record, in front of that 28,000 average crowd remember; well, only Doncaster and Brighton fared worse.

We've never played at the third level of the game and we've never been out of the top division for more than three seasons. That's a record that looks like going by the wayside unless we go up two divisions next May! However, let's look on the bright side. There will be a few new teams coming to Maine Road and we'll get to visit a few new grounds. We'll also rediscover the joys of standing on crumbling terracing in the rain. Roll on August, here we come.

LAND OF SHEEP AND GLORY

Carlisle United

Well, what a difference a year makes. This time last season I was facing the prospect of three months with no competitive football. However, I was looking forward to the new season in Division Two. We had managed to keep together the squad that had seen us win promotion and gain our first Wembley win against Colchester in the Auto-Windscreens. As well as the solid squad, we had also had a great manager in Mervyn Day who had done a tremendous job in guiding us back to the Second Division at the first attempt, in what was his first full season in management.

The summer also saw the club bring in a couple of players,

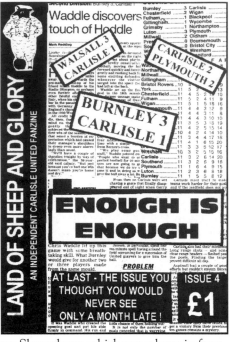

notably Ian Stevens for £100,000 from Shrewsbury, which was a bargain for a player who had a proven goalscoring record in the lower divisions. However, Stevo didn't make the start of the season due to a mystery illness that kept him out until November.

Another summer arrival was Andy Couzens, a former England Under-21 player from Leeds who lightened the club's bank balance by another £100,000. Despite the setback with Ian Stevens we had a really strong team comprised of a mixture of youth and experience. I really did have high hopes for the coming season; well, when Michael Knighton spent £200,000 on players, I was half expecting the catering at Brunton Park to consist of two loaves and five fishes to feed the hungry crowd.

After the run-of-the-mill friendlies it was apparent that maybe this was going to be our year. We'd had some good results and more importantly, good performances, with the most effective new player being free transfer Billy Barr, who put in three or four solid displays in a bid to win a place on the team sheet.

The one place where we were lacking was in defence, where I feel that we could have done with one quality player just to give us that bit of edge. We had Dean Walling but I didn't think that he would be good enough for the Second. We did look at Jason Rockett but the deal never developed despite him being spotted in Carlisle with a group of players and wanting to come. So we were stuck with Deano, who was excellent in the air but not so good with his feet.

The season began with hope as we drew with Southend away from home. Two wins against Chester saw us progress into the second round of the Coca-Cola Cup. However our league form was not as good, losing four on the trot as Merv juggled the team to accommodate new players and suspensions. September saw our first league win against fellow strugglers Wigan, with Darren Holloway, on loan from Sunderland, making an impressive debut. To the average fan, things were looking good; okay, we hadn't had the best of starts but given time we would get things right - or so we thought. After another defeat, against Blackpool, the chairman took the decision to sack Mervyn Day along with physio and coach Peter Hampton, and install himself in the boss' chair.

Michael Knighton had taken the final piece out of a once great coaching team. In the last two years we'd seen Mick Wadsworth leave due to lack of cash for players and Joe Joyce depart in a very secretive manner due to disagreements over a new contract. So at last he'd demolished the coaching team which had helped turn our fortunes around in the last year. But surely he would have a brand new coaching team to replace the former staff? The word on the street was of former hero Peter Beardsley and Nigel Clough getting their introduction into management. However, the word on the street never reached Knighton - he had his own team lined up. There were to be no big names in his revamped formation as in came Sooty and Sweep (renamed David Wilkes and John Halpin) to sit on his hand and do whatever he wanted. The first string he pulled saw Dean Walling banished to the black hole - more commonly known as Lincoln - for £75,000. He was the first in a long line of players to come and go before the end of the season.

The sale of Deano also saw us revert to a 4-3-3 formation. The first test of the change in management and playing style was at Wycombe, where we won 4-1 with another outstanding display from up-and-coming star Matt Jansen. Next up was a bit of relief from the gruelling league fixtures and a trip to White Hart Lane for the Coca-Cola Cup. It was great to get the chance to play against a team like Spurs, and even better when we went in at the break 2-1 up after two goals in five minutes. However, as the game progressed, the difference in class told and we were beaten 3-2 and knocked out 5-2 on aggregate. But a great moment to savour in a bad season nevertheless.

After 11 games we were at last to see Ian Stevens' face in the side as he came on as sub against Plymouth. Unfortunately, he couldn't stop us throwing away a two-goal lead and we ended up with just a point. Stevo's reappearance prompted the sale of Lee Peacock to Mansfield for £150,000, and the Gillingham game signalled the end of Darren Holloway's loan, despite claims that Knighton offered Sunderland £400,000 to keep him after a brilliant spell with us. His return eastwards coincided with a six game losing run, rounded off with a 4-3 beating at York despite being 3-1 up with six minutes left!

Before the Preston game Knighton boasted of his capture of overseas star Laurent Croci, one of six French triallists. Unfortunately, Cumbria obviously didn't agree with him and he left after one game, most likely with more money than he arrived with. The game saw what must have been one of the season's most controversial goals; it's too hard to explain, but suffice it to say that it was later showcased at a referees' conference and they all voted that it should have been disallowed.

Further league woes and FA Cup defeat at the hands of Wigan, meant it was time for some transfer activity - well, we had gone five games without selling or loaning anyone! So after losing to Chesterfield two of our more experienced players headed for the exit, including Archdeacon who'd been Player of the Year and top scorer just months earlier. It had now become apparent that Knighton was asset-stripping the club and taking the first offers to come along. I fully back the selling of players, but only if they're replaced by permanent signings. In our case though, it was another loanee who arrived in the shape of Burnley's Jamie Hoyland and he was followed days later by free transfer Graham Anthony. And the activity didn't stop there. Tommy Harrison left, Andy Couzens was despatched to warm the bench and Nick Wright arrived on loan from Derby. The Rams on the other hand were busy chasing our three young stars Matt Jansen, Rory Delap and Paul Boetien.

At this rate it was strange to see the same eleven play two matches in a row. I mean, where's the surprise that we were struggling at the bottom of the league? We had a revolving door team selection policy, coaching staff patently not up to the job and Michael Knighton too proud to go back on his decision to install himself as manager.

Still, at least the New Year ushered in some better football. Ronnie Wallwork, bought in from Man U, gave the defence a bit of extra class, the starting line-up settled down a bit and we hauled ourselves off the bottom of Division Two. But you guessed it, the temptation to cash in on players was too much for Knighton, and Rory Delap fell to Derby's advances for around a million quid while Matt Jansen rebuffed Old Trafford for Selhurst Park in a deal that at the time was worth two million. Mere peanuts now, with figures of four and a half million now being bandied about for the ex-Brunton ace.

So, deprived of two Premiership quality players and also having to absorb the loss of the classy Ronnie Wallwork, replaced by jailbird Richard Liburd, the pack-shuffling started again. Problem was, we had few good cards left and it was no surprise when we slipped back into the drop zone.

About this time Knighton decided to leave the country and head for the Isle of Mann to live in his tax exile status - and far away from the growing concerns of the fans at the club. With ten games left we reckoned that safety required maximum points from at least five. Ha, despite two defensive signings on transfer deadline in the forms of John Foster from Man City and David Hughes from Villa, the relegation run-in was more like a decrepit crawl as we managed to win just one more game. With relegation duly achieved, the last home game witnessed a couple of thousand fans vent their fury at an *empty* directors box.

That the season ended as it did was as inevitable as it was avoidable. Look at the key events: Carlisle United lost a brilliant manager, replaced by an asset-stripping chairman who failed to provide the necessary financial clout to keep us up. We used 34 different players: seven free transfers, 11 from home grown talent, two who played a single game, six that cost money with the rest being non-contracted staff. At the time of writing we've lost Allan Smart and Nick Wright to Watford for around £175,000. Rumours persist about four other departures and we now have 15 players on the books from last season.

I can't foresee anything but despair and struggle in Division Three, what with a very basic squad and a bad coaching team. But loyal or just daft, I'll be back next year!

Source: The Latic Fanatic

THE LATIC FANATIC

Wigan Athletic

In years to come, people may look back on the '97-98 season, see a final league position of tenth, and be comforted in the knowledge that everything went according to plan: mid-table consolidation being achieved with the play-offs narrowly missed by a few points. In reality it was anything but. For Deirdre Raschid wasn't the only one to get out of jail in the last 12 months. The fact remains that if it wasn't for a rousing finale in the final few weeks which earned Deehan the Manager of the Month award, things could have been a great deal worse.

The season was probably best summed up by a manic few days in April.

The game at home to Bristol Rovers in December had seen four players sent off, and the supporters who travelled down to the West Country for the return fixture at the Memorial Ground where about to witness something equally weird which would turn their Good Friday into a bloody awful one. In his wisdom, Deehan decided to rest several key players (he had spoken about using a squad system similar to Ruud Gullit's at Chelsea earlier on in the season. Mmmmm...). Rovers promptly rubbed their hands with glee and stuffed us 5-0. In the end we were lucky to get nil. An embarrassed chairman later apologised to the fans who'd made the arduous trek, but the manager remained unrepentant. In fact the following Monday, when the same key players helped stuff a piss-poor Burnley side by a similar scoreline at Springfield Park, he felt his decision had been vindicated. Quite how you can feel vindicated for making a tactical blunder that cost your side a 5-0 defeat is fairly bizarre, but then so is John Deehan.

For our one big game of the season, at Blackburn in the FA Cup third round, he managed to astound 5,500 travelling fans by playing Smeets and Lee out of position, dropping our leading goalscorer David Lowe and picking Steve Morgan (the slowest player in the squad) to mark Stuart Ripley. After Blackburn scored their fourth, it began to dawn on him that his tactical masterplan was in fact complete and utter bollocks. Lee and Smeets reverted back to their normal positions, Lowe was brought on, and we finished the match losing 4-2, playing our best football after the changes had been made.

However, don't be misled by this somewhat cynical introduction; there have also been high points to the season. The performances of Carl Bradshaw, recruited following his release from jail in Norwich after he'd developed a distinct fondness for a taxi driver's finger, was one. Roy Carroll, who is destined for far greater things, whether it be at Wigan or elsewhere, was another. And David Lowe's never-say-die attitude, even though he had a half-time bust-up with Deehan at Bristol City, helped him become the club's record goalscorer in the league and Player of the Year.

An opening day 5-2 demolition of Wycombe Wanderers gave us real reason to be optimistic. Brendan O'Connell created club history by becoming the first Latics player to score a hat-trick on his debut, while there were other impressive debuts by Scott Green and David Lee, both recruited from Bolton for £550,000 in total. Unfortunately the trio couldn't maintain that same sparkling form. O'Connell missed more than half the campaign after being diagnosed with a blood disorder. Lee was the perfect model of inconsistency, being able to turn the match in your favour or just not wanting to know. And Green was one of our better performers, until his form nosedived spectacularly following a training ground bust-up with Deehan in the latter stages of the season. Performing in more positions than the Karma Sutra couldn't have helped matters either.

Players who had been the heroes of the Championship-winning side also found life tougher in the Second Division. Graeme Jones began the campaign struggling with injuries and, even when he came back into the team, never looked like repeating the scoring marvels that was one of the main highlights of such a successful previous season. Whether he was hindered by a lack of fitness or ability at this level remains to be seen. Roberto Martinez, the last of the Three Amigos, also had a disappointing time. The tricky and creative play that has become his trait in English football was seldom seen in a 12-month period when he's been up against, and overshadowed by, more skilful and faster players. Although you could hardly describe last season as the best football of Kevin Sharp's Latics career, a bust-up with Deehan (get a feeling of déjà vu?) resulted in him joining the transfer list. This was a bit of a joke considering that our other left-sided defensive players at the time were Steve Morgan, who would seriously need to break sweat to beat a tortoise over 100 metres, and Gavin Johnson, seen more times in town centre pubs than at the training ground. At present, Sharp's Wigan future is in doubt, while Morgan and Johnson have both been released. Wigan nightclub owners are reported to be heartbroken. To compensate for the unsettled left-sided defensive position, Deehan managed to sign ex-Man Utd and Latics old boy Neil Whitworth till the end of the season. Whitworth was given a grand total of 54 minutes football from the final 12 matches to prove his worth, before being released with a 'he's not what we're looking for' statement, despite being heralded as a great signing upon his arrival. Add to this the signing of midfielder Neil Mustoe, again from Man Utd, who made less appearances than Lord Lucan, despite the midfield being continually overrun, and you may begin to understand why so many Latics fans wouldn't be sorry to see the back of Deehan.

Fortunately, things have improved on the ground-move front. You may remember in *SOTF3* how the situation had already changed at least three or four times. Well now, as we predicted, we are going to be sharing a 25,000 all-seater stadium with the Warriors rugby club. By all accounts they were sinking faster than the Titanic (if only...) weighed down by so much financial crap. Then their chairman was ousted and they were bailed out by a certain Mr Whelan. Orrell RUFC will still use the ground but only for big games, while the reserves will be using a pitch laid in the middle of a nearby new athletics stadium. This all sounds hunky-dory, but no-one, as yet, has explained when any repair or re-turfing work is going to be carried out on a pitch that will be used all year round. Another disturbing thought concerns rumours that one of the stands will be named after a famous rugby player. The stadium isn't even built yet and already the rugby mob is acting like German holidaymakers.

Whether John Deehan will still be at Latics when the new stadium has been built remains to be seen. Already, Dave Whelan has issued an ultimatum that if we aren't in the top seven at Christmas, Deehan won't be here to see in the New Year. All contract and transfer dealings have been taken away from him for the coming season, so he can concentrate on coaching, while rumours of a management partnership with Steve Bruce are rife. Roll on August!

LEYTON ORIENTEAR

Leyton Orient

There comes a time when even the most die-hard supporter questions their reasons for devoting time and money to what's more often that not a lost cause. Now I'm not putting the O's in that category, but after missing out on promotion yet again, my faith is being sorely tested.

Looking back at last season I still cannot believe Orient missed out. The omens were favourable at the beginning as manager Tommy Taylor brought in a wealth of experienced defenders to bolster the sieve otherwise known as the Orient back four. Dean Smith, Simon Clark and Stuart Hicks were recruited for the sole purpose of inflicting pain and misery on the

division's unsuspecting forwards. The big question was: could we create - and finish - enough chances to produce a side with true promotion credentials?

The early part of the campaign didn't reveal much in the way of answers. Despite looking tight at the back, the mighty reds struggled to put together any sort of positive attacking game. We also noticed that a touch of 'hoof-ball' had been instated and we lost count of the number of times Stuart Hicks launched the ball towards the corner flag for our minuscule attack to chase. Yet there were times when we played some excellent football on the ground and via the wings. The epic 4-4 draw at Premiership Bolton Wanderers in the League Cup (leaky stadium roof *et al*) was a prime example of what the team could produce.

Despite that encouraging performance, our league form was pretty indifferent (the only highlight being a comical confrontation between the club's chief executive and a drum-wielding supporter during a midweek game against Scarborough). And by the time the FA Cup tie at Hendon came around, many of us were contemplating another first round disaster in the club's recent history. Sure enough, the resident pessimists at Orient were not disappointed as we fought out a 2-2 draw in the driving rain. The match had everything, including a punch-up between three relics from the seventies (probably Chelsea hoolies) and some of the more dubious sections of the Orient support. What made this incident even more laughable was that after getting a real pasting the three 'seventies men' protested their innocence vociferously to the stewards as they were escorted from the ground. So the stage was set for the replay which will go down as one of the - if not *the* - worst nights in the club's 117-year history. The records will show that Hendon won the tie 1-0, scoring from the one clear chance they created. As for Orient, despite making a couple of good openings early on, we fell away badly and ended up sending aimless punts up field in a vain effort to save the game. Tommy Taylor's whole approach, and not just the result, was what angered many supporters. When you have talented players at the club and fail to play to their strengths, questions have to be asked. The cries of "Taylor out" and "Sack the board" told their own sorry tale on the night. Such a state of affairs was reflected in the *Orientear*. A scathing editorial calling for a return to being entertained on a Saturday (allied to an article ridiculing the club's inability to replace the car park with a new stand) brought about an angry response from Barry Hearn on 'clubcall'. The bottom line was that despite all the hype since Hearn's take-over at the club, Orient had achieved zilch and were producing some of the worst football in living memory.

However, that terrible defeat proved to be the campaign's turning point. From then on Orient produced a pleasing style of play that had a nice combination of short passing through the midfield allied to the use of wingmen such as Baker and Harris. Results started to reflect this and the 8-0 destruction of pitiful Doncaster Rovers gave us hope for the second half of the season. Even so, some people still complained that we should have run in a dozen against the poor sods. Living proof if needed that O's fans want the moon on a stick.

With Orient having to play catch-up in an effort to clinch a play-off berth, every game became a six-pointer, Brighton were beaten (yet again) 3-1 in a pulsating encounter as the behaviour of a tiny selection of their support brought back memories of the previous season's shenanigans at the Goldstone. The following Saturday's 2-0 win at Rochdale gave us real hope that an unlikely promotion was still within our grasp. Suddenly news broke that the club had some discrepancies with its suspensions and that a points deduction was possible. At the club AGM, Barry Hearn was pretty sure that the worst scenario would be a fine and a warning, and there was no need to choke on our half time burgers (that's if the E-Coli hadn't killed you first). Nevertheless, this problem just would not go away. Exeter City, Peterborough, Lincoln and Rotherham all protested to the league and wanted to claim points off Orient, although the case had been heard at the FA and a fine of £20,000 - £12,000 suspended - imposed. Meanwhile Orient remained in the promotion hunt as our home form held up well. Come late March we took on Notts County at Meadow Lane in what turned out to be an epic encounter. It will live long in the memory as one of the best performances away from home that ended in defeat. Our defence was so solid, one would have thought it had been given a collective dose of Viagra, but even so a soft goal from the edge of our area heralded the O's downfall. Despite plenty of possession we came up short and perhaps that game more than any summed up our season. When it came to the crunch Orient were lacking that certain something required for success. As for County, they became the first team to clinch promotion in March since the creation of the division. Their 15 wins in 17 games was the kind of consistency we should be aiming for next season.

As Easter approached, the situation at the top of the table became unbelievably tight. As many as ten teams were fighting it out for automatic promotion and play-off places, and for once we were one of them. The crunch game at Barnet produced a fantastic victory (and the traditional punch-up with obligatory red card) after we'd been a goal down and sparked off some wild celebrations. Not least in the social club afterwards with both players and supporters holding a 'love-in' akin to a Roman orgy. What a contrast then two days later as we crashed to a 2-3 home defeat against Shrewsbury having held a 2-0 lead against ten men. If a whole season turned on one incident, the miss by Carl Griffiths, when a simple pass square would have meant a certain goal to put us 3-0 up was it! To say that the stuffing had been knocked out of the club's support is akin to implying that WW2 was just a little dispute between neighbours. Just to top that off, four days later the League docked us three points in relation to fielding suspended players and killed our promotion charge stone dead. With the O's crashing to defeat at Hull the following day, the possible promotion dream had crumbled. From now on we were counting the days to the season's end. To the team's credit the high standard of performance and at times entertainment was maintained right to the end. The 2-1 victory over Torquay was especially surprising given Orient's reputation of gifting promotion-chasing clubs easy points when they most needed them.

So we consign the '97-98 season to history, but for once Orient supporters have reason to be a little optimistic. At long last we have a team that looks like it can play a bit and won't collapse as soon as the words 'away game' are mentioned. We also have the mouth-watering prospect of two derby games with our old mates from Brentford with whom we look forward to renewing hostilities; I can hear the sound of studs being sharpened for that encounter already. Off the park, the club's rebuilding plan is in the hands of the lottery people and it will be touch and go whether Orient grab the three million quid they're asking for. Whether the decision to kick the old scheme piloted by one of the club's directors will help clinch the deal, only time will tell. My guess is that the outcome will go a long way to revealing Barry Hearn's true level of commitment to the club - and the local council's for that matter - and whether he really is involved at Orient chiefly in a property developing capacity. Watch this space.

LOADSAMONEY

Blackburn Rovers

Too Good To 'B' Forgotten

At the end of the '97-98 season every football fan looked towards the World Cup Finals in France... Well... *Almost* everyone. Not many Rovers fans will be cheering on England, what with the treatment handed out by Glenn Hoddle to Chris Sutton. Bring back Graham Taylor!

Our hatred of Hoddle stemmed from his insistence in preferring Les 'if you can play for England so can I' Ferdinand instead of Sutty, who at the time of selection was the country's top goalscorer. He also favoured Dion Dublin, saying that the Coventry talisman could play at centre half in an emergency. So could Sutton.

Everyone knows that Sutty refused to play for England B. But rather than do what hundreds have done in the past and call the coach professing injury, Sutton was honest: "I've nothing to prove to the England manager." Hoddle's mouthpiece Shearer had his say; "It's Sutton's loss, not England's." No other England player commented on the situation, but Colin Hendry was heard to enquire whether Sutty had a Scottish grandparent! Good judge, Colin.

Back to football and a trophy was captured during Roy Hodgson's first week by winning the CIS Trophy against the might of Aberdeen: "Roy Hodgson's Blue 'N' White Army."

The appearance of money promised to the boss had enabled him to strengthen his squad with Henchoz, Dahlin, Andersson, Filan and Valery, but out went Berg and Le Saux. Others left Ewood during the season to take Rovers' profit on transfer dealings to around the £18 million mark since winning the Premiership. Whatever happened to Moneybags Rovers?

Our opening game went well a 1-0 win over Derby and things improved the following Wednesday with a 4-0 win against Aston Villa at Villa Park - Chris Sutton scoring an unbelievable hat-trick. But then seeing was believing as the live *Monday Night Football* produced a thumping Rovers 7 Sheffield Wednesday 2 scoreline. The same team that had struggled the previous season to score goals had now bagged 13 in four games, with Stuart Ripley recapturing the form that got him his only England cap. The only downer to the win was the injury to Rovers' Aussie international goalkeeper John Filan, who was stretched off with a badly broken arm. This meant an early recall for the also recuperating Tim Flowers. To avert a 'keeper crisis we signed Alan Fettis from Nottingham Forest as Tim's number two.

Roy picked up his Manager of the Month award for August in front of the returning *Sky* cameras and we all drew a collective breath, anticipating the dreaded 'MOTM' jinx to strike. Tradition didn't disappoint as Rod Wallace and Jimmy Floyd Hasslebaink ripped our defence apart. The Leeds game also gave Rovers fans the chance to see what a donkey Martin Dahlin was; he goes down better than Devine Brown in the box.

Rovers' poor run in cup competitions continued but at least John McGrath of *Red Rose Radio* brought a smile to our faces when commentating on the Chelsea game. Before getting to the penalty shoot-out, Billy McKinlay had scored a goal in open that was described thus: "If the goal had been scored by one of the Italians they would have been having orgasms in the press box." Pass the Kleenex.

Rovers, up in the top three after 14 games, then entertained Everton. The blue half of Merseyside were severely depleted by injuries and had to play an injured Neville Southall in goal. And despite ending up on the losing side, Big Nev was outstanding on his *one* leg. He really did deserve better that day. But even a fully fit Southall would have struggled to nullify our wonder boy Damien Duff. He got his first Premiership goal and the rave reviews his performance deserved.

Next up was the 'Title Decider'; well that's what the press labelled the meeting with Man Utd. Unfortunately Hodgson made a tactical error by playing Chris Sutton alone up front and packing the midfield. We lost 4-0 and Sutton took the early bath.

With Christmas coming up the trip to Highbury gave the Arsenal defence the chance of handing out some early presents. Tim Sherwood was so busy accepting one that he missed two others. Despite his squandered hat-trick opportunity the Rovers still ran out deserved 3-1 winners. This game proved a turning point for Ian Wright and both teams. The Arsenal striker got himself into trouble with the Old Bill, this time for shouting obscenities at the home fans from a dressing room window. Meanwhile his teammates were just about to embark on a run that would take them all the way to the double. For Rovers the season was about to turn sour. Post Highbury we struggled to win two games on the bounce. We won only six of our last 20 games, collecting a measly 22 points from a possible 60 along the way. What went wrong?

Well, we gave out some belated Christmas presents of our own. On Boxing Day Tim Flowers produced his own contender for 'What happened next?' He allowed a harmless looking ball to bounce over him and trickle agonisingly slowly over the line for the Crystal Palace equaliser. The subsequently doomed South London outfit left with a draw but deserved three points. Hodgson was quick to defend his goalkeeper, blaming the groundsman instead: "The ball hit a divot and bounced over the England 'keeper." Only last season Steve Patrick won the Groundsman of the Year award. A touch of the Alex Fergusons or what?

Then Gally hit a hat-trick against Aston Villa in a 5-0 hammering of the Clarets, and chants of "Are you Burnley in disguise?" echoed around Ewood. The Villa fans turned against their own player Spitalotovich, who cleared his throat and sent its contents towards the travelling supporters sat behind the goal. The chant of "You're not fit to wear the shirt" was a delivered back to the gobbing Serb with equal venom.

Two 3-0 defeats followed, the most embarrassing being at home against Tottenham. It was a clash between a has-been number nine, Les Ferdinand, and as far as Glenn Hoddle's concerned, a never will-be number nine, Chris Sutton. The chance to make meaningful comparisons never arose, though, as Big Les was stretchered off after five minutes.

Then Sutton banged in his second hat-trick of the season in a 5-3 win over Leicester City, and this brought him the Carling Player of the Month award for February. Ironically, Glenn Hoddle was one of the panellists. Did he vote for Sutty?

Rovers' last chance of any silverware was in the FA Cup. A 2-2 away draw at West Ham seemed unlikely after Kevin Gallacher was sent off after 20 mins following some argy-bargy with Eyal Berkovic. But getting a draw at Upton Park convinced many of us that the replay at Ewood would be a formality. Sadly, someone forgot to inform West Ham who scraped home in the penalty shoot-out 5-4.

Come March and April, our European spot was looking more than a little dodgy after heavy defeats against Leeds, Man Utd and Arsenal. But wins against Chelsea and Alan Shearer - sorry - Newcastle lifted us to that all-important sixth spot. Dwelling on Shearer's Ewood return for a moment - it was no different to last time with the chants of "Judas" and "there's only one greedy Bastard" echoing around Ewood. And he didn't get a kick all afternoon. Maybe he *did* miss Neil Lennon's face after all!

At season's end rumours were rife around Blackburn that Roy Hodgson would be off to manage Monaco. I hope not; with the addition of three quality players we might be challenging Arsenal and Man U for that top spot next year. And there's always Europe to look forward to. Let's face it, it can't be as bad as last time...

MAD AS A HATTER

Luton Town

For this writer, the '97-98 season marked the passing of 30 years supporting Luton Town. Supporting them through thick and thin, with plenty of thin in recent years. Of that 30, a total of 11 were spent in the old First Division, and all but five of the remainder in the new First Division. This should go some way to explaining why we tend to think that we shouldn't be floundering at the wrong end of the current version of Division Two.

Football seasons tend to be rated as good (promotion), average (play-offs) or bad (anywhere else). As bad seasons go, '97-98 was bloody awful for Luton Town fans. We'd started out as favourites for promotion, after blowing out in the

play-offs a few months earlier, Crewe proving themselves more resilient than the Hatters. We had basically the same squad with Simon Davies, a £200,000 capture from Manchester United, replacing the departed Ceri Hughes. So, on a sunny day in August, we found ourselves at the seaside (Blackpool) falling to a ninth minute goal in blistering heat. The weather was scant consolation. The first home match was televised, but beating Southend was not the glorious victory we thought at the time. That they failed to get a single shot on target against our crocked 'keeper in the entire second half was surely a sign of things to come for them - as was the injury for us. At the time we achieved our highest league position of the season, twelfth.

By the end of the month we were in the same position and hadn't lost another game. We consoled ourselves with the knowledge that the previous campaign had suffered a slow start as well. However, things were about to take a turn for the worse. We not only lost two of the next three matches, but lost most of the first team squad with injuries as well. We had two loan players at full back, our top scorer was missing and we had a 40-year old on the bench. Andy Dibble, goalkeeping hero of our 1988 Littlewoods Cup victory at Wembley, when he saved Nigel Winterburn's penalty, was brought in on a short-term contract. We held West Brom to a draw in the Coca-Cola Cup, but four days later Wrexham arrived, having never won at Kenilworth Road. Dibble was truly awful, and the Welsh side probably couldn't believe their luck when, with the scores level, Lennie Lawrence substituted a 26-year old with 40-year old Trevor Peake. It was all over in minutes. Wrexham won 5-2, Peake went into the record books as the Town's oldest ever player and promptly retired. Dibble had one more match, at West Brom, where he lived up to his 'nine in a row' tattoo by letting in another four goals.

The following match saw a 3-0 defeat at Ashton Gate and the team given a standing ovation at the end of the game. Their inexperience (most of us hadn't even heard of the third substitute, one Colin Omogbehin) was such that they had been expected to lose much more heavily! As you will understand, this was not the ideal build up to the big match, the home local derby against Watford. By 3.30pm on October 4th, we were 4-0 down and the natives were somewhat restless. At 5pm we were in 23rd position. It was at about this stage that Lennie Lawrence started getting a bit of stick. Well OK, a *lot* of stick. Injuries aside, the team looked unmotivated, and the management seemed incapable of shaping events, at least in a positive direction.

Inevitably, three of the next five games were won and none lost as we shot up to the dizzy heights of 18th. Also, the next four matches were all at home. The revival was nipped in the bud as we contrived to lose all four, including being dumped out of the FA Cup at the first round stage for the first time in over 60 years, and we were back in 23rd place. It was two months since we had spent £400,000 buying Phil Gray, one time top scorer at Luton, from the Dutch club Fortuna (appropriately) Sittard. But he had also joined the injured list, although nobody was that bothered, as most had decided that he was going to be no help in avoiding relegation. Simon Davies was a regular - in the reserve team - and Paul Showler was making his way through the Footballers' Book of Injuries, moving from Hamstring to Hernia via Ingrowing Toenail! But we'd got Chris Allen in on loan from Forest so things were bound to improve. They did, as we only failed to score in three of his 14 games. All we needed now was a defence that could stop the opposition getting more than we did. Two matches over Christmas encapsulated this problem. In losing 4-2 at home to Bristol Rovers, the defence were described as incompetent, gutless, clueless and unprofessional, but the Rovers fans chanted "We love you Luton." On Boxing Day, Northhampton 'One Goal' Town arrived, and fortunately failed to recover from the shock of the generous and comical own goal we provided for their second. As a result we managed to salvage a draw with a storming second half performance. Two days later we managed a bizarre win at Millwall with two goals in the last minute.

We won the next two as well, and then lost four on the trot to ensure another mini-revival went down the pan. These included a 2-1 defeat at Oldham, where the home side scored the same goal twice, and a 4-1 home débâcle against Fulharrods, who were made to look much better than they really were. What ideal preparation for the local derby. Scheduled for February 14th, we had an idea of what the headlines might be the following day (rearrange the words Day, Massacre and Valentine's), but as usual, the Town players hadn't read the script. There was a five-figure crowd, the largest to see the Town all season, and the players seemed to respond with a spirited display. After going behind, Marvin Johnson somehow managed to divert the ball into the net with his knee, securing his place in our Hall of Fame, and salvaging some pride for us. What we didn't know at the time was that this was to be top scorer Tony Thorpe's final appearance in a Town shirt. Allegedly injured for the next couple of matches, we began to smell a rat, and then it was announced that he was off - to Fulharrods. The fans' reaction was predictable, with our top scorer being sold we stared into the abyss of relegation.

All hope of salvation was immediately lost, especially as Phil Gray re-appeared and showed his incompetence as a replacement. For the next few weeks the goals dried up, and we dipped back down to 23rd spot. On transfer deadline day, we signed a goalkeeper. Wow! That was going to help. But then, at the death, we also got a striker on loan. A youngster who'd been out of action most of the season with injury; this was hardly going to inspire confidence. Not only that, but having had Chris Allen on loan, and found out that the original target for a loan this time was Bradley Allen, the one we actually signed was Rory Allen. We wondered how many pages there were in Lennie Lawrence's Book of Players. Rory made his debut at Walsall, scored one and laid on another of our three goals. Of course, we all know about players making an immediate impact, and fading rapidly after that, but this boy was something special.

In the first match of April we were awarded our first penalty of the season, and went on to beat nine man York. Then came a rare win at Grimsby where Allen got the goal. He went on to score in each of the next three matches as we headed towards safety. This was finally secured at Brentford with a 2-2 draw. In the final game, one of the biggest home crowds of the season turned up to pay homage to the youngster who had almost single-handedly saved us from the bottom division. Carlisle failed to read the script on this occasion, and almost snatched a point, but were denied with a goal in the 90th minute, by Allen of course. The cheers could be heard for miles.

We knew that signing Allen permanently was unlikely, but he had been our best loan signing for many years, contributing six vital goals in eight games. He'd saved our season, not just with his goals but also with his whole-hearted effort and the way his play brought others into the game.

The club now has just two coaching staff, manager Lennie Lawrence and youth team coach John Moore. Wayne Turner had been sacked at Christmas and Trevor Peake had gone to Coventry. Many of us would have liked to have seen the back of Lawrence as well, but it looks like we're stuck with him for another year, although he'll have to recruit some assistance. It is a tribute to Moore, and the work he puts in, that his youth team won the South East Counties League Division Two, and the League Cup with an 8-3 aggregate win against SECL Division One Champions West Ham.

Nonetheless, this was a season that was marked by injuries, to such an extent that only five players made more than 30 appearances, only two made more than 40, whilst 35 players were used. With that number of players available, no club in the Second Division should even have to give a second thought to relegation, and we'll be looking for a big improvement next season. The one good thing to emerge was the progress of some of the younger players, which at least provides a bit of optimism for the future. And, inevitably for a club like Luton Town, the promise of a fat transfer fee coming in at some stage.

As an aside to all the action on the pitch, there has been inaction off it. Not, this time, in the boardroom where precious little happens at the best of times, but in the halls of power. In the latter stages of the '94-95 season, a planning application for a new stadium was submitted to the local council, who referred it to the Department of the Environment. A year later (summer '96) a public inquiry was held, and since then nothing has been heard. Whether no news is good news or not, we really don't know, but the waiting is getting to all of us. Perhaps the DOE, Transport, the Regions or one of the many other arms of Government have lost the application. Or, there again, perhaps they've lost the plot. Over to you, John Prescott...

MAN UNITED ARE ON THE TELLY AGAIN

Norwich City

Mike Walker's departure now seems a distant memory. With the Canaries' new continental style team of Bruce Rioch and Bryan Hamilton newly installed, the '97-98 season will be an intriguing one for City fans after the threat of relegation last year.

A disastrous sequence of results during the first few months of 1998 saw the Canaries go 14 games without a win, a run which included a demoralising 5-0 thrashing by arch rivals, Ip*****. Therefore the decision of the club's major shareholders, Delia Smith and her husband Michael Wynn-Jones, to controversially end Walker's second spell as Canary boss by 'mutual consent' (a nicer

way of saying 'you're sacked Mike') was probably a good move. Ironically, Walker's departure came on the back of two impressive 5-0 home victories against Huddersfield and Swindon.

Many City fans that demanded Walker's reinstatement as manager after Robert Chase's demise wanted him out in the end. Walker's exit seemed insensitive at the time, considering that he'd tragically lost his wife Jackie through cancer midway through the season. However football can be a cruel sport, and the Wynn-Jones' have shown assertiveness by doing what they thought was best for Norwich City, not Mike.

Walker made a habit of blaming poor results on City's crippling injury crisis (other clubs have coped in similar situations) and he would regularly claim that "if it wasn't for all the injuries we'd be in the top eight" (this got a bit boring after the fiftieth time). City's coaching method - or lack of it - was regularly criticised, and at times it was frustrating watching a team with no shape, getting turned over easily by the likes of Wolves (0-5), Ip***** (0-5) and Grimsby (0-3). The man we used to call 'Saint Mike' seemed to have lost the plot. Players regularly appeared out of position and poor signings were made, especially striker Iwan Roberts (seven goals at £128,571.42p a time) and Spanish defender Victor Segura. Bruce Rioch is apparently a disciplinarian, so hopefully the likes of Keith O'Neill will be given a long overdue kick up the backside.

Eire international O'Neill spent most of '97-98 on the treatment table and when he did play he was rubbish anyway. Newcastle allegedly bid £3.5 million for this Irish tart at the beginning of the season. Walker should have bitten their hand off!

Another Irishman Bryan Hamilton has joined us as director of coaching, from Ip***** of all places. It's claimed that Hamilton, and not Burley, was the major influence behind the scum's admittedly attractive football last season. Now he's with us, his old club's fate will hopefully be more unpleasant than Tony Mowbray's backside, which must be pretty horrific judging by his face.

The progress of teenager Craig Bellamy was one of the few plus points. The cocky 18 year old cheekily described himself as 'the new Juninho' in a magazine interview, and he really is bloody good, even though he looks like he's just come out of Middle School. Already a full Welsh international, Bellamy's 13 league goals probably kept us up in the end and he was a deserved Player of the Season.

The climax to a poor season.

Walker had left by mutual consent the previous Thursday. Bad signings, inconsistent performances and tactical naïvety had cost our greatest ever manager his job.

The trip to relegated Reading on the final Sunday of the season proved to be a subdued affair. The day began well; the coach organised by the landlord at my local left at 8am. The bar opened at 7am so we had an opportunity to get into the spirit of a football away-day, and to allay the effects of the previous night's drinking, by sinking a few lagers and double brandies. In between the anti-Ipswich chants the general murmured concerns were pertaining to whether anyone knew of a decent pub in Reading, rather than the turmoil of the previous three days.

I personally believe that the City board made a brave, calculated decision in changing the manager. Under the old regime, a change would only have occurred if City really were in dire straits. Since the team appeared to be going nowhere fast, a change could only be a good thing, although many City fans would disagree with me on this point.

There were so many weaknesses in the side this season that we were lucky to finish above the relegation zone. The defence looked fragile in every single game, even against poor opposition, and Marshall in goal made far too many mistakes. There was a desperate lack of quality in midfield, which was even more evident after the signing of Peter Grant. And up front Roberts and Co. never looked dangerous, a fact reflected by the strikers' goal tallies, and on top of all this was the staggering injury crisis (caused by insufficient fitness and match preparation - stand up John Faulkner).

The reasons for staying up were the outstanding crop of 18-year-olds that came through the ranks, and Neal Fenn, who made a vital contribution to the team at a vital time.

In the end, 15th was a respectable (considering injuries) but flattering position for a team who were very ordinary throughout. As we returned home from the final game (where we beat Reading 1-0 thanks to an excellent strike from Craig Bellamy) we were happy, safe in the knowledge that Man City had been relegated, Man U hadn't won the title and that Ipswich never had a cat in hell's chance of gaining promotion.

Top Ten of '97-98

1. *Nothing lasts forever* by Echo and the Bunnymen.
Mike Walker's second spell as Norwich boss ended in tears. He once led us to European glory against Bayern Munich and Inter Milan, but nearly got us relegated to Division Two this time round.

2. *Stop me if you think you've heard this one before* by the Smiths.
Another poor Norwich performance meant another tired old excuse by Walker e.g. "We had all our best players out injured," "we were playing against 12 men" and so on.

3. *Big Mistake* by Natalie Imbruglia.
The signing of so called striker Iwan Roberts was a disaster. He scored just five goals in the league and two against Barnet in the Coke Cup.

4. *Can't see me* by Ian Brown.
Keith O'Neill's hardly played and when he did you wouldn't have known anyway.

5. *Yesterday's men* by Madness.
Walker gave Carrow Road legends Gunn, Fleck and Polston the push.

6. *Who do you think you are?* by the Spice Girls.
The Muppet who spent almost the entire second half of the 3-2 home defeat by Bradford chatting on his mobile in the snakepit. He wasn't remotely interested in the fact that his team (?) was facing a relegation battle, he just wanted to show off. Sadly these people are a growing breed at football grounds across Britain.

7. *Money's too tight to mention* by Simply Red.
With the club debt at £7m, Walker had to sell before he could buy. So exit left midfielder Andy Johnson to Nottingham Forest for £2.2m, with half of the fee being used to buy Iwan 'All I want for Christmas is my two front teeth' Roberts. A shrewd bit of business by Walker? Nah!

8. *The Young Ones* by Cliff Richard.
The performances of teenagers like Bellamy, Llewellyn, Forbes and Coote were highly impressive considering the position we were in. The future looks bright for Norwich City, as long as we don't sell all these youngsters!

9. *The End of the World* by REM.
That's what it felt like after the scum had humiliated us 5-0.

10. *Rubbish* by Carter the Unstoppable Sex Machine.
I think this just about sums up our season!

MANY MILES FROM HOME

Blackburn Rovers

To use a racing analogy that a certain dishonorary Doctor of Psychology at Old Nafford is fond of repeating, Blackburn Rovers started the season like Red Rum and ended it like Devon Loch. Unlike Devon Loch, however, at least Rovers staggered past the winning post and into a UEFA Cup place that at one stage would have been the very least we could have hoped for.

With new boss Roy Hodgson proclaiming at the off that a European place was the season's target, we flew out of the traps. We rattled off four wins and one draw out of the first five matches, notching 15 goals in the process, including four at Villa and putting seven past a hapless Sheffield

Wednesday in Ewood Park's best match of the season. Unfortunately, the first blips appeared on our screen around this time. First, stand-in 'keeper John Filan's excellent run of performances came to a sickening halt after he broke his arm in two places against Wednesday, then a 3-4 reverse at home to Leeds in a game of pantomime proportions brought us back down to earth. The scoring rate slowed down somewhat after that, but with Gallacher and Sutty (the GAS rather than Sutton and Dahlin thankfully) proving the most potent partnership in the Premiership, Rovers were still in the top three come December.

Our most critical result came in mid December when we went to Highbury and played Arsenal off the pitch, winning 3-1. Important as this result was for us, it also gave the Gooners the kick up the 'Arse' they needed to go on their title-winning unbeaten run. However, after the game it was the Rovers who were in the ascendancy and we were being mentioned as title dark horses. Sadly, 1998 was mostly an *Annus Horribilis* as our form slumped from February onwards. The cups offered their usual false dawn as we drifted out of the Coke Cup in the third round after penalties. Then again, who apart from Chelsea fans gives a toss about who won it now? We progressed to the fifth round of the FA Cup after strolls against Wigan and Sheffield Wednesday, only to lose on pennos again after a bad tempered replay with West Ham. This led me to conclude that if the Rovers can't notch a winner before the end of extra time, we should just throw our hand in and let the opposition win without the shoot-out. At least we'd get out to the pub before last orders.

Ironically in February, probably our worst month results-wise (three league defeats and dumped out of the FA Cup), Chris Sutton was voted Carling Premiership Player of the Month by a panel including the man least likely to appear on Sutty's 'Friends and Family' numbers. Glenn Hoddle had the top scorer in the Premiership and a man who could fit in comfortably at centre half for England, and that man was Dion Dublin? Now I've got nothing against Dublin as a player *per se*, apart from the fact he attempted to decapitate Big Colin Hendry earlier in the season. But if Glenda Hoddle took a look at the England side who faced Chile and said to himself "I've seen the future of England and his name's Dion Dublin," then he needs putting away. As another Rovers England casualty Tim Sherwood put it, "the only way to get in the England squad is to go and juggle balls in Hoddle's back garden."

With this in mind, *Many Miles From Home* was proud to be the first to call for Hoddle's head (and other parts) on a silver platter. Our campaign slogan was "You're talking twaddle Hoddle" which followed on from previous England manager crusades, "You're a failure Taylor" and "You've been good Greenwood, but now do one Ron." I'll be giving my support to the only World Cup squad that recognises Rovers talent and gives it a chance. Scotland, with 'Mr Blackburn' Big Col Hendry, Billy McKinlay and Kevin Gallacher, will be leading the Tartan Army's charge for glory (but probable heroic failure). These three were certainly amongst the pick of our squad this season, along with Sherwood, Sutton, Stephane Henchoz and Filan, until he got injured. Our impressive youth policy also threw up 18-year-old Damien Duff, our most exciting new player for years, who left defenders trailing in his wake as he squeezed past them, reminding me of a little Irish Paulo Wanchope if you will. He's certainly our one to watch for the future. As long as he doesn't get burned out playing 50 odd games like Giggs or start believing he's untouchable like Beckham. From what I've seen of him so far, he looks too sensible for that to happen.

There's no doubt that the squad needs strengthening if we're to keep up the challenge next term. The likes of Croft, Fettis and particularly the well overrated (and over-weighted) Martin Dahlin haven't done the business and need to shape up or ship out. Before our last match, our mentor and favourite patron Uncle Jack Walker came on the pitch and announced he'd put his hand in his large wallet again and fork out for a new stand if we guaranteed our European place. With this confirmed, and an alleged £15 million available for transfers, things are looking up again for Blackburn Rovers and we can face the future with confidence. It certainly beats those wet Friday nights in Wrexham; just ask any Burnley or Manchester City fan!

MONKEY BUSINESS

Hartlepool United

Not so much a game as a season of two halves - not so dramatic as the previous one, but no less frustrating for the Poolie faithful. As the season petered out, without the almost compulsorily vague attempt to join the skirmish with relegation to the Conference, we thought it was all over till after the World Cup, but managerial uncertainty and behind-the-scenes rumblings have held the fans' interest to the bitter end.

The first half of the season exceeded most fans' expectations, especially after January 3rd's victory at Colchester left the team in a heady sixth position - oh that it had ended there. From then on we entered our now traditional late

Monkey Business

No 42
Mar 98
Still £1

Farewell to Jan Ove Issue

"He's been like that ever since Jan Ove went home"

season free-fall, although without our previous grim (reaper?) determination to boldly go forth and sample the delights of the Vauxhall Conference. A record equalling 23 drawn league games proved the ultimate frustration, as fans pondered what might have been had we signed a striker to cover a rash of injuries in the new year.

The Norwegian connections of IOR (Increased Oil Recovery), the club's new owners, were much in evidence throughout, and the sight of a full Norwegian international midfielder and an Under 23 goalkeeper were relished by fans sporting Viking helmets. Sadly, none of the rest of the flood of Scandinavians arriving on trial made the grade. Later, players from France, Argentina, Chile and the Cameroons came and went, with only Gustavo di Lella (signed from distant Blyth Spartans!) earning a contract.

IOR bought out 'local guy made good' Harold Hornsey, the popular chairman who had rescued us from a fate worse than death a few years earlier. Being based in Aberdeen, and in an uncharacteristic (for football club owners) display of honesty, IOR admitted that they didn't know much about running a football club and decided to retain Hornsey as their chief executive, with responsibility for the day-to-day running of the operation. To a large extent, HH was thus in a 'win-win' situation - he got his money back (how many chairman can say that?) and yet still continues to do the job he obviously relishes.

Their arrival was broadly welcomed, even though they made no promises about vast amounts of money to spend - more a continuation of Hornsey's prudent stewardship. They have improved several aspects of the club, although most fans were disappointed that they didn't strengthen the playing staff when it was obvious to everyone what was needed. Close links with a local Further Education College have brought superb indoor and outdoor training facilities, better dietary regimes for players and improved catering for match-day sponsors. However, the closer links with Norwegian clubs Brann Bergen and Fana (also owned by IOR) were not always universally popular, especially when coach Arne Moller arrived in a consultancy role and was immediately heavily critical of many aspects of the set-up.

Our campaign started with the gentle away jaunt to Exeter... a journey better made in August than December mid-week, and a 1-1 draw seemed to augur well. The goal bagged by Jon Cullen, signed from non-league Morpeth Town late the previous season, was also to prove significant as the season progressed.

The opening draw for the Fizzy Pop Cup couldn't have been less kind - and Tranmere must have been wondering what they were doing in the first round anyway. The highlight of the away leg was a 40-yard thunderbolt from Steven Howard, but the 3-1 scoreline virtually ended our interest. The first home game saw ever-popular visitors Colchester United defeated 3-2. Manager Steve Wignall had previously been critical of us, and their local paper was particularly scathing about Pools' hospitality, the town, the area, the roads, the hotels and of course - the weather. After the defeat, Wignall announced that if they couldn't finish above teams like us, he would resign.

The return leg with Tranmere unexpectedly held the interest for most of the game, but our 2-1 victory was not quite sufficient. Draws at home to high-flying Macclesfield and Notts County, then away to Scarborough, started us on a trend that was eventually to be our undoing. With three points for a win, draws are the last thing you want; you're better off winning and losing alternative matches. The traditionally intense local derby game at Darlington ended predictably in a 1-1 draw, with midfielder Cullen scoring our goal. He also scored in the 2-1 home win over Shrewsbury - his fourth successive strike in as many games, and was starting to attract the attention of scouts from Premier and First Division clubs.

A home victory over then table-topping Peterborough rounded off a solid October, as more away draws topped up the points total. November 1st saw the arrival of Jan Ove Pederson, a full Norwegian international, on loan from Brann Bergen for the duration of their close season. He arrived by ferry on the Friday lunchtime, accompanied by a contingent of fans. Boss Tait decided that the 36-hour ferry journey was probably not the best preparation for a game, even against Brighton, and he sat it out on the bench. He made his debut in a 2-0 victory at Swansea which featured Cullen's 40 yard lob that beat the goalkeeper and two defenders on the line, and won him *Sky's* Goal of the Year award for Division Three.

Pederson gradually settled into Pools' midfield and the somewhat uncompromising standard of tackling in the Third Division. In spite of many attempts to take him out of the game, he relished receiving the ball under pressure and improved with every game. On some occasions he was simply too quick-thinking for his teammates, but was always a joy to watch. A consummate professional on and off the pitch, he rapidly acquired the tag of 'the best player ever to wear a Pools shirt'.

He scored in our 2-4 home exit from the FA Cup at the hands of Macclesfield... Two cups down, one to go, then we could concentrate on the league! However, the sequence was broken by a somewhat surprising 2-1 away victory at Shrewsbury in the AutoWotsit Shield, with Jan-Ove scoring the winner.

We reached Christmas unbeaten at home in the league, with six home and seven away draws and poised just behind the play-off positions. Offered this situation at the outset, most fans would have settled for it, but the general consensus was one of slight disappointment that we'd been unable to convert enough of the draws into wins. Jon Cullen's 11 goals from midfield had papered over the cracks in our attack, but he couldn't lift the team single-handed.

Joe Allon had scored two goals in the home opener against Colchester but had been missing since then with a mysterious knee injury that was eventually to see him retire. Paul Baker broke his leg in a bruising encounter at Scunthorpe in November, and was also destined to take no further part in the season. This left the striking duties resting on the shoulders of Steven Howard and Stephen Halliday, neither of whom were playing at their best as the pressure of expectation took its toll. A reinforcement arrived in the form of Ian Clark, released by struggling Doncaster, and he was at first not universally welcomed, but his hard work and skill soon won over the fans.

This was to prove to be the turning point and many fans expressed their disappointment that new owners IOR did not fund the purchase of a striker or at least take one on loan. Although Clark contributed four goals and never stopped running at defences, he was not an out-and-out striker. What we needed was an experienced finisher. Stig-Olaf Larsen arrived from Norwegian Second Division club Fana but never made it further than the sub's bench. In February we signed Paul Connor on loan from neighbours Middlesbrough, but the 19-year-old striker, with no league experience, was not what was required either. He went back after a month having been substituted on three of his four starts and starting on the bench twice.

Christmas Sunday saw almost 2,000 Poolies visit Notts County to witness one of our best performances of the season. County gave us a lesson in finishing, scoring two out of their three chances, whilst we were unable to make anything of the vast majority of possession in the second half. January 3rd's trip to Colchester proved to be more productive and the 2-1 victory was celebrated in style by the travelling fans, vociferously reminding manager Wignall of his earlier comments. This was our fourth successive victory over Colchester and took us to sixth in the table. But as often seen before with us, it was not to be the start of an assault on the top; rather, the beginning of a rearguard action.

A predictably lacklustre performance at home to Scunthorpe ended our interest in the AutoWotsit and now we genuinely could concentrate on the league.

Cullen was still attracting the attention of scouts from several teams, and rumours abounded about those interested. Eventually Sheffield United offered £250,000 and he was on his way after scoring at Macclesfield. Some fans cited the sale as a sign of the club's lack of ambition. The truth of the situation was that he was soon to be out of contract and could have gone anywhere he liked without a fee, so the club simply made the best of the situation. The true test would be how wisely the money was spent.

Draws were still coming thick and fast, including four in consecutive home games, and this started a gentle slide down the table. Away games that would have earlier been drawn turned into defeats and the season started to peter out on the pitch. The money received from Cullen was obviously not burning a hole in Tait's pocket as none of the expected signings arrived. The explanation was that previously agreed deals were dishonoured by clubs who suddenly wanted twice the fee for their players once they knew we had some cash. IOR's inexperience in footballing matters appeared to have been exposed - although one would have thought that general business acumen would have taken care of this regardless.

The last remaining positive symbol of the season disappeared on a dismal March night, as we gave up our unbeaten home league record without much of a fight against Scunthorpe. Defender Graeme Lee was tried in the striker's role late in the season, and scored twice on his debut, but he never looked totally happy in the position. Just before transfer deadline day we made our traditional foray into the market and signed Craig Midgley from Bradford City for £10,000 (ten down, two hundred and forty to go!) and Paul Stephenson from York City. York released the latter as he was injured and would then have to serve a suspension - obviously acquired with a view to next season! Both of these players proved to be more skilful than those they ousted but neither is a proven goalscorer.

As the season finally fizzled out, watching the reserves proved to be as interesting as watching the first team. Triallists from all over the world appeared on our doorstep. Frenchman Habib Sissokho arrived and impressed in training, but was poached by Preston, with a little help from a local rival. But this may have been a blessing in disguise as he failed to score and left under a cloud before the season ended. A Cameroon international centre forward turned up but never saw first team action, as did a French full back. Two Argentinians also featured in the reserves - the midfielder looked a bit like Zola, and initially played like him; the centre forward looked like Severiano Ballesteros... and sadly played like him. The only one to make the first team was Gustavo di Lella, an Argentinian with an Italian passport, who made the long journey from Blyth.

The season ended with a trip to Peterborough and a fancy dress party. Just like last year the local plod was not in party mood. The Freddie Mercury look-a-like seemed to have been satisfactorily dealt with by the stewards, until the boys in blue decided they needed some exercise and waded into the crowd, knocking over children and pensioners on the way. Yet again they proved their total lack of understanding of the situation, and football fans were once again treated like second class citizens. Apologies for the injuries caused to the bystanders? What do you think?

Seventeenth position in the league was certainly safe but disappointing after the promising first half of the campaign. The new owners never promised untold riches to spend but the fans certainly expected more than eventually transpired. Money was spent behind the scenes, which will help to build a better future, but most fans simply want to see success on the pitch. Now! They expected to see the money from the sale of Cullen invested in a push for promotion, and the strange lack of signings was never satisfactorily explained.

As the season drew to a close Tait was offered a new one year contract by Hornsey, which should have put an end to speculation about his future and rumours about the arrival of Peter Beardsley or a variety of Scots. However, all had not been finalised and Tait fell out with IOR as they insisted that he "work with" visiting Norwegian coach Arne Moller, and allegedly "adjusted" his retained list. Tait sat in the stand during the last home game against fellow draw specialists Cardiff and walked out before the final day's visit to Peterborough. In the weeks since the end of the season there has been much discussion between the parties and Tait's contract was eventually confirmed. Not an ideal way to build a good working relationship - but then again, what do we know? After all, we're only the fans.

MOULIN ROUGE

Rotherham United

Having suffered probably the worst season in our history, we were looking for positive signs after the appointment of former crowd favourite Ronnie Moore on May 23rd. As I wrote last year, Ronnie was a hero in the early 1980's during our best period and was the only one who could get the supporters believing again. Pre-season provided those signs with Ronnie's 'Coming Home Party' at the Zone nightclub in town. An incredible 1,500 turned up to welcome him and even though it was clearly spelt out that we should not expect an immediate turn-around, the talk was of promotion at the first attempt and FA Cup finals, etc.

MOULIN ROUGE

THE ROTHERHAM UNITED FANZINE

Sponsors of Paul Dillon's Football clothes and now **ALSO** Steve Thompson's kit = over £200 to RUFC this season... so far!

GOOD DECISION MR LEAKE..... AGAIN!!

PLAY ON

-ANDY97-

Included in this issue: Dave Nicholls interview, Paul Dillon interview, a game with the Press, Donny problems, Mystic Mug, the Shrewsbury debate and loads more.....

ISSUE 19   £1   OCT/NOV '97

Friendlies were arranged for July and 8,000 turned up to see us stuff Lager League new boys and local rivals Barnsley 2-1. Aberdeen were dispatched by the same scoreline and even the doubters were beginning to think the impossible was... possible. Ronnie only had two professionals under contract, so there was a lot of negotiating to do. Ten more agreed deals and some new faces came in to give us a squad of sorts for the opener against Barnet. A nightmare start with - I think - the quickest goal of the season for Barnet but we forged ahead at 2-1 before losing both centre backs. Monington was the victim of a horrible challenge by a Barnet player. He was carried off and was then out until the new year (unlike the culprit, who played the rest of the season - where's the justice in that?). Adjustments were made but the damage was done and Barnet scored two late goals to win 3-2.

We then came across our eventual 'Kev' winner (*MR*'s annual award for most inept refereeing, named after Kevin Lynch at Burnley a couple of years ago). Tony Leake of Darwen was the official for our trip to Shrewsbury and he ignored an awful challenge by Devon White on Bobby Mimms (resulting in Mimms being carried off), sent off three of our players, including stand-in 'keeper Neil Richardson for trying to dive for the ball at the feet of an attacker and Lee Glover for reacting to being pulled back twice when clear by the same player - who was only booked! All this sparked a mini riot and CS spray was used on Millers fans in the crowd. We only lost 2-1 that day!

Results were not good over the next few weeks as we struggled to get going. Tall Dutch summer signing Gijsbert Bos fell out with Ronnie when he was substituted for being absolute crap, throwing his shirt into the dug-out. It wasn't until October that we hit some kind of form, a first away win at Rochdale, beating Macclesfield, a 3-3 draw at Mansfield and a win at Brighton. Despite a hiccup at home to Scunny we were showing some good signs. A six goal thriller at home to Barnsley in the FA Cup set up our *Sky TV* debut and we showed the nation what a great side we are! Three-nil at Turf Moor, we out-sang those Clarets who'd bothered to turn up and we were down to play Kings Lynn in the next round. Progress was being made.

The East Anglians put up a brave fight, holding us to 0-0 at the break, but we put six past them in the second half and drew Sunderland in the third round. Meanwhile, league form was continuing to improve and over 1,000 enjoyed a day out at Scarborough and probably our best performance of the season to win 2-1. I must say that the Boro stewards were by far the worst we saw; just looking for confrontation and nicking anyone who looked like they were enjoying themselves. Millers out in town that night will have seen them performing their other jobs outside night-clubs.

Donny were beaten at their place and it was sad to see our neighbours in such a state. (Yes, it's nice to win there, but I recall some great games with them over the past 30 years or so and my Dad always told me about the games and crowds of the 'Good Old Days'. Our fans who laughed at Donny's plight should just think how close we are ourselves to despair. We've been in free-fall for five years now and it could be us next - be warned!) Boxing Day saw us race into a 5-1 lead at home to Hull, their fans singing "six-five, we're gonna win six-five..." How right they nearly were! They put the frighteners on us by scoring three times and gave us a nervy last 20 minutes at 5-4 but we held out.

After losing to Sunderland by a flattering 5-1, league form began to dip and from third place we started to edge our way from any kind of promotion place. We only won five games from then, and one of those was an incredible turn-around against Orient. Earlier in the season we'd been robbed of a win deep into added time by the O's, so we owed them one, but I never imagined we'd turn a 1-0 deficit with a minute to play into a 2-1 win. Someone asked why people leave games before the end and miss things like that... well, it's to sell fanzines of course! Yes I was outside when both goals went in... but I was happy they did.

A few weeks previous to that, we'd been 2-0 down to Cambridge with a minute left and got back to 2-2, and games against Mansfield and Rochdale saw us pull two back as well, so we *can* show spirit if we want.

But why do we go 2-0 down in the first place? At the game with Mansfield, two Stags fans went on the pitch to celebrate when they scored their second and were promptly nicked for it. Just as our second was going in, they were being led away sporting a nice pair of handcuffs each - justice that time then! Macclesfield away saw us meet up with Tony 'Kev' Leake and once again he infuriated the Millers with some awful decisions. He sent off Mark Monington for two bookables which most refs wouldn't have even had a word about. He then ignored similar challenges by Macc players and gave them seven minutes of added time for no reason in which to find a winning goal before giving it up as a bad job. A hard earned 0-0 for the Millers.

The season appeared to be fizzling out but other sides were attempting to avoid promotion as well, keeping us in with a shout right up to the last game. Highlight in the second half of the season was the win at Torquay to shut that slapper from *Sky* up. She and her colleagues have ignored all our letters asking to go on the show as fans of the week, yet they put the same Blunts fans on regularly. They reckon to represent real football fans but ignore those who stick by their clubs, even if they're crap.

On the last day we needed Rochdale to beat Barnet (quite possible, we thought) and then all we had to do was win at runaway Champions Notts County. A shade under 3,000 made the short trip down to impressive Meadow Lane and swelled the crowd to over 12,000. It all looked on when Jason White put us ahead but despite a brave performance and a Lee Glover goal to make it 2-2 in the second half, we were punished for our all-out attack and were beaten 5-2 in the end by a good side.

So we've got another season in the dungeon and Ronnie has been told to make cut-backs. The signings of Jason White and Vance Warner have added quality to the side when they aren't on the treatment table, but more is required to make us into genuine contenders. Bobby Mimms has made some howlers throughout the campaign but did improve as time went on. He appears to have spent too much time in the Pontin's League. Young Irish lad Paul Dillon has established himself in the side with some promising displays and he is our choice for kit sponsorship again next time. Look out for his name in the future. Injuries have played a part in our failure to go up and it's something we need to avoid for the best part of next season.

Highlights of '97-98 were the Burnley away cup tie, Rochdale away, Scarborough away, Lincoln away, Hull at home and Torquay away in the league. Best stewards we came across were at Chester, worst at Scarborough (as mentioned). Best company were the Notts County people at the *No More Pie In The Sky* fanzine, both at Millmoor and Meadow Lane.

Once again May means a trip to Scotland for a match and a new ground for me and son Jonathan at the Kilmarnock v Hibernian game. As I wrote last year, we travelled up for the Scottish Cup final and we promised their fans we'd go up for a game this time. Well, it turned out the first opportunity was on their last day of the season after ours had finished. We travelled up on the morning of the match, having been treated to complimentary tickets by Killie boss Bobby Williamson (ex-Millers hero '88-89) and had an absolutely fantastic time with the lads in the Killie club, met up with Bobby for a chat - and we're definitely making it an annual trip. Several of them promised to come down to Millmoor as well - they're all welcome! All we need now is to get our club to make the kind of progress Kilmarnock have made over the past five years; we can learn so much from them.

Finally, a word for our friends at other fanzines - James and all at *The Seadog Bites Back* Scarborough, Bart and gang at Notts County's *No More Pie In The Sky* and Andrew at Cardiff's *Thin Blue Line*. Keep up the good work on thoroughly entertaining mags. Others to catch our eye this time were Darlo's *Mission Impossible*, Hartlepool's *Monkey Business*, Motherwell's *One Step Beyond* and of course Jackie at Brighton's *Seaside Saga*!

Chesterfield receive crowd boost.........

Right Bob, that's the Main Stand sold out for the season!!

NEW FRONTIERS

York City

A year ago, most supporters would have said that getting past Port Vale in round one of the Coca-Cola Cup and to be in play-off contention as late as mid-March would constitute a successful season.

The reality was defeat by a poor Oxford side in round two and staring relegation in the face in late March as we plummeted down the table.

We divested ourselves of some of our most expensive players during the season, including David Rush (£85,000 written off in six months and later to do a runner at Darlington), Paul Stephenson (surprisingly freed in March when enjoying his best season and said to be on £50,000 a year), Marco

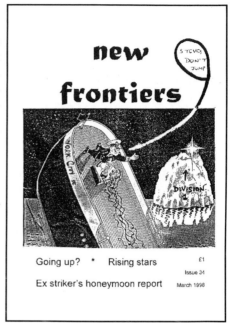

new frontiers

Going up?   *   Rising stars   £1

Issue 34

Ex striker's honeymoon report   March 1998

Gabbiadini (prodigal son returns and gets injured) and Steve Tutill.

In March we netted what is probably a club record fee when 18-year-old striker Jon Greening joined Manchester United. A few days earlier, manager Alan Little had suggested that his best position was substitute, a reference to Jon being physically immature when up against fresh defenders at the start of a game. No fee was disclosed but it was reckoned to be £500,000 now and up to £2 million if Jono goes all the way.

We enjoyed our best spell early on when we had a settled team; we tried to improve it in November and seemed to lose our way, reaching our nadir on the last day of the season when we had no shape and players didn't seem to know what to expect of each other. Perhaps a small squad is preferable to our rather cumbersome 25 or so.

As usual, there was an undercurrent of dissent at the way the club is run. You've only got to look around the empty spaces on the terraces to see that we will never get rich through turnstile income alone. Many supporters feel we would do better with a new regime in charge. Whilst the sporadic "Little Out" chants were the main focus, it is widely recognised that chairman Douglas Craig is the man with all the power. He has always run the club applying strict business principles, never spending money we haven't got. When crowds struggle to top 3,000 it would be foolish to throw money around.

Grimsby and Northampton both took in excess of 20,000 to Wembley for the play-off final, the second Wembley appearance for both clubs within 12 months. On our only visit to Wembley in 1993 we took 11,000; I wouldn't bet on us taking any more than that the next time.

We've always been a net seller of players. With some justification, they point to Darren Williams (England B and Under 21), Jon McCarthy (Northern Ireland) and Dean Kiely (Eire) and ponder what might have been if they were still pulling on the York City shirt. However, the club must be doing something right as next season will be our sixth successive one outside the bottom flight; a new club record.

For me, one of the high spots was the win at Millwall. The most trouble we saw that day was the verbal aggro between the City fans chanting "Little Out" and their fellow supporters who told them to shut up and get behind the team. But that day we played some superb passing football; a few weeks later our passing was described as emulating that of Brazil in a national paper. The home win over ten man Carlisle was another highlight as we came from 3-1 down with eight minutes to go to win 4-3, thanks to three long range efforts. The whole ground was as one, chanting "dodgy 'keeper" at Caig (who was no better in the return match).

We more than matched the moneybags of Fulham. Our London & South East Supporters Club branch played host to some Fulham supporters in March. A good weekend was had by all, culminating in a Sunday morning match on City's new training ground. Alan Little gave up his Sunday morning lie-in to unlock the ground at 9am. His pre-match pep talk worked wonders, as City won 9-1. No allowances should be made for the after-effects of the previous day's proper northern beer on the visitors. Oh, and the disallowed goal is still talked about to this day. The Fulham supporters said it was their best away trip of the season. How different to the tragic events that occurred at Gillingham just a week later.

We finished the season with five left backs and five on the managerial/coaching staff. Admittedly, all the left backs could play elsewhere but it was a bit of overkill, especially as the only good one (Neil Thompson) was only with us on loan. The coaching staff increased by two during the season, I think partly as a result of our desire to enhance our youth development policy.

Looking ahead, it seems the Bosman ruling may even work in our favour as the giants seem quite happy to subsidise clubs like us by buying our promising youngsters before they've had a chance to make a name for themselves. In the same week as Jono went, Newcastle paid a similar sum for two even younger members of Darlington's squad. Alan Little thinks so anyway. He's hoping to recruit lots of free transfer signings under Bosman in the summer; perhaps someone should tell him that it usually means higher wages. History shows we have never signed anyone through the transfer tribunal, as players out of contract have preferred to go where the wages are higher. And anyway, the summer saw a few of our squad players released, but the elevation of three juniors to the professional ranks will leave little room for experienced newcomers.

We've got a squad which has some talented players, but no one performs consistently well. Alan Pouton or Richard Cresswell could be the pick. Mark Tinkler has the class but doubts remain as to whether he has the temperament. We turned down £250,000 from Wigan for Tony Barrass who forms a dependable centre-back partnership with Martin Reed, another youngster who could make a name for himself. What we really lack is a prolific goalscorer. Rodney Rowe, Neil Tolson and Richard Cresswell all look useful as second strikers, but none of them really scares the opposition or is talked about in the same terms as the likes of Paul Barnes, Keith Walwyn or Jimmy Seal.

No doubt we'll be most people's favourites for relegation. Again. Just as we have been for each of the previous five seasons.

Source: Loadsamoney

NO MORE PIE IN THE SKY

Notts County

"THAT'S ENTERTAIN-MENT" { The 7" Radio Friendly Glory Glory Mix }

The Soundtrack to our Season :-

PROLOGUE :- Heather turned over and hit the play on her cassette radio. The familiar voice of Paul Weller illuminated the silence. *"I've got a grapefruit matter, it's as sour as shit, I have no solutions, Better get used to it!"*

The summer months had seen the dark of the last season take a back seat, as the music of life blossomed once again. From a 'Heavy Soul' to the 'Fat Of The Land', there seemed a new-found optimistic vibe, as another summer

Only : £1

THE SKY NO MORE PIE IN [Issue No. 30]: March 86 - April 86

A Notts Co. Famzine

Champions!

NUFF SAID..

ALSO INSIDE :- The Ultimate Football Challenge, The Class Of 1990, Where Are They Now ?, Andy Hughes Q & A, Life Down The Lane, Alas Poor Poric, Dread-Zone, Victory Came So Sweet, The Elephant Files, Jnr. Statto Match Reports, The End Of Season Awards & loads more....

of love touched all that dared to open their hearts. Yes, there was still the threat from the dark side, but good will always come through, even Darth Vader had shown this to be true. Promotion thoughts jumped around in her head, but was it really just a daydream? She toyed with the notion, 'What if her beloved Notts were offered the promise of promotion?' But, if she were to accept, then F****t too would secure the same fate. Would she take it? Last season's dealings with such dreams had taught her one lesson at least: to keep her eyes focused on what she loved, not what she loathed.

Side A: The First Half

Track 1 : - Sunshine - Ian Brown

There are only four times you can be guaranteed the sun during the football season: the first and last games, Blackpool away (unless it's your team playing them then it always rains), and the FA Cup final. The rest of the season is cold, wet and miserable. That's a fact; just you wait and see...

Our season opened on a hot summer's afternoon that rewarded us with a 2-1 home win, thanks to a late goal that for the first time in what seemed like seasons rattled the net in our favour, against long-time Division Three residents Rochdale. Following an unimpressive draw at Darlo' in the Coca-Cola we had to pinch ourselves during the 3-0 demolition over the bullish Tigers. We were playing a style of football not witnessed by the band of travelling supporters since the Mick Walker era. Saturday 23rd. A derby battle with the Imps was full of tabloid drama. The 2-1 defeat seemed incidental after the M.I.B. had enraged the home support with a number of questionable (i.e. shit) decisions. One dedicated fan relinquished the rest of his season by doing what a thousand others dreamed of. The media missed the point, picturing him as the criminal, and although we can't condone we can understand his frustrations. The whole referee débâcle really needs to have some ounce of consistency, for not only the fans but for players and managers alike. The month closed with a late passage to the second round and a couple of away draws. August had finally come, Oasis had eventually delivered a third album and Notts looked in promising shape...

Track 2 :- What Goes Around, Comes Around - Bob Marley

The dark shadow of FA let the Pies off with a warning after the Lincoln drama. But another potentially difficult derby followed. The Stags came to stamp over our stadium, but left empty-handed, thanks to a penalty save from their ex-'keeper Darren Ward and a dubious off-side goal from Gary Martindale. "*What goes around comes around,*" as Bob would say. The new-found winning formula continued to blossom: we took maximum points from Scunny, Shrewsbury and an emphatic performance against the Seadogs. Was this really Notts or was it "*just like watching Juve?*" The golden browns of September leaves began to fall, leaving a Magpie perched on top, looking down on all below.

Track 3 :- All You Good Good People - Embrace

As October sang along to the *Urban Hymns* of The Verve, the Magpie's flight would be one of consolation. A couple of wins and a trio of draws kept us in contention, but rivals Peterborough nudged above us by a point to take the top spot. This month also saw another landmark reached: I left my twenties behind and hit the 30 points spot. The birthday bash coincided with a Tuesday away tie at Millmoor. A 1-1 draw kept all parties happy as the after-match curry with the lads from the *Moulin Rouge* fanzine offered a side of football that never gets a mention in the scandal toilet of the media: football supporters of different factions embraced in a common love.

Track 4 :- The Cost Of Loving - The Style Council

Sat. 1st November. For many, a run-of-the-mill away trip to Barnet. But for one fanzine editor it would turn out to be a rather expensive day. Due to a mix-up between myself and the regular away daze crew (and I *still* say that I asked to be picked up at the Magpie pub!), Joolz and I ended up on a last-minute dash on trains and tubes to get us to Underhill. When you add the cost of that to the gate money, programme, food and drink, you have a rather expensive bill for 90 mins of footy. A 2-1 win however did offer some consolation! But never did I stop to question the cost of loving. Sad, or Mad? Notts failed to win again in the league during November. Both Chester and Colchester took three points off us, while Grecians, O's and the Posh all shared the honours.

Notts made hard work of plucky Colwyn Bay but secured a second round place in the FA Cup.

Track 5 :- Bitter Sweet Symphony (Extended Version) - The Verve

As the barren wastelands of November faded into the distance, the festive season would turn out to be a historic chapter with a present bonanza. The defeat of the Seagulls away at the Priestfield Stadium gave an insight into a rock-bottom landscape that can so easily befit us all. A comical 5-2 over fellow struggling Donny plus away wins against Torquay, Scunny and Hartlepool pulled the curtains on an eventful 12 months. To quote the KLF, "*1997 What The F*** Is Going On?*" The year began with the appointment of the man that would eventually put smiles back on faces, pride in the hearts and bums back on seats. Sam Allardyce now had the opportunity to take this side, *his side*, all the way, and come May, many fans would expect him to fulfil what December and Santa had promised: promotion. And maybe if we were good - very good - the Title.

- End Of Side One -
Side B: The Second Half

Track 6 :- Mad Flava - The X-Ecutioners

The extended break of the new year (the snow making its now obligatory raid on the fixture list) delayed our 4000th league game until the visit to Spotland on Jan 12th. Yet again, we were to return home in joyful mood, as this became just a taster for a month that saw Notts take the top spot of Division Three and remain there until our eventual exodus. Wins over Cardiff, Hull, a thrilling 5-2 revenge over the Imps that saw us not only go 3-0 up, but allow them to pull level before we hit home two further strikes to rub in the defeat. Mansfield offered little resistance as we took maximum points during January. The prospect of promotion had now become a very real possibility, as the Posh began to drop points like pigeons drop shit. The FA Cup campaign closed after a late winner from Preston ended an epic battle over 120 mins that saw the lads leave the field with the knowledge that they could compete on equal terms with the Second Division; a moral victory that played a valuable part in the resurrection of this phoenix.

Track 7 :- Good To Be On The Road Back Home Again - Cornershop

The road back home was still some distance ahead. Cool heads were needed, as members of the chasing pack came forth to do battle. We slayed all but one. Only the Macc Lads offered any resistance as our amazing book of 16 league games unbeaten closed at Moss Rose. The month belonged not only to Notts but to Cornershop, whose indie anthem *Brimful Of Asha*, now in remixed form, enlightened the chart-fodder buying brain-deads to a vibe of Indian promise. Spring looked to be finally here.

Track 8 :- The Private Psychedelic Reel - The Chemical Brothers

The merry month of March held much delight. The long trip south on a damp Tuesday night to far away Exeter saw possibly the best performance of the season. Saturday's defeat was soon pushed aside as Notts out-played the home side; a crushing 5-2 win was like a personal reward to the trusty band of supports who defy work commitments and always seem to make it to these testing fixtures. It felt good to see the side win without all the new-found glory-hunting fans that had joined us along the way this season. Not that we don't want them there - everyone is welcome - but this one was for the hard-core; one for those that saw out last season's nadir; this win was for *us*. Thoughts of the title dream drew ever closer now, as Barnet bamboozled. Chester and Colchester offered some resistance but as March 28th approached the expectations now began to grow to gigantic proportions.

The scenario was simple. We had to win and Scunny had to beat Torquay. The prize: promotion and the title. The day was to be one to remember. A close encounter saw us nudge ahead on 50 mins through Robson, but as news of two Scunny goals late in the second half swept the ground like a Mexican wave, it seemed to give the lads that final lift, to not only win the game, but to take the title in record-breaking time. The pitch invasion afterwards was a melee of joy as fans of all generations sipped (or rather downed in one) the sweet wine of success.

Track 9 :-24 Hour Party People - Happy Mondays

After the jubilation of March, thoughts that April could sustain this 100% were in hindsight foolish. *Sky TV* turned up a week too late as we lost against the Posh. Well, they needed the points and their taunts were met with sarcastic replies of "We'll never play you again" as we just got on with enjoying our own promotion party. The Brighton and Donny games saw Notts playing like a troop of hungover lager louts. But the visit of Torquay saw them back sober to teach a side who had already hit their own self-destruct button a lesson in how to play football. The fully resurrected Gary Jones again came oh-so-close to the Lost Ark of the hat-trick as we trounced the Seasiders 3-0.

Track 10 :- Here Comes The Sun - The Beatles

The End Of Season Gala at Meadow Lane produced our largest turnout. Over 12,000 enjoyed the sun and the football as Ian Hendon finally got his hands on the Third Division trophy. Rotherham, who have become good friends over the last three seasons, had to not only witness our glory, but endure a defeat that sentenced them to another campaign in the basement. Gary Jones scored twice and earned a well-deserved Golden Boot award for a tally of 28 league goals. But again, football was the winner that day, as the after-match fanzine party not only saw us repay the compliment from October to the *Moulin Rouge* crew but we also entertained Norwich, Carlisle and Barnet fans, all locked together in talk of next season's hopes and fears, the World Cup - and of course, the quality of the beer.

Bonus Track - Happiness Is Eggshaped - The Seahorses

After the darkness that enveloped the '96-97 effort, this would soon fade and become but a distant memory for many Magpie followers, as the '97-

98 season came to a close. The team ran the perfect race, a Steve Ovett classic, hanging just behind in the chasing pack during the early stages, but as the others began to fall away, the rebirth of spring saw the side not only take the lead but move ahead, out of reach of all our competitors. Was it that we were just too good or that they weren't good enough? The Chinese 'Ying and Yang' theory again is, as always, present at the Lane. For followers of Notts County there's never a grey area of mid-table mediocrity. Either we're entangled in promotion-hunting raids or battling for survival. There's a sense of optimism around again. The team is taking shape; a few minor adjustments (i.e. a midfield maestro) and the possibility of a second successive promotion could become a reality. The key to this dream is obviously stability and the continued reign of 'Big Sam' as our leader. There's talk of a take-over, investment and new players. But we seasoned supporters take each step one at a time; the roller-coaster ride of Notts Co. never gives you time to speculate as to what can or should happen, but only what might...

See you next season!

- End Of Side 2

EPILOGUE :- The noise next door had kept Heather awake for hours now, but for once she didn't mind. She'd had her own party weeks before and only now, as April rolled into May, were the Red elements of Nottingham able to celebrate their promotion. Thoughts of the World Cup and the united colours of football took centre-stage in her world now. She leaned over and pulled out *Exodus* from her record box. The sweet summer vibe of the reggae bass seemed the perfect solution to quell the non-descript din from the *Smash Hits Party* CD that echoed from next door.

But next season would be different, she thought. They'll never survive in the top flight. An Arsenal annihilation; Murdered by Man United; A Demolition Derby... The lists could be endless. You've had your slice of success, but take care not to became too fat on the fruit cake.

NO-ONE LIKES US

Millwall

After nearly going bust the previous season, this was the start of a new dawn. We'd seen more new dawns than the average sparrow, but this really *was* a new dawn, or that's what we were told. New chairman Theo Paphitis, fresh from his successes flogging paperclips at Rymans and knickers at Contessa, had installed a board of toadies ready to agree to his every word. Having been a rank Millwall supporter for, oh! about two weeks, he knew what we wanted and he was going to give it to us. Passion. The Dunkirk spirit. Never say die. Remember the blitz? And he was going to bring all his wealth of experience gained at Walton and Hersham to turn us around.

the alternative
MILLWALL
magazine
£1.00

ISSUE
55

season's
review

brimful of
theo

the millwall
supporters
club

world wide
'wall

the 8th
annual
reggies

OH! WHAT A SEASON

New sponsors were brought in - *L!veTV*! Resulting In 'The weather in Nowegian' appearing on the shirts. Everyone else in South London was laughing at us - why shouldn't we? Billy Bonds was appointed as manager. Bearing in mind his close association with the Devil's spawn at Upton Park, a brave decision; even braver when Bonds attempted to recruit many of his former players - paper talk or not, the natives were getting restless. The opening day saw 9,000 punters turn up to see Billabong's Bloowarmee stuff Brentford 3-0 with a display of passion, and power. Our new dawn turned out to be a false dawn - it was to be our last decent home performance! We crashed out of the Coke Cup 9-1 on aggregate against Wimbledon, and Bonds got the cheque book out. Paul Shaw was signed from Arsenal's reserves for half a million and Paul Wilkinson from Grimsby along with 63 year old goalkeeper Nigel Spink. Assistant manager Pat Holland saw the writing on the wall and fled to the safety of Spurs youth team, leaving Bonds to soldier on alone.

Home performances went from bad to worse, while away from home we battled to some impressive wins, particularly at Watford and Gillingham. Going into the Christmas period we were still in third place. But a barren spell through December and January saw us in freefall, and a particularly inept performance at Blackpool resulted in Bonds offering his resignation. The team had started to perform like one of those jumpers your Gran knits you for

Christmas - no shape or pattern. Then a spate of draws earned Bonds a reprieve. Andy Gray was brought in from Bury to give our powder-puff midfield some bite and he proved an immediate success. Stuart Nethercott joined from Spurs to form an effective partnership with Brian Laws and then they both joined our ever-increasing injury list for the rest of the campaign. The last we saw of them was in the performance of the season away to Fulham: a goal down and reduced to ten men, we battled back for a 2-1 victory to show what we were really capable of. If Bonds had ever managed to get a grip on them...

With all hopes of the play-offs gone, a few anxious weeks looking over our shoulders was all we had left as the season limped to a conclusion. Bonds immediately started the rebuilding process, releasing nine players out of contract, only to be called into the chairman's office following the final Reserve game and given the boot himself. Paphitis issued a statement saying the club would not rush into a replacement, having already given the job to the club's longest servant Keith Stephens, with Alan McLeary as his assistant. Paphitis proceeded to not so much shoot himself in the foot as blow his legs off by talking about Bonds' Premiership experience being unsuitable for a club in our situation, leading many of us to ask what that said about the chairman's non-league experience.

Under Rhino we'll certainly be better organised and trained, and woe betide anyone who doesn't give 100%. What's that I see on the horizon, another new dawn?

THE NUMBER 9

Newcastle United

The end to last season had us slavering in mouth-watering anticipation at what was to come. Our late burst had seen us qualify for the Champions' League, albeit in second place again, but the prospects of unleashing Shearer, Tino and Ferdie on the likes of Juventus and PSV had us all dreaming of European and domestic glory for the first time in years. Then the pre-season forced many of us to reconsider our betting slips. Clark, Elliot and Ferdinand were all gone, Shearer was out with another long-term injury and Tino was as lethargic and unpredictable as ever. The signings of Tommason, Pistone and Ketsbaia hardly restored the optimism we had felt earlier.

THE NUMBER 9

ER KENNY TEMUR IS A LITTLE TIED UP!!!

THE NUMBER NINE ISSUE 32

DALGLISH INTERVIEW

EXCLUSIVE

5 PAGE EXCLUSIVE WITH THE GAFFER
OCTOBER/NOVEMBER 1997
WIN 24 CANS OF BEER IN FAN'S FORUM

£1

But things started brightly enough and the defeat of Croatia Zagreb in the qualifying round of the Champions' League saw us drawn in the nicknamed the 'Group of Death' with Barcelona, Dynamo Kiev and PSV. What a way to make your entrance on club football's greatest stage: Barcelona at a packed St James' Park. There was something in the air that night, it's something you can't describe, you just knew that tonight was to be our night. From the moment the lads in black and white emerged from the tunnel to the chorus of "Toon army," you just knew. Tino played like a man possessed that night, and although the Spanish giants managed to claw back two consolation goals, nothing could take away the headlines from Asprilla and his magnificent hat-trick. A 3-2 defeat of Barca, Nadal and all, and now the world would see who the greatest team in black and white *really* were.

Our league performances began to dip by early November and to be truthful they never really improved. We had made the transition off the pitch from FC to Plc; on the pitch we had transformed from the entertainers to the out-and-out defenders. Very hard for those Newcastle fans who had just arrived five years ago to accept, a lot easier for those who had been there BK (before Keegan). The Coca-Cola Cup, as always for those struggling, brought a welcome break, and for the second year in succession we reached the quarter finals, only to fall at home to Liverpool after extra-time. To be fair, had Owen and Fowler had their shooting boots on, the inevitable would have become reality somewhat quicker. So out of the League Cup and with the Champions League mathematically out of reach after defeat by PSV, we had only the FA Cup to aim for. Sir John Hall announced his retirement to coincide with the return game with Barcelona at the Nou Camp and handed the reins over to Freddie Shepherd and his son Douglas. The trip to Spain was one to savour. To hear the Spanish say "Haway," and "Whey aye" was one for memory banks. But the visit was soured a little by the fact that it was virtually empty and pissing down, but we made the most of it as Newcastle served up another magnificent 1-0 defeat.

The turn of the year had every Geordie making at least one New Year wish: the speedy return of Alan Shearer. It also witnessed the media witch hunt stepped up against our great club. Having been the darlings of the British media under Keegan, we'd become the scourges under Dalglish. Why? Only the press knows. But the whole saga was brought to a head by two events. First, the Stevenage FA Cup tie was billed as David and Goliath, with the home side tipped to knock Newcastle out as Hereford had done in the seventies, and it all made for a mouth-watering tie. The non-leaguers had hinted at the tie being switched so they could make more money, but changed their minds at the last minute, upsetting the Newcastle hierarchy, who in turn made an issue of safety at the non-league team's ground. The media, TV, radio and newspapers then all jumped on the bandwagon and publicly castrated Shearer and Co. At the forefront was Stevenage chairman Victor Green, to whom I personally gave a few choice words when I saw him loitering with intent outside the ground. As it happened everyone went home happy. They got the replay, we won the tie, and *Sky* and the *Sun* made millions.

Amidst the Stevenage fiasco, Shearer made his return and within two minutes was doing what he does best… scoring goals. He was back and boy, did we need him. A serious lack of league form had us hovering perilously above the relegation trapdoor for the first time in our Premiership lives. Enter stage right the *News of the World* and one of their worldwide exclusives, "Soccer Chiefs' Shame." In a wonderful Beadle-like set-up our chairman and vice-chairman had been lured into Marbella and taped insulting their fellow north-easterners and paying public. Any true Newcastle fan was obviously upset, but when it really comes down to it we only care about the football. Who gives a shit about what happens upstairs as long as they run the club to the best of their ability and make funds available for the manager's transfer activity? So with Sir John's son caught with his pants down he had no choice but to return to the helm himself and steady a possibly sinking ship, or should that be nose-diving magpie?

Amidst the sleaze allegations, bad public relations and relegation battles, our first FA Cup Final appearance beckoned. With just Sheffield United between us and the twin towers the Geordie masses marched on

Old Trafford, and just like Hillsborough in 1974 the *Number 9* came up trumps with the match-winner. The season drew to a close with the Toon scraping clear of Nationwide football, the key game being a 2-1 home defeat of Barnsley, a game in which Shearer was lambasted for leaning on a defender to get the winner. If he'd had the white of England on, would he have had the same treatment? I think not. So onto Wembley and the Champions Arsenal, who'd already done the double over us in the Premiership. Great day out! But the team selected was, on the whole, a great disappointment, which really summed up our season. What lies ahead I am not too sure. Dalglish will have to do some serious tuning to his engine I feel, or he will once again suffer a breakdown when chasing some honours. It was gratifying however to see a team lose a 12 point lead in the Premiership! And fancy the second place team qualifying for the Champions League! After all, it's supposed to be a cup for Champions isn't it?! He who laughs last laughs longest, Alex... Ha! Ha! Ha!

Source: Chelsea Independent

THE OATCAKE

Stoke City

Power, Corruption & Pies

The '97-98 season added another chapter to the book of misery for Stoke City supporters, as once again we saw opportunity and potential converted into neglect and dismal failure. It is a constant source of amusement for Potters to hear Everton or Spurs fans being classed as 'long-suffering'. Yes, year after year of Premiership football and occasional Wembley Cup Finals must be more than it is fair to ask any football supporter to have to endure. They haven't got a clue!

For those who don't know, Stoke City left the oldest surviving league ground in the world, the

Victoria Ground, and moved to a new purpose-built stadium about a quarter of a mile away. The move to the Britannia Stadium (named after the locally based building society and not a deliberate continuation of a regal theme) was trumpeted as the dawning of a new era for the club and its supporters. The board talked excitedly about having all the facilities in place "when we get into the Premiership," yet never explained exactly how they saw the team managing to achieve such a feat.

Their first fatally flawed decisions of the season came before a ball had even been kicked. With Lou Macari having quit as manager, the board decided against making an inspirational appointment to boost interest in the new stadium and gave the job instead to Lou's genial, though somewhat limited, assistant Chic Bates. The selling of our best player, Mike Sheron, to QPR and a decision to spend virtually none of the £2m proceeds on new players then confounded this move. Not to worry though, one of our big pre-season acquisitions was Paul Stewart from Sunderland, who had finished top of the scoring charts for the Roker men the previous year with a whopping four goals. Just the tonic to get the new stadium packed to the rafters!

Many were predicting relegation but Stoke confounded the critics with a surprisingly spirited start to the campaign. Because of the completion date on our new stadium we were forced to play our first four games away from home. Even so, we managed to get two wins and a draw, including an excellent

1-0 at Middlesbrough's Riverside Stadium in what turned out to be Fabrizio Ravenelli's last game.

The scene was set for the curtain-raiser and Stoke showed once again just how effortlessly they can make the easiest thing in the world seem incredibly difficult. The official opening was pencilled in for the league game against Swindon Town on August 30th. However, the Coca-Cola Cup had paired us against Rochdale on the 27th. The club decided to stick with the original date and tried to pretend that the Rochdale game was nothing special, and that it wasn't *really* our first game at a new stadium after 119 years at the Victoria Ground. Still, more than 15,000 turned up, mainly out of curiosity, to see mighty 'Dale hold Stoke to a 1-1 draw; a chilling portent of things to come.

A highly suspect and deeply unpopular new ticketing operation for the Britannia Stadium had many people vowing never to set foot near the place. Nevertheless, more than 23,500 did put in an appearance for the Swindon game and, somewhat predictably, they witnessed Stoke lose 2-1 to two late goals after they'd looked all set to make a winning league start at 'The Brit'. The result wasn't the most abiding moment of the day though; that came before the match. As part of the opening festivities and celebrations, Stanley Matthews, whose job it was to conduct the official opening, had been given the task of kicking a ball into the net in front of what had been designated as the 'home end'. Sprightly and fit Sir Stan may be, but he's also 83 years of age and people wonder whose decision it was to have him try and kick the ball in from over 20 yards!? The net may have been empty but we have first team players that have difficulty hitting the target from that range, never mind an octogenarian! Stan stroked the ball towards the net but it was clear that it wasn't going to reach the line. Thousands of Stokies behind the goal tried to suck the ball in, but no, it stopped about two yards short. There was an embarrassed silence and nobody quite knew what to do. Eventually, the on-pitch compère with the microphone ran up and booted the ball over the line and everybody politely cheered, but again, it was another pointer as to the type of season we were going to have.

In a thriller in front of the TV cameras, we beat our local rivals Port Vale in the first ever Potteries Derby at our new home. Our near-neighbours harbour serious grievances (most of them imaginary) about the Britannia Stadium, which Stoke built with the generous assistance of the Stoke-on-Trent City Council authority. Having voluntarily turned down the chance of a ground-share arrangement, Port Vale supporters and sympathisers consequently ran a campaign alleging "council corruption" and bias against them at every opportunity. Vale fans are difficult to tolerate at the best of times. Had they won at the Britannia they would have been unbearable!

The zenith of Stoke's season came on October 22nd when they won 1-0 at Maine Road to go fifth in the First Division. In fact, had Charlton not sneaked a deflected late equaliser at the Valley three days earlier, in another televised clash, Stoke would have been in second place! From that point on it was all downhill. It is perhaps ironic that the high point of our season should have come against Manchester City. Some five months later it would be a very different story in the return.

Stoke's season quickly began to fall apart. Our away form was pretty bleak and at home we started losing a little too regularly. Initial talk about the play-offs turned into a grudging acknowledgement that mid-table was a more realistic target. A 2-0 home defeat by South Cheshire neighbours Crewe Alexandra sounded the alarm bells ringing and the spectre of relegation was already starting to haunt the thoughts and conversations of many Stoke supporters. We were still comfortably placed in the middle of the pack but the club was in a downward spiral, and with no money to spend few had much hope that things were going to improve.

As if things weren't bad enough on their own, Stoke were suffering from a major shortage of good luck. Twice in December they completely outplayed high-flying Sheffield United, only to be denied on both occasions by late goals. A Christmas game at West Brom saw the home side grab an equaliser against a stand-in goalie after the referee, Paul Danson, made the Stoke 'keeper leave the field for treatment to a head injury. In the same match he also denied Stoke a penalty, which he conceded was a mistake (after the game), and disallowed a goal straight from a free-kick because he saw that we were trying to make a substitution. Nothing was going our way.

If we were justified in bemoaning our misfortune up until the turn of the New Year, then on 10th January 1998 it's fair to say that we ran out of hard-luck stories. Birmingham City came to the Potteries and played their part in a seven-goal thriller. Well, maybe 'seven-goal thriller' isn't quite the right way of putting it. In fact they won 7-0, thus inflicting on Stoke City the worst home defeat in their entire 135-year history. It was the most harrowing day in the life on any Stoke City supporter and for many it was the final straw.

It was a hugely embarrassing experience, but most supporters' first reaction was one of rage. From the very first days of the season there had been a growing campaign against chairman Peter Coates, his board of directors and the chief executive Jez Moxey. The powder-keg of emotions that had been building up for weeks finally exploded with this mauling. A stream of supporters spilled across the pitch to voice their protests and were promptly arrested for their troubles. There had been a number of previous pitch invaders throughout the season but nothing quite as dramatic as this. Hundreds stormed onto the pitch and dozens broke into the executive suite in an attempt to get at the chairman. It's not the sort of thing you want to see at your club, but enough was enough; *something* had to be done.

For years now, Stoke supporters have been in direct opposition to the club's board, who'd clung limpet-like to power and taken full advantage of the 'truce' called by the fans to help facilitate the move to the new stadium. But now the gloves were off and there was a call to boycott all Peter Coates' catering products (he's the owner of 'Stadia/Lindley Catering' who provide matchday nourishment to a great many grounds throughout the four divisions). A threat to pie sales aside, Peter Coates decided to step down as chairman in the wake of the Birmingham defeat and the FA Cup exit at West Brom (the first time we'd lost to the Baggies for almost ten years!). Mind you, he retained his substantial shareholding and position on the board, and as far as many were concerned he was still the real power at Stoke City.

It was also inevitable that Chic Bates wouldn't survive the Birmingham débâcle. The dreaded vote of confidence was a precursor to the mandatory separation by "by mutual consent." Typically, the Stoke board kept the faith after a 7-0 defeat and then sacked Chic following a 2-1 win at Bradford!

The club already had his successor lined up. Chris Kamara, a former Stoke City player, favourite with the fans and a young manager seen as having plenty of potential, burst onto the scene. Having been the first black manager to lead a club to promotion (with Bradford City), Chris wasted no time in placing the noose around his own neck; on his first day in charge he stated that he wanted to get Stoke into the Premiership within two years. It might have been wiser if Chris had looked at what he had to work with before shooting his mouth off about breaking into the élite of English football.

'A nightmare' best sums up Chris Kamara's short stay at Stoke City. Anything that could go wrong did go wrong. He got off to a flyer by immediately selling popular 18-year-old defender Andy Griffin to Newcastle United and then buying Kyle Lightbourne from Coventry City. Andy Griffin may not be in the Michael Owen mould but he was a firm favourite with the fans and was seen as a real star of the future. As for Kyle Lightbourne, well, it's difficult to know where to start. He went down with a debilitating mystery virus on the very day that he signed, and looked so lifeless in subsequent performances that one Stokie wag nicknamed him 'Stillborne'!

Chris Kamara's hold on the managerial reigns at the Britannia Stadium lasted for 14 games, during which time we won just once and slid from 16th to 24th in the table. His style of management didn't work and the players hated him. To be fair he suffered miserably with bad luck, especially late goals from opposing teams, but few Stoke supporters had any faith left in him when he resigned with five games remaining.

Alan Durban moved out of the backroom shadows to take the helm once more (he was manager between 1978 and 1981) with a mission to keep us in the First Division. In doing so, he became our fourth manager inside 12 months! He calculated that we would stay up if we won three of those final five games and though few of us had much hope that we'd get nine points, it certainly wasn't an impossible task.

The first part of the mission was accomplished in thrilling fashion with a dramatic win against fellow strugglers Portsmouth. In an exciting game Pompey took the lead with 15 minutes left. Stoke equalised with 12 minutes to go and then, deep into injury time, grabbed a winner. Scenes of unbounded joy and ecstasy greeted that strike, and for the first time in many weeks supporters started to believe that we might just escape... The poor fools!

The quest for survival continued at nearby Crewe, owners at that time of the worst home record in the division. We travelled with high hopes but came home with our tails between our legs after a 2-0 defeat. Other results had gone our way though and while our performance had all the hallmarks of a team doomed to relegation, the mathematics of the thing still gave rise to unsubstantiated hope.

A surprisingly comfortable 2-0 home victory over Norwich meant that we'd gained six of the nine points deemed necessary with two games still to go. But you could count out the visit to Premier-chasing Sunderland where, in a cauldron of noise and the biggest First Division crowd of the season, Stoke were swotted aside to the tune of three goals to nil.

But there was still a chance, if we won our final game, and other results went our way. To add spice (if any were needed) to the proceedings, our final day visitors were Manchester City; themselves dangling over the precipice...

There was a clamour for tickets and *Sky* recognised the importance of the occasion by bringing their cameras along. Not happy with their generous allocation of nearly 5,000 tickets, scores of desperate Man City fans travelled down to Stoke-on-Trent, bought tickets for home areas of the ground, and ensured that there was going to be trouble inside the ground, regardless of the result and outcome for both teams.

The match turned out to be another, ahem, 'seven-goal thriller', though one not quite as harrowing as the mauling received at the hands of Birmingham City. This time we actually managed to score, twice in fact, to finish off the season with a 2-5 defeat. Once the initial fighting amongst supporters had subsided, and the Man City infiltrators had been flushed out of areas of the ground they shouldn't have been in in the first place, we sat back and watched Stoke get relegated. There was an almost surreal atmosphere inside the ground though. Even the Mancs had nothing to cheer about, despite the romp their team was enjoying on the field of play. Bury, Portsmouth and Port Vale were all winning against 'couldn't-care-less' opponents and that meant that Stoke and Manchester City were doomed to the Second Division.

In the end relegation was almost a merciful release. We had been limping lamely for months and a drop down into Division Two was all the team deserved for their uninspired efforts. But it wasn't what the supporters deserved. In the past decade and more we've endured much - too much - but we've still stuck firmly by the club. Even in such a dreadful season the average attendance at the Britannia never dropped below 15,000 and that says a lot for the tenacity and loyalty of the support.

The story of Stoke City's '97-98 season was one of relegation, a power struggle, allegations of corruption against the club and a pie boycott by supporters. It's enough to test the patience of a saint. How much longer will Stoke fans put up with being subjected to all this? Well, that may well depend on just how quickly they get their act together in Division Two.

ON THE TERRACES

West Ham United

Although we didn't end up qualifying for the UEFA Cup, I still think season '97-98 should act as a benchmark for the future, for the overall way the team has begun to gel and grow together. The manager has assembled a squad with the likes of Rio Ferdinand, Lampard, Sinclair, Lazaridis, Hodges and an excellent youth team set-up including Joey Cole, whose 'contract' made front page news in several Sunday papers in March, (and who looks set to bear the dreaded 'England's hopes for the future rest on his shoulders' tag before long). So Harry has set both himself and the club up for what should be a very exciting and adventurous leap into the next Millennium. I was just a bit too

young to appreciate the achievements of the Ron Greenwood side that put West Ham on the world football map in the early and mid 60's, so I can't really say whether the team that we have now can be favourably compared to that one, but I think the present squad has the *potential* to be the best we've had since then. If Harry can continue to improve the team like he has over the last two years, we could flourish and possibly match, if not eclipse, the achievements of Greenwood's FA and ECWC winning sides.

For all that, I still have reservations about Redknapp and his approach, both on and off the field. Off it he has consistently failed to fully research the players he buys. Marco Boogers (who played barely 90 minutes during his four year £8,000 per week contract which only ended in May) and Ilie Dumitrescu (who he spent three months trying to sign and then sold at a knock-down price to avoid having to give him away) are good examples. As is Florin Radiciou, "a disgrace from day one..." according to Redknapp, who neglected to mention that it was he who chose to pay £3m+ for the Romanian and then sell him back to Espanol for £2m. Other poor buys include Richard Hall (always an injury liability and only a handful of appearances in two years), Paul Kitson (ditto) and John Hartson (who could be a brilliant player, but due to his off-field antics and pathetic temperament on it, is unlikely to EVER fulfil his potential). On the field, Redknapp's tactics and the timing of the changes (when he decides to make them), are rarely those of a man in control of the situation. Too often, his decisions are just as a reaction to what the opposition manager has done, when he should be taking the bull by the horns and making changes which force the opposition to re-think their tactics. On the all-too-rare occasions when Harry's strategies *do* work, it is usually down to nothing more than fluke (Ian Pearce's performance as an overlapping right wingback in the 3-0 home win against Leeds being a case in point).

Although I say that West Ham has its strongest squad for many a year, there are still some areas that need strengthening, beginning in goal. Despite the very favourable impression Lama made when he finally got his chance, and all the good PR done by West Ham, I doubt very much that there was ever any intention by the club to sign him. Word that Shaka Hislopp would be signed leaked out at the turn of the year, and although Lama was also available for free, the club claim that his wage demands priced him out of the race. It seems to me that the decision was made purely on financial grounds; never mind who the better 'keeper might be. The right-hand side of the defence is also a weak point, just as it has been for a few years; Tim Breacker has made a valuable contribution in the past, but to be fair he's been going downhill for a while. And in a season that has seen him spend longer out with injury than available for selection, Impey has not really convinced me, and you have to wonder about his overall fitness (another one for that previously-mentioned list).

Most of all, I think that we are lacking someone big and strong to help us take hold of a match in the middle of the park; someone with the presence and authority to keep the team driving forward for a second goal when we're 1-0 up, or to keep things tight at the back to stop opponents grabbing (late) equalisers. I think - and hope - that Lampard will be a good enough player to perform this duty in four or five years (if he's still here). However, the qualities that are needed only come with age and experience, and we could do with someone to do that job now. How many games were either drawn or lost by the odd unnecessary goal? We were left to wonder whether we'd have got some sort of result out of at least a dozen games, if only we'd had a strong character like Billy Bonds, Julian Dicks, or even (dare I mention them?) Paul Ince or Slaven Bilic leading the team. Maybe Marc Keller (signed at the tail-end of the season) is the man; we'll have to wait and see. Someone like that would definitely have made the difference between qualifying for Europe and not, just as John Hartson not missing seven league games, or playing without the desire away from home (like Iain Dowie) too often would have done.

I am pretty certain that Harry recognises these chinks in his squad's armour, and will continue building on the good work that he and his coaches (particularly Tony Carr) have done, to make West Ham even better for next season. It is noticeable how much favourable press and media attention he and the team started accumulating over the course of last year, but even the exciting football that the fans were treated to (sporadically, but more often than in the past) I don't find too surprising. Anyone who has followed the team since Harry stepped into the manager's seat cannot fail to see that this is the best team since he took over; things are on an upward curve and even if the progress that has been made these past few seasons slows down a bit, you can sense that some sort of success is, whilst still unattained, but a fingertip away. UEFA Cup qualification would have been a brilliant boost for all of us, for a number of reasons. For a start, it would be the first time ever in the club's history and it would've helped put us back on the football map in European terms (and therefore make it easier to attract good players). Second, there was the potential for a few more unexpected million quid to he banked from TV, advertising; etc.

Which brings me on to our board of directors, their appalling abuse of the meagre league success the team has achieved and their similar treatment (by no means for the first time) of the awe-inspiring loyalty of West Ham's long-suffering fans. Followers of the game may recall West Ham's ill-considered decision a few years ago to follow Glasgow Rangers' and Arsenal's example of issuing Bonds (a scheme whereby fans had to pay for a Bond in order to buy a season ticket), and the fans' response to it. It caused an outcry that led to thousands of supporters of many years' standing to resolve to never set foot inside Upton Park ever again. A steadfast refusal by chairman Terence Brown and Co. to make any apology for the scheme is only matched by Hirohito's stand on war crimes - and at least *he* has the excuse that it was his father who was responsible. If an apology had been made; if there was any chance that the board could've learnt from their mistakes, I am sure that many would forget (if not forgive), but it doesn't seem as though our current chairman is capable of that. Recent increases in season ticket prices, stopping concessions for the unemployed, and even reducing the number of cup matches covered by season tickets all show the voracious greed now at work within the West Ham boardroom. (Sadly it seems to be the same story in too many football clubs today).

Being one of those under the 'unemployed' category, I can tell you that for '96-97 I paid £180 for my season ticket, compared with £520 for '98-99. Disenfranchised? Feeling unwanted? You bet. Last season, notification that our free cup games were being reduced from three to two came only after we'd won the second game! This time, the club waited until they thought the time was just right before announcing increases of between 20 and 30% in season ticket prices, undoubtedly banking on UEFA qualification; I couldn't help but laugh when I thought of the looks on their faces as failure to win at bottom-of-the-table Crystal Palace ended up meaning we missed out by a single point. To avoid what would undoubtedly have been a very heated meeting, the club even went to the trouble of moving a Fans' Forum forward by a week, which meant that letters detailing the increases arrived two days after the meeting, rather than five days before.

I thought that my last *SOTF* article was depressing enough, but this time I really do feel that '98-99, the eleventh season of *On the Terraces'* existence, will be its last. I believe that football as an affordable and enjoyable spectacle, at Premier League level anyway, has become a thing of the past. Its once vibrant heartbeat is now little more than a murmur, and having been treated like an inconvenience by West Ham's board (only temporary custodians, after all) for so long, like so many other fans I know we'll turn our backs on the game without a second thought.

ONE MORE POINT

Crystal Palace

The final whistle blew. Within seconds the scoreboard was flashing up the number of Samaritans and the first line ("I get knocked down...") of Chumbawamba's *Tubthumping* blared out. Palace had lost 3-0 at home to Manchester United and the relegation which had been a formality since mid-March had been confirmed. The roller-coaster known as Crystal Palace had had yet another season of not even hinting at slowing down... just going down. Each of the reviews I've written for the three previous versions of this book have contained more incidents and excitement than most teams have in five years and this year was no

THE FANZINE OF THE LEAGUE'S YO-YO TEAM

ONE MORE POINT

PRICE £1.00   ISSUE 25

MEANWHILE, OVER AT FULHAM

IT'S TERRIBLE RAY, MY WIFE'S RUN OFF WITH THE MILKMAN, I WAS BURGLED THE OTHER DAY AND MY JAG GOT CLAMPED THIS MORNING.

COULD BE WORSE ALAN, YOU COULD STILL BE AT PALACE!

REVEALED - OMP PLAYER OF THE YEAR FOR 1997

different. Yet, when Uncle Ron finally loosened the purse strings last summer it looked like it would be different this time and a long-overdue season of boring mid-table consolidation could be ours to savour. But then again, if I wanted that I wouldn't support Crystal Palace.

The season started at a time when my life was in turmoil. I'd gone into sales at the start of the summer and it had gone horribly wrong. I had hardly any money and if I didn't get a deal by Tuesday I'd have my meagre basic taken away and be on commission only. Nevertheless, I spent just about every penny to my name for the opener at Everton. It was good to see everyone again, many for the first time since that wonderful day at Wembley when we'd secured promotion with the last kick of the season. Hoppo, the play-off hero, had gone but in his place we had a new 'keeper in Kevin Miller, the experienced Paul Warhurst and best of all, the Italian superstar Atillio Lombardo. Arriving at Goodison, the Ladbrokes board advertised example bets. 'Palace to win 2-0 - Lombardo first goal 100/1'. It had to be done. A cool one'er in my pocket could see me through two weeks at a push if I lost my basic.

The game started and after half an hour Warhurst teed up Lombardo who stroked the ball past Southall. Bloody hell! The bet was well and truly on. With 12 minutes to go our Italian god raced towards goal before being hauled down. PENALTY! I could hardly look. There was a hundred pounds riding on this. Dyer converted!! Palace then tried their best to ruin it with a succession of counter attacks and I found myself cheering Southall as he made some great saves. But with four minutes to go Ferguson pulled one back for Everton. I was gutted and felt like a tosser for wanting Muscat to miss when he'd been one-on-one. After a nervy finish we held on and a quick totting up showed us to be in second place. We'd have been top and I'd have been a ton better off but for that Ferguson goal. Still, it was a great day out.

Our first home game pitted us against Barnsley with the lure of going top of the league for only the second time in our entire history, if we won. I needed cheering up because my deal hadn't come in... Despite dominating the game we somehow managed to lose 1-0. In the pub afterwards I was suicidal. Eighty quid in the world to my name, no cash coming in, rent due and worst of all we'd lost at home to Barnsley. Little did I realise how indicative of our home form that game would be.

However, things picked up on the job front and by the time the next game came around 11 days later I was in the City, working for a major bank, and on more money than I'd ever been on. When Palace beat Leeds 2-0 to go fifth after three games, life couldn't have been better. I must have been supporting them too long, as my own life seemed to mirror the Palace team's roller-coaster nature! However, from that moment Palace would decline, slowly at first, followed by freefall after Christmas. Three defeats including a hammering at home to Chelsea exposed our weaknesses. We were signing million pound players every ten days or so. Zobar arrived from Israel with the club sending out signals hinting that we'd got the steal of the century. Emblen breezed in from Wolves and the unknown Hreidarrson came from Iceland on the recommendation of DJ David Jensen's wife. For the first time ever Uncle Ron was throwing money around to ensure we actually stayed up this time.

A Lombardo goal in the away leg of the Selhurst derbies ensured we halted the mini slide. October was solid if not spectacular and even contained our first win at Hillsborough since the 1920's. It also marked our first win without Lombardo, one of only two all season. The constant transfer dealing continued with Muscat and the skilful Dougie Freedman going to Wolves in a swap for right-back Jamie Smith.

With work going nicely I managed to get my own flat, just five minutes walk from Selhurst Park. I moved in the day after we beat Wednesday 3-1. What more can a man ask for in a weekend!?

November started spectacularly as we raced to a 2-0 lead at West Ham in a *Sky* televised game. Unfortunately, the Hammers stormed back with Hartson and then Lampard scoring within 20 minutes of the restart. As Lampard ran away celebrating, the floodlights went out. Another *Sky* gimmick, I thought, but after a few minutes of darkness it dawned on everyone that there was a problem. Palace fans then started getting their lighters out and waving 50p coins 'for the meter'. Despite the banter and spontaneous songs and chants that sprang up around the away end, it was frustrating to finally have to leave wondering how the game might have finished.

It was around this time that millionaire Mark Goldberg came to the fore. It was known that he was largely responsible for the wads of money being thrown around at Selhurst. A lifelong Palace fan, he'd built up a £100m computer recruitment company from scratch and made no secret of his desire to own the club. Great on paper, but in reality his zealous approach often conflicted with the more experienced Noades and this would lead to disaster by the end of the season.

Sky was on hand again to witness one of my highlights of the season, our 1-0 win at Spurs (and yes, the goal was clearly offside). Having won five of eight on our travels we were being dubbed 'away day specialists'. The away form was good enough to put us tenth, and the following Saturday's *Sun* had a major article on Palace, and Coppell in particular. They claimed that we would be the surprise packets of the season and were a good outside bet to get a European place... We didn't win again for four months! When Newcastle went 2-0 up after an hour that afternoon I decided to go home and have a bath. "We won't score today," I said to the others as I walked out. Shipperley pulled one back before I even got out of the ground. Bollocks! I kept on walking though and there were no further goals.

The re-arranged West Ham game took place without Lombardo, who'd been injured whilst training for an Italian World Cup qualifier, and we duly went down 4-1. Still, Neil Shipperley managed to score in that game to support his selection of the *London Evening Standard's* Player of the Month for November. It also highlighted a bizarre scenario where, thanks to the previous floodlight failure and a friendly in Gothenburg, Shipperley scored in seven consecutive matches, yet officially still only had five goals all season!

December, usually a good month for us, was poor. We were robbed of three points at Leicester in the last minute, despite having controversially been down to ten men for an hour. Muzzy Izzet went off for an injury but came back on to the pitch without permission and then scored a good goal. It was my birthday weekend and the bastards had ruined the day. Four years previously, on my birthday, I got beaten up after the game. Please don't make us play Leicester in the first week of December again! Just to rub it in, *Match of the Day* included it in Goal of the Month. According to the laws, it shouldn't even have been allowed for God's sake!

A battling 0-0 at Derby was unexpected and welcome. We were completely outplayed and thanks to injuries we fielded a team without a single striker. The Boxing Day game was sublime. Southampton were somehow 1-0 up at half time despite our domination. Shipps, seemingly back from injury, pulled us level then had to go off as his groin injury returned. With ten minutes to go we won a penalty; finally our barren home run could be banished. We had two very competent penalty takers on the pitch and surely one of them would win us the game. Unfortunately, Israeli import Itzik Zohar (whose name sounded remarkably like 'he's shit so far') decided to wrestle the ball from Bruce Dyer and demanded to take the kick. What was going on? This was mad. This bloke's crap! The 'keeper saved and I was in the Selhurst Arms cursing into my pint by the time the final whistle blew. Coppell went to the press saying that Dyer was injured and was in no fit state to take the penalty. What bollocks - you only had to look at the player's body language on the pitch. This point was confirmed when I bumped into Simon Rodger whilst having a leak in a Croydon pub. A battling 2-2 draw at Blackburn rounded off the year. We weren't in the bottom three but there were definitely problems at the club.

January, and one-time great Tomas Brolin joined us on a free transfer and played brilliantly in his first two games. Once he'd won himself a ten grand a week contract he was crap for the rest of the season. Bloody typical.

A midweek 6-2 thrashing at Chelsea was the final straw and on Friday 13th (you knew it had to be on *that* date with Palace, didn't you) March, Palace shocked the football world by announcing that Lombardo and Brolin were to replace Steve Coppell. Atillio was loved by everyone at Palace but from a purely objective viewpoint having a man with no coaching experience and an almost non-existent command of English did seem extreme, even by Palace standards.

Lombardo's first game in charge was at Villa. The Palace faithful were hopeful and full of voice. "Lom-bar-do's Red and Blue Army" we sang. Ahem, we were 1-0 down after a minute, 3-0 by half-time. After the break a section of us stripped to the waist and twirled our shirts around, something that even made the nationals on Monday. It seemed to work a little as new signing (yet another one) Matt Jansen opened his Palace account with a wonder goal. Some hope for the future?

Our next game at Newcastle coincided with the row surrounding their director Freddie Shepherd. Playing us seemed to offer them the chance to get back to winning ways and appease the fans. GMTV's presenter even had the nerve to comment, "All the Newcastle female fans will turn their back on the game after each goal they score tonight in protest." Lombardo and Jansen had other ideas and we secured a brilliant 2-1 win that ended our Premiership record of eight straight defeats. This went nicely alongside our other Premiership record of nine games without a goal the last time we were in this division! It also got us thinking about a possible escape.

But after more defeats and with relegation looming, the only thing occupying our minds was whether we'd win at home before the end of the season. Leicester at Easter looked a good chance. I left before they made it 3-0! A narrow defeat at Liverpool on Easter Monday, which included a great goal from another new youngster Marcus Bent, a £300k signing from Brentford in January, was followed by the visit of Derby. We'd still not kept a clean sheet since we played them in December, and when it got to half time and they still hadn't scored we began to think that maybe, just maybe, we could get a home win.

Lombardo came on with the score 0-0 after 71 minutes and the whole team seemed to raise itself. The effect was stunning. Matt Jansen made it 1-0 five minutes later and it was like we'd won the league. Four minutes later Lombardo was instrumental in putting the ball on a plate for Sasa Curcic (yes, you guessed it, another recent signing) to make it 2-0. "We're gonna win at home," we sang. With five minutes to go Derby scored. With two minutes to go they hit the bar. With one minute to go they forced a wonder save from Miller. In injury time Lombardo set up another, this time for Bent, to finish off a crazy 20 minute spell and finally end the most embarrassing statistic in British football. WE'D WON AT HOME!

The visit of Man Utd sparked a lot of emotions. Not least because it was the first time they'd played us at Selhurst Park since three of their fans murdered Paul Nixon before the FA Cup semi back in 1995, which in turn was a result of the Cantona kung fu incident three months earlier. With this still fresh in a lot of people's minds, the United fans (who are always quick to complain when teams sing the Munich song) decided to sing Cantona's name throughout. Still, we drowned them out and created an unbelievable atmosphere even when we were 2-0 down in the first half. And who gives a shit that we went down that night. I know who I'd rather support; I'm Palace and proud.

For the first time since 1992 our season was over before May. Lombardo resigned as manager and for what it was worth Ron Noades took control over team affairs. The last three games would be treated as a party. Bolton away was crazy. Thanks to diabolical trains and the world's worst cabbie, my mates and I got to the ground half an hour late by which time it was already 2-2 and I'd missed our *two best goals* of our season. I'd been in the ground for one minute and it was 3-2 to Bolton. Doh! By the end we'd lost 5-2 but yet again our fans stole the show with 20 or so running around the away end dressed as Red Indians! Top stuff. The thing is, as I write, I still haven't managed to see either of our goals from that game. A mad 3-3 draw with West Ham saw us scrape to the 30 point mark with a game to go.

The last day saw some great fancy dress, although without doubt the best was a guy who led a conga around the Holmesdale in flippers, snorkel and diving mask. Sheffield Wednesday were the visitors and they represented our only chance of doing a double. In a mediocre game it looked like both teams would settle for a point apiece. Two minutes into injury time Pressman made a minor error in the Wednesday goal and who else but Lombardo was on hand to pounce on the mistake and pass to Clinton Morrison to score into the open goal eight minutes into his debut. Like the Derby game we went nuts and from the reaction you'd have thought we'd won the World Cup. The last few weeks had seen brilliant crowd support and some blinding moments. Blimey, we should get relegated more often if it's always this fun!

With El Tel in charge and the likes of Lombardo, Curcic, Jansen and Bent around we'll be straight back up - no worries. But knowing Palace, we'll be straight back down again. I wouldn't have it any other way. The only problem is, having seen England get robbed in the World Cup two days ago I wish I'd made a note of the Samaritans' number when it flashed up after the Man Utd game!

ONE-NIL DOWN, TWO-ONE UP

Arsenal

Gooners will surely remember '97-98 as the season from heaven. Both major domestic honours were scooped as Arsenal romped home comfortably. Even more satisfying is the fact that we were two wins away from the treble and Spurs so nearly went down. Arsene Wenger is magic and he wears a magic hat (probably one of those red and white Viking-cum-Dipsy-Teletubby efforts).

But who would have thought that any of this was possible in the dark days of November and December? In the fanzine, many despairing words were used to describe our league form but none served so well as 'crap'. Embarrassing losses to Derby,

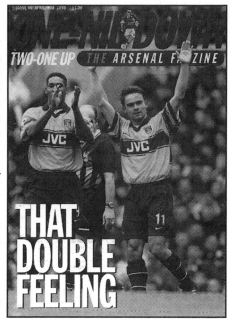

Sheffield Wednesday, Liverpool and Blackburn cast a very gloomy cloud over N5. Most humiliating was Blackburn at home; not only were we completely outplayed but also Blackburn wanted it more. For an Arsenal side to show no will to win was nothing short of scandalous. As the team trundled off to a crescendo of boos, we in turn trundled down Avenell Road to be greeted with the sight of an almost naked Ian Wright standing at the changing room window informing us that we were "tossers" for having the temerity to question his and the team's woeful performance.

The general consensus was that Wenger was an interfering French busy-body who had ripped the heart (the 'magic man' Paul Merson) out of the team and replaced it with foreign dross like Grimandi, Wreh, Boa Morte and Anelka. Overmars just never got stuck in and Petit was a graceless centre-back masquerading as a midfielder, clattering anyone in his path, whose passing appeared entirely random. The erudite Mike Collins remarked that "Wenger's real problem is that he's French. When we had to evacuate the beaches at Dunkirk we did so in the full knowledge that we'd be back for more - and we were, if only to rescue the Frogs from another fine mess." *The One-Nil Down* postbag was full of letters bemoaning the disastrous situation.

The winter of discontent reached its nadir with the Port Vale home cup-tie. The game had all the ingredients of a superlatively crap day out.

Torrential rain and gale-force winds made fanzine selling impossible and various soaked malcontents fled to the safety of the Arsenal Cafe. When I finally took my seat in the North Bank, I realised that I was practically at pitch level with no cover and an assortment of young children to give the section all the atmosphere of a crèche. The game was bloody awful too. Travelling home on the train, I vowed never to waste a Saturday afternoon again in such a pointless fashion.

Of course, things had been different in the halcyon days of summer. Not even a useless third album from Oasis could stifle my enthusiasm as Arsenal played even better than the 1970 Brazil side. Goals flew in from all over the place, most of them coming from the divine Dennis Bergkamp. The three he bagged at Leicester made surely the greatest hat-trick of all-time. Shame about the defending, though. Sides of the calibre of West Ham, Barnsley and Bolton were dispatched with ease, as Arsenal stood proud at the top of the table. Tony Willis described Gilles Grimandi as having "more than a touch of Franco Baresi about him." Arsenal then, as described above, collapsed at the first sign of winter.

Then, as winter turned to spring, Arsenal's form changed too. Finally, the foreign misfits began to gel. Anelka began to score regularly at last and was starting to live up to the tag of 'the new Platini'. Previously he had swanned around like a French Emerson looking like he didn't give a toss about playing for the Arsenal, much to the annoyance of the fans. There were odd flashes of brilliance - his goal against Man United - but generally we saw nothing of note. Now it looked as if we had a replacement for the ageing Wrighty. Overmars was tearing down the wing, turning various right-backs' shorts a curious shade of brown. The strike at Old Trafford was the sweetest we had seen from a winger since the golden days of Anders Limpar. Petit had formed a formidable midfield partnership with Patrick Vieira and they brushed aside anyone who dared stand in their way. They were far better than Keane and Butt anyday. Petit inspired surely the best chant of the season - "He's blond... He's fit... His name's a porno flick... Emmanuel... Emmanuel." However, he took some time to find his shooting boots. The legend of Jensen's number 17 shirt lived on after Manu's efforts concussed various fans. But he hit his purple patch in April with two goals in three games - the second being a cracker against Derby. Even Christopher Wreh managed to endear himself to the Highbury faithful with crucial goals against Bolton, Wimbledon and Wolves. He has it in him to be a Highbury cult hero: although your granny is probably a better player than he is, he has the knack of getting vital goals.

Some things never changed though - Grimandi, Garde and Boa Morte were just crap. But this didn't matter because Arsenal were thrashing everybody with 11 wins in 12 games. By the Everton fixture we knew that we were home and dry, needing just one more win, and of course you know what happened next. Massive partying ensued in Islington. However, the FA Cup run wasn't the steamrollering performance that the league run-in was. Endless replays meant that the season seemed like a continual set of matches with Chelsea, Crystal Palace and West Ham. Never mind though, because the Double is most certainly not to be sniffed at. The final seemed almost too easy with Arsenal showing a quiet dominance with a polished and forceful performance. Unfortunately, the vagaries of Cup Final ticket allocations meant that I sat at home watching it on TV. The FA *must* increase the allocation given to the finalists - a mere 25,000 is a disgrace when 30,000 go to sponsors and representatives of clubs.

Speaking of Wembley, a major issue of the season was the relocation debate. As The Clash pondered - should we stay or should we go? If we stay there will be trouble with the Highbury residents putting up a strong fight to resist any redevelopment. But if we go there would be possibly double our present capacity at a new super-stadium. The ideal solution would be to build new stands on the south and west sides to reach a capacity of around 55,000. Those living around Highbury, especially those on Highbury Hill opposite the West Stand, would perhaps be forced to leave their homes. Their arguments against are somewhat spurious - they see the venture as a simple moneymaking move for the board and urge us to oppose the redevelopment so that we can keep our nice, compact stadium. Bollocks! For a start, we want an increased capacity so that we can actually get in to see the games. Secondly, Arsenal have been at Highbury for 85 years. The majority of residents have lived there for under five years or less. Thirdly, the residents feel that an increased number of fans would simply make their lives unbearable. But when the ground had terracing, crowds of 55,000 were common. *And* they were more unruly then. The current Highbury art-school bohemians have it easy compared to the previous generation of residents. Besides, you don't move next to a football ground and then complain when crowds converge on your home every other week. I happen to live under the flightpath of Luton airport and have the M1 around 150 yards from the bottom of my garden. I can't object - I knew full well what it would be like when I moved there. Finally, we must look at the logistics of the situation. There are around 90 or so people on Highbury Hill whose homes would possibly be demolished. A redevelopment would benefit up to 20,000 fans, not to mention the local chip shops, pubs and the like. Think about it.

The alternative is to leave Highbury for pastures new. This would probably be a greenfield site off the M25. But this prospect horrifies many. Imagine ten years in the future if we are mid-table and playing Sheffield Wednesday at home to a half-empty, soulless concrete bowl and the old ground exists only as a plaque, telling us that one upon a time there was a famous old stadium where there is now a hotel. Would we, as one reader noted, be called Potters Barsenal? Even worse, can you imagine another club moving in to Highbury? God, it could be Wimbledon! It would be like someone burgling your house whilst you were on holiday and moving in, using your sofa as a bed for their Rottweiler and your CD collection as Frisbees for it to play with. At least we're not moving to Wembley, though. Thankfully, the board have decided not to buy the dilapidated relic "in the interests of English football." Yes, of course. It wasn't just a bargaining tool used to put pressure on Islington Council, was it?

The fanzines have set up the Arsenal Fans For Consultation (AFfC) consisting of the editors of *One-Nil Down*, *The Gooner* and *Highbury High*. A letter was sent to David Dein and Ken Friar asking for a meeting between the group and the club to air the fans' views. The board, though, maintained their usual silence on important matters and all that was received from the club was a bland letter from the head of communications Clare Tomlinson and a set of press releases from Islington Council. Isn't it nice to see the Arsenal board moving along with the times and being open with the fans?

The other debate around Highbury is the Wrighty issue. Some feel he is an egotistical and ageing striker who is way past his best and should be packed off to somewhere like Palace. Others feel that the man walks on water and to criticise him is tantamount to heresy. The realistic view is somewhere between the two. Yes, he is past his best and has lost a lot of his pace. But he is still one of the best finishers in the country and his goalscoring record proves this. He is still good for another season yet, and will provide competition with Anelka to partner Bergkamp. The fact that I have Wright on the back of my away shirt (which must last another season) has no influence on my opinion whatsoever.

Player of the season? Ray Parlour for his conversion from boozy, inconsistent wide-boy to one of the best midfielders in the country. How he isn't in the England squad is beyond me. He is the ideal player for the right wing back role as he can tackle like a demon and run all day, providing reasonable crosses. I write this before the World Cup so these words are either incisive and well informed or hopelessly wrong and naïve, depending on England's performance this summer. Transfer targets? Alan Wright and Rob Jones as new full backs and Darren Huckerby as a striker to work with Anelka and Bergkamp in the long run. See you next year.

ONE TEAM IN BRISTOL

Bristol City

It all started with the memories of last season's play-off defeat at Brentford still fresh in our minds; a route we didn't want to go down ever again. This time around, so high were the expectations that even a defeat in the play-off final at Wembley would be looked upon by the fans and directors as a failure.

The signing of Steve Torpey for £400,000 from cash-strapped Swansea showed that desperation had crept in at an early stage. The team coach on the way to our very first game was made to wait in the car park while he signed the relevant forms. With the season just 27 mins old, we thought we'd got our money's worth; a torpedo of a strike from the new boy. But before we had even thought of a relevant chant for our new hero, his season was nearly finished. A sickening head injury four minutes later kept him out for a month, and he never seemed the same after his come-back.

Our perennial problem - inconsistency - arose in the first month, when we slumped to 19th position, yet the disappointment was helped by the more important fact that we had dumped our rivals Rovers out of the Coca-Cola Cup. Will they ever beat the Reds?!

Promotion, our only aim this season, seemed about as likely as buying an edible pie at Ashton Gate, a fact backed up by the Colman's survey, which showed that our food rated 91st out of the 93 footballing venues. Yes, we certainly are the Doncaster of catering. However, our season completely changed with the introduction of Tommy Doherty. No, not *him*, but a teenager with a talent unseen at City for a decade or more; a ball-winner in the centre of midfield, and one who can link play with the front men with quick-thinking through balls. It was no coincidence that after his debut, we started an incredible sequence of results, amassing 41 points from a possible 45. It saw us climb from our previous anxious position to the dizzy heights of second. Our superiority was highlighted further by the fact that the team in third place were closer to being relegated than promoted! But the most important result in that run was the game down at the local rugger pitch. Our visit to the home of the odd-shaped

The fanzine for the only __permanent__ team in Bristol

Championship Special

ONE TEAM IN BRISTOL

Cheerio, Cheerio, Cheerio,

54

Golden Touch
Grand Prix Finish
Better than Sex
Vergard Hansen

32 champion pages

Still Only

£1

balls, Bristol Rugby Club, the latest stopping-off point for Bristol Roamers, saw us yet again beat the Rent Boys: Goater 2, Rovers 1.

Shortly after, we travelled to Watford for a game billed as 'Part One of the Championship Decider', amazing as it was still early December. It showed graphically the enormous potential our club could realise if football was regularly played at a higher level: a massive 6,000 City fans made the long trip to Watford. There, fans and players alike were in a state of shock, staring in disbelief at the massed ranks for 85 minutes, and it even looked like we would deservedly grab all three points until a late equaliser by Giften Noel Edmonds! In my view the acid test of our new-found ruthless confidence was against Grimsby. They visited Ashton Gate in red-hot form, yet after only five minutes we had completely destroyed them. It was so good it was frightening; the Fishermen were sunk in a 4-1 tidal wave but it could have been many more.

As the season unfolded, the gap between Watford and ourselves to the chasing pack was growing; analogies between us and the infamous Grand National horse Crisp were becoming more common. But unlike that race, *this* one rewarded the first two, and not just Red Rum. The 16 point gap we had opened up around February was still not enough for some nervous City fans to be able to claim promotion, but it would have taken a collapse even beyond our capabilities. The only uncertainty really was the exact date that we would wrap up promotion. Favourite was March 14th, the day the Rovers came to town. Unfortunately, due to a minor splutter in the preceding weeks it was not to be, but what a day it was. Billed as the 'Last Ever Bristol Derby', due to the fact that we were going up and they weren't, and furthermore because it was patently obvious that in the future we would never again slump to their level, and they certainly will never aspire to greater heights. It was probably the most one-sided derby ever witnessed. The salt was rubbed in Rovers' wounds even more with the news at the final whistle that the 2-0 victory had taken us to the top of the league. Even more degrading for them was that with that news, City fans refused to leave the ground, staying on for seemingly ever to sing "We are top of the League" to the Rovers fans who were held back in the ground by the police until we had dispersed. Saturdays don't come much better!

Transfer deadline day came, and top-scorer Shaun Goater, who had not kept a secret of the fact that he wanted to play football at a higher level, like his best mate Kyle Lightbourne (then of Coventry reserves), finally left for £400,000 to Manchester City (later described as the career move of the century!!). This was not looked upon as a major blow as we had promotion sewn up and we would have got nothing for him at the end of term. That was until it was announced we had signed, thankfully on loan, Oldham's over-weight, over-the-hill Sean McCarthy for the remaining games.

Even our jinx of never winning in front of the *Sky* camera team was ended in this unbelievable season, when we turned over 'unbeatable at home' Oldham in their own back-yard.

Our promotion party was a strange affair; it happened without us kicking a ball when Grimsby, who had to win all their remaining games, slipped up in midweek, but the 3,000 fans travelling to Burnley the following weekend weren't complaining.

The 'Championship decider' at home to Watford in front of 20,000 decided nothing, but our impressive scoring record throughout the season was disappearing quickly. Key injuries were taking their toll in our quest for the title. During the penultimate away game at Chesterfield, we lost our goalkeeper with a career-threatening pelvic injury, but more spooky was that the match programme named Ade Akinbiyi as City's top scorer. Obviously their editor is Mystic Meg...

The final day will live long in the memory. For many years, the 'Second of May' has had negative connotations, thanks to a one-off defeat on that date by our rivals. But no longer; this was the day we will remember forever as the conclusion to one of our greatest ever seasons. A victory at Preston would have given us the title, but it was not to be (with two tiny wingers as the only front men in the club without a sick-note, it was probably on the cards). But if you'd said to City fans in August that we would finish second, streets ahead of the chasing pack, they would have bitten your hand off - just think what happened to the team who beat us in last year's play-offs, Brentford!

A question asked regularly to fans with rival teams in the same city is "would you swap two victories against your most hated rivals for promotion?" Well, this season that was irrelevant; we did both!

On a personal note, *One Team In Bristol* were proud to receive the award from Teletext as the Best Regional Fanzine in the South West and Wales area. Robbo, Phil, Matt, Julia, Martin, Kev, Smiffy, Dalziel, Finbar, Nytram, Mike, Elljot and all our contributors received the trophy with pride.

THE ONION BAG

Chester City

"Yes! Yes! Yes! Oh yeah! Yeah! Oh God! Yes!"

Not, as you might expect, the script from a low budget blue movie, but the words on the lips of all but the most masochistic of Chester fans at the final whistle on May the 2nd 1998. At last! At bloody last! The league campaign had come to an end. The abject misery of watching a team with nothing to play for - seemingly not even pride - was over. Dreams of holidays watching scantily-clad young Scandinavian ladies on sun-kissed beaches could finally become a reality. What bliss.

It seems strange that the onset of another close season (in truth, typically spent standing at deep square-leg in summer drizzle on a cricket field rather than ogling topless Swedish birds) could have been greeted with such wild enthusiasm, considering the optimism of four months earlier. Back in January, City's supporters had emerged from Sincil Bank in jubilant mood. The double had been completed over the Imps with consummate ease and Kevin Ratcliffe's men had moved up to fourth place in the process. Unbeaten at home, and with away form on the up, a position in the play-offs looked a formality. Little did we realise the traumatic weeks that lay ahead of us. What was to dramatically turn the season not so much pear-shaped but more like one of those phallic vegetables everyone used to giggle at on *That's Life?* We'll come on to that later.

The Blues began the season with the addition of just two new faces to the squad. Rod Thomas, so often a tormentor of our defence in the past, had arrived from Carlisle while, starting his third spell at the club, Gary Bennett had re-signed from arch-enemies Wrexham. The latter's controversial return was greeted with mixed reaction. Some welcomed his undoubted goal-scoring prowess whilst others still regarded him a quisling for wearing that loathed red shirt with such apparent enthusiasm. Fortunately, Psycho's early strike rate in the penalty box won over most of the zealots to help ensure City a solid start at home to the campaign - only Macc and Cambridge sneaking draws.

Onion Bag 25

A singularly strange Chester City fanzine *April 1998 Price: £1*

Leave go of my head or I'll rip your bollocks off!

Murphy Lays Down The Law

IN THIS EXCITING 20P DEARER ISSUE:
Vox-Pop, Scored Against The Wrexham, Letters Page, Expert Analysis, Helena Bonham-Carter Reveals All, Four Pages Of Incredibly Dull Match Reviews, Lots Of Other Things In Tiny Print, Plus Rod Thomas Takes Us Fly-Fishing For Grayling On The Palindromically-Named River Tanat.

Away from the Deva though the team had big, big problems. Uncustomary four goal stuffings at Rotherham, Mansfield and Scarborough (plus defeats elsewhere) had staff and supporters scratching their heads as to the reason why. Were they missing the charging-rhino style tackling of Shaun Reid - whose services we were to be denied the whole year due to a knee injury - or were the card school's games of snap simply proving too mentally exhausting for the team by the time they took to the field? Despite a shock win at Notts County, it was inevitable that the lads would be the first to succumb to the league's whipping boys Doncaster Rovers. To compound the misery of that humiliating, frosty December night in South Yorkshire, three days later Chester lost 2-0 at home, and live on *Sky*, to Wrexham in the FA Cup. With the gulf in class between the two divisions so patently obvious, I doubt I have endured such a debilitating experience since a dodgy lamb souvlaki in Corfu in 1985.

To be fair, City kept on doggedly, if unimpressively, grinding out the results. A run of four wins from five games, including a memorable late rally at Hull, brought us to the aforementioned win at Lincoln. The following Saturday though Barnet ensured the home record went up in flames and quickly, after ugly rumours of impending financial ruin became rife. The signs were there for all to see. The club shop had had stock removed by disgruntled creditors to leave it resembling, in the words of one local hack, an Albanian supermarket (not that you could buy framed photos of Enver Hoxha - more's the pity). The official kit washers retained City's rather unpleasant green away shirts on solicitors' advice over unpaid debts. The manager wasn't allowed to sign anyone due to the club's non-payment of instalments re: the Gary Bennett transfer. And so it went on. At the centre of all the hearsay lay City's corpulent thirty-something chairman Mark Guterman. Although an impassioned speaker on behalf of the welfare of the lower divisions, he had few admirers despite his constant insistence that it was his personal money alone that was keeping the club afloat. Cries of "Guterman out" became commonplace as the team's form went well and truly down the pan. A winding-up order from the Inland Revenue duly arrived, and fans deliberated over whether they'd support Witton Albion or Northwich Victoria next season.

Eventually, as so often is the case, the club survived by the skin of its teeth on transfer deadline day. As had been expected, some money was raked in by the sale of the relatively accomplished defensive duo of Iain Jenkins and Julian Alsford to Dundee United. (Mind you, the Tannadice faithful will quickly see Jules is better suited to facing the likes of Forfar or Brechin on a regular basis rather than Celtic or Rangers.) However, the remainder of the debt was to be wiped out from a most unusual source - a certain 17-year old named Matthew McKay. Hopefully Mattie will go on to become the star of England's heroic 2002 World Cup victory but when Kevin Ratcliffe gives up football management (sooner rather than later some would wish), he must surely have a job awaiting him at Saatchi & Saatchi. What marketing skills and powers of persuasion the man must have to have coaxed Howard Kendall to part with £250,000 for someone who could boast just three full first team appearances.

OK, the lad had shown some promise, it has to be said, but the deal, not that Blues fans were complaining, smacked distinctly of a favour from Howard for his war-horse skipper during his glory days at Goodison.

Of course, the players were suffering too during these financial traumas. If the PFA weren't paying their wages they were being presented with cheques that had the potential to bounce like superballs. Some were advised not to turn up for training to save on petrol costs. Labouring under this huge disincentive, and further hindered by the loss of two key defenders, it was little wonder form was so appalling. Losses at lowly Brighton and Swansea were bad enough, but the 5-0 stuffing at Exeter was perhaps the nadir. Indeed, so inept was the performance on that April day, Gary Bennett, himself without a goal since early November, felt obliged to come over to the disgruntled visitors' enclosure to apologise for events before slagging off the chairman.

So, in the end, a hugely disappointing placing of 15th - or was it 16th - but then again, who really cares? All we know is next season is a frightening prospect. The summer pay-cheques are already bouncing. Player of the Year Nick Richardson is refusing to sign a new contract and club record scorer Stuart 'The Master' Rimmer has been released. The lumbering John Murphy has another 37 years to run on his contract, and we've yet to sign anybody to set the pulse racing. Ah well. Hereford and Doncaster have done the honourable thing and saved Brighton from the trap-door. Guess it might be our turn this time around.

P.S. Anybody who attended the Chester/Rochdale game, when both sets of players wore yellow arm-bands, may have been under the gross misapprehension they were a sign of support for the convicted child-killer Louise Woodward from nearby Elton. This wasn't the case. It was simply a tribute to that great record by Dawn (featuring Tony Orlando), viz. *Tie A Yellow Ribbon Round The Old Oak Tree.*

OVER LAND AND SEA

West Ham United

Looking back at last season, I still can't get it out of my head that in real terms, as usual, West Ham United kicked us in the collective nuts. I'm sure I'm not alone in coming to that conclusion, but saying that, I do appreciate how others might look at the events, and how their opinions may differ. But it's their fault if they are easily pleased. Personally, I'm not. Never have been. That's why I write my own fanzine I suppose.

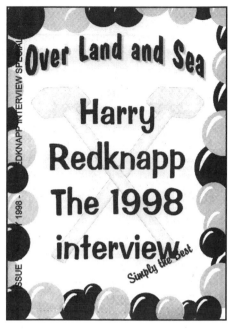

But whatever anyone says, fact is, all we ended up with from a season that showed so much promise was a final finishing position of eighth. And that is it. No silverware, no European place, just a lonely eighth position, two places above the middle. And I find that hard to accept. Especially when, with just six matches remaining, we were bankers to be heading through the countryside on the Eurostar Express just a few months later.

And as if that wasn't already enough, the second and probably biggest of all bombshells arrived in the shape of a season ticket increase announcement. Nothing new here, I suppose; most clubs are equally greedy come the end of the season and most would have tried to squeeze a few more quid out of you, but West Ham didn't just want a few quid. Oh no, they had the audacity to ask some of us to suffer ticket inflation of 40.9%. A whacking £150 increase.

Few would take that too kindly, so I think that I speak for the majority of Hammers fans when I say it ruined what was, in West Ham's terms, a somewhat above average season. When I say above average, I suppose there are one or two of you that will start shouting 'hypocrite', given what I said in my first paragraph. But that couldn't be any further from the truth.

You see at West Ham we get used to fighting a relegation battle every year. And if we're not fighting one, then we're doing the opposite and scrapping for promotion. So anything other than a relegation struggle is deemed something of a successful season. It's weird I know, but that's the way West Ham fans are, no matter who tells you otherwise.

So in that respect, you can now begin to understand the logic.

And then, as I have mentioned previously, if the Hammers *do* string one or two results together over the course of a season, then we are told we should be grateful for what we have had, and we are therefore lucky to have season tickets. So up they go in price - just to punish us for having the slightest bit of success! I sound bitter don't I? Well, it's not really surprising. You have to support the club to understand what I mean.

Politics aside, bitterness aside, sarcasm aside, even I'll admit that there were some very special moments last year. And not just by our standards; special by anyone's. For instance, totally dominating anyone who came to Upton Park - except Arsenal of course and, strangely enough, Southampton. Oh yeah, and Newcastle. But, almost as astonishing was the fact that apart from winning at Barnsley on the opening day, we still managed to lose eight consecutive away games before Christmas.

Talk about *Home and Away*; it was like watching two different teams.

Week by week, Harry Redknapp claimed almost parrot-fashion that we had played well but were unlucky. And although he was basically right, it didn't make things any easier to deal with. Travelling around this beautiful country of ours, the claret and blue army lost the overwhelming sense of optimism that we are renowned for. No-one among us expected to get a single point. Because that's the way we are. But it still didn't stop us turning up in the same usual numbers and having the same crack. After all, partying all day long is surely what away trips are all about. Even when you lose.

However, the same claret and blue army descended on Upton Park for the home matches certainly more buoyant, knowing all too well that they would return back home to their loved ones just a few hours later, with three points safely tucked away in the bag. It was a very odd feeling week after week; emotions going into overdrive either way. Very odd indeed. But I suppose that was half the fun of it. We probably wouldn't want it any other way.

It wouldn't be an over-exaggeration to say that it was one team alone that totally destroyed our season last term. One opposing team that is. After all, we self destructed more times that I care to mention. But if I am going to have to point the finger, I'll point it at the main men: Double-winners Arsenal.

We met (and failed to beat) the Gooners on no less than *five* occasions, including defeats in both domestic cup competitions. And that hurts. But I'm not going to diss them. As far as I'm concerned the Gooners were the best side we played last season and I personally think that they are going to go from strength to strength and will possibly dominate the English Premier Division the way the Mancs have done over the past few years. We'll see.

Highlights of the season were plentiful in reality. Beating the Geordies at St James' was one of them. Another, oddly, was clawing back to 3-3 at Selhurst Park against Palace at the end of the season. That result effectively meant that Europe had gone out of the window, but it was still magic to see a couple of goals from substitute Manny Omoyinmi. He was one of the ex-South East Counties League Championship winning side of a couple of years ago, and a player that we have been screaming for to be given a chance for at least the last 18 months. But what do *we* know? After all, we're just fans aren't we?

Another high point for me was the emergence of assistant manager Frank Lampard's son: the originally named Frank Lampard! Young Frank played in the same Championship side as Omoyinmi, and for that matter Rio Ferdinand; to get not one or two, but three great players from the same youth side is very encouraging.

Rio has made his own headlines and I'm certain that even though he didn't actually get a game in the World Cup Finals he will be captain for the 2000 Euro Championships. Frank however, has had to work even harder. And not for any lack of ability; he always had that in abundance, but purely because of his dad's job. It may not seem that bad a reason, but remember, Harry Redknapp is Frank's dad's brother-in-law, thus his uncle. And for that reason alone, young Frank had everything to prove. I think he went a long way towards doing that in our very first match of the season when he came on as sub and scored the winner at Barnsley.

Talking of youngsters, last year our South East Counties side once again took the Championship. With our youth sides doing that twice in three years, even the most pessimistic amongst us have got to be happy about the way the club is growing in stature at that level. It's often said: get the youth policy right and everything else becomes less of a problem. I hope that's right.

For the season ahead, I doubt you'll be surprised to hear that I have got mixed feelings. The little angel on my left shoulder is telling me that this time we're certain of at least a European placing. But the little devil on my right is saying we'll be lucky to finish as high as we did last term. I'm going to ignore the pair of them. Nosey bastards, they should keep out of it. *I'll* decide what I think.

So it's a mid-table position then, with maybe a cup run or two thrown in for a bit of extras. However, if we can maintain the astonishing home form of the last 12 months, and improve just a tad away, then, after all is said and done, I can honestly see no reason why we can't end up in at least sixth place.

Has this been a hypocritical piece? Probably. No, *definitely*. But I'm a dedicated Hammer. What else would you expect?

THE PIE

Notts County

Hello, it's me again. You may remember that I wrote to you last year to explain that my old man couldn't write for your book about fat men. Well I am afraid he can't write for you again this year either. It's not that he doesn't qualify, in fact he is even fatter (and uglier) than before. No, the reason is that he has got terrible bad feet; so painful, or so he reckons, that he can't walk upstairs to his computer - although miraculously it doesn't stop him walking to the pub! But I have no sympathy whatsoever as it is all his own fault.

Let me explain. He has suffered from excema on the soles of his feet for some time, but the

No. 50
ONE POUND
December 1997

The Original Notts County Fanzine

STRIKER CRISIS?

" I am sorry Mr. Allardyce but I am afraid it is not possible to clone you a new striker from one of Tommy Johnson's old jockstraps! "

odd thing is that it tends to get worse at weekends. Eventually we worked out that he is allergic to real ale which he drinks by the bucketful, particularly at weekends. So does he give up drinking? Does he hell! "There is just too much celebrating to do" he claimed. "Besides I would sooner give up sex rather than real ale." Which came as a surprise to me as I thought he already had.

But celebrate he certainly has, ever since March. You see he is the co-editor of this flanzine thingie called *The Pie*, which isn't about eating pies, although, given his weight, for years I thought it was. He writes for this flanzine under the name of Electric Steve. What a stupid bloody idea. I overheard someone describe his writing style as self-defecating, which sounds like a load of crap to me.

But in fact it's about Notts County, which he tells me is the biggest and best football team in the area, if not the country, world and universe. I asked him about that other team whose ground he hurls abuse at as we drive over Trent Bridge, but he went berserk and used some very unsavoury language. He says they are called "the f-word" but I have never heard a team called f**k mentioned when they read out those boring football results on the wireless. Oh, and what *is* a bung by the way?

Well this is where his feet problems come in. Apparently Notts have been what he calls "shit hot" all season and by the end of March they were Champions, which he says nobody has ever done before. And that is when things went downhill chiropody-wise as the bugger has been on the piss celebrating ever since. In fact he has set up a direct debit to pay £100 a week to the pub. "It saves carrying money about, and with my feet any reduction in weight is a blessing" he says. That's alright, but by Thursday evening he's in the red with the pub again.

He now has a hero, Big Sam, who can do no wrong. He is some geezer called Allardyce who apparently is 'the messiah, the saviour, a genius'. This is odd because 12 months earlier he reckoned this Sam bloke hadn't got a clue. He used to walk around like Fraser in *Dad's Army* saying "we're doomed, doomed I tell you, the bloke can't hack it." Well he has certainly been proved wrong yet again. In fact I reckon I know more about this football lark than my old man and I haven't seen a game since Jeff Astle played for them, although thank goodness he didn't sing in those days.

So in awe is he of this Allardyce guy, that he had a beer commissioned in his name! He got Castle Rock Brewery to brew Big Sam's Mighty Magpies Ale, and so popular was it that the brewery sold out within days and it even featured on radio and television. I haven't got a clue what it tasted like, as I don't drink the stuff, but his lordship drank gallons of it so it must have been pretty good.

He didn't start the season happy though. Even though they were winning by the odd goal he used to come home moaning. Reckoned the strikers were "crap" and this bloke Gary Jones was "chuffing useless." Bloody odd that, because by April he was bragging about them being top scorers in the country. And as for Gary Jones he reckoned he should be in the England squad: "Scored 28 goals for the season, better than Sheringham he is," his lordship pronounced to his cronies in the pub, "and he doesn't do the naughties in the Algarve either." Although they weren't his exact words.

The team made the papers back in February, which he says is unusual as "the buggers usually ignore us, unless the manager's in the Sundays for being pissed up" which is a reference to somebody called Howard I believe. Well anyway, they were on the way up the A1 to Darlington when the team coach broke down. So the players changed into their kit in case they were late and eventually they had to thumb lifts from passing supporters to get them there in time. "Last season they would have left them at the side of the motorway" commented my better half.

Talking of the press, he's been waging war against *BBC Radio Nottingham* all season. He keeps writing them letters because they don't broadcast commentaries on Notts away games like they used to. Instead they broadcast 'f-word' games every week, even though the same game is also broadcast on another local station and sometimes on *Radio Five Live* as well. At first they reckoned it was because of the fees that the clubs charged, but they soon changed the story when the *Pie* offered to pay the costs to broadcast a game!

So he keeps writing them letters and they keep writing back replies that don't really justify what they are doing and he prints them in his flanzine and at that end of the day I reckon the radio station are starting to look right pillocks. He even had a letter from one sports journalist that read "I would ask you to refrain from any further correspondence that refers to my job description. For my part I won't tell you how to do your job." So good are these replies that he has put them on the *Pie's* website!

Well that's about all I know really. Big Sam is the almighty, Gary Jones is better than Alan Shearer, Notts are the best team in the world and my husband can't walk due to celebrating too much.

Electric Sue.

"In a few hours, after more views and analysis of todays goalless draw at the City Ground, we'll be popping over to Old Trafford for a few brief words on Notts County's Cup win there today"

PIE MUNCHER

Preston North End

Last season was a nightmare, but I've now realised that when you support Preston North End it's the same every year. Well I'm not watching North End anymore and I'll tell you why I'm not watching North End anymore:

Because you spend all summer saving your 20p's in a jar for a season ticket and eagerly counting the days to mid-June when the fixtures come out so you can plan your away trips to Walsall and Lincoln and Brentford and everywhere else on the Second Division map and then you find that on Boxing Day we're away at Stoke and it's Wycombe away on a Tuesday night in September and the home games against Blackpool,

Burnley, Man City, Oldham and Wigan have been brought forward to 11am kick-offs on police advice and you just know we're gonna get hammered by York cos it's the first match and, like, we haven't won on the opening day for 14 years, and we've got Mansfield home and away in the first round of the Coke Cup and Mansfield away in the opening game of the AutoWindscreens and we're drawn away at Mansfield in the first round of the FA Cup (sponsored by Littlewoods - I ask you!) and then we play Mansfield at home in a friendly cos neither of us have a game on FA Cup third round day because after beating us Mansfield got slaughtered 7-1 by Tamworth Tarantulas in the second round and by then you start thinking to yourself... Well, is it worth it?

The season begins and the entire population of York turns up in the new Bill Shankly Kop and sings "Down with the City, you're going down with the City," as they cruise to a 3-0 victory even though we bring Lormor on in the second half. And then our Coca-Cola Cup dreams of reaching the second round have to be shelved for another year, then some Blackpool fans turn up at Deepdale the night before the derby and daub the Shankly Kop in tangerine paint, then Burnley fans smear claret and blue all over the place, then hundreds of thousands of Man City supporters arrive in town and remind us what real football hooliganism used to be like and then we find ourselves drawn away to Kettering Town in the FA Cup and it costs £20 for the coach fare, £15 to get on the ground, £3.50 for a sodding souvenir programme full of adverts, £4.72 for a cup of coffee and half a dozen chips at one of them rip-off service stations where the coffee's lukewarm and the chips have been stood under warm lights for a week and the shop wraps the dirty books in cellophane so you can't take a peek as you pretend to be interested in reading *Anglers' Weekly*.

Then it's Christmas, and North End release their 15th new kit in five years which costs £45 but you've just got to have one because, well it's a new kit innit, and you find it's as cheap and tacky as were all the other new kits you've ever bought and the 'revolutionary new breathable fabric' gets your armpits smelling like a monkey's cage after about ten minutes and you think to yourself why doesn't the marketing department come up with 'Deepdale Deodorants' but if they did it would probably cost a tenner a tin and contain cheap scent manufactured by child slaves in Haiti and give off enough CFCs to melt the polar ice caps and turn the underarm part of yer new shirt green after three washes. And if you took it back to the shop to complain they'd probably say something like 'think yourself lucky, green splashes under the arm is next season's new shirt design'.

Then on Boxing Day you turn up outside Deepdale at 7.30 on a freezing morning to catch the coach for Stoke after having walked eight miles cos there's no buses at that time of day only to find there's no coach either and the only sign of life are scores of people knee-trembling against the Town End wall after a typical Friday night in neighbouring nightclub 'Legends', then at quarter past six the coach turns up and you find all the seats are double-booked and by the time *that's* sorted the bus leaves three hours late and you're bursting for a piss cos it's still freezing but the driver says he can't stop till Keele Services and the bus heater isn't working and the guy sat next to you chain smokes and farts all through the journey and reminisces about all the fights he's been in while supporting North End over the years and you finally arrive at Keele with a bladder the size of Richard Branson's balloon to find all the bogs closed cos the pipes burst on Xmas Eve and "have you ever tried getting a plumber over Christmas?" so you go for a steam behind a bush and halfway through a security guy catches you so you end up with a big wet patch on your jeans and a bollocking off this jobsworth and all the men's magazines are wrapped in cellophane covers then you get back on the coach only to find that everyone who brought what you thought were flasks of coffee on board at Preston was actually carrying whiskey, gin, vodka etcetera and they're all pissed and having a roaringly good time except that the closer you get to Stoke the more the coach has to stop to let somebody throw up until the driver frustratingly shouts out that he's not stopping for anybody else otherwise we'll be late, and ten minutes later we're parked up in a lay-by while the driver's having a row about whose going to clean vomit off the back seat with a green-faced guy whose blaming the driver for not stopping and claims it was the winding roads that caused it even though he smells like a distillery.

And when you finally arrive at the Britannia Stadium it's three minutes to kick-off but there isn't a soul about and you wander aimlessly around the stadium then stumble across the groundsman just locking the gates as he's leaving who tells you the match was called off yesterday on account of a frozen pitch and it's not his fault if PNE failed to inform their fans.

So you're *that* pissed off all you want to do is get back on the coach and go home as quick as possible but you find that the driver can't leave until 5pm because he's required by law to have a two hour break so everyone goes to the nearest pub en mass only to find it shuts at 3pm. So you follow the crowd to the next pub but they refuse to let you in because you're away supporters and when you point out that you can't be away supporters because there's nobody to support they get all stroppy and call the police who are bored stiff cos it's Boxing Day and sod-all ever happens in Stoke on a normal day never mind Boxing Day so five minutes later the entire Staffordshire Constabulary and their dogs roll up and there's utter bloody mayhem, meanwhile three hundred yards away our coach driver is stretched across the back seat blissfully sleeping.

Footballing giants such as Wycombe, Bournemouth and Blackpool all record wins at our part-Premiership, part-Third Division stadium as we plummet towards our inevitable final resting place of 15th in Division Two, and as another season's end draws near you see the next new shirt but instead of green stains under the arms it's got blue flashes and it looks, well, stylish, even though £50 is a lot then you realise how God-awful summer is without the World Cup, how utterly dull cricket and tennis are, so you take to wandering the streets on a Saturday afternoon or going to the pub or taking the wife to Asda or mowing the lawn or shooting up or staying in bed or trainspotting or reading your old programmes or painting the gutters or buying one of those cellophane-clad magazines or taking up brass rubbing or going to the cinema to see *Titanic* again or playing ten pin bloody bowling for Chrissake or jogging around the local park or delousing the dog or trying to save some money by giving the car a home service or fellwalking or trying watercolours or going swimming or getting round to finally re-upholstering the three-piece suite or canal fishing or joining a vintage bus preservation society, and when all that fails you realise what a totally and indescribably dull and uninteresting life you lead until it dawns on you that it's not yet the last day in June and it's still possible to buy a new season ticket at the previous year's price and what the hell if the limit of North End's ambition is to sign up three free-transfers and consolidate in the Second Division, and Lancashire Lynx, the rugby team that play at Deepdale, are currently rendering the pitch as lumpy as the half-time Bovril and we've just brought John Beck back as Director of Football and the Town End's been closed for safety reasons and worst of all Owen Oyston's finally out of prison and promising to rapidly make up for the last few years of under-investment in the team and ground at Blackpool.

So you go down and buy yourself a new season ticket in the full realisation that this act of folly keeps you on North End's mailing list and every so often you'll receive a crisp white A4 sized envelope containing the 'The Official Newsletter of Preston North End' which you're convinced is written by Mormons or Jehovah's Witnesses cos it's all touchy-feely-good-news-let's-all-smile-and-dance-and-hold-hands sort of thing and do these people not realise that the essential part of being a North End fan is being miserable and who gives a shit if it costs £75 for a ticket to the Player of the Year dinner and last year you drew the short straw cos you were sharing a table with Kurt Nogan and consequently you were pissed by ten o'clock just trying to keep up with him.

And spare a thought for those poor folk who live adjacent to the new stands and find their lives blighted by constant noise and dust and workmen's arse cleavages and the sun doesn't shine in their living rooms or back gardens anymore and their TV and radio reception is crap and one bloke's homing pigeons keep clattering into the stand and they're living in negative equity cos their property values have dropped by 30% and "so what?" I hear you say, "they chose to live there." Well that's not the point is it given that we're all supposed to be environmentalist these days it's just a shame English Heritage never got round to making the old West Stand a listed building cos none of this new development would have gone ahead then.

And talking about the environment I hope you're boycotting North End's pies like me I mean who needs a bloody pie wrapped in a cellophane with a PNE logo stamped on it and they're charging 10p extra for the packaging I mean it's not as though you can eat the bloody wrapper is it? The first thing you do is chuck it away and then there's no litter bins so it eventually ends up getting blown into the gardens of all those houses near the ground adding to the torment of the local residents.

I wouldn't mind but North End already appreciate the need to save on things like paper for example just go for a shit in the Town End bogs if you dare cos you'll soon find out where a few cutbacks have been made in order to fund another private registration plate for one of the directors' swanky new limousines. Anyway don't get me going about North End cos once I start I'll never shut up and I can't sit here banging my keyboard all day when I've got work to do so I'll say Ta ra, and by the way, what about Glenn Hoddle dropping Gazza, and then starting with Anderton of all people, he must be mad, I mean...

RAGE ON

Oxford United

The close-season saw a momentous change at Oxford United. No, not a new manager (*that* joy was yet to come), or news about completion of the new stadium at Minchery Farm (we're still waiting), nor were there any particularly noteworthy new signings. The news that everyone on The Manor terraces was talking about was the change at the fanzine. *Raging Bull* was no more; long live *Rage On.*

We changed name for a number of reasons, all of which are too boring to be of any interest here, and which no-one but the editors particularly cared about anyway. The first *Rage On* appeared in September, featuring reserve

RAGE ON

No. 4
March 1998
One Pound

An Independent Voice of
Oxford United Supporters

OFFICIAL SPONSOR OF
JAMIE COOK

The Messiah has arrived

Life   **The Universe**

& Everything

goalkeeper and Son of God Elliot Jackson on the front cover (God being first choice 'keeper Phil Whitehead, naturally). Unfortunately, 'Son of' turned out to be some kind of fundamentalist bible-thumper. He took exception to us proclaiming that he "looked good on crosses" and, on the advice of his mum (the Virgin Mary?), he took it upon himself to rip asunder the famous yellow pages in the Manor Ground changing rooms.

This historic first issue coincided with United's first live *Sky* game against Wolves, when two goals from Joey Beauchamp and another from Bob Ford sank the so-called Premiership contenders out of sight. Whilst this was enough to raise a smile, the main talking point in the initial *RO* was United's finances. Especially the débâcle surrounding the half-built stadium on the edge of town, work on which had halted the previous January as contractors Taylor Woodrow realised what the rest of us had known for some time: United were skint.

Issue two came out at the start of November and continued the blasphemous front cover theme. 'God' was still injured and Denis Smith refused to place continued confidence in Elliot 'Jesus' Jackson (despite some assured performances). After the signing of Bruce 'Antichrist' Grobbelaar fell through, Port Vale kindly lent us Arjan Van Heusden. He was pretty good too, so we had no choice but to salute our new Holy Trilogy, the front cover featuring The Father, The Son and Van Heuligheust. Our previous issue had enraged at least two 'Christian' supporters who wrote to criticise our sacrilegious stance. There's just no pleasing some people.

In the time between issues #1 and #2, Oxford had gone from the sublime (that leisurely 3-0 win against Wolves) to the improbable (an away win, of all things, at West Brom) to the embarrassing (Middlesbrough outclassing us with consummate ease to win 4-1 at The Manor). We'd also have liked to include some reaction to major news regarding the future of the club and the re-start of work at Minchery Farm in this second issue. One of our editors had spoken to Denis Smith during a *Thames Valley FM* phone-in, and was told that a major announcement would be made on 10th October. Needless to say the 10th came and went with a deafening silence.

Issue three hit the streets at the start of the new chronological year, making in-roads into the metropolis of fanzine culture. Not the usual boring load of cobblestones, but a veritable trove of tarmacadam that paved its way into the annals of time. The 'SOS' used as a protest slogan to show the concern of the supporters at the club's mismanagement would have a new meaning on the cover of *Rage On #3*. It started as 'Save Oxford Soccer' - yeah, we know, soccer is a shite American term for the beautiful game, but it was chosen with majority support at a special meeting. It was also a continuation of the theme from the Maxwellian era and the ludicrous proposed merger with Reading as the Thames Valley Royals. Although Reading are doing their best to keep up with us by having the opening of their new stadium delayed, betcha can't beat 18 months with no new work done? 'SOS' then stood for 'Shotton Our Saviour'. On Xmas Eve, Neil 'Shotts In' Wakefield, an exile from the famed village of Garsington (it ain't just operas, you know), had taken it upon himself to chase the favours of an Oxford United ex-skipper. This was the day after it had been announced that Denis 'Smith Out' Smith was to go, at last, to West Brom (which made my festive period far more festive). On hearing of his communications with the moustachioed Malcolm, us editors thought: what an excellent idea for the traditional, jokey cover slogan of our magazine. Little were we to know the prophecy of our jesting. The middle pages, as yellow as the outer and reserved for 'special' articles, featured the letters that Neil had written to Keith Cox (managing director of the club), ourselves at *Rage On*, Maurice 'Put The Kettle On' Evans (the Mighty Yellows chief scout - dyb dyb dyb) and the man himself, Messiah Shotton (then reserve team coach at Barnsley).

It certainly was a hectic time between issues #2 and #3. We had: 1) seen the departure of our chairman, Robin Herd; 2) a meeting between fanzine editors and independent supporters group members with the new board; 3) the SOS protest, and 4) Smith Out.

The meeting was not hurriedly called to placate the revolutionaries into stopping the pending protest, or at least that was what the board said. Even though afterwards it was stated in the programme that they had met with "supporters' representatives." We disclaimed this as we see ourselves as a mouthpiece rather than a voice.

The actual SOS demonstration at the QPR game (call anything a demo and people start panicking - we were accused of nearly trebling the police bill) was a huge success. Yellow slogan cards, banners and placards resplendent around the pitch were seen by the nation's live TV audience. And after the match, there was a vociferous but peaceful sit-in followed by a gathering outside the boardroom; a wonderful example of 'fan power' and a big thank you to all those who participated.

The meeting with directors also threw up a few interesting statements which needed to be put into print. Things like the sale of The Manor Ground to be announced by 23rd December 1997, the new stadium to be 'dried out' (by Betty Ford?) in January 1998 and completed six months from then. Both things we took with a pillow-full of salt, and we were slightly cynical in the way we reported them in the fanzine. Best of the lot was the directors accepting 'corporate responsibility' for the crap running of the club and producing an 'unnecessary' deficit of £3m. But it's OK, cos they're gonna introduce budgetary control. Yeah right, talk about shutting the stable door after the horse has bolted, shot-pinned and riveted the Forth bridge.

It was the fourth issue of *Rage On*, dated March 1998, which gave us something extraordinary to celebrate. The front cover proclamation said it all: "The Messiah has arrived" (a term that was picked up on by the local media and used for the remainder of the season). This was the announcement that the 'Shotts In' campaign mounted by Neil Wakefield and supported by ourselves and fellow fanzine *Yellow Fever* had achieved success. Former United hero 'Sheeney' Shotton was appointed manager, following Smithout's departure and a disastrous spell as caretaker by Malcolm Crosby. More fan power. It is highly unlikely that anything like this had ever occurred before in the crazy universe of football, and many saw it as a calculated gamble to try and garner support by a board which had come in for much criticism in its handling of the Minchery Farm affair in particular, and the club's accounts in general.

Another issue *Rage On* was getting its teeth into was the Open Meeting called by the beleaguered board in January, just prior to the announcement of Shotton's appointment. At this meeting we came in for a fair amount of criticism and abuse from some board members for daring to be critical (they didn't like our "snide remarks" in our editorial following our meeting with them), an attitude for which they themselves were chastised by Jim White in a lengthy article in the *Guardian*. The other noteworthy event at the meeting was the remark by club secretary Mick Brown that the SOS demonstration we organised was for "no apparent reason." Even those who normally support the board through all its ineptitude found this statement reprehensible, and it was met by a loud chorus of boos. He was forced to retract his foolish words and even other board members started to call the demo "a good thing" to placate the crowd.

The food at the Manor was also coming in for a lot of stick, as United finished 88th out of 93 in a survey of catering at all the league's football grounds (plus Wembley). The fact that Cambridge United came first somewhat defeated our caterers' claims that the survey was "unfair because Oxford was being compared against the likes of Manchester United" (who finished 12th). The fact is that the food at the Manor is barely edible (at best) and the catering staff are often rude and unhelpful. When questioned on this at the Open Meeting, the club manager Ian Davies could only respond, "Well, would you rather support Cambridge United?" which is not really the attitude we were hoping for from a former fanzine editor.

Issue five coincided with our last game against Birmingham. The Messiah had continued to work miracles during the final run-in, and a series of comfortable victories (Stoke, Norwich, Swindon and Reading to name just four) had taken us above mid-table. Kevin Francis had continued his fine scoring record, Beauchamp was as lively as ever, and *Rage On*-sponsored Jamie Cook had repaid Shotton's confidence with goals against Tranmere and at Maine Road in front of 30,000. With a fine run of form and oodles of teen appeal (if he wasn't playing for Oxford he'd be playing for FC Boyzone) we had to make him our end-of-season cover star. We'll be sponsoring him next season too, although the club hardly made it easy by asking us for nearly £600, upping the fee by 67%. And we'll still be accused in some quarters of not getting behind the team.

The *Rage On* readers' survey produced some interesting results, and some predictable ones too. Joey Beauchamp won our Player of the Season award by a mile, scoring three times as many votes as his nearest rival. Our readers also demonstrated their affection for the departed Denis Smith by voting him our second worst manager ever, hot on the heels of Brian Horton. Despite two open meetings the results illustrated a deep distrust of Keith Cox and his fellow directors. Fifty per cent of respondents felt the club's financial future was bleaker than the previous year, only 3% felt the club was well run and one in four thought the new stadium would never be built. Judging by the current mess they could well be right.

POSTSCRIPT: Since Issue 5 none of the announcements about the new owners, sale of The Manor or restart on the new stadium have come to fruition. Blimey, maybe we're prophets not cynics, although the last thing any of us want to see is the death of our club . So let's finish on a high note; all together, in falsetto: "Malcolm Shotton's Yellow and Blue Army."

RED ALL OVER THE LAND

Liverpool

Nothing Was Delivered

They say it's not over till the fat lady sings. Well, I got worried when she started to clear her throat before August was out. By then our beloved team had been less than convincing against Wimbledon (nothing new about that) and bloody useless against Leicester. Added to this was the first episode of what became a long-drawn-out and boring soap opera called 'Macca for Barca'. With a start like that, is it any wonder that Liverpool fans spent most of '97-98 in a state of depression? To pinch a phrase off Tommy Docherty, it started bad and got worse. If '96-97 had

been bad, then just what was this all about? "But you finished third," I hear you shout. Well so what; so bloody what?

Some of the stuff served up at Anfield was so bad that at times I wished I'd bought a programme so that at least I could have had something to read - and it's not exactly the most riveting of tomes. There is another saying: You could write it on the back of a postage stamp. It perfectly sums up the highlights of Liverpool FC's season. If you don't believe me, then pop down to your local GPO and purchase a normal sized stamp and write on the back of it: *Owen*. What more proof do you need?

During the months that spanned the close of the anonymous '96-97 season and the bright new dawn of '97-98, our manager 'The Grey Goose' purchased four new players. Paul Ince came from Inter Milan and was given the captain's armband to lead us out of the wilderness. Well, he didn't. It wasn't his fault - not all of it anyway. He was given a bunch of misfits and we wondered if his mind ever wandered back to his time with Milan (or, worse still, United). There were times when we thought that he was taking control and turning our team of perennial also-rans into something decent - like the time when he gave Robbie Fowler the mother and father of a rollicking against Spurs because 'God' had chosen not to chase a loose ball. He also whacked in the occasional goal, but in all honesty the jury is still out on 'the Guv'nor'.

Roy also gave Wimbledon four million notes for one Norwegian International named Oyvind Leonhardsen who came with a reputation of having a 'good engine' - someone who liked to work from 'box to box'. Our ever-astute boss decided his best place was on the left wing (despite him not having a left foot), just in front of his comrade from the land of Vikings, Stig Bjornebye. If you ever wanted to find a steward at Anfield, you only had to wait for Stig to take a corner, because almost without fail the ball would hit one standing halfway up the KOP. So Roy paid £4 million for someone who couldn't play were Roy wanted him to. However, rather than bring in someone who *could* play in that role, Mr Evans left things alone and left out little Danny Murphy.

Now Danny was another of the close season purchases. Only he was young, came from Crewe and did not carry a big reputation on his shoulders. Danny made his mark on his debut against Wimbledon, leaving Roy to say, "These young lads are the future, but the future is now." He promptly turned back the clock so that the future was still - well, in the future! It was back to the old tired and worn-out team selections and performances, some so mundane that you started to wonder if this outfit had any future at all with Mr Evans in charge...

Roy also popped into Germany for a bit of duty-free and came back with World Cup/European Nations Cup/European Champions Cup/German League winner KarlHeinz Riedle. The final piece of the jigsaw, we thought; our version of Klinsmann, we thought; a genuine world star, we thought. Well we thought wrong again, didn't we. KHR spent more time on the sick than a social security scrounger, and more time on the bench than your average judge. But Roy told us all that he was a model professional; one of the best he'd ever worked with. *I'd* have been a model professional if I were getting 20 grand a week for doing sweet FA.

Roy's summer shopping spree wasn't exactly bargain-basement. Nothing new there, though. For two years David James had looked less safe than the old Tory government, and his handling of crosses was certainly out of the Dracula books. Roy woke up one morning and finally saw the light as the 'CALAMITY JAMES' headlines screamed at him one more time. So he went stateside and after a long drawn-out battle against red tape and more red tape, signed Brad Friedel. Then didn't play him. At any other club he would have been shown the door for wasting his employers' cash but fortunately (for him) Liverpool appear to be slightly more tolerant. After all, prior to the Friedel farce Roy had spent a cool £40 million to win nothing; I suppose another £1.3 million wasn't going to do any harm. Finally though, Friedel got his chance - whether he gets another work permit we don't know. And after James had almost invited Everton to win the Anfield leg of the derby (thankfully refused), even Roy had to admit that the fans (who had been whispering rather loudly that David wasn't using his hands as he should) were right. Not that it made a lot of difference - we were still crap.

All in, all we made no impact on the league whatsoever, unless you count drawing at OT and helping Arsenal along a bit. So maybe we could do better in the cups? We know the answer to that one now. In fact, if our league form was bad, our cup form was worse - and *that* took some doing.

In Europe we at least had a night of passion - two, in fact - with Celtic. The game at Parkhead will long stay in the memory; not for the football, but for the atmosphere. We got through thanks to a wonder goal from Steve McManaman in the last minute of the first leg. We managed to hold out 0-0 in the return at Anfield, and as we left we laughed with Celtic fans because Rangers had gone out to some lowly team from France. Little did we know... Yes, we went back to play Strasbourg. Our previous visit to France had been the nightmare result against PSG the previous April, but we'd learnt the lessons from that painful night - or so we thought. Over the Channel we went and out we went. If PSG had been bad, then this was worse. The night was memorable only for the local branch of the Gendarmes - the CRS. They have a warped sense of humour, do the French police: they like to bang you on the head with their batons and then wonder why you don't laugh! I had nowt against the French until they sent over Cantona, Ginola and latterly Madarse (Everton) but even without those three I would still despise them now, just because of their police. Here Roy used all his tactical know-how and decided that Razor Ruddock was just the man to play in the middle of a back five against fast-running French forwards (the tactics that had served us so well the season before in Paris!). We've not seen Razor since that night. Rumour has it he is still running round Strasbourg trying catch the man he was marking. This was the night when the travelling fans greeted the team at the Airport with a few lines of "All we want is pride." The team looked bemused, just as they had on the pitch.

So we were out of Europe for another year, our proud reputation more than severely dented. Never mind, there are always domestic cups to strive for. Ah, if only... In the FA Cup (bloody sponsored by Littlewoods) we had a nice home tie in the third round against Coventry City. There was definitely a time when this competition brought people out in a rash (cup fever they called it). Well, our team has become the perfect cure. In fact the FA Cup has become a bloody phobia; I've no idea what you might call it, but whatever it is we've got it. After the losses earlier in the decade against the might of Bolton and Bristol we'd had the 'White Suit' final against the Mancs and then our part in the 'cup tie of the decade' (if you support Chelsea). Well, the Coventry one was something else. There must be a word for it; I just don't know what it is. The only consolation about going out of the FA Cup was no worries about getting tickets and the happy knowledge that the team wouldn't be making another version of the *Anfield Rap*. Small mercies for which we were grateful.

Then there was the Coca-Cola Cup. Well, whatever fizz there was, our lot ensured it went flat. It wasn't too bad at the start because we saw Michael Owen score that hat-trick against Grimsby and then we had the night at St James' Park when the Newcastle stewards tried their hardest to empty the way end during the game. An extra time win and we had a semi-final to look forward to against First Division Middlesbrough. We took a 2-1 lead to the wasteland of Teeside and our man in charge - still Roy Evans - had another brilliant and cunning plan. Maybe we should call him Baldrick because his plans are about as successful as those of Blackadder's side-kick. Yes, it was time for another outing for 'five at the back'. This fragile form of defence fell apart inside two minutes (a good eight minutes before it usually does - we surpassed ourselves). By then we were two down and in arrears. Oh well, another trip to Wembley cancelled... Most of us who had gone to Middlesbrough returned home more than a bit pissed off.

So all that was left of our season was the league. We knew we wouldn't win it; our lot had thrown in the towel months before the Fizzy débâcle. We couldn't even capitalise on Manchester United falling apart at the seams, losing against teams like Coventry, Southampton, Leicester and Sheffield Wednesday - OK, *we* didn't beat them either, but that's not the point. The thing was that every time United left the front door open for us to simply walk through and take the silverware, we went round the back and knocked.

If it had been a horse race, you could have said that as the leader slowed up thinking it had won, we hit every hurdle and finally fell. Meanwhile, the French-trained horse came through on the blindside, eventually strolling past the blinkered leader, leaving the beaten owner to mumble something about the conditions of the race being unfair.

It has come to something when the fans of Liverpool have to share in the pleasures and/or failures of others, but sadly that's how our life is at the moment. It doesn't appear to show signs of getting better.

ROUTE ONE

Wimbledon

There is a time in a football fan's life when things get really bad. For most, this concerns relegation or the failure to win promotion. A long losing streak is bad enough and all teams have those, but the failure to score a goal must be one of the hardest punishments to take. The very joy of seeing the net bulge, the realisation that your team has actually managed to perform the basic function of the game is what it's all about.

In the period from the 28th March to the 29th April, Wimbledon Football Club played eight Premiership games and failed to score a single goal. Now I know the record book shows a

'goal for' against Southampton but it also suggests that Carl Leaburn 'scored' with his foot, therefore it must be a higher life form messing with our minds. I am reliably informed that even in training this has never happened, although he is alleged to have notched against his son in his back garden! Now eight games is a long time not to endure the joy and emotions of scoring. Losing each one would have been an easier pill to swallow, but in six of those eight games the opposition also failed to score! That fine line between three points and one was continually in the balance. Each attack, each shot, each save, each miss was a cruel punishment. The 5-0 stuffing by the deserving Double winners was the equivalent of a prisoner's weekend parole, a chance to relax in the knowledge that the team were not going to win and could totally concentrate on scoring that elusive goal. To lose 6-1 would have been manna from heaven compared to another blank day at the office. Alas, the players were intent on making our agony last longer.

The final release from our suffering was the equivalent of a man on death row celebrating the good news that he had only been given a life sentence rather than the march to the gallows. Tottenham Hotspur are the one team that virtually every Wimbledon fan has a real hatred for; we respect Arsenal, have a soft spot for Chelsea, an artificial dislike of Palace and we even appreciate Manchester United's mutual respect for us. But

Spurs have conspired against us once too often. Perhaps it was Hoddle and Waddle's strikes against us in the 1987 FA Cup Quarter Final? Or was it the disgraceful Nico Claesen play-acting to get Brian Gayle sent off? What about the Jellyfish's comments about preferring to watch us on Ceefax? And then there's the continual whinging whenever we play them, either about our robust style of play, or perhaps... I could go on, but you probably get the gist. Who else could it be that performed the act of our release but Spurs?

Personally, I've had a recurring dream for many years now: it's the last game of the season and poor little old Spurs stand on the edge of the relegation abyss and the fixture computer has conspired to give the Dons the opportunity to nail the lid on their coffin. In '97-98 this dream could have come true. Although not the last game, a victory for Wimbledon would have meant an extremely uncomfortable last day for all their followers; not just the travelling masses but, perhaps more significantly, all those armchair Spurs fans.

The prospect of rectifying our lack of goals and consigning the boys from White Hart Lane to the Nationwide was the sexiest combination on a football pitch since Gregory's Girl. A real buzz of expectation was in the air as people took to their seats; the previous eight games seemed to be forgotten and the team appeared keen to end their home account in a real stylish manner. Even going behind did not seem to stop the inevitable, especially when Peter Fear volleyed home a fantastic goal. Oh the thrill of seeing the onion bag bulge, it was just too much; people around me had to listen to their radios to confirm that we'd actually scored a goal. Belated cries of joy were heard all over the ground (okay, just in the one end as Spurs fans were everywhere else). Then Fearo scored his second and my dream was coming true. The world was suddenly a better place; famine in Africa would now cease, tension in the Middle East would evaporate, the stock market would rise 50% overnight, Sam would get planning permission in Merton for a new stadium. Even a lucky equaliser could not stop the inevitable.

Er, in the second half Spurs scored four goals after Ben Thatcher had deservedly been sent off for a two-footed lunge that would only look good in a Danny Baker video. A 6-2 defeat by the Spurs; my dream had turned into a nightmare, the magnitude of which even Hammer couldn't recreate. Jurgen the German helped himself to four just to rub salt into the wounds. Why did one of the most despised players in World Football suddenly become one of the favourite players in this country? Just because he likes to drive around in a VW Beetle and does a few interviews, and then reminds everyone about his diving antics when he scores his first goal. What short memories we have. Spurs stayed up, and although we had at long last scored a goal, I was left thinking about our numerous goalless draws and reminiscing about what great games they really were.

The beauty of the defending, the tracking-back of midfielders, even the hard work of the forwards at set-pieces: Alan Hansen eat your heart out!

After the previous season had yielded so much promise, what with two cup semi finals and a potential European place, '97-98 was a thorough disappointment. The woeful finish to the campaign only compounded our disappointment. Wimbledon Football Club is a remarkable institution. It makes up its own rules as it goes along. This season the Dublin issue took most of the attention and the boys on the park were a side issue. The future is wholly uncertain and the summer months shall drag on while we await the next instalment of our remarkable adventure. However, when those fixtures are announced, I for one will be looking out for the games against Tottenham, just to see whether my dream has any chance of coming true in 1999.

Source: Monkey Business

RUB OF THE GREENS

Plymouth Argyle

Basement Bargains

Well, if we thought season '96-97 was bad, then this one was worse. What makes it even more galling was that at the start of it most of us could see it coming, and were powerless to stop it.

Most fans have that pre-season optimism, usually boosted by the arrival of some donkey from your most hated rivals - because we all know he will play better for us than for them (not!!) - but in our case the only arrival of note was Jon Sheffield, and an Argyle fan who used to live in Essex kept telling us how he had seen him concede ten goals whilst playing for Aldershot. We lost one international, the eccentric Mr Grobelaar, but gained

RUB of the GREENS
The original Plymouth Argyle fanzine

No. 41 February 1998

50p

The "World Wide Company" who are planning to sponsor Argyle seem very appropriate for the club....

another in Earl Jean, who was top scorer for Rotherham in their relegation campaign. We also saw the arrival of Paddi Wilson and Graham Anthony, but they were the sort of bargain players we expected, especially when our chairman allegedly scuppered a deal to sign Steve Guinan from Nottingham Forest without consulting the manager Mick Jones.

Still, the first day of the season beckoned, and it was a gloriously hot day. A local derby to start off with (especially for those of us living in Bristol) and the chance of a good 'sale' to start the season off with a bang...

Carlo Corazzin obviously had the same idea as he left the field rather early after using his elbow for violent purposes. Now with us 1-0 down at the time, most of us expected the worst, but for once we actually played better with ten men and a Heathcote goal salvaged our first point of the season.

The Coca-Cola Cup provided a brief distraction to our pools-winning form of score draws, as we lost 2-0 in the first leg at the Manor Ground. With 50 minutes of the second leg gone we were 3-0 up, but injuries forced a reshuffle, and we conceded five goals rather too rapidly to give the fans an optimistic view for the rest of the season.

Things resumed as normal in the next game, as we shared a point apiece with Chesterfield, before Watford returned up the M5/M4/M25 with all three points. We then had to play at Fulham just after the Diana incident, and were not helped by a referee who was obviously a royalist as he allowed a Fulham defender to stay on the pitch despite hacking Littlejohn down with only the goalkeeper to beat (OK, *we* know he would have put the ball into the Thames but it's the principle of the thing...).

Another draw at home to Brentford was followed by our longest trip of the season, to Carlisle. A glorious day, a scenic town to wander around, and another bloody draw, again after having a lead. We'll remember September 27th though, as we finally gained our first win, at the expense of Walsall, with midfielder Martin Barlow getting both goals. Of course, it couldn't last, and the trip home from Bootham Crescent seven days later was made even longer as we returned, pointless as a condom vending machine in a nunnery.

A spineless display away to a Luton side ravaged by injuries was followed by the visit to Home Park of Southend, who took all three points. Now, the alarm bells were ringing loud and long. Off the field, things were even bleaker. We had to reduce the ground capacity due to essential safety work, although our lack of wins ensured that even the lower limit was not being tested. Chairman Dan made rumblings about no longer being in a position to support the club and its overdraft, and even went to the PFA to ensure that the player's wages would be guaranteed.

The daft thing was, that there would be talk of consortiums of businessmen willing to buy him out, but discussions would always break down once negotiations looked like being finalised. This left most of us wondering what exactly his motive was. Dan was finding it more uncomfortable to attend matches as hostility grew; he was losing money but he would not surrender control.

Against these off field troubles, we did well to hold 'Chris Waddle's Burnley' to a draw before the team put in a gutsy display at Gillingham, only to lose 2-1. However, those fools still mad enough to venture to northern climes saw us gain our first away win (and second of the season) away to those rich kids of Preston. Amazingly, seven days later we had doubled our total of wins as Wycombe and Bournemouth were well beaten. So we were hopeful of a good FA Cup run, as we had drawn Cambridge at home, but a poor performance meant we had to travel to East Anglia ten days later, where we threw away a two goal lead with 15 minutes to go...

Amongst these matches, Bristol City totally played us off the park, although we somehow kept the score down to 2-1. The next game was a crunch match as Neil Warnock returned to Home Park with his Oldham team, and his reception turned from warm to distinctly frosty as Ronnie Maugé gifted the visitors an early lead, and they wrapped up the points with a very late second. Christmas definitely came early to the West Country for the Boundary Park team...

Our annual trip to the North West coast on the first Tuesday in December failed to raise the temperature as neither team hit the target, but the week off for the second round of the cup obviously worked wonders, as we soundly beat Millwall the following Saturday. This was despite a midweek defeat on penalties at Northampton in the AWShield.

So we returned to the County Ground, in one of those strange coincidences football throws up, and played the home side off the park. However, the man in black/white/whatever needed a home win to complete his fixed odds coupon, and two very debatable decisions (including not allowing a central defender back on the pitch at a corner) meant we all had a miserable Christmas.

The festive gloom deepened on Boxing Day as big-spending Fulham came, saw and totally conquered our ever-struggling side. So we were not exactly full of hope when we travelled to Vicarage Road two days later, but when we went a goal up with five minutes to go, we could see the first signs of recovery. That hope soon disappeared as the home team equalised in injury time, demoralising the fans almost as much as the players.

The new year started late, due to Grimsby's cup commitments, and started badly as Bristol Rovers returned up the M5 victorious. This was followed by a defeat at Saltergate that was a whimper compared to the shenanigans of the previous season. By now the favourite joke (and I apologise for using it here) at Home Park ran along the lines of 'Why don't Argyle players take the dog for a walk? - Because they lose the lead...' This was something we'd done about ten times by now, and you can understand why we would prefer to concede the first goal.

However, at 2-0 down at home to Wigan even the most dyed-in-the-wool optimist had resigned themselves to another miserable Saturday night, but in a strange twist of fate we staged the comeback of the season to win 3-2. With a long list of games against teams in the lower half of the table to come, we could once more see that light at the end of the tunnel. The following week that light was extinguished as we once more threw away a lead, but in a true six pointer at Brentford. The irritating thing was, we were all discussing how bad Brentford were, and how they deserved to be in the bottom four. What did Mick Jones tell the team at half time? Perhaps he too needed a home win for his coupon...

Fortunately, we scraped through in another relegation battle with Carlisle, before York came to town and obtained their customary away point. The travellers amongst us were happy again the following week, as we effectively ended Walsall's league challenge. The next two games were vital, away to Southend, and home to Luton, a minimum of four points were required. Of course, we got none. The display at Southend left the fans angry and resigned to our fate; the Luton game was one neither team deserved to win, but we gifted them two late goals to leave that relegation trapdoor firmly open.

Time was running out. We went to Bournemouth in torrential rain, went a goal down, 2-1 up, gave away another goal, went 3-2 up in injury time and *still* managed to allow our hosts to equalise once more. If the loss of points were not so vital, that would have been one of the best games I had seen for years. Then, our first double of the season was achieved against Preston, although Richard Logan was sent off late in the game. He then decided he needed an even earlier bath the following week at Wycombe. We managed to equalise after his departure, but the defence was too disorganised in the second half, and we conceded another four goals. With two games against high flying Bristol City and Wrexham, that was our last chance of points for a while, or so we thought. However, Phil Starbuck joined on loan, and we won both games by two goal margins.

The situation at the bottom of the table was becoming more clear: there now seemed to be five main contenders for the bottom four places, with Southend and Carlisle looking favourites for two of the positions. However, neither Brentford, Burnley nor ourselves would take anything for granted. We travelled to Oldham knowing that a win was vital, a draw acceptable, and a defeat a disaster. So, when former crowd favourite Adrian Littlejohn scored both their goals, it added huge insult to fatal injury.

An Easter Saturday win at Blackpool kept hopes alive, although any hopes were mainly due to the ineptitude of those teams around us. We travelled to The New Den and gained a draw that most of us would have settled for beforehand, but in truth it left most of us disappointed because the game was there to be won. We settled for a point early in the second half, with the obvious intention of gaining wins in our last two home games.

However the aerial power of Northampton battered us into defeat, and Gillingham gained an undeserved last minute winner. This left us in the position we'd feared almost from the beginning: we had to go to Turf Moor and win to stay up. To add spice to the game, *they* had to win to stay up as well, although if Brentford won at Bristol Rovers we were both down.

The game had added poignancy, as the previous week, one of Argyle's best known (and loudest) fans, Noddy, had passed away after the Gillingham game. The huge importance of the game was put into perspective by that event, and the main chant of the 3,500+ fans who travelled was "Let's do it for Noddy."

The game itself was rather good, despite the tension, and when we equalised there was mayhem in the stand. Unfortunately, we let Burnley gain the advantage just before half time, and never looked good enough to pull back in the second half. Full time came with another venture into the Fourth Division, and tears on the faces of the players and fans.

As for next season, we have a new management team, the chairman is still there, and as yet we have no budget for players. Will we escape first time of asking? I think it is unlikely, but just watch this space...

THE SEADOG BITES BACK!

Scarborough

"Football's a funny old game." It's a phrase that seems so commonplace when talking about this beautiful game of ours, yet it's only really been used by Jimmy Greaves, and he probably only ever said it once... Ah, what the hell!

Boro's '97-98 season culminated with a 16 hour round trip to Torquay United in the play-offs. We lost 4-1 and 7-2 on aggregate. The damage had been done in the home leg after a 3-1 defeat in front of our highest gate for five years. I'd dare Jimmy Greaves to walk up to any Scarborough fan at Plainmoor that night and say *that* was funny. No, it wasn't a laughing matter. Boro had worked hard all season to reach

the play-offs, and when we finally did, the players cracked under the pressure.

Otherwise it was a very successful year throughout the entire club. Apart from the first team finishing sixth there were many other successes. Our reserve side, led by former player, manager and current assistant Ray McHale, who is due a testimonial next year, beat a Newcastle United side comprising of nearly £10m worth of talent to win the Pontin's League Division Three title. Our youth team knocked Premiership Bolton out of the FA Youth Cup, and finished the Northern Intermediate League season in seventh place. Former Leeds United star Glynn Snodin, whose younger brother Ian signed for Boro in the pre-season, coached the juniors to their success.

But it was the senior squad's Third Division campaign which sparked most interest within the town. It took a lot for Boro to get the armchair fans off their backsides, and those that stayed at home before turning out near the end in their part-time thousands missed some crackers.

At the McCain Stadium we finished with 44 goals, the most of any club in the Third. We thrashed Donny (obviously) 4-0, Chester 4-1 and, ironically, Torquay 4-1. We knocked in three past sheepish sides Swansea and Cardiff and we only failed to score in two home games... *the last two*, against Scunthorpe and Shrewsbury - a couple of goalless draws with plenty of spurned opportunities that cost us an automatic place.

Away from home we weren't so hot, despite having five fine wins at

Darlington, Doncaster, Cambridge, Shrewsbury and Scunthorpe. Our biggest defeat of the season was 4-0 at Rochdale on Easter Sunday, and we conceded three and lost at Hull City, Hartlepool, Leyton Orient and Macclesfield. We scored three at Lincoln and would have won but for Gareth Ainsworth who scored a hat-trick and two days later moved to Port Vale. Why couldn't he have left two days earlier?

Conceding goals was a problem all season. It wasn't until Tony Elliott signed from Cardiff in February that we tightened up properly at the back. Elliott played 15 league games, conceded just 13 league goals (including the four at Rochdale) and kept six clean sheets. He has already become a cult hero with us Seadogs and young 'keeper Kevin Martin, who was badly injured at Scunthorpe in the FA Cup - forcing him to miss the rest of the season, was offered just a monthly contract this summer due to Elliott's form.

Our two centre-backs this year were mainly picked from Paul Atkin, Gary Bennett and Jason Rockett. Atkin, mainly a squad player having joined Boro from rivals York City in the summer, was released after a year and became a driving instructor! Thirty-six year old ex-Sunderland captain Bennett was voted Boro's Player of the Year in three of the season's four polls, and led by example from the back after starting the first few games in midfield.

Rocky would have won the Bravest Player of the Year award, had there been one. In almost every game he battled through severe pain from his Paul McGrath-like knees, and he barely trained more than twice a week. The measure of his courage was shown at Doncaster when despite limping heavily from an earlier knock, he rose above everyone to head Boro's winner with just three minutes left. Unfortunately, his injuries mean he will have to retire from the game. He will be a great loss.

Another former Sunderland stalwart, John Kay, was the regular holder of the right-back slot. His 'the ball or your legs' attitude cost him ten bookings and a couple of suspensions. He regularly won tackles which were 30/70 against him and he also compiled a winger and striker casualty list. When he was suspended, young YTS right-back Richard Jackson filled in and did well enough earn a professional contract, along with YTS centre-back Michael McNaughton and youth team captain midfielder Neil Radigan. Again, Sunderland connections helped fill the left-back spot. Young Paul Hockingbottom proved a good acquisition after he came in on loan.

Our midfield was a mixture of toughness and skill. Ex-Everton star Ian Snodin was Boro's captain throughout most of the season, and had it not been for a couple of nasty injuries, he would have led us to more wins without a doubt. His passing ability and mental strength helped a lot of the younger players.

One shock at the end of the season was the release of Michael McElhatton, an Irish midfielder we signed from Bournemouth last year. 'Macca' had been one of Boro's most consistent players, and had won many fans over with his never-say-die attitude. He also won a strong female backing from the young ladies at the McStad who couldn't resist his 'Cantona' of an up-turned collar! Unfortunately, he wanted more money than we could offer.

Despite only playing a handful of games, former Swindon midfielder Ben Worrall was a fans' favourite. The five-foot nothing, bald-headed battler scored the goal of the season at home to Cardiff, a 25-yard belter. He then followed that up with a second - his first Boro goals of '97-98 and his first brace since he was 12!

Dutchman Carel Van der Velden came from Barnsley in pre-season and promised much, but he left three months later, looking as if he'd spent too much time in the town's seafront ice-cream parlours! Van der Chunky, as he became known, went back to Holland, before almost re-signing in January. Apparently he rang Mick Wadsworth and said he'd lost two stone and was 100% fit. But by that time we'd already signed Paul Conway on loan from Northampton.

Steve Brodie was our main striker but not our top scorer. That honour went to Gareth Williams, who was on fire in the first half of the campaign. Yet he only managed three goals after December and finished with just 15. And despite scoring four penalties in that total, he miss-hit a spot kick in the play-off from which the Gulls took full advantage. Still, it's good that 'Gripper,' as he's known for his likeness to the old *Grange Hill* character, will be a Boro player for a further two years having extended his contract in December, although he is set for a role as left wing-back next season.

Three of the seven strikers we used were under-21. The most popular was Neil Campbell, signed on a free from York City in September. The tall shaven-headed Campbell is good in the air and on the ground. Once he realises this himself, and does a bit more work, he'll become a constant threat.

Chris Tate was signed from Sunderland (yes, another one) in pre-season and was top scorer in the Championship winning reserve side. He only got one for the first team, and, like Campbell, once he realises how good he can be he could do well. But Jamie Mitchell's Boro career is over. After scoring seven goals last term, he lost form and confidence and played just nine games. But he did manage to notch three memorable goals - an individually brilliant effort at Mansfield, a 20-yard thumper at home to Rotherham, and a last gasp equaliser at Brighton. He was also the winner of the super sub award - coming off the bench 31 times during the season!

Liam Robinson added a touch of experience when necessary, but more often that not he lacked the pace and ability to outwit defences. He scored an ingenious goal at Scunthorpe as we bowed out of the FA Cup - a 45-yard chip over a 6'4" 'keeper! He was placed on the transfer list at the end of the season, and would have been released had he not been under contract for another year. Linton Brown was brought in on loan during August and September from Swansea, but the less said about him the better!

So there you have it. Scarborough FC's '97-98 season in a nutshell. Oh sorry, no it's not, it's in *Survival of the Fattest 4*, with no nutshells in sight! Nevermind! Anyway, look out for the Seadogs next season. After our play-off loss this year we are looking to bypass the lottery of death, especially when changes for the better are planned. We are changing our chairman, changing our sponsor, changing our game plan, our formation, our midfield, our strike force and even the colour of the little trays the chips come in!

SEASIDE SAGA

Brighton & Hove Albion

"Are we nearly there yet? I feel sick..." The all-too familiar cry from one's offspring, as a traumatic journey gets underway.

Actually, no. This was me, as we made our way round four (or five, depending on map-reading ability) motorways on our way to Gillingham. I know... I shouldn't moan. The previous season ended with our triumphant survival in the Football League, and that 1-1 'victory' over Hereford United. But the glow of complete happiness ebbed away as we took stock of our situation. We didn't actually have our new board in place, and we didn't have a ground. The only arrangement was to play our home games at Gillingham. None of us

A Brighton & Hove Albion Fanzine

BRING HOME THE ALBION *BACK WHERE THEY BELONG*

BUMPER 44 PAGE ISSUE - FREE COMPETITION

Issue 20 January 1998   £1

was keen on this, for various reasons. Mine was fairly basic - I suffer from travel sickness. Very girlie, I know, but Gillingham is 70 miles away... so it's kill or cure for me this season.

To start at the beginning:

August - the season kicked off, and being on holiday I missed the first home and away games, and our Coca-Cola Cup 'run'. Ahem. Anyway, bright-eyed and bushy-tailed, I prepared to make my first trip to Gillingham on August 30th. Jonathan (8˜) was keen to come with me, so we booked ourselves onto the Supporters Club coach for the game against Leyton Orient.

It suddenly occurred to me just how much of the enjoyment of matchday is in the repetitive and ritualistic behaviour unique to each individual. Mine included driving to pick up my Dad, walking up the road, buying a programme from the same bloke, going into the ground, sitting in the same place, enjoying the same company and chatter. Mundane? Perhaps - but all of that was part of the experience, part of a matchday. It was this routine of the home games that I loved so much. And now it had been taken away. I'd have to make myself a new pattern, draw up a new routine. Except looking back on this season, I never did. Going to Gillingham never was a comfortable or enjoyable day out. I never made it without either getting lost, breaking down (the transport, not me) or some other catastrophe.

Don't get me wrong; it hasn't all been bad this season. We had some mild flurries of excitement. The first was our run of two wins in a row, (Rochdale and Doncaster) when Steve Gritt started talking about pushing for the play-offs, and later our away win at Peterborough, to name but erm... two.

Anyway, where was I? Ah yes, my first trip to Gillingham. I took my travel tablets, made some sandwiches and set off at 11.30am. I didn't quite get the dosage right on the tablet front. I was so concerned not to throw up on the coach I took more than was necessary, and ended up in a coma for much of the day. I hope you're not expecting a match report or anything here. All I can say is that we got there and back, and didn't really enjoy it. The team lost 1-0.

September began with the news that Bellotti was, at last, out, and we had the new board in place. Dick Knight was in control, and stated that his first priority was to end the controversial ground-share with Gillingham. Well, that never happened, but he has done lots of other good things. We now have a shop in Brighton town centre, a mobile shop and two of 'our own' running the PA system at Priestfield, thus ensuring good quality music? (Long Live Supertramp!) Other occurrences during this month? We were playing away at Torquay on the 20th - what a golden opportunity for a weekend at Pontins in Brixham! We (husband, Jonathan, teenage daughter and myself) set off on Friday night, arriving at 'The English Riviera' in time for a couple of drinks and a quick 'in, out, shake it all about'. Gosh, you can't beat a Hokey-Cokey before bedtime can you? The weekend was ruined by a particularly inept Brighton performance, as we went down 3-0. However, the shopping in Brixham and the visit to the Golden Hind did much to make up for this, and we came home Sunday afternoon in good spirits.

October - and having beaten Rochdale in late September followed by our win over Doncaster, I got totally over-excited and thought we were on an unstoppable winning run. The next home game was against Exeter on the Saturday, when unfortunately my husband was to be in the USA on business. This meant convincing my daughter that a day out to Gillingham was an unmissable treat, and wasn't I a wonderful mother for arranging a trip out for us all? I virtually promised her an Albion victory. We lost 3-1, and she hasn't been back since. I decreased the dose of travel tablets this time and ended up pleasantly dreamy.

November was another red letter day for us - the first time we drove *en famille* to Gillingham. A forgettable game was livened up by the last five minutes when we almost managed a draw, but we went down 2-1 to Rotherham. Husband and daughter don't share my love of the beautiful game, and found a very nice shopping centre in which to pass the 90 minutes. The following week, fate stared us in the face as we played Hereford in the first round of the FA Cup. It had to happen didn't it? Needless to say, they won this time, 2-1. The game and the victory meant a lot more to them than us. We weren't expecting to progress very far in the cup anyway.

Also in November came the shock announcement that cash was in short supply and our top earners were being given golden handshakes. Several players left, and we found ourselves with only 15 professionals. However, most of us were glad to see the back of these high earners, Craig Maskell in particular. Leyton Orient - you're welcome to him!

Towards the end of November, and with things looking bleak, a group of supporters met in a pub in Hove. The team were struggling, relying on Doncaster to save us from going down, the crowds were too small and the players uninspired. We needed some way to kick-start the season, something to encourage supporters to return in numbers, some way to make the players feel more at home. And thus was born the 'bring home the Albion' campaign. The idea? To lovingly blanket Brighton and Hove in a sea of blue and white ribbons. We were going to Bring Home the Albion.

December - Posters, car stickers and blue and white ribbons were handed out to supporters and to local Albion-friendly shops, offices and businesses, and one evening, under cover of darkness, several supporters donned balaclavas to go out draping blue and white over local landmarks and historic monuments in the towns. Queen Victoria was not amused, although I'm sure she understood we meant no real harm.

December 15th, and the board held a public meeting in Hove Town Hall. It was packed out with over 1,000 people, showing the level of public support and interest. Over Christmas, the team pulled back from being 3-0 down, to draw 4-4 with Colchester, and then travelled to Peterborough and beat them 2-1. Bizarre! But why didn't we play with such spirit for all the other games?

January dawned with the news that the site of the old Goldstone ground had been re-sold. The buyers paid an eye-watering £24 million for it, more than three times the original sale price. Heartbreaking? Oh yes, but someone must have come out of it smiling. The 3rd of January, and the one away game everyone wanted to go to: Macclesfield. Newly promoted, and the only 'new' ground for all the anoraks. The game was postponed with everyone at least half way there, and rearranged for an evening later in January. Not many people could make that date, but they philosophically reasoned they could make it next season instead. Doh! Ah well, congratulations Macclesfield. Next, Walsall dumped us out of the AutoWindscreen Shield. I won't mention the score, as losing 5-0 is so embarrassing. January 11th, I was up and dressed bright and early on a Sunday morning. The Supporters Club launched a 'Buy a Player' appeal. Yes - a seaside sponsored walk in early January. Great idea - how could I resist taking part? Back in the seventies another similar appeal had resulted in the purchase of Bert Murray, the 'People's Player'. He very kindly came down to Hove from his pub in Lincolnshire to start off our walk, and strode off at such a pace he almost lost us all. It's nice to see he hasn't let himself go.

February, and Valentine's Day was our 'Heart of Football' day, as the fixtures kindly threw ourselves and Doncaster together for this 'love-in'. Crowds turned up from many different clubs, but our love for Doncaster didn't extend to giving them a helping hand up the table, and we shared the points in a 0-0 draw. Two losses later and Steve Gritt was sacked. Stunning news, and at first no one could believe what seemed to be very poor treatment of the man to whom we owed our Football League life. So he hadn't worked miracles this time around, but he could have been given until the end of the season, surely? The following day old Brighton favourite Brian Horton was brought in. Obviously we're right behind him, but we still remain eternally grateful to Steve Gritt for what he did for us.

March and April: On the pitch, consistency ruled - we ended up 91st again! Off it, we were canvassing the public with petitions to show how many supporters wanted to Bring Home the Albion. We finally gained over 32,000 signatures, with thousands of letters written to local councillors. This has been one of the hardest things I've had to do this season: writing to someone, trying to tell them what your club means to you, and why its very survival depends on it coming home, when you're not sure whether they're even a football supporter, let alone if they understand what the whole beautiful game means to you. A place called Withdean had been earmarked, with elaborate plans in place by the Brighton board to ensure limited nuisance to residents. It would only be temporary; we needed to borrow it for three years.

And despite the threat of a Public Enquiry, the Government signed off on the Withdean move. So it looks like Brighton and Hove Albion will celebrate the Millennium on a site where they actually played at the end of the 1800's. Now *that's* what I call a long-awaited home-coming!

THE SECOND OF MAY

Bristol Rovers

There was an air of despondency hanging over the Memorial Ground at the start of '97-98. Having hovered precariously just above the relegation trap door for too long the previous season, many 'pundits' had Rovers down for their first ever visit to the basement division - including some of our very own. "I reckon Bater'll be manager by Christmas" was one bar-room pessimist's appraisal of Ian Holloway's chances of lasting the duration, prior to the arrival of Plymouth Argyle for the opening game.

At the end, the despondency was probably far greater than anything evident on that opening day, but it shouldn't have been.

THE SECOND OF MAY

An Independent View of Bristol Rovers F.C.

£1

Oi, Don't Touch What You Can't Afford

We're Not Tenants Anymore....

The truth is that despite being knocked out of the play-off semi finals in bizarre fashion, Gasheads were treated to one of the most entertaining seasons for years.

Little did we know it at the time, but the game against the subsequently relegated Pilgrims highlighted everything that was different from the previous campaign. Then, entertaining football had been at a premium and the spirit of certain individuals left plenty to be desired. Gasheads don't ask for much, but commitment is a basic necessity. The lack of it was not the manager's doing. His blood is blue and white and he'd inherited a side too full of slackers and shorn of the thing which had undoubtedly made things seem a lot better than they actually were the previous two seasons: Marcus Stewart's goals.

But new-found spirit was evident even before the kick-off. Walking around the back of the new West Stand, you go straight past the changing room windows, and all you could hear from the Rovers dressing room was the players screaming "Come on Gas!" Then, when the teams came out, we were treated to a new innovation - the Rovers 'huddle'. Later in the season, they even started playing Chumbawumba as the teams ran out. Surely there's no other team in this country where the words "We get knocked down, but we get up again" are more apt. Yes, the famous Rovers spirit had returned.

There were also a couple of other things that were blatantly obvious within 45 minutes of the new season: silky football was back on the agenda, the new non-league signings Barry Hayles and Steve Foster were gems and we had a new 'psycho' cult hero in Jason Perry, signed on a free from Cardiff City. With regard to the latter, Rovers - in their wisdom - had decided during the close season that the West Stand Enclosure, directly next to where Perry would spend the first half patrolling, would be a designated 'no swearing' zone. In a thinly disguised attempt to keep the corporate suits in the seats happy, it was decreed that any offenders would be instantly ejected. Unfortunately, there simply weren't enough stewards to eject all of those who joined in the collective "f**kin' hell!" for our first ever experience of Psycho's version of a sliding tackle.

Anyway, without boring you too much with individual match statistics, the most entertaining season for years saw Rovers finish a highly unexpected fifth as leading scorers (70 goals) but with a goal difference of just plus six! During his first outing in league football, Barry Hayles netted 24 goals to be the undoubted bargain buy of the season at £250,000. How many clubs - our nearest and dearest neighbours included - then clambered out of the woodwork saying "well, we looked at him two years ago" after Hayles passed the 20 goal mark. We've only got one question for them. Who put their neck on the line? Ian Holloway. However, any thoughts that we were a one man show (yes, that's you *Sky*) can be dismissed straight away, given that Peter Beadle and Jamie Cureton also both finished in the top 20 goalscorers for the division.

In a season where we lost a total of 16 games, notably eight at home, there were numerous times when it seemed we'd taken a hammer blow from which we couldn't possibly recover. Every time though, that never-say-die spirit, which had seen us claw back from 3-0 down in 20 minutes at Oldham to gain a 4-4 draw, brought us back from the brink. I lost count of the number of times that I said, "Ah well, good effort, but that's the season over." But each time they came back.

We even survived our now infamous trip to Wigan. From the moment we stood on the freezing terrace at Springfield Park (there's something to be said for spending that extra couple of quid for a seat), we worried about the state of the pitch. When the players came out our suspicions were confirmed. The game degenerated into a farce as referee Kevin Lynch made decisions seemingly without taking the conditions into consideration; Dave Pritchard's sending off was testament to this. Rovers ended up with seven players after a series of dubious dismissals, and although the game was lost the remaining players rallied magnificently. Geoff Dunford echoed the thoughts of every Gashead at Springfield with his outspoken and justified criticism of the referee, although all it gained him was a trip to Lancaster Gate (where a number of our players followed later in the season as we topped the disciplinary table). Mr Lynch, not surprisingly, hasn't been seen in charge of a Rovers game since. Come to that, it's rare to see him taking charge of *any* league game at all these days...

Five losses on the trot in February and March had us resigning ourselves to a spot in the top half of the table, which was at least better than fighting relegation like last season. But the final game at home to Brentford really summed it all up. We'd looked out of it after the previous week's results, especially when hitting the post three times at Blackpool in front of 3,500 travelling Gasheads before losing 1-0. Suddenly, we were reliant on other results. In front of a packed Memorial Ground (my God, people were even paying up to £30 for a ticket!), we had to win, and Brentford had to at least avoid defeat to stay up. After quarter of an hour, the battle looked lost. The normally amiable Gary Penrice had floored Warren Aspinall with an elbow after Mr. Blobby had been indulging in a spot of intimidation. Pleas from the terraces that such an action deserved a medal, not a red card, fell on deaf ears.

Not surprisingly we had to ride our luck on occasions, but that commitment and willingness to work for each other, which Bees' boss Mickey Adams (a far better manager than Wilkins or Keegan by the way) manfully acknowledged afterwards, paid dividends when Jamie Cureton put us one up. Cue pitch invasion number one. Then, with news going round the ground that Fulham were losing, the Bees equalised. Minutes later, Jamie Cureton had his leg broken by a challenge from behind, which would have had any self-respecting commentator jumping out of his seat screaming, "He'd be off in the World Cup for that!"

But each time they came back, refusing to feel sorry for themselves. The resulting free kick was played out to the left wing from where Matt Lockwood put in the cross he'd been threatening to deliver all season. Hayles' head connected. The crowd seemed to fall silent for half an hour. The net rippled. Gooooooal! F**kin' Heeeellllllll! Gooooooaaaaal! Cue pitch invasion number two - an even bigger one. At this point we should clear something up for Bristol City fans - the reason we weren't called hooligans after the pitch invasions is because we applauded the Brentford fans, failed to attack any players and generally didn't threaten anyone.

After the final whistle, Ian Holloway appeared with the players on the balcony. He uttered a mere four words: "Never, ever, give up." If ever there was a statement which summed up our season, that was it.

Unfortunately, the play-offs summed up everything that was good and bad about Rovers' season. We dismantled Atkins' long ball hoofers with a dazzling display of football, going 3-0 up, with each pass being greeted by "Olé!". Barry Hayles then had a one-on-one saved with the Cobblers 'keeper and minutes later hit the inside of a post. It was the turning point of the whole season. Moments later, John Gayle lobbed (yes, lobbed) 'keeper Lee Jones to give the Cobblers hope for the return leg.

Never ever give up. This time, devastatingly, it was the Cobblers who lived up to Olly's war cry. On a pitch waterlogged down the sides, so that our wingers who had ripped Northampton apart just four days earlier spent most of their time on their arses, the nightmare scenario became reality. We were defeated 3-0 in what Cobblers manager Ian Atkins described as "an awesome display of power football." It's hard to argue, but I couldn't watch it every week.

And finally, we come back full circle to the point made at the start of this piece. The way we missed out on another trip to Wembley was heartbreaking. During the summer months, it will be all too easy to dwell on that night at Northampton and think of what might have been, especially when you look at how hard Division Two will be to get out of next season. Loaded Fulham's failure (ha, ha) and the likes of Manchester City and Stoke coming down to meet us will see to that.

However, the biggest cause for celebration last season happened off the pitch. When did Bristol Rovers last own their own ground? Now there's a pub quiz question if ever there was one. The answer? 1940. And now, after half a century of tenancy and our recent nomadic existence, Rovers finally have a home to call our own. The significance of the purchase cannot be underestimated and it gives the club a solid basis on which to plan future investments, whether they are at the Memorial or at another site. Many of us would have put owning a ground as a higher priority than reaching the play-offs this season, and to have achieved both really is beyond our wildest dreams. And not only do we have a ground - there's even reports that we might have four sides and a roof within the next two years.

So before we get too suicidal about losing to a team more suited to the wrestling ring, let's remember season '97-98 for the numerous good things which occurred. Never, ever, give up.

THE SHEEPING GIANT

Wrexham

I can't believe what has just happened! I, Dai Shovett, investigative journalist and winner of the Jean Rook Local Paper Sportswriter of the Year award in 1983 for my thrilling expose of Limahl's twisted love for Mick Mills, have just been told by my boss that I've failed to make *The Wrexham Pleader*'s team to cover the World Cup! I'm sick as a carrot! I can't believe I didn't get into his final squad of 22; after all, we only employ 12 journalists, and I'm the only football correspondent! Even the bloody receptionist is going - she boned up on Jamaicans all Summer apparently. I was so furious that I burst into tears and trashed my room. Then I realised that I was at

THE SHEEPING GIANT

Issue #35

The Wrexham Fanzine

50P

After the defensive debacle against Blackpool, They've left me no choice.........

It's time to bring back ....Nigel Beaumont!!

home and had just wrecked my bachelor pad. It'll take mum ages to clean it.

I suppose I'm a victim of my own success. Little did I know this time last year, as I completed my entry for *Survival of the Fattest 3*, that top talent scouts were monitoring the purpleness of my prose in my unparalleled, unreadable coverage of Wrexham, judging the time to be right for them to make a move. Chris Evans' call came in early August, saying he wanted to hang around with me and could he join me when Wrexham played at Fulham. I agreed, of course, although I'd never heard of him, and we enjoyed a booze-soaked Friday night of indulgence with Anthea Turner and some nurses which led to my failing to turn up to the match or file a report - a minor detail which seemed to irritate the boss. He threatened to punish me, but backed down when Chris launched a furious attack on his radio station against "stupid editors who expect journalists to turn up and write about stuff just because they're paid to." Too right! I thanked him by giving him a copy of 'David Letterman's Bumper Book Of Copyright-Free Jokes And Formats' which I signed "From your favourite Wrexham correspondent."

Oh yeah, Wrexham! How could they blow it this season? Primed with one of the strongest teams assembled in Western Europe since the Reformation, they seemed certain to at least win the league and the FA Cup, while forming the basis of a successful Welsh team in the World Cup.

I mean, look at the opposition - it's not as if any Second Division teams were about to get taken over by the owner of *Harrods*, employ two all-time great England internationals to run the side, and spend millions on glamorous strikers! Some people accuse me of raising false expectations among the fans. Do you know what I say to those people? I say "Could you wait a second, I'm busy interviewing our new manager, Pele." That usually shuts them up. Anyway, if a team who often play before huge crowds of up to 4,000 and had a princely sum of £60,000 to spend on new players last year can't get into the Premiership, then who can? Huh? Huh?

Wrexham went from strength to mediocrity in the early stages of the season. Their best performance, and another disaster for me, came at home against Blackpool, when they raced into a 3-0 lead after an hour. I'd seen enough to write my report, so I joined Danny Baker and Zoë Ball in a pub crawl through Caego. It was only two days later, when letters of complaint came in, that I discovered Blackpool had come back to win 4-3. Doh! The boss was furious, but I cried all over his desk and promised I'd make a new start and never ever do anything like this ever again ever, and he said he'd give me one last chance. What a sucker!

I continued to cover matches while enjoying my new status as a showbiz personality. Of course, Danny and Chris didn't fancy going to places like Northampton or Carlisle. There's very little scope for getting their pictures taken by the paparazzi there. It's a pity they didn't come to Walsall, though, as we had a great sending-off. Battling Basile Boli's Brother was dismissed for something he said to the referee. I thought the Foul Frog'd accused him of cheating, or even worse, flawed dress sense, but when I spoke to the ref afterwards he explained "I took objection to the way he kept referring to me as 'vous' rather than 'tu'. I took this as insolence and dismissed him under Section 12a - foul and abusive language, or provocative use of the second person as a form of address." I rubbed it in by pretending to play a flute in front of the Walsall journalists; the locals claim the Pied Piper came from a hamlet off ye olde M6 and get sick of the people of Hamlyn, with their provocative marches and penalty shoot-out re-enactments. Fortunately, I escaped disciplinary action by claiming ignorance - a quality I seem to have no problem simulating.

It was brilliant to have a good cup run this year. After beating Rochdale we met our deadly rivals, Chester City. The lads weren't interested in coming down until I told them it was live on *Sky*. They never made it, though, as none of them had any idea of how to find the North, so they missed our glorious victory. For the rest of the season Wrexham fans had the pleasure of watching Chester suffer further. Their problems started in March when their players were asked to film a *Nike* advert in Manchester Airport. Unfortunately, their ball-juggling skills were not what *Nike* expected, and the resultant bill for damage to three x-ray machines, a luggage carousel and a display unit in a Sock Shop was what nearly drove them bankrupt. However, they survived. It was the saddest moment in football since Andy Goram pulled out of the World Cup after his life was blighted by a personal tragedy: a lorry full of oranges had crashed into both his local Ladbrokes and the pub next door, wiping them both out.

In the third round we met Wimbledon. I went down to Plough Lane and spent a pointless afternoon watching a housing estate (there was no score). Typical! Again the boss was less than pleased, especially when pictures appeared in the tabloids the next morning of my subsequent night on the town with that gawky bird from Texas and the truncated Spice Girls (by that I mean the four remaining members, not the Scandinavian dwarf tribute band). Indeed, the *Pleader* splashed a huge picture of me seeing how many kebabs I could fit in my mouth (twelve in case you're interested):

HAVE YOU SEEN THIS MAN?

At last, we can feature Dai Shovett in our pages. If you see him around, please ask him if he has any plans to report on a Wrexham match for us in the near future.

Wrexham continued to press for a place in the play-offs. A long unbeaten run took them into third place, which was awful - a successful team gives you nothing to write about! When you make up stories about back room bust-ups or drug probes at a flourishing club no one takes any notice - that's how Phil Neville got away with exporting arms firm to Eritrea through Bury's commercial department for so long. It was much better at the start of the season, when we didn't score for ages, enabling me to run a daily feature, 'WREXHAM GOAL WATCH'. Thankfully, a trip for the squad to the filming of *T.F.I. Friday*, followed by a huge booze-up at a dentist's ended that good run, and they went into a tail-spin which left them out of contention.

Of course, I pretended to care while laughing up my sleeve at their misfortune. It gave me the chance to run lots of spurious 'What on earth can we do to rescue dismal Wrexham's crappy team?' features. I enrolled the help of Uri Geller to get us into the play-offs, but to no avail, although he did get my microwave to work again, which is amazing, as it's a television. In the final analysis, it was the lack of a centre-forward who played like Duncan Ferguson with a gutful of aftershave which cost us dear. You'd never catch him in a Portuguese night-club at six in the morning. Mind you, you'd never catch a Wrexham player there either, despite my front page splash 'CAPTAIN ALGARVEL - Bryan Robson and Brian Carey in Women's Lavatory Shocker Probe.'

Everything seemed to be going fine, but then I got careless and got into more trouble, this time with the NUJ. They regularly send instructions to tabloid sports writers, reminding them of the clichés they have to feature in articles on certain subjects. Basically, I wrote a piece on Barnsley, but forgot the statutory instructions which were established when they got promoted. In case you're interested, here they are:

1.   Each of these words or phrases must be mentioned at least once every 400 words: 'Whippet', 'Pigeon, 'Grim' , 'Miners', 'Cobblestoned Hills', 'Clogs', 'Dickie Bird', 'Michael Parkinson', 'Skinner Normanton', 'Unemployment', 'Cheap Foreign Centre Back', 'Flat Cap'.

2.   The tone of all articles must not veer from the patronising.

3.   Disparaging comparison must be made between a Barnsley player with a suitably homespun name and an international star (irony is a bonus) e.g. "Gianfranco Zola might be able to cope with the biting cold of a miserable January night in the shadow of the dark, satanic, filth-belching mills, but will he be able to cope with Matty Appleby?"

4.   Accompanying photographs in colour publications MUST be sepia.

Thankfully, I got away with it. They didn't fine me a penny, although the boss wasn't delighted with the £40,000 fine the *Pleader* received. He insisted I should go to see a faith healer, who might be able to exorcise the demons in my mind, but I never made it to her office as Danny's local, 'The Pet and Prize' is on the way, and the lads were holding a party for David 'Five Bellies' Mellor and Ally McCoist. Never mind.

The Boss wasn't happy though, and insisted I got in shape and kept my mind on Wrexham if I was to make it to the World Cup. How many times had someone said that to me? Still, I made the usual noises, saying I was so sorry to have caused offence, and made it look like I was trying really hard to get fit. In fact, I wrote my coverage of the last month of the season wearing a bin bag.

Despite the lack of league success or affairs with pop stars, the season wasn't totally wasted. Wrexham did win their first trophy since before, when they claimed the inaugural Welsh Invitation Cup for the first time. Funded by BBC Wales (a professional outfit committed to providing quality coverage of South Walian issues), carefully selected classic ties, and the odd mid-table bandana, were screened live - usually they were selected on the basis of whether a team from South Wales had to come all the way up to the North. It was a brilliantly organised competition which had the entire nation on the edge of their seats as they stretched for the remote control, based on the infallible format of a knock-out cup in every respect except the 'knock-out' bit. By ensuring that no-one could be eliminated from the competition in the thrilling seven month first stage, no matter how hard they tried, the Welsh FA guaranteed breath-taking action between full strength teams while coincidentally making sure every South Walian side got through the quarter finals. Once the tournament got to the knock-out stage, matches went to extra time and, if the scores were still level, were decided by a game of conkers between both goalkeepers. As Reliable Andy Marriott had been soaking his forty-niner in vinegar for three months, The Reds were quietly confident.

We faced Cardiff in the final; a clash of the titans played out before a heaving Racecourse crowd and millions at home. Our victory literally drove the fans apathetic, while the six Cardiff fans went on the rampage, damaging several programmes as they ran amok in the stand.

Excitingly, Wrexham emulated top European team Real Madrid by trying to lose their manager after a successful season. Burnley sacked Chris 'Brooding' Waddle, the most amazing news since Gazza went to a health farm to buy half a kilo of organic stamina with the mud still on, and Little Brian Flynn was linked with the job. He seemed ideal as he's single, leaving little scope for disgruntled Burnley fans to set fire to his wife if form slumps. However he turned the job down on the grounds that he's not mad. I mean, if the Burnley job's worth taking, Rod Stewart's a Londoner!

I was sad to see Flynn stay, though. He has been at Wrexham for ten years now, and no journalist likes stability at his club - what the hell am I supposed to write about? If it gets any stabler I'll be back to writing 'Rhosllanerchrugog News' on page eight again - month upon month of 'DOG MIGHT BITE MAN' and 'WOMEN'S INSTITUTE IN MEETING SENSATION'. Other journalists get to invent lists of people they think will become their next managers, and I'd got mine written and everything. It had all the usual faithfuls: Johann Cruyff; Bobby Robson; Ron Atkinson; Wim Jansen; but I'd added a couple of new faces to spice things up: Jeremy Clarkson, Jools Holland and that magician bloke who's married to Victoria Wood. I'd have loved to see Clarkson get the job as the post-match interviews would be brilliant. His original, nay, ceaseless use of the word 'apocalypse' has revolutionised the world of journalism, and made us think of the end of the world in a new, gentler way, more related to a flippant noun in a video about helicopters exploding than the end of everything, which has got to be a good thing.

So, with my World Cup over before it began and my showbiz friends strangely hard to get in touch with since my popularity waned, there's nothing left for me but to look forward to next season. Wrexham have been linked with top Elvis impersonator Neil Ruddock, but big transfer swoops are hardly their thing. We are a very traditional side. For a start, we don't have any of those new-fangled foreign players (we call them 'bookreaders'). We may build a new stand though; we only got money promised for it because the managing director thought he was being asked to fund a news stand.

Next season will be a strange one though, with many absent friends. Sadly Neil 'ex-chiropodist' Warnock is no longer with Oldham, which is a shame as his teams always play great football. I was waiting at the players' entrance this season when they arrived. They play in blue and white, but as they got off the coach they were wearing their club uniform of animal pelts, wode and clubs. I asked their charming striker Sean McCarthy for a quote but he was busy studying the coach's wheel with a confused look of fascination on his face. Warnock's pre-match comment was "Ug. Creegah mangani! Fire bad. Woman good." It was a tough match, with Steve Redmond picking up a booking for threatening the referee with a rudimentary arrow head carved out of flint. There was also a nasty incident after the match when their goalkeeper walked into the dressing room door and fractured his protruding eyebrows. I'm sure the atmosphere at Boundary Park next season will still be brilliant, especially if they develop bronze in time to complete the main stand.

Despite my World Cup sickener, life is still exciting. Football is the new rock'n'roll (As a matter of interest, rock 'n' roll is now the new reading,

reading is the new opera, and going to the pictures is the old watching television. Fishing is still fishing.) We are now truly living in Planet Football. Sainsbury's have even introduced football currency at their petrol stations, although my attempts to buy a trial price bag of Giant Smarties brought home to me just how little Andy Hinchcliffe is actually worth. There's bound to be plenty of exciting action for me to report on next season - if only the boss would tell me where the paper has relocated to. Never mind. Catch you later, as I once said to Dave Beasant, with painful consequences. That guy's got no sense of humour.

Dai Shovett is brought to you in association with ink - the lead of the next millennium.

SHRIMP SEASON

Southend United

Déjà-vu Or What?

Ever had that feeling of déjà-vu? Well, two relegations in as many seasons wasn't déjà vu, it was bloody reality!

A new season. A new government. A new division. A new manager. All these greeted the faithful as they returned to Roots Hall for the '97-98 season. Welcome back OUR all non-conquering losers - Southend United. Alvin 'Chipmunk' Martin had taken over from ex-Liverpool favourite Ronnie Whelan. Whelan had resigned during the summer after he had successfully taken us out of the First Division at the first time of asking, and into the Second. He had left

RELEGATION PARTY ISSUE!

Uncle Vic: "I see Alvin Martin as a very good manager for the future. Given time and resources he will create a better team...."

ONLY £1

ISSUE 9
APRIL/MAY
1998

Shrimp Season

A
SOUTHEND
UNITED
FANZINE

OUR beloved Leader is seen here licking his lips at the thought of OUR trips to Hartlepool, Halifax and Hull next season!!!

Picture nicked from The Evening Echo with apologies to Robin Weaver

us with a team that war poor by anybody's standards and was especially lacking in spirit, including players with long term injuries, weight and attitude problems. OUR so-called star players had already become liabilities. There were rumours and innuendoes about drinking bouts, constant back and knee troubles and non-payment of signing-on fees, etc. Just before the season started, OUR beloved chairman Uncle Vic Jobson announced that he was going to make drastic cutbacks, this included scrapping OUR reserve team and getting rid of some back room staff. Motivation or what?

Chipmunk's appointment mystified many of us; he wasn't mentioned in any of the press rumours that circulated during the summer of '97. His subsequent team selections and substitutions are still a mystery. Chipmunk's first match in charge was a pre-season affair at Canvey Island which the non-league side won 3-1. Other warm-ups at Gravesend and C********* United saw a slight improvement. A quickly organised re-match at Canvey saw us lose 4-2. They say friendlies don't count for much, but these results were a sign of things to come.

Like most football supporters up and down the country, we were confident about the forthcoming season and there was little sign of the disasters that lay ahead. Mind you, we did have just two new faces in OUR opening day fixture against Carlisle. Carl Beeston, a loan signing from Stoke City, who left us after nine matches to join non-league Hednesford Town and Nathan Jones, a 24-year-old from Numancia in Spain. Nathan Jones? Sounds more Welsh than Spanish... Exactly right. Born in the valleys, he spent last season playing Spanish football and helped his club gain promotion. He played a trial match for us against Purfleet and was by far the best player on the pitch. He looked to be the solution to OUR left back problems of last year, and was promptly offered a contract, which he duly signed.

Guess what happens when a talented player signs a contract for Southend United? It's remarkable. They lose enthusiasm, confidence, form; call it what you like. Something happens when they come to this part of the East Coast. Mike Marsh was a classic example: played in the top division with Liverpool and West Ham but when he came to Roots Hall, 'it' happened. His form went out the window. Maybe it's something in the sea air that causes it. Marsh subsequently retired from football through injury. He is now playing for Barrow and has helped them to win promotion. Either OUR club is jinxed, or is it apathy from the board downwards? I put it down to the latter. It's pulling OUR club down and the supporters with it. A prime example of supporter apathy was the red card demonstration planned at the last game against Wrexham to protest against two consecutive relegations. Every supporter was handed a red card and a P45, but nobody bothered to hold them up as the players came onto the pitch, most just laid down and died even though there was an after-match pitch invasion by a few anti-Jobson protesters. Perhaps now we've been taken over, it will be a 'new dawn' for OUR club and the apathy will disappear down Victoria Avenue where it belongs - along with the departing chairman, Uncle Vic, although under the terms of the deal we've still got to put up with him for the next two years. OUR new bosses are a property company and land developers, so does this mean a new stadium? Will there be greyhounds running around Roots Hall? Or will we, as season ticket holders, get a special offer for one of the new apartments that could spring up on the Roots Hall site? As long as Brighton don't get that feeling of déjà-vu when they visit us next season, we'll be all right.

So, it was basically the same team that was relegated that kicked off the '97-98 campaign. Last season began with a home game against Tranmere Rovers, where we took a 1-0 lead. Tranmere equalised. Final result 1-1. This season we took the lead against Carlisle... Carlisle equalised... Final result 1-1. Déjà-vu?

The regionalised draw in the Coca-Cola Cup gave us a local derby against - Cardiff City! The first leg was drawn 1-1, with the second-leg won 3-1 by the blue of Southend. Chipmunk blasted the players for their performance. I bet he wished he hadn't bothered after some of the results we subsequently witnessed! He didn't blast them again (not in public anyway).

We made a guest appearance on *Sky* for OUR first away match of the season. A boring game that finished 1-0 to Luton. *Sky* didn't invite us back again!

The campaign didn't start as badly as it finished (it didn't, honestly!); we were unbeaten at home until the middle of October. Bristol City were the first team to win at Roots Hall, a 2-0 victory that started their run to eventual promotion. Typical! On the other side OUR away form was atrocious. The last time we'd won an away match was November 23rd, 1996, a 2-1 victory at Stoke City. Twenty-one games and 11 months later we won away for the second time. This time we beat Plymouth 3-2, and we even made hard work of that. Two goals up we allowed Plymouth to pull it back to 2-2. With 15 minutes to go Sada 'Pepe' N'Diaye, a French bloke making an excellent debut, scored the winner. Had we unearthed a new Stan Collymore? No, was the simple answer. Out injured for quite a while, he never reproduced his opening form. He subsequently left during the summer. Remember apathy?

The first round of the FA Cup (sponsored by Littlewoods) gave us an away tie at giant-killers Woking. The bookies made Woking favourites to go through to the next round and the staunchest Southend supporter probably would not have argued with that (except for Argie Pete of course!). Hundreds of Blues fans made the short trip round the M25 with loads of them piling onto the pitch in celebration, as two late goals from Jones and Gridelet beat the odds and put us in the hat for round two. You'd have thought we'd just won the whole damn thing, not just beaten a non-league team in the first round! This was the highlight of OUR season! Yes, this is what it had come down to. Mind you, we don't get many away wins, so we really celebrate when we do. The second round took us to Millionaires' Row against Al Fayed's Fulham. They say money can't buy you success. Maybe not, but it might influence some people! We were doing okay in this game when Mr Karren Brady found himself with a one-on-one against OUR 'keeper, Simon Royce. Roycie brought him down - penalty, fair enough, no complaints. Then the ref sent him off. Again, no complaints. Fulham duly scored from the spot. He then sent off OUR substitute Ben Lewis, who had only been on the pitch nine minutes when he was accused of stamping on a Fulham player. It looked no more than a tangle of feet to us. Down to nine men and Tony Henricksen, OUR reserve goalie, also brought somebody down to give away a penalty. Red card offence? No, he just booked him. Surely the same offence should produce the same punishment? Henricksen saved the resulting penalty... Small consolation! Fulham won 1-0 and the ref still got paid for his afternoons' work!

OUR one realistic chance of reaching Wembley was blown in a whimper, when Wycombe visited Roots Hall in the first round of the AutoWindscreens Thingummy. The ref might as well have tossed a coin to see who went through to the next round, as either side didn't seem to be bothered. The only goal went to Wycombe, which they didn't even celebrate. You'd have thought they'd just been given their P45s (now *there's* a thought!).

With Roycie's sending off at Fulham earning him a ban, which began with the Boxing Day game at Brentford, we just naturally assumed Tony Henrickson would play in goal. Apparently he wasn't experienced enough! So Chipmunk went for experience and brought in The Welsh Legend, Big (sic) Neville Southall saying, "This was a major coup for Southend United to be able to bring in somebody of Southall's quality and stature." Now *there's* an understatement if ever there was one. Reality was that Big Nev's agent had rung round every club including all the Scottish ones and nobody was interested apart from good old Southend United. Big Nev's stay at Roots Hall saw him play nine matches, seven of which were defeats and two were draws, conceding just 18 goals. Roycie was finally re-instated in goal (sorry Stoke) with a little bit of pressure from the fans. Nev may have been a legend at Goodison Park, but a legend he was not at Roots Hall. He only came down to train on a Friday before a home match, then returned home to Merseyside straight after each match. The club's excuse was that we were only paying part of his wages, and his experience would help the lads around him. It certainly did the trick. The opposition lads had loads of fun putting the ball past him! Isn't it funny how these 'legends' come down from Merseyside to the seaside, and we always manage to bring them down to OUR level! Whelan, Marsh, Southall: who's next for a piece of Southend rock?

Roycie was restored in goal for the next two home matches, which saw us gain all six points and only concede the one goal. Was this to be the turning point of OUR season or was it just a false dawn? Ahem, defeats at Bristol City and at home to Grimsby saw us back to where we had started. The Grimsby manager Alan Buckley said that Southend were the best team he had come up against and he couldn't understand why we were bottom of the league. It's quite easy Alan; we'd conceded more goals than any other club in the Football League apart from Doncaster and Barnsley, and we were the lowest scorers in the Second Division. It doesn't take a genius to work that one out.

So Chipmunk had followed in the footsteps of Ronnie Whelan and took us to the heady lows of bottom spot in Division Two. Just as last season, Southend had gone down without a fight. Déjà vu? No, just the pure reality of Division Three football next season!

SKY BLUE ARMY

Coventry City

1998 will go down as a momentous year in the history of Coventry City.

...Not because we finished in a higher league position than I care to remember - although not having to endure a last-match-brown-trouser-day was something of a new experience.

...Not because only Arsenal, Man United and Liverpool lost fewer games than us, and that we only lost two games at Highfield Road all season, our best record since joining the top flight in 1967 - although it does prove that we've now become a difficult team to beat.

...Not because we have more internationals in our team than at any time in our history, with

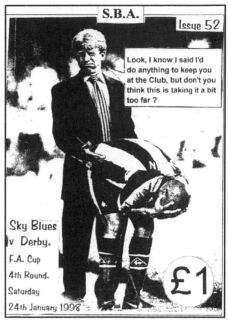

Dublin, Huckerby, Moldovan, Breen, Nilson, Soltvedt, Hall, Hedman, Boateng and Howarth all playing for their country at one level or another - although it shows the club is heading in the right direction with the players at last getting the recognition that they deserve. In fact our squad has never looked healthier. In Magnus Hedman we have the next Peter Schmiechel (he's that good!) and in Gary Breen we have one of the coolest young centre-halves in the country. In George Boateng, at £250,000, we had the bargain of the decade; he must have Duracell batteries up his arse 'cos he never stops running. In Dublin and Huckerby we have the best striking partnership since Wallace and Ferguson were scaring defences shitless in the seventies (mind you they were ugly f**kers). They're so good that our record signing Viroel Moldovan can't get a look-in!

...Not because Oggy got a 'special' award and Dublin and Huckerby were our first ever nominations for 'Player of the Year' and 'Young Player of the Year' respectively - although needless to say it was a great honour for the club.

...Not even the fact that Dublin took an equal share of the 'Golden Boot,' again our first ever - although it was uplifting for the club when he decided to stay after all the silly talk of a move to Middlesbrough. His form was pivotal to the success of our season, and besides, all this talk of Dublin moving to Middlesbrough was confusing the f**k out of the Wimbledon fans!

...Not because Paul 'get up you cheating diving Dutch Bastard' Williams nearly won us the fair play league single-handedly (despite being out half the season injured) with his impressive array of red and yellow cards. I assume we would have got a cup or something for getting the most points?

...Not because for the first time in our entire history we managed to win seven games on the trot, scoring 15 goals and conceding just two along the way - although it was a fantastic achievement and a joy to behold.

...Not because Huckerby won more Goal of the Month competitions this season than we've had since Jimmy Hill's chin was making his mum's eyes water during childbirth - although some of those goals were a bit special to say the least.

...Not even the fact that in Gordon Strachan we have found a manager who I believe is one of the best in the league. He is loyal, astute, forthright (not always a good thing as far as the suits are concerned) and above all passionate for the club, and I believe one day will lead us to glory. (Hang on, I'm getting carried away now!)

No, No, No... 1998 was a momentous year because we beat Aston f**king Villa at Villa Park! Viroel Moldovan's name will go down in Sky Blue folklaw as the man who finally beat the Villa Park hoodoo or jinx. Call it what you may but we hadn't won there in 600 years of trying. His goal put the icing on the cake of what had been a memorable season. Being able to walk out of the Witton End smiling - delirious more like - was a new experience and was the best feeling in the world. I was so happy, Savo could have gobbed at me for all I cared. We had won, and did we enjoy it! It was all part of a fantastic cup run which included a brilliant victory over Liverpool at Anfield, including a Huckerby Goal of the Month. It all ended in tears with a penalty shoot-out at Bramell Lane after we'd been on cruise control for 85 minutes of the match. To concede a goal so close to the end was a sickener, but the victories over the Liverpool, Villa (yeesss) and Derby gave us plenty to cheer about.

Other highlights of the season? Trashing Spurs 4-0 (two crackers by Huckerby) was particularly pleasing. Beating Bolton 5-1 at the Reebok was a bit special (two each from Huckerby and Dublin). Beating Chelsea 3-2 on the opening day of the season (a Dublin hat-trick) was a thriller. Doing the double over Southampton, our first over them since Oggy was a good-looking young man, was also pleasing (another Huckerby contender for Goal of the Season). But other than beating Villa, the main highlight of the season was our 3-2 win over Man United. One-two down with minutes to go, first Dublin and then Huckerby, with another Goal of the Month strike, gave us a shit hot win. To cap it all, deep into injury time, United got a dubious free kick on the edge of the box. Up stepped Beckham with 23,000 fans holding their breath, fearing the worse and - whoops! - he slips on his arse and the ball ends up half way to Leicester. "Does she take it up her arse?" was still echoing around the ground as the ref blew the final whistle!

Down-side? Well, despite our win over the Villa in the cup, we still managed to let the bastards do the double over us in the league - the only team to do so this season! The only other team we managed to lose to at home was the sad bastards from up the M69. You'd have hardly chosen Villa and Leicester to be the only two teams to beat you at home, especially as those defeats were the difference between Villa qualifying for Europe and us not. Although the damage was really done with too many home draws at the start of the season when victories looked certain.

A major disappointment was Dublin's (and Huckerby's to some extent) exclusion from the England squad for France. Dion has been superb throughout, both in defence and attack; his leadership and versatility would have made him a great asset for the World Cup. Hoddle dropped him for an apparent lack of pace (since when has Ferdinand been a Linford Christie?), so in that case you won't get many quicker (and trickier) than Huckerby. They have both been on fire for us and Hoddle wouldn't have gone far wrong taking both of them. By the way I'm writing this pre-World Cup, so no doubt by the time you're reading this, England have won the World Cup and Ferdinand has scored a hat-trick in every game. And Glenn Hoddle knew what he was doing after all...

In a strange sort of way I also missed the torture of having to win our last game to stay up (I think us Coventry fans have a sadistic streak!), although for once the boot was on the other foot with Everton having to endure a nerve-wracking game against us, whilst we sat back and relaxed. It was a strange atmosphere with 40,000 yampy scousers going delirious. I think there must have been about 39,000 of them on the pitch at the end celebrating their luck. I say 'luck' because they would have still gone down if Bolton had managed a draw at Chelsea. But they didn't and as they say, the rest is history. The Evertonians were in joyous mood, even applauding our supporters, although if we'd beat them I'm not so sure that we would have got the same reception! Having been there and done it so many times ourselves I knew exactly how they felt. So if you can't beat 'em, join 'em, which is exactly what we did. After all we had a damn site more to celebrate than they did!

After all this had been a momentous season - and for once we can actually say we "shit on the Villa!"

SON OF A REF

Scunthorpe United

I Wish I Never Saw The Sunshine

In *Fever Pitch* there's a section where Nick Hornby rattles on about 'catching a glimpse of a world that doesn't stop in May and begin again in August' Yeah, right... What ever really happens between the last match of one season and the first of the next? Well, loads, actually. But, for me, once the last whistle of the final game has been blown (and once that same evening's beery post-mortem of the previous nine months is filed away in the draw marked 'Underachievement'), the onset of the close season is an uncomfortable prospect. It instils in me a kind of paralysis, almost an inability to function properly. Outside the structure of a football season, everything cracks slightly, with the very constant danger of falling completely to pieces. I never quite know where I am, or exactly what's going on. It's as if everything outside of me has shifted up a gear while I'm stuck in neutral. Don't get me wrong; I don't get so gauche that I have to lock myself away in a darkened room and sit very very still for three months. But a night out can suddenly develop that 'one-nil-down-ten-minutes-to-go' cup-tie tenseness, with an edge that can only be blunted by too many spirits and 40 B&H. Some years - a World Cup year for instance - everything's alright; there's plenty to talk about, but I'm afraid I can't kick the habit of starting three out of every four summers with toes already dipped into a pool of depression.

So - 'real' life? If it's all the same to you, Mr Hornby, I'd rather not. But, then again, what can you do when 'real' life batters down your door and grabs you by the arm, shouting 'come out and play'? In the close season of 1997 the stretch of rumbling emptiness was full to the brim. But then, I may well have ended up with Hornby's words tattooed across my buttocks, so high did I soar as I fell for someone who was holidaying in England. I can't say for sure how it happened, but meaningful looks across pub tables turned to kisses in the dark, turned to hours sat on a park bench sharing the night: the profound night; the one where you talk forever and the other person lifts you right out of

a
scunthorpe
united
fanzine

Yes, Mr. Wagstaff.
Last year total rubbish,
this year - TOTAL FOOTBALL!

issue 5   £1

16 August 1997

yourself, above yourself, and as the sun comes up you do indeed see that there *is* 'a world that doesn't stop in May and begin again in August'. But, of course, this is Scunthorpe we're talking about, so a Hollywood ending would not be at all appropriate. She went home to Canada and I was left with a couple of photographs in one hand, the new fixture list in the other, and a headful of "What the hell was *that* all about?...."

Driving down the motorway for the first game of the season, the previous miserable couple of weeks seemed to disappear in my rear-view mirror. It was as if a page in my story had been turned somewhere - bathed in beautiful sunshine and The Big Fella upstairs smiling down and saying "Go on, son, clean slates for you and for United. Write yourselves a good year" in his Charlton Heston-type voice (see, Hollywood *does* come to Scunthorpe sometimes). Seeing our chairman get off the team coach at Peterborough in regulation formal club attire, but also sporting massive cuban heels lent the pre-match atmosphere a bit of a frightening edge, but once safely positioned away from him on the terrace there was nothing to be scared of. The fans were magnificent, and the team were, too; absolutely steamrollering Barry Fry's much-fancied boys in blue.

Half-time with the beautiful, beautiful sunshine still beating down and Shola Ama's aural honey *You Might Need Somebody* dripping through the P.A. The Big Man upstairs gave me a nod and a wink and I suddenly realised that Everything Was Going To Be Alright. I knew I'd get me some happy, and United would get themselves promoted. I said to my mate, "Is this as good as it gets?" as we watched our fellow supporters dancing around like they really *were* watching Brazil. For a while afterwards if seemed to get better. A few weeks in, we were in second place in the table and even the nosebleeds couldn't stop the party.

And then, the September morning of the Saturday we were due to play rivals Hull City at our place, I got a letter from Canada. I felt about twice as old as I should be - everything suddenly seemed so very long ago. That night on the park bench, the glorious murder of Peterborough... I put the letter away and trudged down to the ground, sure it had been a portent of doom. Even the welcome visit of the rarely-spotted Uncle Vern to the game could do nothing to rid me of the sickening feeling in my stomach. But United turned in their best performance since that opening day, and we trounced our visitors. Uncle Vern was most impressed. So was I wrong to have been worried? Well, no, as it happens. Our tallest-of-the-tall goalkeeper, Tim Clarke, went down for a harmless looking through-pass only to receive the full might of renowned tough-bloke Gregor Rioch's boot to his face. I'm a terraces man myself but for the sake of Uncle Vern I'd sat down in line with the goal that day, and I'm glad I did. If I'd been in my usual position I'd have seen what appeared to be nowt but a scuffle, but from my new vantage point I saw it all, in full Exorcist head-spinning horror. As soon as he was hit, Clarke's body flopped, it has to be said, lifelessly. I looked at my father's brother and he looked back at me with a face that said "In nearly 60 years of supporting these, I've never seen owt so bad." I honestly thought Clarke was dead, and sat open-mouthed at the awful deafening silence that followed a very sober PA announcer calling for an ambulance to drive onto the pitch immediately. As it turned out, he only suffered a severe concussion. Well, I say 'only', but when you'd thought your 'keeper had actually died on the pitch you'd have been relieved if you found out he'd only lost his arms. I actually saw him in the shopping centre three or four days later and asked him how he felt. "Who, me?", he said, a little unsteady on his pins, with the little birds still tweeting around his head, "I'm fine mate. I'll be fine for Saturday." Jesus! And off he went, that brave walking bruise...

The other interesting thing about the Hull City game is that it was the last one we won at home for another four months. The second half of that period saw us lose eight games on the bounce; a club record. At our level you can't realistically expect Keown and Adams-standard defending (apart from Chris Hope - how this lad hasn't ended up in the Premiership I'll never know. He's not *quite* Matt Elliott, but he's good enough to be up at the sharp end) and you know very well that you begin every game with a good chance you'll take a goal or two, so the team's sustained lack of success seemed to indicate one thing: the strikers were misfiring on all cylinders. Even when we had ended that disastrous record-breaking run it was still another three weeks before a striker found the net.

My theory is that the front men just didn't feel the pressure of real competition for their places. What had the intelligent John Eyre and the inventive Jamie Forrester got to worry about, when the only real replacement in the reckoning was Ian Ormondroyd? The ex-Villa chap was brought in on a short-term contract by manager Brian Laws to put himself about a bit, and to use his height (Laws' belief in Proper Football, after a stubborn struggle, soon gave way to the realisation that you probably have to tough it out to get promotion from Division Three), but the man failed to perform. Most were left feeling quite sorry for him in the end as he sounded like a thoroughly decent bloke when he co-commentated on a United match for local radio. He retired from football at the end of the season. Stamp, a reserve team prospect - another lanky front man - forced his way into the reckoning by consistently scoring for the B-team, and is sure to feature strongly next season. The reserves themselves almost got promoted (losing a crunch tie at home to Newcastle United in front of a record crowd). Laws has signed up several strikers this close season, and has vowed to play with three up front in '98-99. Can't wait!

The manager himself is a passionate man, almost volcanically so (Ivano Bonetti might agree), and rumours were rife all season that in the dressing room he doesn't take defeat lightly. I've heard it said that the players don't like him, but I find that hard to believe - on the occasions I've met him I've found him to be polite and courteous but, admittedly he does have a weird edge, almost as if he's working hard at stifling a perpetual rage. "People might think I'm one of the lads because I still play occasionally," he told me in an end of season interview, before exploding: "That's *bollocks!*"

We ended up playing 'fingers crossed' catch-up for the last quarter of the season, desperately clinging to the notion of a play-off place, but following that our terrible run of defeats had left us with precious little room for error. When the errors came, in our last four or five games, and the season finally ended with us one place and one point beneath the play-offs it was hard to reconcile our failure with that perfect day at Peterborough in August, but not impossible. We've been through it so many, many times. The worst thing was that long-ball merchants Lincoln got promoted, when we were the only team locally who tried to get the ball down on the floor and *play*. And what can you say about the tragedy of Doncaster? Only the very cruel could really feel pleased at what happened to them.

Our season lurched from highs to lows and ended up so painfully close I still don't reckon I've worked out whether it was all to do with her or just the football. '97-98 - The One that Got Away. We nearly made it, but nearly's not quite enough, is it? But we are stronger. We have learned. We are ready for the next war...

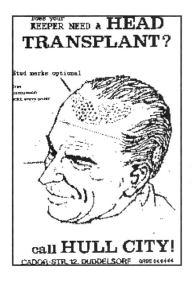

SPEKE FROM THE HARBOUR

Everton

Having parted with Joe Royle 'by mutual consent' on transfer deadline day of '96-97, Peter Johnson, the Everton chairman, informed the fans that they would be "pleasantly surprised" by the appointment of the new manager in the summer.

"We are looking at bringing in a coach with knowledge of the European game," was Johnson's claim. What he should have said was, "We're going to waste two months trying to entice Bobby Robson from Barcelona whilst all the other clubs are buying up the cream of the players available for transfer."

SPEKE £1
FROM THE
HARB UR

The Other Everton Fanzine
issue no. 21

Andy Gray was offered the job, but lost a lot of Evertonians' respect by appearing to use the club as a bargaining tool to up his (already considerable) *Sky* wage packet. He claimed that he wasn't aware that Johnson was offering him the job. What did you want him to do, Andy? Draw a little white box around you and put an arrow towards the managers' office? Howard Kendall, was, with all due respect to the man, probably the last person on Evertonians minds to fill the vacancy. However, Howard it was who was appointed manager for the third time, two days before the players reported for pre-season training, having dumped another of his mistresses (Sheffield United) and decided to give it another go with the old ball & chain.

It was going to be a long season.

£££ CASH WATCH £££ The bank statement on August 1st '97 must have read at least £15 million as the club attempted to persuade £8.5 million pound Fabrizio Ravanelli and £4.5 million pound Paul Ince to sign (taking any wage demands into account). This figure was to dwindle mysteriously as the season wore on. It goes without saying that these two managed to resist the temptation to come to Goodison and play with the likes of Claus Thomsen and Earl Barrett. And so which big names would we actually end up signing before the start of the proceedings?

Step forward Danny Williamson, Gareth Farrelly, John Oster and Tony Thomas...

All four for a little over £4 million. Still, nobody had ever heard of Trevor Steven, Peter Reid or Kevin Sheedy before Kendall's first reign, so we decided to sit back and see what happened.

An opening day home defeat at the hands of Crystal Palace was to set the tone for the season as Everton were led a merry dance by one of Serie A's former stalwarts in the shape of Attillio Lombardo. Was it the sun bouncing off his head blinding our defence or was it just the fact that we were just plain shit? All would, no doubt, be revealed in the fullness of time. We should have savoured the home win against West Ham, as we were only to see this phenomenon another five times. Our second was to come against Barnsley, or 'Brazil' as their rather unusual chant would have us believe. A young man by the name of Danny Cadamarteri scored on his full home debut. The baby-faced John Oster also got his first for the club and a few of the more wildly optimistic Blues were beginning to dream of a top ten place, come May. The Coca-Cola Cup saw us travel to Scunthorpe and come away with a 1-0 victory secured by a goal from another of Kendall's Kids, Gareth Farrelly. The way he slotted that one away, I thought to myself, I'm sure it won't be long until we see another!

Off the field, the club had finally managed to get the new home shirts in the shops, (Mid September) but the fans weren't very happy with the insipid, pale blue colour and the appearance of an errant yellow stripe across the chest.

October brought the bad news from the treatment room that crowd favourite and 'Chief Dog of War' Joe Parkinson was to miss the rest of the season with a bad injury. This discovery was probably more significant than anybody realised at the time. Joe's work-rate, tackling, stamina and sheer presence in the Everton midfield was probably the difference between staying up and going down the previous year. The 4-1 away defeat at Coventry in the Coca Cola Cup prompted some bizarre scenes on the Highfield Road pitch with Kendall and his players having a public set-to. All was not well; what we really needed was an easy game to boost the players' confidence. Cue the Goodison derby match. A superb own goal by Fatty Ruddock and the sight of Norwegian 'star' Bjorn Tore Kvarme disappearing up his own arse as Danny Cad turned him inside out and slotted the ball past David 'Nintendo' James had the Blue half of Merseyside in raptures. It was, however, to be yet another false dawn, as Evertonians would have to wait two months to see another victory. Abysmal performances against Southampton and Villa saw us hit rock bottom of the Premiership on November 22nd. The knives were out for Peter Johnson and the hunt was on for his cheque book...

£££ CASH WATCH £££ The bank statement as at December 1st reads... **NIL.** Everton, the club once dubbed the 'Mersey Millionaires' are told by chairman Peter Johnson to sell before they buy. (Hold on, £15 million minus £4 million equals NIL - that can't be right?)

Graham Stuart was sold to Sheffield United and two of Kendall's former charges Mitch Ward and Carl Tiler moved in the opposite direction. Very little money actually changed hands in this deal, with United coming out with perhaps £1 million.

Having had his chance earlier in the season and blown it (again), Paul Gerrard was pushed down the goalkeeping pecking order with the arrival of a promising Norwegian unknown, Thomas Myhre. Once again the club's hierarchy contrived to scupper the deal by haggling over a few Krone, but it eventually went through. The appalling 2-0 home defeat at the hands of a David Ginola inspired Spurs team at the end of November saw the end of an era with the last appearance between the sticks of a certain Mr N Southall. Regarded by many as the best goalkeeper in the world during the mid eighties, Neville appeared to have finally succumbed to the ravages of time and was made available on a free transfer. Neville, along with Dave Watson, are amongst the last of a dying breed of footballers: players who love the game and the club, more concerned about the results on the pitch than zeroes on their bank statements. It has been a privilege to have been around to see them play. I wonder how many true Blue Evertonians will be around for *their* ten year testimonials come the year 2008?

And speaking of true Blue Evertonians, how nice it must have been for Gary Speed to have been given the honour of captaining his boyhood heroes in only his second season at Goodison Park. Or so you'd have thought. Speed decided to ditch Everton (last trophy 1995) for Newcastle (last trophy 1969) in order to further his career - oh, and I suppose he got a hefty signing on fee as well. Not that I'm suggesting he's a mercenary, you understand. Andy Hinchcliffe also moved on to Sheffield Wednesday in an altogether more distinguished manner for £3.5 million. This deal went ahead mainly due to the emergence of a young left back by the name of Michael Ball (no, not *that* one). Michael made himself indispensable by turning in a series of consistent displays (which earned him many people's vote as Player of the Season). However, as one full-back emerged, another, Jon 'O Connor, regarded by many as the best right back at the club, was almost given away for £500,000 to Sheffield United.

Meanwhile, new captain Duncan Ferguson decided that he would try to make the back pages by firing in a superb hat-trick against Bolton, having already managed to make the front page of the *Liverpool Echo* with some 'hotel room shenanigans'. Kendall's revolving door transfer policy was further in evidence as he picked up Frenchman Mickael Madar from Deportivo La Coruna on a free transfer to bolster an attack too reliant on the skills of our flying Scotsman. He began to repay his transfer fee (erm, well his signing on fee then) straight away with two goals in his first three games. Yet another signing arrived in the shape of Manchester United reserve John O'Kane, as Kendall continued his master plan to build a team full of right backs. (He has just signed another, Alex Clelland, as I am writing this!) The chance of an FA Cup run had been dashed by our arch nemesis, Ian Rush, at Goodison, where the nasally-challenged one swooped to score one of his few goals all season. Well, at least we could now concentrate on the league...

£££ CASH WATCH £££ Bank Statement as at February 1st reads £6 million. (So that's £6 million from Speed, £3.5 million from Hinchcliffe and £500,000 for O'Connor minus £500,000 for O'Kane and £1 million for Myhre...

$$6 + 3.5 + 0.5 = 10 - 1.5 = 6 \ (?????)$$

A trip to Anfield was only spoiled by our new Gallic striker's inability to put the ball into an empty net on *Sky's Monday Night Football*, and our loveable neighbours were let off with a 1-1 draw. Still, the Liverpool fans had at least one precious point from us this season to comfort themselves with on their long trips home to Devon and East Anglia. Cries of "Down the line, Robbie" and "Cut it back to Charlie, Robbie" were mixed with less subtle chants like "He's on the gear, He's on the gear, Robbie's on the gear" and "Smackhead" which were aimed at the mysteriously out of form Mr Fowler.

Not for the first (or last) time this season, Mr Kendall punched in the short dialling code for Sheffield United FC into his novelty whiskey bottle shaped desktop phone. The result was the arrival of ex-Liverpudlian Don Hutchison, as quick as a flash. Don's first meaningful contribution in a blue shirt was to miss a vital penalty at Southampton. In the same game Slaven Bilic extended his lead to 3-1 over Duncan in the 'I'm a stupid wanker who keeps getting sent off' competition, and Everton found themselves one place above the relegation zone.

With only nine games left, reinforcements were required. The injury list had forced Howard into fielding young, inexperienced teams and some older heads were needed. John Spencer was taken on loan from QPR and old crowd favourite ('old' being the operative word) Peter Beagrie came on loan from Bradford. The season which had started with Everton bidding £8.5 million for one player had seen them not spend that much on eleven! A sorry state of affairs indeed. An unexpected 2-0 win against an out-of-sorts Leeds side secured our first excursion into the top 15 of the Premier League for over two months. This was, however, to be a minor blip which lasted for only two days. With a series of inept displays we found ourselves staring down the barrel of a gun on the last Sunday of the season.

In seventeenth position and one point behind Bolton, we had to achieve a better result than they did to stay up. Our fate had been taken out of our own hands. If they were to win, we would be playing football out of the top division for the first time in 44 years. The tension around the city was almost tangible. I would say that 75% of Evertonians had already resigned themselves to relegation, and in the week running up to the game our beloved red neighbours had a new joke up their sleeves every day. The game itself was going to be tricky enough against Coventry, against whom we had still to register a Premiership win. The newspapers pointed out that Bolton's opponents Chelsea had the small matter of a Cup Winners Cup Final three days later, and would either field a weakened side or one that would only turn up to show their faces.

And so 40,109 packed Goodison to watch and pray for a miracle, but realistically expected a long, slow and painful execution. With seven minutes gone, Duncan Ferguson headed the ball into Gareth Farrelly's path and the Blues in Row ZZ of the Park Stand clutched their heads in anticipation. However, the law of averages had finally come into play: Farrelly: shots at goal during season - 100, on target - 3, goals - 0 (in the league); that was up until now. The first half ebbed away with the news from Stamford Bridge that it was still 0-0. There was still a chance. The second half saw a Coventry onslaught, but with some 20 minutes to go a chant rang out praising a player wearing Blue who was not playing at Goodison Park. Mr Gianluca Vialli had put Chelsea into a 1-0 lead and now a sense of belief gripped the supporters as they realised that the pendulum had swung our way. Cadamarteri was sent on for a tired looking Madar and his first significant contribution was to win a penalty which Nick Barmby stepped up and... missed. Here we go again, we thought to ourselves. Coventry went up the other end of the pitch and scored. It was 1-1 and if Bolton equalised we were down. I suddenly find myself ensnared in the plot of one of those cheesy spy films where the baddie has set the bomb to go off in two minutes, and each second on the clock seems to last for ever. Then, more news from Stamford Bridge, 2-0 and then, having endured another elbow-biting Coventry attack, the final whistle...

Joy, delight, exultation, rapture, ecstasy, happiness, relief, surprise, amazement. Goodbye '97-98 and good riddance.

SPITTING FEATHERS

Sheffield Wednesday

Up Wednesday!
or A Roman Tragedy

Greetings Good Citizens... My name is Lurcio and I am the long-suffering servant of my master, Emperor Biggus Diccus... who has the responsibility for making sure that Stelia Halfdayclosingus (that's Sheffield Wednesday to you, mate!) stays in the Liga Premierus.

The Prologue! And it came to pass that the city of Sheffield was built on seven hills, just like the Eternal City of Rome... and seven was the position in the Premier League to which Senator Pleatus guided the football club of Sheffield Wednesday. The plebeians of the blue half of Sheffield were undoubtedly salivating at the prospect of conquering the rest of Europe next time round. Unfortunately, seven was the number of goals that the tribe of the Black Burnt Rovers (so called from their charcoal war paint) slammed past us four matches into the season. It was round about that time that I began to doubt the wisdom of Pleatus... Well you would, wouldn't you?

We suffered a slow pre-season where the only action seemed to be the rapid uptake of season tickets for the amphitheatre, borne on the promise of new arrivals. The citizens of Sheffield paid out their hard-earned denarii, sat back and waited for something to happen. The crack French international full-back Patricus Blondus was already champing at the bit to get a piece of Premiership action, but the wily Pleatus had promised the people a big name... and while everybody seemed to be joining everybody else, he merely philosophised; all the while observing a certain *crise de coeur* over Hadrian's Wall at Celtic Park.

From his first appearance at Nova Castrum, it was obvious that Paulus Di Canius was 'different'. (No, no, I don't mean in that way. Oooh! Common as muck you are!) His arrival in the brilliant sunshine of Northumbria was a sight to behold. He nonchalantly sauntered onto the field in white boots, shorts hitched up into the veritable crack of his backside (my eyes watered just looking I can tell you!) with sunglasses perched upon the top of his head. OK, perhaps I'm exaggerating about the glasses...

The game was not remarkable apart from a beautifully executed overhead kick by our little Calabrian genius, Benitus Carbonus, which, as we have come to expect at Sheffield, never got a look in on Goal of the Month (after all, Bergkamp had scored one good goal and two tap ins - so no contest really).

That Di Canius was not your normal run-of-the-mill footballer became ever more marked when, on scoring his first goal for the club, at Wimbledonia (a deflection off his backside which, had Bergkamp scored, would have easily won Goal of the Month... Again), he hitched up his shorts and bared his cheeks to the crowd. The FA took a dim view, appropriately enough, and fined him 1,000 librae.

Now it came to pass that things started going rapidly downhill and Pleatus appeared to be fiddling whilst Rome (sorry, Hillsborough) burned. His speeches at the Senate, offering tactical advice to the likes of Celtica and Liverpulia, were embarrassing especially when being delivered either side of an embarrassing two-legged defeat at the hands of the tribe of fishermen from Grimsbus Marinare. Hear now the wise words of Pleatus!...

On Celtic's Enrico Anone: "I see him as a hacker-whacker-blocker kind of player." You see my point?

Our Roman tragedy took a turn for the worse when we were visited by the tribe from Pridus Parcus in a game which started with both our Italians scoring and ended with both their Italians taking the points. The misery was compounded when Blondus got himself sent off (playing his last game for the club) and perennial crowd favourites Benitus Carbonus and Pyntus Tones took umbrage with each other at the game's end and gave a demonstration of gladiatorial combat... both using a leather pouch at ten paces.

Respite was brief against Evertonia, where the introduction of Pyntus Tones in the last ten minutes led to a remarkable transformation as Carbonus netted two and Di Canius took an eternity to score a goal, turning their goalkeeper not once but twice before eventually netting. This was Pyntus' last game for the Owls. We will not see his like again... Unless we sign Oliver Reed.

It was merely a deferment, as the beginning of Pleatus' end came when we were soundly beaten at home by Cristalus Pallas. And seeing as the next fixture on the horizon was Mancastra Unitas - away - things were not looking good!

After an inspired 20 minutes, in which Unitas were run ragged mostly due to our two Italians and our new import from the frozen wastes, Petter Rudi, it all went fig-shaped. Our normally reliable goal guardian Pressius Maximus let in two soft goals and we were 4-0 down by half time. Rumours abound that Di Canius and Carbonus decided that they had just about had enough and were heading back to Sheffield in the next hired chariot as Wednesday took the field for the second half... *and* that a certain Biggus Ronnus was driving that taxi. These whisperings have never been proven.

Within a few days, Pleatus was ritually sacrificed. The emperor Biggus Diccus had put an end to Pleatus' *annus horribilis* (which as we all know is Latin for making a horrible arse of things). The embarrassing process of appointing a new senator was undertaken. Serganus Wilko looked favourite...

Meanwhile, the day-to-day matters had to be carried on and I was honoured when I was asked to manage the team until someone could be appointed. To everyone's surprise, except myself, we annihilated the Wandering tribe from Boltonia. Longus Andreas scored a first half hat-trick... it was as if the débâcle at Mancastra had never happened.

The citizens of Sheffield were nonplussed when the new senator was announced - Biggus Ronnus. He had left us six years earlier, amid accusations of treachery after stating that he would be a fool to leave a club like Wednesday. Fool he was because he turned his coat and joined Aston Roman Villa. Many were undecided about the return of this 'Judas' and had it not been followed by a month in which we beat Arsenae (2-0), Ancient Dellas (3-2... another Di Canius masterclass goal) and Barnslius Bitterus (2-1... yet another Di Canius... zzzzzz) a local tribe who occasionally attack the more civilised areas. Biggus Ronnus was back. Now don't titter. Titter ye not! The Barmy Army was on the March and there weren't any Ides in sight... except Graham Ide.

But we should have known. The omens were there for all to see....

"Woe! Woe! And Thrice Woe!" Here she is, Senna, the soothsayer. Poor soul! "Beware of Hidings in March!" (Well what do you expect - wit?) Chelsaea came to our home and crucified us 4-1 without breaking sweat. The diversion of the FA Chalice paired us with Senator Turnipus' Watfordia side. After an evenly matched game on their marshlands, we brought them back to our amphitheatre for the old thumbs down. What we were to witness that night was a display of sheer petulance that the Emperor Caligula would have been hard put to beat, had his horse ever told him it had a headache. Paulus Di Canius decided that both referee and linesman were wrong in giving a meaningless throw-in to Watfordia (as it happened they were both right). Paulus wouldn't let it lie and gave an impromptu performance of arm waving that could only be matched by a semaphore signaller attempting "Supercalifragilisticexpialidocious." Wednesday were still the better side despite playing for 90 minutes with ten men, and eventually won on penalties thanks to a Pressius Maximus thunderbolt that removed the Watfordian 'keeper's hand from his wrist.

Things picked up when we hammered Nova Castrum with a quite wonderful display of football from Di Canius, Carbonius and Rudi. Yet once again Wednesday showed the viewing public that we were surely the crappest team in the Premiership by rolling over (once more) to the Black Burnt Rovers in the cup... Surely we can plead a case for not appearing on television ever again. No? But we always were miserable pleaders! Oh, please yerselves!

The rest of the season panned out into a string of pathetic away defeats (except one) and a smattering of wonderful home performances including Liverpulia (3-3) and a hard-fought 2-0 win over Mancastra Unitas. Relegation loomed with every inept performance; all the bottom three clubs beat us. Pallas even did the double over us! Now don't laugh... Ooooh, it's wicked to mock the afflicted!

It was a glorious day at Evertonia that saved our club. We were on fire that day. Our little hero was Gingerus Pembo, who gave us a two goal lead. The Evertonians came back in the second half and pulled one back. Longius Andreas was sent off and the ten men held on. The police, at the behest of the Evertonian authorities, demanded that the Wednesday band stopped playing as it was inciting the Evertonian hordes... Yeah.

Cometh the hour and all that... it was a battle-weary Paulus Di Canius who received the ball on the halfway line, danced between two players and ran towards the advancing goalkeeper (Wednesdayites knew it was no contest... we'd seen it all before). It took Paulus another age to put the ball in the back of the net, but then it always does. Just like his Roman compatriot Julius Caesar before him, Paulus came, saw and conquered the hearts of Wednesday fans. We have something special in this player. At times his ability takes your breath away. Finishing third in the Carling Opta index for strikers while playing for the club who finished sixteenth in the league *must* say something about him. The big problem with Paulus is harnessing that talent and building a team round it. Pleatus failed and so, in the end, did Biggus Ronnus. The non-renewal of the corpulent one's contract came as a big shock to the staff as well as the fans. There hadn't been such a surprise to my knowledge since the Man from the Pru nodded a hearty "*Good Morning!*" to Lazarus three days after the funeral.

DRAMATIS PERSONAE

LURCIO - Peter Shreeves
BIGGUS DICCUS - SWFC Chairman, David Richards
PLEATUS - David Pleat
PATRICUS BLONDUS - Patrick Blondeau
PAULUS DI CANIUS - Paolo Di Canio
BENITUS CARBONUS - Benito Carbone
PYNTUS TONES - David Hirst
PETTER RUDI - Himself
PRESSIUS MAXIMUS - Kevin Pressman
BIGGUS RONNUS - Ron Atkinson
SERGANUS WILKO - Howard Wilkinson
LONGUS ANDREAS - Andy Booth
SENATOR TURNIPUS - Graham Taylor
GINGERUS PEMBO - Mark Pembridge

STAND UP

Bristol City

The objective for this season was perfectly clear: GO UP. Nothing else would do in the eyes of the fans and justifiably so. After surrendering to a heavy-handed Brentford in the play-offs the year before and then spending £1 million in the summer we expected success and goddammit, we were going to get some.

The signing of Steve Torpey for £400,000 in the close season proved to be a major talking point throughout the ensuing nine months. Conversations on this subject always seemed to include words such as "money," "waste of," and "shit donkey." A minor section of our fans who never really identified themselves in the ground,

only in writing, had nothing but praise for the man. "Get off his back, at least he's trying." "He had a horrific injury in the opening game of the season so he's still not fully fit." An eight goal tally after a nasty head injury isn't too bad I suppose, but it was his unique ability to expertly combine a constant semblance of lethargy *and* apathy on the pitch that brought the boo-boys out. And this in a season which, overall, couldn't have been further from deserving them. Promotion we wanted and promotion we got, but I believe the aforementioned boo-boys can take some credit for kick-starting our season. Languishing in 19th position after six or seven games, we conceded a late equaliser at home to Bournemouth and as the final whistle went the jeers rang out. John Ward (later to be named Manager of the Year by the way) mused in the press that "it seems we aren't allowed to draw at home to sides like Bournemouth." To be honest John, you're damn right we're not, if we want a top two finish. The squad reacted angrily according to the manager, but instead of isolated violent outbursts in the press directed at the fans, the boys 'bonded' apparently, and found an inner strength and desire to prove everybody wrong. Despite sounding more like an excerpt from David Icke's autobiography than a recipe for success, it certainly worked.

From that moment on there was never really any doubt in my mind that we would go up. We soon embarked on a 15 match unbeaten run, 13 of them ending in victory. Barnsley sang "It's just like watching Brazil" last season. I think you'll find it was just like watching BCFC. The samba football played by the club in the run-up to Christmas was the most flowing, clinical, incisive, and exhilarating stuff I'd ever seen at Ashton Gate. Performance of the season at home came against Grimsby, arriving at the Gate with a record of 11 clean sheets in their last 13 games. We were 1-0 up after 17 seconds. Two-nil after three minutes. Three nil after 30, and we added a fourth straight after half-time. This complete and utter shoeing of what was considered our nearest rivals for an automatic spot created a two horse race for the title between ourselves and Turnip Taylor's Watford. The constant annoyance of seeing Watford come from behind to win in the last minute on numerous occasions, as we strove for our first Championship trophy for over 40 years, was somewhat vindicated as we entered the derby game with Bristol Rovers. Nearly 20,000 packed out the ground, and the customary win followed against what must rank as one of the poorest Rovers sides I've seen in ten years. All bar a man named Hayles that is - but he was suspended that day anyway!

Providing the goals all season, including three in the two derby games, was the main man Shaun Goater. Twenty five goals last season and knocking on the top scorer's door again this time around, the City strike force looked to be in good shape. However, in December, strangely enough coinciding with our marvellous run, The Goat slapped in a transfer request. His justification for such action was "ambition to play at a higher level," and it WAS NOT financially motivated. Hmmm. City top of the league, Division One beckoning... A level that the big man was untried at. Rumours shot around that Forest were interested, but his form dipped and it seemed unlikely he would go.

Deadline day came and the true scale of his ambition was realised as he put pen to paper in a £400,000 deal, moving to those giants of football Manchester City. Obviously the thought of another season in the Second Division was too irresistible an offer to turn down. Rest assured, his wages went up despite his new club going down. It was disappointing to say the least. Not only did he always score against the Gas, a knack which pretty much guarantees legendary status amongst the fans, but his move effectively lost us the Championship. We drafted in Sean McCarthy and Jason Roberts on loan to solve the striker crisis and the instant result was two away wins and our first ever victory on *Sky*! Roberts then decided to chip off to Grenada for a couple of weeks, and McCarthy didn't score until the final day of the season.

Second spot was where we ended, though it could and should have been first.

No matter, next season is already being eagerly anticipated by all Cider'eds as the striker crisis has been well and truly solved. City's first £1 million player joined in the shape of the dark destroyer Ade Akinbiyi from Gillingham, and he was shortly to be followed by the second £1 million player, Tony Thorpe from Fulham. A Danish striker, Soren Andersen, along with Leicester defender Julian Watts, and midfielder Carl Hutchings should all be following shortly. We're more interested in next season's fixture list rather than some poxy kick-about in France. I sense an underlying self-confidence amongst City fans at the moment, and let's face it, if Charlton can do it with Mendonca and Old Man Brighty, we should have a decent chance of the play-offs in '98-99. The emergence of young Tommy Doherty in midfield has given the team a tenacious yet creative look in a department that has so often accommodated fat has-beens. At only 18, I will tell you now, he could play for England. Everton have already been sniffing about as subtly as a dog on heat, so remember the name and where you heard it first!

Optimism is a wonderful thing, but probably second only to the ability to gloat horribly and unashamedly at the plight of our second-rate neighbours. They stole a play-off place, led 3-1 after the home leg, but then, in what must rank as the greatest result of the season, lost 3-0 at Northampton and sensationally crashed out. People at work had already booked coaches to Wembley after the first game! Superb. It just completed a wonderful season for Bristol City and their fans, and of course Harrods failed promotion attempt placed a cherry on top of the already delicious cake!

Next season will no doubt be less successful on the pitch, and the fans will have to get used to losing again - I'd forgotten the verb existed over Christmas! Nonetheless, Premiership football before the millennium is not out of the question. Consolidation and then a real crack at it the season after would be sensible, but I reckon we should have a bash at it now. Confidence high, two brilliant young new strikers and a couple of the best lower division players around should ensure that we will not disgrace ourselves this coming August. The future's bright, the future's Red and White.

Oh, by the way Mr Goater, enjoy your trips to the Memorial Ground and Macclesfield next season. What dictionary were you using when you picked out the word ambition? Or maybe you just confused it with money?

THE SUNDERLAND FANATIC

Sunderland

It may be one of the oldest clichés around, but Sunderland fans will tell you that football REALLY is a cruel game. Neutrals will remember the 1998 First Division play-off final as one of the most exciting games at Wembley in recent years. Sunderland fans will only recall the agony of a sudden death penalty shoot-out defeat.

All this, remember, after a season in which Sunderland finished third with 90 points (a record for a club not to win automatic promotion), scored 86 goals (the highest in the league) and lost just three of their last 36 league games. Yet it wasn't enough for automatic promotion, and counted for nothing in the play-off lottery. The fates decreed that Michael Gray's failed spot-kick would give Charlton victory and a place in the Premiership. To describe Gray as the villain of the piece, however, would be a bigger travesty than the fact that Sunderland missed out on promotion altogether.

No disrespect to Charlton, but they'll suffer exactly the same fate us Barnsley *et al* in making an immediate return to the Nationwide League after one season.

Cynics might ask why Sunderland fans have any more confidence in their own side's ability, given recent failed returns to the top flight. However, a visit to the Stadium of Light last season will have convinced any neutral that Sunderland AFC truly have what it takes to establish themselves, not only as a Premiership side, but as one of the leading clubs. A magnificent stadium (possibly the best in the country), huge support (40,000 crowds on a regular basis) and the potential for a lot more. Sadly, the failure to win promotion meant that plans to increase the stadium capacity to 46,000 were put on hold, but believe me, when Sunderland do go up (and I firmly believe that will be next season), that still won't be big enough.

An important reason for the renaissance of the club, in addition to the new stadium, has been the quality of the football on offer. Whereas the Reid vintage of '96-97 was dull, functional and on a scale of 1 to 10 for entertainment value, scored 0, that of '97-98 was invigorating and exciting to watch. In fact, and although ironic, there is much in it, many drew comparisons with the Newcastle sides of Kevin Keegan which only knew one way to play: attack. Unfortunately, Sunderland also shared the same flaws as Keegan's teams: an inability to defend which cost them dearly in the big games when the points mattered far more than the performance. The change of style under Peter Reid came as a surprise. Most thought he was incapable of playing anything but a defensive, negative line-up, but key personnel changes followed relegation which transformed the team.

In came Lee Clark from close neighbours Newcastle, a surprise signing to some, not just because he was making the short journey to Wearside from the old enemy, but also because Clark himself was a Geordie lad and self-confessed Newcastle nut. However, any doubts supporters held about him soon vanished in the wake of a series of magnificent performances in the middle of the park, providing the craft and guile that had been sadly missing the previous season. Partnering him to provide the steel was old war-horse Kevin Ball, who loves the club with a passion and will have been as gutted as any supporter about the club's relegation and subsequent failure to win promotion. In Ball's absence the superlative Alex Rae, who can count himself unlucky not to have played more games, also showed his ability as an attacking midfielder. Some fans thought he should have been picked ahead of Ball in the team. In truth, both gave everything they had and it was hard to fault either one.

If you thought old-fashioned attacking wingers were extinct, you were wrong. On the left, Alan Johnson had already shown glimpses of what he could do in the latter stages of the Premiership campaign, and is undoubtedly a throw-back to those magnificent breed of Scottish wingers such as Jimmy Johnstone. On the right, Nicky Summerbee came to Sunderland from Manchester City in a swap deal involving Craig Russell, and soon proved his skill and subliminal crossing ability. Both gave Sunderland an attacking dimension that had simply not existed previously. Up front, out went the ineffective Paul Stewart (yet still joint top scorer with four goals in '96-97) and in came Kevin Phillips from Watford. "Kevin who?" thought supporters. Little did we know that Peter Reid had just signed the club's most prolific striker since WWII.

All round, Sunderland were a far more attractive attacking side than they had been previously under Reid. In defence, injuries to key defenders saw young players such as Jody Craddock, Darren Holloway and Darren Williams given their chance, while the impressive Michael Gray at left-back, who linked up superbly with Alan Johnson on the left, completed Sunderland's attacking new line-up.

To summarise the season briefly, which is difficult given the thrills and spills it provided, Sunderland opened life in their new home (after a friendly with Ajax) with a magnificent 3-1 victory over Manchester City in front of a near-40,000 crowd. This was a truly memorable night, with a fantastic atmosphere and a win against what we thought would be serious promotion rivals. Little did we know! However, we lost five of our first ten games, a statistic that Peter Reid blamed for our failure to win automatic promotion. Given that both Middlesbrough and Forest made flying starts to their respective campaigns, there is something to be said for this view.

Sunderland's season eventually turned on the recovery of Niall Quinn from a long term knee injury. Quinn had played at the start of the season when clearly unfit, much to the wrath of the fans, and the general consensus was that he was finished. However, the game at Portsmouth on November 15th saw Quinn back with a vengeance, scoring two goals in an impressive 4-1 victory. Sunderland never looked back as the team started to click. This was particularly the case up front, with Quinn and Phillips forming a lethal partnership. Between them, they scored 50 goals over the campaign, with Phillips bagging a post-war club record of 35.

There were many highlights, but the outstanding games in my mind are the 2-0 defeat of Bradford City at the SOL on Boxing Day, the scoreline scant reward for Sunderland's domination, and the thrilling 4-2 home victory over Sheffield United in January. In truth, many other performances could have been mentioned in the same breath. The 3-0 demolition of Nottingham Forest at the City Ground is a special case - unfortunately I missed it!

Despite a run of only two defeats in 28 games, we were still adrift of both Forest and Middlesbrough by the end of March. However, two costly successive defeats by Middlesbrough against West Bromwich Albion and Sheffield United meant that on Good Friday, Sunderland were four points clear of Boro' with a home game against QPR (televised live on *Sky*) to come that evening. With only six games remaining, four points seemed an unassailable lead, and leading QPR 2-0 with just over ten minutes to go, the Premiership seemed within touching distance. Then, a suicidal back-pass let in Mike Sheron, who made it 2-1; minutes later Sheron made it 2-2 and 40,000 stomachs collectively turned over. We've read the script so many times before - Sunderland build up your hopes and just as quickly bring them crashing down again.

Sure enough, a last minute goal conceded at West Brom on Easter Monday cost us another vital two points. The initiative had swung back to Teesside. The Premiership, which had been within our grasp, was now slipping away fast and we knew it.

Ipswich provided the *coup de grace* - a 2-0 defeat when victory was needed to keep hopes alive in the final week of the season, although only a point finally separated us from second placed Middlesbrough.

Despite the massive disappointment of missing out on promotion, '97-98 was a season which Sunderland supporters can be rightly proud of. The move to our new home has been a resounding success - average crowds of almost 35,000 testify to that. The football had, after a sticky start, been outstanding and the players, in this age of the mercenary footballer, had worn the red and white striped shirt with genuine commitment and pride - including that worn by staunch black and white Lee Clark! Sunderland, so long touted as one of the game's sleeping giants, is finally starting to wake from its slumber, but only Premiership football will satisfy supporters.

So, congratulations to Nottingham Forest, Middlesbrough and Charlton on winning promotion from undoubtedly the strongest First Division in recent memory, and a warning to the rest of the clubs in Division One: Sunderland will be back, and even stronger next season with money to spend on new players. Failure this time round has only made the whole club and its supporters more determined to succeed. And we will.

Source: Super Dario Land

SUPER DARIO LAND

Crewe Alexandra

Fifteen years into the most stable managerial reign in the club's history, and the Alex have become a First Division side. Some onlookers may feel the need to pinch themselves; indeed, some Alex fans still fear waking from dreamland. The reality is, however, that Dario Gradi has guided Crewe Alexandra safely through one of the most turbulent seasons, while several of the game's so-called giants continue to slide down the leagues. Without being malicious - honestly - the failure of certain clubs (we won't mention Man City and Stoke) can only be good for the game. Perhaps the small fry *can* prosper in shark-infested waters, where money rules in an increasingly cut-throat business. It's this hope that fuels football, that drives the underdogs and allows supporters the fantasy that their passion will bear fruit. The Alex had a superb season, thank you very much.

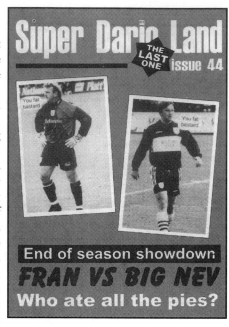

One thing for sure is that you can forget your daydreaming when you're 5-2 down at home to Huddersfield a few days before Christmas. Talk about low ebb, with the doom and gloom merchants spouting their predictable "told you so" line, while the frustrated hard-core vented their spleen on Gradi. Yes, I even heard one request for the manager's head during our most disappointing period of the season. But the boss is made of sterner stuff, and is certainly no quitter. In fact, our season was transformed by the sweetest of moments; the high-point in any supporter's calendar - a crushing victory over your local rivals, in our case Stoke City at their swanky new Britannia stadium. Most had feared the worst before this fantastic day, our first league meeting with the clayheads in years. Enter Shaun Smith, captain fantastic, whose goal at Wembley the previous May had secured our place in the First Division. Once again he silenced his critics and converted yet another long-range free kick to commence the celebrations. If the truth be known, fans from most clubs would gladly trade some of the so-called high-profile victories for the simple pleasure of triumph on their rival's patch. Such is the importance attached by the die-hard fan to being the best locally. Forget trophies, cup victories and spectacular goals, this inaugural season in the First Division would have been perfect had the Alex finished one place above the relegation zone and beaten Stoke 1-0 by the scrappiest goals in the final minute. Okay, so Stoke's relegation iced the cake perfectly.

To be honest, we would quite happily have seen the season end after that derby victory, with three points in the bag, local pride ours for at least another season, and the dreaded relegation zone falling away beneath us. But there was better to come. A blip against Sunderland was followed on Boxing Day by the scalp of another fallen giant, Man City. A ticket couldn't be had for love nor money as hundreds milled around the cramped Gresty Road streets in search of those golden bits of paper. City could have filled our compact and bijou stadium with their travelling army alone, but impressive support doesn't necessarily secure points.

Being honest, it wasn't the prettiest of passing games, but stuffed with post-Christmas pud we'd have settled for one shot on goal if it had silenced the Mancs. Saturdays usually see several hundred of them returning to Crewe having made their desperately sad pilgrimage to Maine Road. For some, supporting their local side had never been an option. This time, however, they had just a short stroll to their homes after the match, but the smiles and condescending comments were absent following what was, for them, perhaps the most humbling of moments during an horrendous season. Losing to the Alex confirmed their fall from grace but, more importantly, opened the eyes of supporters who still pigeon-holed Crewe as a no-hope lower division side. Enjoy your 'Oasis' of despair next season...

With preconceptions shattered throughout this opening season on the higher stage, supporters nationwide looked on in awe at several players who in no way fitted the Dario Gradi mould. Dele Adebola was one such player. A monster striker at 6'3" and weighing in at over 15 stones, the big fella was a terrifying sight. From Autumn onwards he was linked with a switch from Gresty Road to numerous Premiership and Division One sides. It was just a question of money. He hit a sackful of spectacular strikes before the Blue Nose Brummies splashed £1 million to take him to St Andrews. But there's life after Dele, no doubt about that. The Alex would finish just a few points short of Trevor Francis's points tally at the end of the campaign, and Dele will visit Gresty Road once again during the '98-99 season. Money doesn't always guarantee success.

One final change emerged at the end of the season. For several years the Alex have been one of those clubs who sport a shirt sponsor which remains obscure to everyone but those directly connected with the company concerned. Boldon James, a local IT-related company, confused many who watched the Alex play. But the much-publicised tussle for car maker Rolls-Royce saw a new name hit the headlines - VW, the eventual winners in the race for the world's most admired marque, now adorn the Alex shirts courtesy of the local Crewe dealership. The only question is whether the Alex lads will shed their goody-two-shoes image of perennial Fair Play victors and become rampant Beastie Boys? Somehow, we think not.

TALK OF THE TYNE

Newcastle United

Supporting a team can bring with it an unusual set of unwritten rules. "We'll support you evermore," and all that goes with it. But does that mean a supporter should continually sit with his head up his backside?

This was without doubt the most frustrating season I have ever had the misfortune to sit through since my first visit to St James' Park back in 1967.

I said after the 0-0 draw against Wimbledon, and it has been well documented in local newspapers, that there were periods in that match when I almost lost the will to live! What you had that day were teams content to play for a goal-less draw with neither making the slightest effort to muster a shot on target. But that was just one of many of such experiences. Visits to Derby County, Bolton Wanderers and Leicester City were just as bad. The home games against Derby, Coventry and Crystal Palace... no better.

Kenny Dalglish openly declared that his tactics for away games were simple:

1) Kill the game
2) Frustrate the crowd
3) Try and pinch a goal on a breakaway

Point two was most apt, because his team managed to do just that with clinical effect.

Tino Asprilla returned to Italy with a parting jibe at his old manager: "Kenny Dalglish lost the plot." To be honest that was an overstatement because I don't believe King Kenny had a plot in the first place!

He inherited a team that was two players short of a Championship winning side, yet within 14 months he'd drafted in no less than 20 players and his side avoided relegation by winning the last home match of the season. While some of those 20 were teenagers 'for the future', three of them (Pearce, Barnes and Rush) had ages that totalled 104 years. But it should be said that Barnes and Pearce were two of the better performers.

The match that probably said more than any other about our approach was a midweek fixture. It didn't make it onto *Sky TV*, and to be honest there wasn't even a match programme printed for it. It was a reserve team fixture against Scarborough's second string. King Kenny's elite signings were at home against a mixture of YTS kids and players who couldn't hold down a place in a Third Division side. Newcastle had no less than SEVEN internationals playing, but Scarborough still ran out 3-2 winners and went on to win the Pontin's Reserve League Division Three. If that doesn't speak volumes about the standard of his acquisitions, then nothing does.

Although league form was pretty dire, the European Champions' League provided us with two never to be forgotten highlights. The 3-2 win over Barcelona was spectacular and the 2-2 draw in Kiev was tremendous. The FA Cup run coughed and spluttered along all the way to Wembley. But even that was partly overshadowed by an horrendous PR stunt that sadly transformed Keegan's 'entertainers' into Kenny's 'moaners' and heralded a handbags at five paces verbal battle with little Stevenage Borough. Why oh why Freddie Shepherd fell for their bait was beyond belief. Then our dear chairman even managed to top that with the infamous 'Toongate'.

Shephard and fellow director Douglas Hall flew to Marbella after the Barnsley FA Cup tie and subsequently dragged the club through the sewer with allegations of prostitutes, hand-cuffs, egg whisks, and God only knows what else. They laughed at Toon fans who'd paid £50 for replica shirts that cost just a fiver to produce, and called the ladies of Newcastle 'dogs'. Nice work lads; just the sort of publicity we needed when facing a dog-fight (pardon the pun) against relegation.

Rather than stand up and be counted, the pair of them buggered off abroad hoping the din would die down. But as it happened the din only got louder. Eventually the pair of them reluctantly left the board, threatening to return at a later date! What I couldn't understand was that none of our other fanzines condemned their actions, even though a public opinion poll showed 97% of the Geordie public wanted these men to resign.

The FA Cup Final, as far as the nation was concerned, was a formality. But, as always, we locked ourselves in our own little black and white cocoon and convinced ourselves King Kenny would at last get something right. Sadly, he messed up big time with a formation that was described to me by one player (off the record) as looking like a rabbit's hind leg.

Stuart Pearce admitted nine months earlier that his playing days at left-back were over, and that Dalglish had signed him as a central defender. After a run out at left-back in a pre-season friendly against Birmingham, when he was left for dead on more than one occasion, it became blatantly obvious why. So, who filled in at left-back for the Cup Final, playing on one of the biggest pitches in the country? And why was Newcastle's fastest defender (Steve Watson) dropped to make way for Pistone, playing out of position, who was officially there to "counter the pace of Overmars"?

The thing is, under Keegan we really believed we could challenge for the Premiership. But with Dalglish there are still many questions left unanswered. Before the World Cup he'd spent almost £22m on players, but how many of his buys would make their way into the Manchester United or Arsenal teams? Shearer and Batty definitely, but they were bought by Keegan!

To end on a happy note, here is the *TOTT* report on the best performance of the season: a trip to the Ukraine to play Kiev.

D. Kiev 2 Newcastle Utd 2

(1st October 1997)

Europeans Champions' League

An incredible voyage to a place tucked away in a corner of the world, somewhere between Norway and Outer Mongolia. On a 7.30am flight from Newcastle airport we were among 300 Toon fans destined for Kiev. All of us had heard rumours of Mafia-led crime, dreadful food and leaked radiation from nearby Chernobyl. We hadn't a clue what to REALLY expect. Would we be struck down with cancer or just have slight side effects, like pissing a luminous green substance?

Once an integral part of the old USSR, Kiev is now the capital of the new independent state of Ukraine, and the place holds the scars of continued poverty and depravation. Never has a city suffered so much through war and disaster. There are very few buildings left standing older than 40 or 50 years. Here is an ancient city that has no signs of a history; the Nazis flattened the place when they retreated at the close of the Second World War. The only impressive structures are the war memorials, the most impressive of all being McDonalds!

After the tragedy of war came the biggest man-made disaster in history - Chernobyl - just 60 miles away. It happened ten years ago but still we were told to avoid the water, milk, vegetables and fruit, so still the effects remain.

On arrival at the airport it took us almost two hours to get through customs and board the buses to the city centre. Just off the town square we took a 40-minute tour of this fascinating city. Keen to sample a few bevies, it took us almost an hour to find the first pub! Beer prices ranged between £1.50 to £3 for a pint, which obviously explains why the poor Ruskies avoided it like the plague. Vodka worked out around 50p for almost half a pint!

At the pub we met three of the Winlaton Mags who had travelled to Kiev on the Tuesday. They had a right horror story to tell. Their hotel was dirty, freezing, had no hot water and was used as a brothel! "We got in during the early hours of the morning. I kept my jeans and shirt on when I went to bed, then I got up five minutes later and put my coat on! It was bloody freezing!" Some gentleman called Oleg Racz, from the *BBC World Service* and writing for *The Journal*, said the place was not as cold as people would expect, describing the temperature as "Indian summerish." Well, when I tell you it was cold enough to freeze the bollocks of a brass monkey, you can draw your own conclusions about how reliable a source Oleg was. Some of the lads on our flight took his word for it and travelled without coats: boy, did they suffer.

With only an hour left to kick-off, Mark Thornton and myself decided to mix in with the crowd outside of the ground to pick up on the atmosphere. It was incredible. On the one hand there were lads trying to sell us souvenirs - anything from Russian war medals to wood-carved images of ex-Russian prime ministers; police hats to army log books. Then there were the fans that couldn't believe we had made the trip from Newcastle. "Newcastle, Newcastle, sign our programmes." Mark tried to explain we weren't players or Newcastle officials, just supporters, but they formed a queue and asked us to autograph their match programmes. Poor deluded buggers.

The Olympic Stadium was impressive from all angles. In the 100,065 all-seater stadium there was a very small block of unsold seats at the far end of the stadium of no more than 50 or so, and the Geordies mocked: "Sell all your tickets - yer couldn't sell all your tickets!" The one fault with the place - and it has to be said it's a bloody big fault - was that there were no toilets! Can you imagine 3,000 plus pissed-up Geordies trying to 'tie a knot in it'? Those that couldn't were given an escort outside by the Ukrainian Army, and what a sight that was.

The Ruskies in front of us were friendly enough, but I have to admit I felt sorry for them. The teenagers and youngsters were dressed in the sort of jumpers and cardigans your dad gets for Christmas. You know the sort of thing, the Val Doonican winter special.

As early as the fourth minute Belkevitch outstripped Stevie Watson down the left and his cross into the six-yard box had several United players in two minds. While the players were deliberating what to do next, Roebrov burst in to slide the ball into the net. One hundred thousand voices hit treble figures on the decibel meter. After a dreadful blunder by Darren Peacock, Belkevitch set up Shevchenko who wasted no time in firing inside the post to put his side well and truly in command.

At long last someone took responsibility. Steve Watson started the killer move with a long throw, John Barnes missed it completely but Beresford seized on the opportunity. His effort was enough to have goalkeeper Olexandr flapping, and somehow the ball had enough momentum to squeeze between his legs. Fortunate? Probably... Decisive? Certainly!

Beresford then tried a 'hit and hope' strike from 30-yards that had the goalkeeper scrambling to his left, but the trajectory was changed by a cruel deflection. No matter how desperately the 'keeper groped to reach the ball, it was always just that fraction out of his reach. An amazing fight-back.

As the six coaches of fans left the ground at the end, several hundred of the home supporters stood outside looking at the euphoric Geordies singing and chanting. Through the glass we could see them looking at us as though they had never seen anything like it before. I couldn't help wonder what was going through their minds. We went back to our world, and left them to theirs.

THE TEA PARTY

Stockport County

In '96-97, Stockport County enjoyed the most successful season in their 115-year history. I feel the need to remind - or, indeed, inform - readers of this fact because, by and large, the national media tended to ignore our promotion, Coca-Cola Cup semi-final and 67-game season. Then again, as many readers will be aware, the national football media *do* tend to ignore clubs like County, Oxford, Crewe, Bury...

For similar reasons to those which compelled me to remind - or inform - you of our most successful season, I also feel the need to remind - or inform - readers that in '97-98, County maintained the success of the previous year, and finished in their highest ever league

the **tea** **party**

stockport county fanzine

You see, I'm not a Burnley fan by birth, Roy, but by choice

issue 73   **price £1**

position - eighth in the First (Second) Division. Okay, you might think that such success, whilst worthy of comment, hardly merits open-top bus journeys through town. Eighth place, huh? Wow. Big deal. Eighth place for many of the teams in Division One would mean disaster. Well, whilst for some johnny-come-latelies proudly sporting the latest Man Utd (oops, sorry, it's Arsenal this year, isn't it?) replica kit, that might seem a pretty pathetic boast, to those football fans who recognise that teams like Stockport County are an integral part of what has sustained the professional game in England for all of those 115 years, and more, it's an achievement well worth celebrating.

Thing was, of course, we weren't really supposed to *be* in Division One. Bit above our station, in the same way teams like Sunderland and Middlesbrough were below theirs. In fact, fans of both these clubs took great delight in informing us of our true status when they visited Edgeley - or at least that's what I took the many cries of "fucking Mickey Mouse club" to mean. Odd, then, that both sets of fans then seemed so happy with the single points their teams managed to scrape, Sunderland in particular being strangely delighted with a last minute equaliser.

They weren't the only side to be outplayed at Edgeley; the success of the season was based almost exclusively on excellent home form. Edgeley Park might not have quite the same ring as Highbury, Old Trafford, or Anfield (come to think of it, Anfield doesn't have the same ring as Anfield these days), but when you consider that we had the grand total of five wins on our travels, a mere two draws, and a staggering 16 defeats, it was all the more surprising that we didn't fulfil most pre-season predictions of a swift return from whence we came.

I must admit, if I'm honest, that the thought of experiencing my first ever relegation as a County fan did flit across my mind more than once. When we clinched promotion on a memorable night in Chesterfield (and you don't often see those last five words in close proximity) in April last year, I genuinely thought that the Division One play-offs weren't beyond us in the coming season. After all, we'd already shown, by beating four Premiership teams in our Coca-Cola Cup run - three of them on their own grounds - that we could live with teams not merely in the division we were joining but those in the one above.

However, Dave and Paul Jones (whose managerial acumen and goalkeeping skill respectively are evidenced by Southampton's first season without a relegation battle since the middle ages) departed, along with full back Lee Todd (who has apparently been less of a success at Southampton than the other two), the board turned to the relatively unproven Gary Megson, poached from Blackpool, and the fans' thoughts turned to a season of struggle.

To Megson's immense credit, it was not so, although things started inauspiciously at Bradford with a 2-1 defeat. We then went to Field Mill for the first leg of the competition that had brought us so much glory the previous season, and got absolutely - and deservedly - thumped 4-2. Dispirited, I went on holiday, only to ring Clubcall for the second leg result and to be astonished by the 6-3 score, which meant an aggregate 8-7 win. In many ways, that game was a turning point, reinforcing our belief that anything was possible at Edgeley Park, and that we were actually capable of playing good football. We began a long, slow, haul up the table, although, with the first league win not arriving until September 20th, relegation thoughts weren't totally banished until the turn of the year.

By that stage, however, things had been turned around to such an extent that we were actually sitting in a play-off position. Sixth in the table minus the Jones boys left most of us wondering just what we might have achieved had we kept last year's team intact. Whether the board were thinking the same way is open to debate, however, as they oversaw the systematic dismantling of the side - if rumours were to be believed, to the distress of the manager. First to go was arguably the most consistent player of the previous year, Chris Marsden, to Birmingham - a team in danger of replacing the pathetic Burnley as our *bêtes noirs*. The board trotted out "free under Bosman in the summer" platitudes, but most people would have preferred to "pay" the depreciation and hang onto Chris at least until May rather than sell him, for a relative pittance, to a divisional rival. However, that's not the way County do things, and if proof of this fact were needed, it came with the sale of Alun Armstrong to Middlesbrough for just over £1million (net - we owed Newcastle a cut). This was a slightly less disappointing sale, as a star of the type Alun is destined to be does not reach the heights whilst at a club like County. He was destined to leave, and at least we got decent cash for him.

Once the board had been seen to have given up on promotion, the old "number of points needed to avoid relegation" chestnut was actually aired again, although most fans now knew that we were destined for a top-half finish. It didn't help that we had what seemed a pretty tough run-in, one that had somewhat chilled the warm glow that promotion brought over the summer, once the fixture list for the First Division was published. Looking at County's final games - Forest at home, Wolves away and Sheffield United at home - most of us had hoped that a position of fourth from bottom would be secured before those last three games. Little did we know that, in beating Wolves (4-3), Sheffield United (1-0), and drawing with the Champions (2-2), County would take seven points from the final nine, securing that highest ever place.

Those were the bare bones of the season, then, but as ever, there was more to a footballing year than simply games of football. One of the undoubted highlights was Gary Megson's genuine appreciation of the supporters who pay his, and the players,' wages. Apart from continual references to the support in the printed media, we were treated to three separate instances of Megson grabbing the radio mike off the half-time announcer and, standing in front of the Cheadle End, addressing the crowd directly. He made his debut at the first home game of the season - stating that as we hadn't had any home friendlies (new pitch being laid), he hadn't had the opportunity to introduce himself to the crowd. He next appeared at the game following the sale of Armstrong, explaining the reasons for letting Alun go, and making what some saw as a few barbed comments on the parsimony of the board. Finally, he was there again after the final home game. He thus made himself many friends and helped smooth over a potentially rough transition from the previous manager. If more people directly involved in the game - and I mean players, managers *and* administrators - showed the same appreciation of the fans as Megson does, the football world would be a much better place.

Slightly less enjoyable than Gary's karaoke were our clashes with Birmingham City, the frequency of which has become ridiculous in recent seasons. After going out of the cup to them last season (yeah, like as if we were bothered with a CCC quarter final replay the following Wednesday!), we drew them in the second round of the CCC and, as well as two league games, the FA Cup again, at the same fourth round stage as last year. In the FA Cup game, Brett Angell was sent off early after a clash with Steve Bruce. Certain County fans around me claimed that Bruce had feigned injury in order to get Angell into trouble; I couldn't possibly comment. In the second half, with County 1-0 down, the referee - that splendid practitioner of his craft, Gary Willard - decided that Birmingham's advantage still wasn't enough and sent off Martin McIntosh. Nine man County then stormed back to equalise through Alun Armstrong, before Birmingham's greater numbers finally told, and they scored the winner. Mr Willard now looms as large as Mr Elleray in the County legend.

Three days later we were back at the theatre of porn for a league game, and a 4-1 defeat that no County fan gave a toss about. The reason? A broken leg for Tom Bennett - the unassuming and unsung star of our promotion campaign - that threatened his career. It was purely accidental; in attempting to hammer a left wing corner goalwards, his shin impacted against the studs of a Birmingham defender and his leg was shattered. Tom suffered three separate breaks, and was left with two bones protruding from his leg. He required oxygen whilst lying on the stretcher, the pain was so bad, and as sawdust was being sprinkled on the bloodstained pitch, the County players lost interest. A doctor who treated both Bennett and David Busst stated that Bennett's injury was worse, and with Tom approaching 30, many people expected never to see him play again. It was with amazement, then, that we saw Tom limp onto the pitch towards the end of the season, and pledge to be back playing by Christmas. I'm already looking forward to the ovation he'll receive when he does take the field again.

It was the fifth time we had played the Brummies in as many months, and any gloating at their missing out on the play-offs was tempered by the fact that we've got at least two more games to look forward to this coming season.

Two games with City also provided no little excitement. We took them apart at Edgeley, and the 3-1 win was hardly a reflection of the play. County were three up after half an hour, in the first league game against our nearest neighbours since pre-war, and City's consolation after half time in no way diminished our achievement - although the local Manchester-biased media tried desperately to make it do so. The return at Maine Road came when our season was over and City's wasn't, and our 4-1 defeat was down in part to an abject performance from one of our ex-City players Eric Nixon. The other ex-City player was Eddie McGoldrick, on loan to County, and who endeared himself to us by not only stating on local radio the previous day that he was hoping for a draw, but also by applauding the Kippax at the end of the game. And we wondered why his loan agreement didn't state that he couldn't play against City... Needless to say, once Megson heard of his radio interview, he didn't play for us again. You might put it down to disappointment at the result, but we honestly weren't hammered, as City were at Edgeley. Indeed, I was telling anyone who would listen after the game that City were deluding themselves if they thought they'd turned the corner - as most callers to local radio phone-ins insisted. Who was proved right?

City's eventual demise undoubtedly provided much mickey-taking fodder in the schools and workplaces of Stockport. And let's be honest, it wouldn't be football if you didn't allow yourselves, whilst not losing sight of the fact that your own team's performances are paramount, pleasure at the misfortune of others. City went down, United won nowt, Burnley went backwards and Birmingham missed out on the play-offs. Oh yes, and we finished in the highest position in our history. Not a bad season.

THE LION ROARS

Millwall

The abject disappointment of the '96-97 season, when Millwall Plc ended up in administration and the team languished in 14th place despite being top in November, allowed for low expectations for this campaign. Indeed most Millwall supporters were just relieved that they still had a team to support. The first task confronting our new chairman Theo Paphitis was to deal with the numerous creditors and satisfy the company's bankers.

A new manager was next on the agenda. Step forward one Billy Bonds, who beat off the threat of 40 other applicants to land the Millwall hot-seat. Despite his status as one of West Ham's all time greats, the expected backlash from the Millwall support didn't materialise, although Bonds quickly learned that he would be in for a rough ride if the team failed to deliver again.

The immediate task wasn't an easy one. Due to an FA imposed transfer embargo, Bonds was a month behind other clubs in his season preparations. A major source of disappointment was the police refusal to allow Brighton's proposed ground-share; something one suspected that Paphitis based much of his take-over plans on. The extra income would have helped fund the necessary team-strengthening, as well as utilising our white elephant of a stadium. The decision didn't exactly do the Seagulls any favours either, as they were confronted with the nightmare trip to Gillingham every fortnight.

By the opening day of the season, our only new arrivals were freebies in the forms of Brian Law from Wolves, Paul Sturgess from Charlton, and Paul Allen from Bristol City. Small fees were paid for Kenny Brown from Birmingham and Scott Fitzgerald from Wimbledon, but the search for a new striker had proved fruitless. Just before the opening game with Brentford, the previous season's top scorer Steve Crawford was sold to Hibernian, with Bonds claiming that he "didn't want players who weren't fully committed to the cause." As a stop-gap, Kim Grant arrived on loan from Luton and duly scored on his debut as Brentford were whipped 3-0. Maybe our prospects were better than expected after all, and Grant was quickly snapped up for £120,000.

As Bonds had openly stated that the side were at least three players short of being able to mount a decent promotion challenge, it came as a pleasant surprise to see the Lions sitting in third position by early October, tucked in nicely behind early pacesetters Watford and long ball merchants Northampton. The only blip had been a 9-2 aggregate defeat against Wimbledon in the Coke Cup, but this was a sign of how far Millwall had fallen in recent years, as Wimbledon fielded a virtual reserve side in the second leg and still beat us with ease.

The squad had by this time seemingly been strengthened by the arrivals of two vastly experienced professionals, Nigel Spink and Paul Wilkinson, together with the surprise half a million pound purchase of Paul Shaw from Arsenal, who became our first slaphead in well over a decade.

It didn't quite work out how Bonds planned though, as Wilkinson, after a bright start, soon became the latest South Stand boo-boy. A distinct 'going through the motions' approach and a general resemblance to something often found strolling down Blackpool beach quickly began to fray tempers, but Shaw's goals would prove vital come the season's end.

After an excellent 1-0 win at table-topping Watford, roared on by 4,500 away fans, the garden of Millwall was looking distinctly rosy. Then our season took a distinct turn. The first disaster struck when Bristol City visited The Den and turned us over 2-0 with consummate ease, showing up every weakness and beginning their surge up the table.

All of a sudden the players began to doubt their ability, and the now all too familiar nose-dive down the table began in earnest. And with Watford and Bristol City pulling away at the top with every passing result, our season was as good as over by the end of November. Performances at home were both nervous and uninspiring, and the defence had been badly affected by the loss of Alan McLeary who picked up a season-long injury during our annual defeat at Bristol Rovers. Bristol quickly became every travelling Millwall fan's least favourite city, as aside from the defeat at Rovers, neighbours City beat us three times in two months at Ashton Gate. This included defeats in both the FA Cup and the AutoWindscreens, and a 4-1 league drubbing on Boxing Day.

By now, home games were simply too tortuous to mention. Crowds began to hover around the 6,000 mark, which meant that the club were still losing money hand over fist. But Bonds had been allowed to dabble in the transfer market again with mixed results. Two Palace rejects arrived at The Den; firstly there was Carl Veart who lasted for about four lack-lustre appearances before being dropped to the reserves. Indeed, rumours flew around about interference from above and that Bonds hadn't actually wanted to sign Veart. However, the second signing quickly endeared himself to The Den faithful with his no-nonsense battling style. Andy Gray was our first player in this mould since Den legend Terry Hurlock bestrode the park.

Gray's arrival helped to reverse an alarming slide, but Bonds still had to read the riot act after a predictably gutless display in the 3-0 defeat at Blackpool. Still, at least the players responded with positive displays that including an excellent 2-1 win at Craven Cottage, which once again was just like the old days. Even the home form picked up enough to see off the dreaded threat of relegation with a couple of points to spare.

Whilst no one could argue that Bonds' season in charge was anything other than unsatisfactory, there were some mitigating factors. The club's injury crisis was so bad that a record 32 players were used, which prompted the manager into admitting that he had never seen anything like it in all his years in the game. On top of the expected casualties, we had the kind of important long-term injuries that would have had Alex Ferguson justifying a Manchester United relegation. Included among the long term sick was Lucas Neill, the club's most prized possession and highly rated Australian international, who managed just a handful of games. Young Irish centre forward Richard Sadlier, who started the season superbly and was looking very much like the player we had needed for the past three years, was ruled out from the beginning of September! Alan McLeary, so consistent at the back since his return and a dead cert Player of the Year, also missed half the proceedings. Andy Gray managed to crock himself in a pointless reserve game and missed much of the vital run-in. And almost typically, Stuart Nethercott, who arrived from Tottenham in February and helped plug the gaps at the back in superb fashion, broke his collar-bone at Fulham.

By the end we were all just grateful it had ended with us still in the same division. Next season sees Millwall going back to basics, with club veteran Keith Stevens appointed manager after the surprising (some might say harsh) dismissal of Bonds in June. With McLeary to back him up as his Assistant, Rhino will have to learn the managerial ropes fairly quickly if the Lions are to get back on their feet.

It appears that most of the players have come to terms with the fact that they are not the First Division superstars they thought they were when we were relegated. If the club can avoid a comparable injury crisis, and with no fear of contradiction it really could have been the worst in Football League history, there might be some light at the end of the tunnel. The most positive aspect of the summer so far has been the lack of signings. Usually we see a transfer rush hour with average players coming and going, but instead it looks like we're undertaking a period of reflection and hopefully consolidation. We have seen first hand that money doesn't necessarily guarantee success, so we're not that bothered about the likes of Manchester City and Fulham. So, this season might just be the first step forward for Millwall FC for FOURTEEN years.

It has been an amazing roller-coaster ten years since we started *TLR*. A decade that has included a promotion, two relegations, two play-off appearances, one ground move, eight managers, three chairman, not to mention the best team in our history sold off bit by bit. And it will all be recorded in our *Best of TLR* book, which will be commemorating this most exciting period in the club's history and a hundred issues of the magazine.

THERE'S ONLY ONE F IN FULHAM

Fulham

It's been one surprise after another at Craven Cottage following the shock arrival of Mohamed Al Fayed as chairman last summer. Whatever next? The Pope installed as spiritual advisor? George Michael recruited as unofficial Cottage guide? The whole World Cup winning squad bought *en bloc*? Or, crazier still, the Supporters' Club being allowed to have a pukka bar again?

Last season was, quite probably, the season no Fulham fan wanted. True, we made it to the Division Two play-offs; on paper a creditable achievement, having been promoted from the basement division only 12 months before. Yet it was all so curiously unsatisfying.

There's only one **F** in

FULHAM

AN ALTERNATIVE LOOK AT FULHAM F.C.

SCARFACE ROBSON CELEBRATES BY THE POOL

STOP PRESS: *Please note the above headline should've read "Scarf Ace Robson Celebrates by the Pool". Tee-hee!*

INSIDE: *It could only happen at Fulham, King Kevin, a present for Pesky, spicy pies, flying the flag, fans file special...*

Issue 57   MAR/APR 1998   £1.30

The euphoria and undoubted expectation following not only the appointment of Kevin Keegan and Ray Wilkins but also the very un-Fulham-like levels of spending actually led to problems, not least of which was the death of a supporter.

Keegan's unexpected arrival had been heralded as a major coup by the fans, although the jury was very much out as far as Wilkins was concerned. The replacement of the hugely popular Micky Adams - unquestionably the catalyst in the club's latter-day change in fortunes - by a man with an unproven track record in management led to a heated exchange of views in the fanzine. And, although the season promised much, the feelgood factor and sense of togetherness, such strong features of the previous regime, became seriously under threat.

The incredible change in circumstances, not least from being paupers to stinking rich, was something supporters found difficult to take in. This was Fulham, after all, where principles were still high despite (or maybe because of) the fact that just a couple of years previously the hardcore of supporters had led the fight for the club's very existence.

Suddenly, lapsed fans made their way to the Cottage once more, as did hundreds of inquisitive new ones. With no real period of transition, it made for an awkward mix at times. Although the bottom line was that every Fulham fan was delighted that their club had been 'saved' and the freehold of the ground re-acquired, people found it difficult to adjust. Some maintained Adams should never have been shown the door (as he effectively was); some maintained they preferred the down-at-heel existence; some feared for Fulham's traditional homely appeal; others shunned the new fans (where were they when the club was in trouble?); while others didn't like the new 'big business' approach, which included the Supporters' Club bar making way for a corporate hospitality lounge.

New players arrived almost weekly. With an ever-lengthening 'gelling' period being demanded on the pitch, terrace 'discussions' often erupted into arguments. Mind you, Fulham being Fulham, these were usually no more than lover's tiffs. But there was a huge, and ultimately tragic, knock-on effect. You see, we were no longer perceived as 'Friendly Fulham' by most opposing fans. We were now considered the 'Flash Moneybags' and not only the team they wanted to beat (fair enough) but ours were the fans they wanted to goad... and fight.

How different from just a few years ago, when we received such magnificent support from a host of other clubs when the ground issue was raging. Subsequently fans from all round the country chipped in to the *Fulham 2000* fundraising appeal. Sadly, some of our new-found support and regretfully, one or two of the stalwarts, were more than prepared to argue the toss.

Events on the park were doing little to appease the disgruntled. Millions of pounds were spent on players, yet apart from a purple patch in January it was all rather sterile stuff. A patient, steady passing approach is all very well but if there is no apparent passion, no final 'killer' ball, no raising of tempo or, most importantly, no end product then the troops will become restless.

That's not to say the new players weren't up to it. Far from it. In Paul Peschisolido, the Second Division's first £1m player, we had an energetic and very pacey striker who suffered from a lack of decent service and later from a dip in confidence. Meanwhile Chris Coleman (two million quid for a defender... blimey!) was arguably the bargain buy. He offered style aplenty together with a superb attitude and was captain in all but name. The other new purchases were far from mugs either but many were plainly played out of position. With the balance all wrong plus an apparent lack of heart, the team tended to stumble and stutter rather than purr as expected. It was all Austin Allegro rather than Rolls-Royce.

The team needed time to gel, we were told. Fine. (Goodness! How many times have we been asked to be patient?) Except that it never really happened. Enough points were being banked however to slip into one of the play-off berths. But this was as much down to other teams dropping points as anything else. At one point Bristol City and Watford were wobbling and a decent run of results then would have put pressure on the top two. But a pretty successful policy of playing three up front was abandoned when loanee Kyle Lightbourne went back to the Potteries. And the chance was gone.

With all the money about it was strange we had so little cover up front. The burgeoning squad contained midfielders in abundance, so much so that the £500,000 buy from Arsenal, Ian Selley, badly injured just as he was beginning to flourish in his second game, was barely mentioned for the rest of the season. Up front it was a different matter. Last year's goal machine Mick Conroy - who netted in spectacular fashion from Wycombe's half-way line in August - picked up a long-term injury, as did Darren Freeman, Division Three's Player of the Season for '97-98, while Paul Moody spent much of the season trying to shrug off a series of niggles. This left Pesky Paul, not the biggest striker the world has seen, to valiantly take the brunt of the rugged Division Two defences. Oh for another forward, or at least someone who could open up the play and feed the front men.

Cue first Tony Thorpe from Luton and then Peter Beardsley on loan from Bolton. Thorpe, clearly out of shape, made his bow in a poor showing at a windswept Blackpool in February. But as his fitness improved so his penalty box prowess increased - he was after all the division's top scorer. Yet the potentially predatory front pairing of Pesch and Thorpe (dubbed 'The Krankies'!) never got going. The service was virtually non-existent! It was a sad indictment of the midfielders in particular that it took the reintroduction of the lofty but still only half-fit Moody to get us back on the rails. Moods, you see, could knock down high balls and generally be a nuisance. A relevant tactic, but where was the guile?

When Beardsley arrived in late March, however, things changed somewhat. He went on to mastermind a terrific, gutsy 2-0 win against Brentford - Micky Adams, Glenn Cockerill, Danny Cullip, Paul Watson and all - at Griffin Park (where the first foul was committed after just six seconds!) then a 5-0 drubbing of Carlisle at the Cottage. Was it all coming together at the crucial time after all? Not exactly, as it turned out, but we squeezed into the play-offs nevertheless.

However, Beardo's Fulham debut (a pretty unforgettable encounter as, not for the first time, we were outmanoeuvred by a far less expensive outfit) was totally overshadowed by dreadful scenes off the pitch. Gillingham away on March 28, 1998 will go down in the Fulham history books as one of the club's lowlights: it was the day Fulham fan Matthew Fox was killed.

The press had a field-day, of course, making several wide-of-the-mark assumptions. Three things are patently clear, however: 1) Any fan attending a football match should be able to do so without the fear of being killed; 2) The ever-worsening atmosphere between some sections of the crowd that day suggested that trouble was in the air (stewarding and policing left a lot to be desired); 3) All football fans should learn from the appalling tragedy - it's only a bloody game after all's said and done.

The atmosphere on the day was particularly unpleasant. Players and officials came in for a furious amount of stick as bad feeling which stemmed from a previous highly-charged encounter resurfaced. Before long, some sections of the crowd became intent on out-abusing each other. In short, it was all set to 'go off' - a fact seemingly overlooked by those in charge who had added to the problems by allowing opposing supporters to mix. Bloody crazy! One guy next to me spent the entire match hurling abuse at Wilkins. Towards the end, when he finally stopped to take a breath, I asked him what was the point of the sustained vitriol. "He buggered up my QPR," came the reply. He wasn't even a Fulham fan!

Anyhow, for the second time in an 'unreal' Fulham FC season we had a 'special' game as FFC and Preston fans honoured a minute's silence in Foxy's memory. It was impeccably observed. Plymouth supporters were equally respectful back in September when an eerie piper's lament wailed around an otherwise silent Craven Cottage to mark the awful Paris car crash which killed Dodi Al Fayed, son of the Fulham chairman, and Princess Di. Although a tragedy of international significance, there was still the chance for Fulham folk to pay their respects in their own way and the main Cottage gates became engulfed in flowers, football shirts and scarves.

You'll gather this was no run-of-the-mill season, even if the end product probably was. Highlights included 4-1 wins at both Plymouth and Luton, a dalliance with the big time with a respectable effort at White Hart Lane in the FA Cup and a solid 2-0 win at Chesterfield where one of the 'old guard', ex-captain Simon Morgan, was inspirational in a tremendous team performance. Behind the scenes, the Youth Team under Alan Smith's guidance made tremendous strides and the club was given the all-clear to set up an Academy of Football under the FA School of Excellence programme. The reserves have been elevated, too, to the Football Combination.

Unfortunately there were far too many lowlights. And ultimately Ray Wilkins - the ultimate nice guy - paid the price. The stats show we used 37 players and spent around £8m but only got into the play-offs thanks, ironically, to Gillingham slipping up on the last day of the season.

KK couldn't steer us past Grimsby, who deservedly took the third promotion spot, but he subsequently confirmed himself as team boss for the new season. So what's in store for us lot now? Maybe the vision of Ronaldo as centre forward and Zidane pulling the strings in midfield is a little too far-fetched, but certainly the script suggests a roller-coaster season ahead. Things won't ever be boring at FFC again, that seems certain! C'mon you Whites!

THE THIN BLUE LINE

Cardiff City

Okay all you fans out there, when did *you* give up on last season? At what point did *you* decide that your club wasn't going to get anything out of the '97-98 term? March? April? Perhaps you were lucky, and went all the way to the play-offs. Down here in Cardiff it was a very different story. At Ninian Park, home of the once-mighty Bluebirds, the club gave up on the '97-98 season after just three matches. Hard to believe? Maybe. But sadly it's true...

It's now three years since chairman Samesh Kumar rescued Cardiff City from the clutches of Rick Wright and embarked on a five year plan to reach Division One. Progress has been remarkable. We

THE

THIN BLUE LINE

SEEMS LIKE OLD TIMES - WITH CARDIFF CITY

CAN HE DO IT AGAIN?

So who were you expecting...
......Ruud Gullitt?

39

THE STRANGE RETURN OF FRANKIE BURROWS

ISSUE TWENTY FOUR   FIFTY PENCE

finished his first season ('95-96) in a club record all-time-low position of 22nd place in the Third Division. The '96-97 campaign saw a vast improvement, with City reaching the play-offs (somewhat luckily, it has to be said) before being knocked out by the eventual winners. So could we go one better? Was '97-98 to see us promoted and back on target? Well sadly, the simple answer is No. We finished back down at the bottom, in 21st place, dazed, confused, and wondering where it all went wrong. In fact, as I've already painfully stated, it all went pear-shaped within three games of the start of the new season...

Kicking off with an away win at Leyton Orient seemed like a good start, except for an ankle injury picked up by striker Carl Dale. This put him out of contention for months, and when he did return, it was only ever in fits and starts. In our second match Kevin Nugent, who'd been brought in specifically to partner Dale up front, was also injured. Once again this was to keep him out for a long time - for almost the entire season as it turned out. Two devastating blows that any club would struggle to cope with, you'd agree. Manager Kenny Hibbitt moved midfielder Scott Partridge up-front, and he combined either with 37-year-old Steve White or loan signing Chris Greenacre to create some semblance of a forward line, but it was a distinctly second-rate one, and all of a sudden goals were hard to come by. The team slumped into a run of draws that was to last almost the entire season, even when some sort of 'proper' attack had been restored. We didn't lose too many games - the solid defence built to help win promotion meant that for most of the time defeats were a rarity - but we didn't win many either.

Perhaps that ability to avoid defeat contributed to the lack of urgency at the club when looking for replacement strikers. Drawing games sounds much better than losing them, and an unbeaten run sounds much better than a string of defeats. Don't panic, was the message. They'll be back soon (our missing strikers) and, as long as we don't lose too many games, we'll soon catch up. That was okay for a few weeks, but as the drought stretched into September, October and November, with no new blood arriving, it was clear things were going just a bit too far. Our missing men weren't going to be back soon, and what was worse, we were never going to be able to catch up.

So why did it take so long to find someone - *anyone*? We can understand that at the start of a season clubs may be reluctant to let players go; after all, they'd probably spent the summer building their sides in much the same way we had, and didn't want to start selling their players off after just a few games. But surely players are always available if you offer the right money, and if money was a problem, why not take a chance on a non-league player? For whatever reason Cardiff seemed to make hard work of tracking down a striker, apparently approaching dozens of clubs without success. We even got involved in a bidding war with Gillingham over Leo Fortune-West, who couldn't even get into their first team, but was still expected to fetch a good price. Fortune-West couldn't make up his mind about the move - never a good sign - and the deal fell through, with Cardiff's board getting a lot of stick in some quarters for being unwilling - or unable - to pay an outrageous £130,000 for him.

Although it seemed that every club in the league knew our predicament, and were therefore asking ridiculous prices for players, for a club sliding rapidly down the table Cardiff seemed very loath to spend any money. There are numerous rumours as to why this was. You may recall from last year's tale that halfway through the season Cardiff had received a large financial boost when the owners of the local ice hockey side, the Cardiff Devils, bought into the club. They too had their own five-year plan - and it certainly didn't include lounging around in the Third for God knows how long. But the story goes that their opinion on who to buy did not match that of Kumar and Hibbitt, and so a stalemate ensued. Eventually though, they settled on a compromise, splashed out on a new striker and Andy Saville duly arrived. So we now had Saville and White with a combined age of 70 leading the line, and as you can well imagine, it didn't make a whole lot of difference to our goal average. But the side seemed to stabilise enough to put a good cup run together, and as our league form nose-dived we bobbed along merrily in the cup, until the two came together just days before our fourth round tie with Reading.

During the '96-97 season we had started off with Phil Neal as manager until he left for Manchester City. Kenny Hibbitt took over until a replacement was found in the shape of Russell Osman. Then just eight games later Osman was removed from office for no particular reason - his results were no worse than Hibbitt or Neal's - and Hibbitt was reinstated. Rumours at the time were that Osman objected to Kumar's very 'hands-on' approach (allegedly to the point of ripping up team sheets just before a game and insisting on the selection of certain players) and so had been ousted from his post. But they couldn't afford to sack him. So Osman stayed and for some odd reason was getting all the stick for the poor results when everyone knew that it wasn't him picking the side. Anyway, by the middle of the season the board wasn't happy with results and had by now twigged that there wasn't much difference between Hibbitt and Osman - both were crap. With promotion out of the question why didn't they bring in a new man then and have a real shot at Division Two next year? Well first off, Hibbitt had a five-year contract, which meant that poor old Russell got the sack instead. Hibbitt, who was responsible for the side and therefore the results got moved sideways into the post of director of football. Cosy, eh? The search for a new manager took nearly as long as the search for a striker. As usual we had the long lists of names, some stupid, some unrealistic, and some far too expensive. The fans thought that we should get another 'name' manager along the lines of Neal, so many were disappointed when the announcement was made heralding the return of Frank Burrows who had led us to promotion back in 1988. While many bemoaned yet another lost opportunity, the more realistic amongst us knew we would be better off spending big wages on players rather than on a manager, and on the basis of experience at this level Burrows was probably the right man for the job.

From day one Burrows did things his way; old favourites were swiftly dropped and replaced by some of the younger players who'd lost their way under Hibbitt and Osman. Centre-back Lee Jarman in particular deserves a mention. Tipped for stardom and a big-club signing a few years ago, Jarman was by now a shadow of his former self - he'd lost his regular spot and seemed nervous and error-prone. Within a few weeks of Burrows arriving, Jarman was back on form, dominating the box, attracting the scouts again, and wearing the captain's armband - a remarkable transformation. Another player to get a chance was youth team striker Christian Roberts, who hit three in his first four games to signal the arrival of yet another homegrown goal machine.

But at the final reckoning we finished in 21st place. We didn't even break the record for most draws in a season, managing only to equal the old record of 23. Strangely enough Hartlepool also managed the same total. We reached the fourth round of the FA Cup and the final of the new FAW Invitation Trophy, losing to Wrexham in extra time. All things considered it was a pretty drab season. Burrows' retained list showed where he thought the blame lay as half of the defence was released. The only player to come out of the season with any real credit was goalkeeper Jon Hallworth, who won all the Player of the Year awards, ours included, and by a pretty massive margin. It just goes to show that you can sign good players on free transfers. A good thing too, as that's where our future seems to lie.

Off the pitch the continuing developments down in Cardiff Bay look set to include a massive 'sports village' complex to include facilities for athletics, skiing, football and ice hockey. "Hold on," you might say, "haven't we heard ice hockey mentioned before in this article?" Well yes, you have. The three owners of the Cardiff Devils Ice Hockey side are Messrs Guy, Temme and Phillips, who coincidentally are all directors of Cardiff City. The Devils have to quit their city centre rink within two years and a move to the Bay seems their best (and cheapest) option. But the complex wouldn't be viable without the inclusion of a football stadium, and so it is in their interests to ensure that the football club moves to the Bay - hence their joining the board. Needless to say they deny that there is any connection, but you'd have to be pretty stupid to miss that one. Most fans are quite agreeable to the move, as long as we get a decent ground; not some tin shed like Chester's (sorry, but it's a bit poor, isn't it?). Many prefer the historical associations of Ninian Park, and there is no doubt it is eminently restorable, with plenty of room to expand. The only drawback is that it doesn't come with its own ice rink.

Behind the scenes there have been some changes at the club, with long-serving fan Steve Borley spending his own money to buy into the club and becoming something of a fans' spokesman. We have also had the regular outburst from the Cardiff-born owner of Birmingham City, David Sullivan, who is claiming once again that he wants to save the Bluebirds. As usual his rantings came to nothing, but he is seen by some as the only hope for a failing club. Say that to the board though, and they come out guns blazing. They have a new five-year plan, and their target is the First Division - something we have heard before from Kumar. I wonder if the new board will have any more success than the old one.

But the long poor season has taken its toll, and morale amongst supporters is now at an all-time low. We really need to do something big, new and exciting to attract back some of the missing thousands. A new stadium in the Bay could just be the kick-start we need, but in the meantime it's up to Frankie Burrows to work his magic. At least Hibbitt isn't in charge any more.

THOSE WERE THE DAYS

Ipswich Town

Into the Valley of Death

Last year I sat and wrote a piece for this book whilst the nasty taste of undeserved defeat remained in my mouth. This year I'm sitting and writing this piece a few weeks later with exactly the same feeling. I'm starting to get disillusioned with all this, you know. Anyone would wouldn't they?

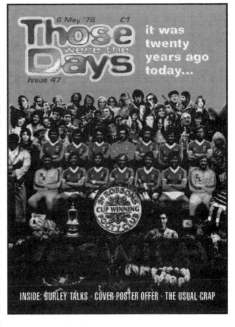

Town's season was that most rare of things: a game of three halves. Back in August we started the whole thing confidently (well, we had only just failed to go up via the play-offs after all), with great hopes of doing even better. We had Alex Mathie, out for nine months after having his shoulders rebuilt, back in the fold and in terrific pre-season form. At least we had him until he did a hamstring at Rushden and Diamonds. Hmm... Perhaps we should have seen this as a warning that things weren't going to go exactly to plan. Ironically, it turns out, our best early season performance was away at Charlton where we won 1-0 but really ought to have scored ten. And that was the general problem; we were playing well in most games but failing to get the goals that turn good performances into points. As the months wore on, and despite a victory over Manchester United in the Coca-Cola (including ten internationals before you all start saying that they put out a load of unknown bloody reserves and by the way shouldn't Man Utd be able to afford to employ reserves who could beat a club like us???)... where were we? Ah, Town found themselves in the bottom three with our displays now dropping to the level of our results. We finally hit a new low with a 3-0 defeat at Charlton on November 1st when we were truly appalling. Injury, illness and bad form had hit the side by then and we had to field David Kerslake, triallist David Whyte and Neil Gregory all at the same time. No wonder we were doing so badly. Added to the inabilities of these three, both Kieron Dyer and week-to-week prodigal son Jason Dozzell both went off with 'a virus'. Jason's unexpected and sudden departure a few weeks later led to much speculation over their withdrawal and the club later released a statement saying Dozzell had been let go because he broke a curfew, a charge he still strenuously denies. In addition to these problems Alex Mathie had forgotten how to score and Jamie Scowcroft was getting grief off a section of the crowd for his failures in front of goal.

After Charlton, things couldn't get much worse, and most who had been present at the Valley considered the 2-0 home defeat by Stockport to be an improved performance. We then entered the second half of the season with the introduction of goal machine David Johnson and new coach Bryan Hamilton. Johnson was a bit of an unknown to Town fans but it didn't take him long to assume the mantle left by his seventies namesake, quickly becoming the King of Portman Road (to the North Stand) and The Bargain of the Season (everyone else). It was goals, goals, goals from now on, with us rushing up the table like a particularly hungry whippet. Victory after victory, home and away, even that defeat at Charlton in November was avenged with a 3-1 destruction at Portman Road. We even came close to adding Chelsea to our Coca-Cola scalps after coming from two behind, only to lose on penalties. By mid-March we were asking "Any more fives?" as goal after goal flew past opposition goalkeepers, with Johnson and Mathie both going goal crazy and Dyer and Petta waltzing through opposing midfields. Bradford, Huddersfield and - most sublimely of all - Norwich were all given five goal thrashings they won't forget. And neither, dear Budgies, will we! Five-nil. Think about that scoreline for a bit. Imagine beating your local rivals like that. Superb!

Onward and upward we went, the only sour note being the hate campaign against Jamie Scowcroft. Why slag off one of your own players like that? Makes no sense to me. By April it was clear that we were one of the best sides in the division and that a place in the play-offs was now a formality. After making friends in our last home game with top Nigerian and Crewe goalkeeper Ademole Bankole, we all prepared for Charlton, the opposition we most wanted to meet of the three other play-off teams. We'd by now beaten them three times (twice in the Coca-Cola Cup and once in the league) with only the November reverse in our four games up to now. And with Sunderland beaten easily at Portman Road towards the end of the season and Sheffield United's form having fallen away we were, if anything, more confident than the previous year.

Thus began the third half of the season: the sweaty bucket of tension that is the play-offs. Things went badly from the start in the first game at Fortress Portman. The nice passing side we had expected Charlton to be turned out to be a vicious clogging bunch of thugs reminding us of a John Beck side at their worst. The referee, to everyone's shock, allowed them to get away with it and we never got into our stride. Jamie Clapham, a mid-season signing from Tottenham, mis-directed the ball into his own net and Charlton shut up shop completely. Belatedly, the referee got his act together and sent off Danny Mills who should have been showered, towelled down and changed, if not by half-time, certainly well before he kicked Mauricio Taricco up in the air for the nth time. All in all we weren't pleased to be down 1-0 after the home leg. We were even less pleased to hear that Neil Heaney had hit Mauricio Taricco in the Players' Lounge after the game, although we weren't surprised to hear the rumours around town that Gus Uhlenbeek had 'more than held his own' in the incident. The two managers were said to have met for lengthy discussions after the game and I think I can guess what George Burley had to say.

At least we didn't have to travel across half the country to lose in the second leg I suppose; that is the only bright side I can see. The trip to the Valley, an hour or so away, started brightly but was effectively over once Shaun Newton scored in the first half. Charlton weren't allowed to be as aggressive but once again defended stoutly. That was all they needed to do and we failed to break them down. I still can't bear to go into any more detail, even now.

So a strange and ultimately unfulfilled season for us once again. Why did things change so dramatically during November? Obviously David Johnson's goals were a major factor, as was Bryan Hamilton's influence on the training pitch, but a key move seemed to be putting Kieron Dyer into central midfield. Up until just after Christmas young Kieron had been at wing-back and seemed wasted. The reshuffle led to the dropping of ball-winner Geraint Williams and a more attacking outlook for Town. Others came into their own: Bobby Petta came of age in the Norwich thrashing, Matt Holland gained greater stature and started scoring from midfield and Jamie Clapham came in and looked assured in defence. All in all we were playing better football than we had for years, scoring goals seemingly at will. We might have even survived in the Premiership!

And so what for '98-99? Hamilton is gone, to Norwich of all places (he has already been airbrushed out of the team photos), and we have (at time of writing) kept all our young stars. Stewart Houston has come in as a coach and we've signed a couple of youngsters and another Dutchman, Marco Holster, and the club has decided that we really should start playing properly prior to November. Where will we be come May? Bloody play-offs again I don't doubt...

THE TRICKY TREE

Nottingham Forest

The Rottweiler Bites Back

Kevin Campbell writes exclusively on a season of ups and downs in the nightclubs of Nottingham...

August

After a long hot summer chasing the babes along the beaches and bars of Ibiza (including a soft shoe shuffle at the Café Del Mar) it's time to return to Nottingham and get out of shape for the football season. Well, it beats having to work for a living.

Reality bites as Harry names the team for the trip to... Port Vale? Shit, I'd forgotten all about our relegation from the Premiership. No returning hero's welcome at Highbury this season then. The Bart-Man kindly reminds me of my opening day hat-trick at Coventry 12 months previous. Unfulfilled promise my arse! Uncle Frank, he really knew what he was on about when he signed me for two and a half million quid.

Still, never having been one to turn in the same performance twice - especially when it's a good 'un - I decide to grab just the one goal this time and save my energies for a night of hot-stepping at Black Orchid. Celebrate National Campbell Day (the anniversary of said three goal salvo at Highfield Road) with an impressive strike against Norwich. Thing was, those bastards at *Sky* had switched it to a Friday night. A *Friday night* - I ask you. Don't they know that's Seventies night at Rock City? Eventually get there an hour later than usual and miss *Staying Alive*. Pull my hamstring making up for lost time (but she was worth it) and sit out the next three games before returning to partner Deano against Uncle Frank's new team because The Dutchman's away on international duty. Sitting on the bench getting splinters, more like. Don't know why he bothers, it's not like you get to tour the bars and check out the foreign talent afterwards. Thing is though, Saunders and me, we're too similar in our styles. Give us the ball in the box and three times out of ten we'll force the 'keeper into a save but outside... well let's say I do all my best work in confined spaces. Naturally we pose as much threat as Leicester in Europe and Manchester's other team give us the run-around. Can't help but think they might be going places this season.

September

The Dutchman's back and with yours truly averaging a net-buster a game it's Deano who gets to pick splinters. And he's not happy, spitting out his dummy and muttering something about not buying a Ferrari to keep it in the garage. Don't know what it's got to do with football but I can see his point. I mean, Bart may only have a soft-top BM (don't worry, his contract's up for renewal at the end of the season) but it doesn't stop us burning up and down the streets of Bridgford impressing the chicks. And who knows, if he had a Ferrari we might even pull.

Must check the family tree again - Harry's sticking up for me in the papers, telling the fans to get off my back. I'm touched - and go down for the penalty - before the bionic Scottish poodle has to stick his handbag in with a line or two about City Ground fans "giving the away team the advantage." Now I know he means well, but as Scot's softly-spokens are taken as seriously round these parts as a Bill Clinton testimony under oath in the Supreme Court, he really would be doing me a favour by keeping quiet. He'll be offering 'em outside for handbags at ten paces next.

Play my part to the full in a turgid League Cup performance at Walsall which leaves us once again giant-killed. Not quite a Chesterfield but near enough. More importantly, and away from football, it leaves Tuesday nights free for grab-a-granny at Ritzy's. Now *that's* what I call getting your priorities in order.

October

Really worried about Uncle Harry. First he alienates the fans by slagging them off at every opportunity, then he tries to flog Coops to West Ham. He calls it "a good deal" but I soon put him right about that. "If it's a good deal you're after," I tell him "then meet me in the Market Square toilets at half past two next Sunday morning." Surprisingly, he doesn't show.

He's probably too busy making up with The Dutchman... except, err, they never fell out, *oh* no. Whoops, must remember to cross that bit out. Off the pitch, October is never the best of months. The odd pair of tights here, the occasional cardigan there. Criminal. Wonder if I could get Uncle Harry to agree to a three month loan spell with Canberra Cosmos?

November

I knew it, I knew it. Suddenly I find my level, the goals start flying in and cousin Kenny's on the phone asking whether I might be interested in spending Christmas and the New Year "oop north." Newcastle... well, there's Funk 'n' Soul night at the Riverside, but the VIP card for Faces drops through the door the following morning and it's no contest. Nottingham loves me, she has taken me to her bosom. I haven't been accused of hitting anyone - especially ladies, because hitting ladies is bad form and that's just not my style - outside Ritzy's for a good few months now. In fact, such is my inspirational form at the moment that Uncle Harry feels confident enough to let Italian international

Andrea Silenzi leave the club on a free transfer. Can things get any better? Well, it's only eight months to the World Cup and Alan Shearer hasn't kicked a ball in anger yet this season... not that I'd be interested if Glenn called. Me and the boys are spending next summer in Goa (which we hope describes the ladies there too).

December

First Silenzi, now Saunders. He's off to enjoy the benefits of a fat signing-on fee while the club is left empty-handed. Which is nice on the face of it, but not when I think (well actually I let Stoney do the thinking for me seeing as he's out injured again) a little deeper about it. If we're to get back into the Premiership - where, incidentally, a goalscoring record such as mine undoubtedly belongs - then I'm going to have to remain virtually injury free until the end of April. Because there's no way The Dutchman, much as he'd like us to believe otherwise, can do it on his own. And we'd be better off saving on the washing powder than have Ian Moore soil a shirt for 90 minutes in my absence. Toy with the idea of getting Bart to call Uncle Harry a crafty cockney bastard but decide against it when he gives me the Saturday before Christmas off to do my last minute shopping. Get back to the car just in time to hear Martin Fisher commentate on Stoney's late winner. Funny, didn't know The Geordie Genius was off the treatment table. Mind you, it's been so long since I've been on it myself, I'm beginning to forget what it feels like. That's the treatment table I'm talking about by the way.

Enjoy gobbling the turkey and return with a brace against Swindon on Boxing Day. All in a day's work for the man they're now hailing as 'King Kev' in the local press. They're right of course, but kind words do not help when the clubs are all shut. Nothing for it but to stick on *Ibiza Dance Anthems 2* (my prezzie from Bart) and dance around the living room. Alone.

January

Half the season gone, we're top of the league and the so-called fans are still moaning about the ticket prices, quality of football and lack of atmosphere about the place on matchdays. Like it's *our* fault. Bloody supporters, they act like they own the club and expect us, the players, to show the same sort of devotion. But will they still remember me after I've moved on (should some club be prepared to cough up the huge amount of cash it would take to entice me away, of course)? Will they bollocks. £20 is nothing nowadays, don't they know you can pay that for a drink in Lizard Lounge on a Saturday night? Peasants.

Uncle Harry decides we'd be better off out of the FA Cup so he leaves The Dutchman out at the Valley and allows Ian Moore the opportunity to show once again that he's not really up to it in big boys' football. Consider giving him my boots to clean after the game but Bart says he'll do them instead. The way he looks after me you could be forgiven for thinking he's my only friend at the club. The long term psychological effects of having to carry Moore for 90 minutes are such that I reckon that it will be March before I score again.

Every game the pressure mounts, it's like being back in the Premiership. The Dutchman reckons that if I'm thinking that way it's no wonder that I can't find the net. Like he knows. All he does is take a few free kicks here and the odd penalty there and all of a sudden he's the D's B's. Look at how many goals *he's* scored from open play in comparison and then tell me who's the better player.

February

Strange month. First Chetts scores the winner at Portsmouth, then Moore gets a last-gasp equaliser at Stoke. Talk about planets and juxtapositions. After such happenings it can only be a matter of time before I get lucky both on and off the pitch, but no. The Black Orchid is closed for a refit and the Dutchman edges further ahead in the race for top scorer. Still, it's a two horse marathon, not a sprint, and my time will surely come again at both work and play.

March

Worry no longer, 'the Rottweiler' (my new nickname courtesy of Ian Ladyman at the *Nottingham Evening Post* - and he better not be taking the piss) is back breaking hearts and nets. In that order, naturally. Brian Robson brings his Middlesbrough muppets down for a top-of-the-table clash and it's time to dig out the old red scoring boots and treat the watching masses to another display of world-class finishing. A 4-0 win ensues but the best of the quartet (mine - so Bart says) is overshadowed by yet another brace from the bloody Dutchman. Why can't he just bugger off on international duty permanently? Robson has the audacity afterwards to accuse the ref of being a homer but I'm not fooled. Fat and bald he may have been but yellow-skinned he most definitely was not. It's my birthday! Well it's not but it feels like it as Uncle Harry lets me play with Bart at Crewe. We enjoy ourselves so much that we get carried away and within 20 minutes it's over. Three for me and one for him. And it's the same story later that night at The Zone. The Dutchman's back for the trip to Birmingham a fortnight later and, loath though I am to admit it, it's a good job. Two long-range efforts inside the final eight minutes turn a 1-0 reversal into a valuable 2-1 victory. Don't tell anyone, but I am beginning to fancy our chances.

April

Deano returns with his new mates from Sheffield but forgets to take the Ferrari out of the garage. He doesn't even come close to troubling the Trent End while I bag a brace. And it's a Wednesday night into the bargain, which means only one thing - Funk revival night at Essence. Pound that dance floor, King, and let the carnival begin. Ipswich the following Sunday is such a huge game I am home before dawn breaks to catch a few hours' sleep. We sneak a 2-1 win, you-know-who scoring his 93rd free kick goal of the season, but it's a blank weekend for yours truly. Unusual I know, but I like to look upon it as offering hope to all those less blessed than myself. Back in the old routine the following week, however, with a goal a game in 3-0 strolls against Bradford and

Wolves. All of which leaves the team on the verge of promotion and myself tantalisingly close to that crate of champagne Uncle Harry promised me for bagging 25 league goals. With two to get and three games to go it's all set for a dramatic finale before I am clogged out of it at Stockport. Woany comes on in my place and hits the post when it was easier to score. Well, that's how I saw it. Other results conspire to leave us needing four points to be mathematically certain of returning to where I belong but Uncle Harry seems convinced a win against Reading should do it. Not wanting to give up on my chance of winning the champers I pass myself fit but fail to last the 90 minutes. *Knew* that Sunday night out at Isis was a bad idea. With me off the pitch it looks as though we are going to draw a blank, until Bart, pushed up-front in my absence, pops up with the winner three minutes from time. Couldn't have happened to a nicer bloke, and what's more, the club have installed pitch-side speakers which pump out a funky tune in celebration. Forget I am supposed to be injured and complete three back flips before a stern look from Uncle Harry catches my eye and sends me scurrying for the sanctuary of the dugout. Unsurprisingly, I'm not picked for our final game of the season but it doesn't matter as we are already up. Ipswich beat Sunderland 2-0 on Tuesday night. At least that's what some drunken idiot told me in the taxi rank at half three on Wednesday morning. "Congratulations Kev," he said, "you've done it." It had taken a trip to over-30's night at the MGM but, yeh, after a punishing evening of blood, sweat and tears, I'd done it. Thing was, how did he know?

TRIPE 'N TROTTERS

Bolton Wanderers

In Todd We Truss

Bugger.

If one word had to sum up our second sojourn to the Premiership, no other could do a better job. But life's like that. And that's the way it is. Bill Shankly once said, "Football isn't a matter of life and death - it's more important than that." He's dead. We're not. So balls to him.

During the summer Mixu Paatelainen (that will thankfully be the last time I have to spell that) parted company, David Lee left, and Scott Green gambolled. Neil Cox came (knak, knak), Robbie Elliott eclipsed (our previous transfer record), Peter Beardsley

BOLTON'S LONGEST RUNNING, BIGGEST AND LEAST EXPENSIVE FANZINE, GOOD WITH CHILDREN AND AVAILABLE FOR KIDDIE'S PARTIES!

became Bolton baggage, and Arnar Gunnlaugsson galumphed. Unfortunately, Cox was to injure himself 110 minutes into his Bolton career and not return until 1998, while Elliott was only to play four games before breaking his leg on his home debut.

The season started on a bright, bright, sunshiny day with a trip to Southampton, and a victory seemed to emphasise the Wanderers' phoenix-like return to the top. However, a defeat at a wet, nay very wet, Oakwell soon dampened the aforementioned planetary rotation.

The first match ever at our super-duper-state-of-the-art-not-exactly-in-Bolton-but-what-the-hey-sponsored-by-a-sports-firm-just-next-to-Kentucky-Fried-Chicken, £25 million Reebok Stadium saw Everton concede a goal. Unfortunately the referee didn't, despite what Andy Gray's new Virtual Reality thingy machine showed. But we're not full of sour grapes, never mind what the local press tell us. The evening also saw the arrival of South African Mark Feeeesh from Lazio, tweed jacket and all (and we thought they had style in Italy). With the earlier departure of the Wolverhampton-bound Mixu, we'd lost a Finn and gained a Fish. Ahem.

Over the course of the season the Reebok proved to be the place to get sent off. Blake, Pallister, Todd, Collymore, Fowler, Benali, Hartson, Bergsson, Ullathorne, Keown, Wilcox and Ismael all received ridiculously rampant rollicking ratty referees' raging red rectangular retributive wrath (we know, it's cheating).

This gained our new stadium tabloid notoriety as 'Red Card Reebok'. Blimey, a soft drink as well as a sports firm sponsoring the stadium name (how witty).

The Reebok nets refused to ripple, until one stormy night, as the Coca-Cola Cup was being watered down like a pub draught, and we were being overcharged as well. Someone jokingly predicted a 4-4 draw. The final score - Bolton Wanderers 4 The Mighty Leyton Orient... oooh, let me think... 4. Bloody hell, and we were beginning to think the goals didn't work.

The aforementioned fracture of Elliott's fibia (or is it fibula? Or is that just a kind of cheese spread?) made Colin Todd buy a second left back in as many months. Previously in Bolton, we were lucky to see two left backs in as many decades (one of those was born in Bolton), and to see good ones bamboozled us all. Mike Whitlow waltzed into the team and left Brylcreem® boy Beckham in a great heap, becoming a firm favourite immediately. Unfortunately (again) he was to become another victim of the injury jinx that seemed to spread through the team as the season went on. Scott Sellars became a victim of sciatica, while Gerry Taggart injured, suspended, suspended and then injured his way through the first three quarters of the season. But hey, never mind. Worse things happen at sea. Ask Kate Winslett.

The main problem for the Whites, surprisingly after last season's 100 league goals, was in scoring. To try and alleviate this drought, Dean Holdsworth headed North in a club record £3.5 million move from Wimbledon. His reputation was for scoring of a different kind after his reported rendezvous with pig-ugly big-breasted buffoon Lindsey Dog McKenzie. John McGinlay, a hero to a generation, sadly departed to Bradford. Throughout the transitional period of the Trotters, McGinlay had been a cornerstone of the Bolton attack, but following the arrival of Beardsley was restricted to mainly pointless cameo substitute appearances.

Bolton bungled their way to a sorry state, ending October in a position perilously close to the bottom of the table. Holdsworth's first ever Bolton goal arrived as a last minute winner against Chelsea. Ooh, we were happy. It was to be five and a half months until we witnessed Deano scoring again. One (lucky) woman did, however, win a prize of sharing a bed with him in a competition run by a local sports superstore. Yes, more sponsorship news. Welcome to the game of the people.

One thing missing from the Reebok was atmosphere. Lofty the Lion's roar was just a weary whine as half-time (and match-time as well, for some people) became just a time to watch the television and have a pint under the stands. It wasn't until March, when people finally realised Bolton were in dire danger of relegation, that the lethargic hordes began to make noise of an enthusiastic manner. The Burnden Roar was replaced by the Reebok rendition of *The Great Escape*. And to think we used to sing real songs...

As Christmas approached, a chill had descended over Bolton. A chill that blew hot and cold, but mostly the chill's central heating thermostat was knackered. Barnsley arrived at the Reebok, and 'babe magnet' Georgi Hristov gave the Tykes the lead. Gudni Bergsson, egged on by Danny Wilson, shot from 45 (some said 70, but it was 45) yards. It took some fans the time to say "Oh my God, it's going in!" before it nestled lovingly into the good old onion bag. How's that for a Boxing Day hangover cure?

A week later and the FA Cup took us to exotic Oakwell for a right old mudfight. 'Fight' was the operative syllable, as a 22-man melee introduced physios, managers, substitutes and stewards to the Queensbury Rules. It also introduced a steward to Barnsley nick for hitting Jamie Pollock. Probably for his own safety. We don't lose many fights, it's games we have trouble with. Barnsley won 1-0, and took the scalps of Spurs and Man United on the way to the last eight. At least now we would be able to 'concentrate on the League'. (As if.)

Bob Taylor trundled to T'Reebok as Bolton goals were as commonplace as Robin Reliants over garage inspection pits. Five million quid of attacking force, and we rely on a First Division reserve's rescue.

The day after the 40th anniversary of the Munich Air Disaster, we had to travel to Old Trafford on a wave of anxiety. After all, Bolton fans have a reputation of revelling in the complications of that disaster. Pleas came from managers, presidents (Nat Lofthouse and Bobby Charlton), and fanzine editors for restraint and respect. Thankfully, silence reigned during the silence - apart from one solitary mobile phone (we know who you are!). The build-up to the event featured the first misquote of the season in the press of a *T'n'T* editor. We'll get used to it. Anyway, we did play United that day, and loan striker Bob Taylor bundled his way to Bolton folklore as the Whites took a point.

Taylor became a sort of talisman for the Trotters as our attempted Great Escape began. A victory over Sheffield Wednesday heralded another unlikely hero. A Bolton-born one at that. Jimmy Phillips. Jiminho. Bobbins for most of his Bolton career, but something happened once local press started to draw pictures of Bolton managers doing naughty things to animals (drawings of Toddy strangling an owl and punting a fox up the bum appeared on the front page of the town's paper - wonder why they didn't do one for Arsenal?). Alternatively it could have stemmed from a change in tactics or the players' realisation that relegation loomed. Either way, it worked. Sort of. Well, nearly. Never mind, at least we're not Man City

Jamie Pollock, disgruntled at being played out of position, moved to Manchester City to further his career. Poor, misguided man. We'll miss him - after all, it was he who scored our 100th league goal of last season. His commitment to the cause was more prominent than many around him. With that face, what choice did he have? The man who pushed Pollock into second place in the Ugliest Bolton Player award, Peter Beardsley, bogged off to Fulham for the rest of the season. With Gerry Taggart's pop star looks, and Mark Feeeesh's funky sideburns, we'd turned into the Spice Boys (hur-de-hur!).

Derby County reminded us that playing football sometimes helps if you want to remain in the top flight, scoring four goals in the space of 19 minutes. "Those four goals could well be important at the end of the season," said Mr Hindsight. A week later, Leicester did exactly the same to them at exactly the same place. Let that be a lesson to you. Our second away victory of the season finally arrived at Villa Park, with Neil Cox scoring his first bulbous Bolton goal on the same weekend that he became a daddy. Aw! He was quoted as saying, "The manager left it up to me, but my wife said, 'go up and do your job' ." Not for the first time, I bet (knak, knak).

A 5-2 victory against Crystal Palace, coupled with an Everton defeat a day later at the hands of Champions Arsenal, set up nicely a last day drama. We had dragged our way out of the relegation zone at the expense of the Toffees, and Steve McQueen was revving his motorbike up nicely. Unfortunately, our motorbike was being ridden by Barry Sheen. Or Mr Sheen, for that matter. Yes, more sponsorship news from the game of the people.

Stamford Bridge was the venue for Everton's self-styled Chelsea reserves, featuring second raters such as Frank Lebeouf, Roberto Di Matteo and such, against Bolton Wanderers. All we needed to do was match Everton's result against Coventry. Did we do it? Did we balls. "It all smacks of sour grapes," a *T'n'T* editor was misquoted by the press. We'll get used to it.

Relegation ensued. We'll get used to it. We've no choice. Never mind, at least we're not Manchester City.

If it's so tough at the top, why does everybody want to be there? Well, everybody except Jamie Pollock? I know why - because it's lucrative. The sponsorship deals can make you so much money in the top flight, along with TV deals, player sales, and fleecing the fans for every last penny possible. This is football. Welcome to the people's game.

Bugger.

THE UGLY INSIDE

Southampton

Saints finishing spot of 12th and victories against all the top teams, bar Arsenal, exceeded our wildest expectations. Indeed, our wildest expectations after nine games and four points would have been fourth from bottom. The turn-around came with a solid 3-0 home victory over West Ham that coincided with a SISA-inspired protest emploring the board to start investing in new players before it was too late. Our protest, though muted because of the victory, did work to an extent as David Hirst arrived from Sheffield Wednesday soon afterwards. Hirst made an immediate impact on his home debut, as a kamikaze Spurs side

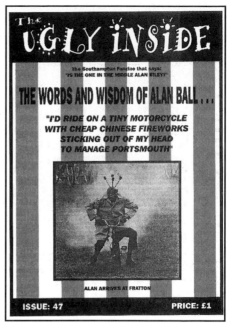

were beaten 3-2 with the Yorkshireman grabbing a pair. Unfortunately, David made more of an impact to the bar takings in Southampton than he did on the pitch, joining up with his old drinking buddy Carlton Palmer who we'd bought from Leeds a month earlier

Carlton Palmer was the catalyst for our upward surge in form. Football fans around the country think of Carlton as a struggling member of the worst ever England team managed by Mr 'Do I not like that' Taylor. However, when Carlton is playing for your side he is like a man mountain (or is it man possessed, I'm not really sure). He is here, there and every fuckin' where; athlete supreme! You half expect him to get on the end of his own crosses. His footballing ability may be limited but the spirit and determination are phenomenal and that spreads to the other players.

Astounding really that Carlton didn't get Player of the Year. That went to goalkeeper Paul Jones who, despite his dodgy start and end to the season, produced a string of brilliant saves, especially in the live televised games. Indeed, the home games against Man U and Chelsea, where Jones excelled, were followed by a most unlikely victory at Anfield where we had terrible injury problems. A return of nine points was like manna from heaven and shot us into mid-table safety.

Cynical Saints fans, and let's face it we had every right to be suffering from vertigo and nose-bleeds at this stage, scoffed as "We're all going on a European Tour," boomed out from The Bikeshed. It was great experience for our younger fans who had only ever known relegation dog fights, (woof woof) and for us old 'uns the prospect of returning to Europe, where we'd been annual visitors in the early eighties, was knob out!

Sadly of course normality returned, but we did hold on to our mid-table respectability, which is a massive stride forward given the off-field débâcle that we shall shortly visit. Selling Kevin Davies was yet another major blow, which you unfortunately get used to being a Saints fan. I don't care how much we got for him. He is one of the best young players in the game and selling him to bloody Blackburn Rovers - again - made it even worse. They started all these silly money transfers of recent years, which is now reflected in the fact that you have to pay over £20 a game. Now we are surrounded by middle class Johnny-come-latelys who are only there cos football's trendy. Where were they when it was shit? Anyway, as always they got our best player and we got their worst, moneybag bastards. Good luck to Kevin though, who, barring injuries, will definitely be a star for England in the future.

Talking of England, why oh why didn't Hod pick Le God for The World Cup? Yes his injury took a long time to clear up but when he hit form he was back to his magical best. His omission from the final 30 after a sensational hat-trick for England B seems to give credence to Chris Sutton's claim that such games were meaningless. Matty had a major bust-up with Saints manager Dave Jones after being needlessly substituted at Sheffield Wednesday in March. I just hope they sort their differences out before next season. So far Le God has let his football do the talking; one thing Dave Jones never did.

The best thing about being a Saints fan is the feeling you get when you knock over one of the big boys, and we certainly went to town this season. They hate coming to The Dell because the crowd are so near the pitch and certain players just can't handle it. Poor old Schmeichel just went to pieces, nervous as hell he was, as we yet again turned over the Red Army. Can we do it again? Who knows, but with United now, it's a psychological barrier which seems to keep haunting them. Let's hope so anyway.

Summing up then a very good season, but the Saints are falling further and further behind in the financial stakes and thousands of would-be fans are missing out. We're the team in the iron mask, but unlike Louis' secret brother, we're not sure how to feel about our strange shackle. Yes, we want to break free of our constrictions and burst into the real world, but we also realise that our iron mask - or the Dell as it's more commonly known - is one of our biggest advantages.

Sadly, the club's much vaunted stock market flotation has yet to result in the construction of a new stadium, even though this event was trumpeted as the main justification for the arrival of new chairman Rupert Lowe. What has happened is that the club have ignored a development deal involving three local councils and plonked a 100,000sq ft commercial development onto the site. This was clearly at odds with the designs approved by the councils and the Government Inspector in 1994.

As a result, two of the councils, Eastleigh Borough and Hampshire County, have made it clear that they will shortly reject the plans. And so, fans who have campaigned for seven years are left marooned in the political fall-out, with Mr Lowe and his chums claiming that the original agreement was "unrealistic and never financially tested" and that the commercial additions are necessary in order to fund the development. Mr Norman Best, a local councillor and former mayor, however, states that he asked the directors three times whether they could afford the project, this on the day of the enquiry and prior to the councils signing the brief. Mr Brian Hunt, a local builder, assured the politicians that the club had the necessary dosh. Mr Hunt is still on the board and indeed saw an investment of less than three thousand pounds turn into a cool million on the first day of the float! And then there's another fellow director Keith Wiseman, whose shameless profits from a similar investment are even more morally questionable, given that he is the chairman of the FA. The Southampton flotation has received much national publicity in the press, and has featured in a *Panorama* investigation into the activities, profiles and profits of various Premiership directors.

Now that the dust has settled, too many Southampton supporters are still ignorant about what it really means when a club becomes a PLC. There is as yet no stadium and Southampton will continue to play in a pitiful 15,000 capacity ground. Mr Lowe and his partner Andrew Cowen are cushily installed on executive salaries of £118,000 and £89,000 a year. The original directors have made personal share fortunes and the club is trying to make the familiar, pathetic justifications for once again selling off its best young players.

It's business as usual at The Dell, with far too many people failing to see the facts in their excitement over a mid-table finish... Remember, not too many years ago Southampton fans would have expected that anyway. Rumours that Southampton City Council will rescue Saints with a new ground site in the city are as yet unproven, but one thing is certain: the directors can construct as many smokescreens as they wish but without a new stadium, Saints will be doomed to a Nationwide future. Those of us who actually understand the workings of PLC's - and their threat to football - have still got a lot of work to do before the majority sees the light. We live in hope!

UNITED WE STAND

Manchester United

Well, that was the season that was. Three Championships in a row, and only the fourth side this century to do it. Our third double in five seasons, clearly ahead of anybody from Merseyside, and of course the Holy Grail came home. After a 30-year absence we finally lifted the European Cup; 30,000 adoring Mancunians turning the Amsterdam Arena into the biggest foreign jamboree since 1991, when, 40 miles away, we lifted the European equivalent of the fizzy pop cup, a tournament we don't even bother to enter these days. Yep, it sure was the season to be a red.

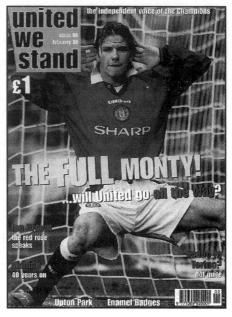

How do we begin to summarise a season when whichever way we tell it, it will sound like gloating? We could try and be modest and talk through a few of our defeats. The one in Turin, the one at Highbury that gave them false hopes, or the one at Barnsley that gave them the FA Cup. But what would be the point? It would all seem so sycophantic. After all, rubbing our rivals' noses in it wouldn't be fair would it? I could mention a few of our more important victories: at home to the Arse and Liverpool, away at Juve in the Champions' League semi, or even the defeat of Madrid in the final, the latter obviously being my personal favourite.

In the end though, I've decided to summarise our season in such a way that results are irrelevant and merely the garnish to the plate we call our main course, that of being a football fan. We want our team to win. They don't always, so we enjoy the good times as the catharsis of the darker winter evenings when not only has McClair started the game but our only three chances have fallen to him, and he's simply just fallen over. A season where we learned to laugh at Poborsky running at a defender for 20 yards before coming to a dead stop, spinning around on the spot shouting "I'm a dog, I'm a dog called Dill," chasing his imaginary tail, before the defender politely took the ball off him. We laughed, though I'm sure it would have been easier to cry. But of course we're made of sterner stuff than are those from the North East.

We learnt to sympathise with the plight of poor Jordi Cruyff, who after being told he'd inherited all his father's footballing talent, had to learn the hard way that he'd been adopted. A string of such inept performances that Johan took out an advertisement in *The Times*. A man so injury-prone he's taken to asking Bryan Robson for fitness tips.

Now let me shock you. Our season, far from being the ultimate triumph you all thought it was, actually had a few down moments.

To moan about injuries would be unfair, particularly as our squad had such strength in depth we couldn't fail to win every game by a margin of at least seven goals. I know this to be true as both Alan Hansen and Andy Gray said so. "Call yourself a United fan for doubting it?" I can hear them scream, "just look at your bench against Monaco." Pilkington, May, McClair, Berg and Clegg - pure European strength in depth there. Then came the month of May when the final silverware was dealt out and of course they were right and we were wrong. That's why they're experts I suppose. Oh we of little faith.

Another talking point in our historic treble-winning season was the performance of the mighty Edward Sheringham. Ted, as his fans know him, "fuckin' Sheringham", as he affectionately became known to the Old Trafford faithful, didn't have the best of seasons. It started off OK, when on his league debut at, of all places, White Hart Lane, he missed a penalty. Unfortunately it went downhill from there. "But he missed," I hear you cry. Yes but at least he hit the post. Gary Birtles, Alan Brazil, Peter Davenport, Terry Gibson and now Teddy Sheringham; why is it they have all come to OT and failed? Too much pressure? No, they all had the one thing missing that could have made all the difference: ability. Pity, because 'Teddy' fitted in well with the current "Stand up if you hate Man U" jocularity. We even began to stand up ourselves when he got the ball. The club said that there was an unfair anti-Sheringham attitude from within and pointedly cited the game in April when he broke into a sweat. Unfortunately, we had to point out that it was for England. "We were never going to replace Eric" they also shout. No perhaps not, but did the owner of Shergar buy Trigger? If only he'd taken to staying up drinking and smoking to all hours of a Saturday morning. Act like Best, play like Best. Even with the customary blonde on his arm, he couldn't compete. He may have dribbled like our hero, but Bestie wouldn't have shot wide. So the blonde says, anyhow.

Yep, the season of triumph ended amidst failure and conspiracy theory. Of *course* there was conspiracy theory - we're United. I mean, our youth team even suffered. The young reds, after a 1-0 win over Brazilian side Irineu, were looking forward to their next game in Viareggio, Italy, in the prestigious 1998 Coppa Carnevale world youth tournament, when news came through of the mysterious disappearance of their team photos. No photos, no more matches. The non-development of the team photo resulted in three points deducted and automatic elimination from the knock-out stage. Would we have won it? Well Arsenal hadn't entered, so who knows.

The summer finally came at the right time, and we can sit and watch the World Cup in the knowledge that up and down the country, clueless nineties football fans, dressed in shabby replica shirts, will be "standing up to hate Man U" at every opportunity. Myself, I'll be looking forward to the Champions' League draw. Just as long as we don't get Arsenal in the group of course.

THE VALE PARK BEANO

Port Vale

We can't understand it either! The club avoided relegation by the skin of its teeth, leaving it until the very last game to confirm that the coming season would again be played in Division One. Supporters endured one of the most depressing successive runs of results that anyone can remember, setting what must surely be a record for number of games played without winning... And yet, in spite of everything, Port Vale supporters are their usual cheerful selves.

Manager, HRH John Rudge, who has been in charge since the Crimean War, is still there, chairman Bill (watch the pennies) Bell, likewise, and it's hard for us to imagine Port Vale

THE VALE PARK

Come on Vale!
Come on Vale!

Free with Beano 5   The Survival Special

without either of them. Gates of over 10,000 are the exception rather than the rule, so HRH John Rudge has to sell to keep Bill Bell quiet, and Bill Bell is determined that Vale Park can at last truly be an all-seater stadium to compete with any other with the redevelopment of the last terracing section. Criticism of either of them is rare; in fact we've never had a letter sent to the fanzine with the usual supporters' comments, i.e. "Sack the manager", "Resign chairman." Come on, I hear you thinking to yourselves, where are you lot living, Fairyland? Are you all like John Boy in *The Waltons*? Is 'Port Vale Land' somewhere akin to Shangri-La? The answer is NO, certainly not. Like most supporters, we moan and complain, but instead of targeting our anger towards club officials we have a far bigger enemy: Stoke-on-Trent City Council. Briefly, this is what it's all about:-

Port Vale cannot be found on a map. It's not near Portsmouth, neither is it in the Vale of Evesham; it is in Stoke-on-Trent, home of another football team, albeit playing in a lower league, who use the city name. Going back a couple of years or so, the Council decided to build a brand new stadium (with tax payers' money - which means we helped pay for it) and install as tenants the area's other football team, whose existing ground was just about on its last legs. Cleverly, they said that it would be a 'Community' Stadium, holding a variety of events that everyone would be attracted to, such as concerts, festivals, etc.

Even more cleverly, the 'Community' bit was soon dropped and, apart from a 'Festival of Erotica' which upset local church groups, businesses and families, the only people that have visited the new stadium are Stoke City supporters. Now don't get us wrong, we're not blaming Stoke City Football Club, or their supporters, it's all a wonderful blag - one of the best imaginable - a dream come true. Wouldn't you like a brand new stadium provided by your council?

Meanwhile, in 'Port Vale Land', for 15 years we'd held a very successful weekly market on the car park, which had contributed a crucial £150,000 to the club annually. Suddenly, at the same time as the new stadium was being planned, the Council refused to renew the market's licence, claiming that they wanted to start their own market nearby and there wouldn't be enough trade to support two similar operations. As if this wasn't enough to antagonise the Vale fans, they also placed an injunction on the club, forbidding them to hold fund-raising events such as car boot sales, fairs, etc. In fact just about everything except football was banned. Unbelievably, this wretched injunction is still in place today. Well, how does it sound to you? One city, two teams; one playing in a Council-funded stadium, the other forbidden to raise money on their own premises. Perhaps this helps to explain our attitude towards the manager and chairman: we all pull together and are united in our disgust at the Council. Perhaps if we didn't have this common enemy, and having had such a rotten season, we might well have started this article with 'It's time for a change, John Rudge is past it, Bill Bell must go'... But somehow I don't think so.

As the '97-98 season approached, we hoped the team could repeat the success of the previous campaign when we just missed out on the play-offs. Incredibly, we deployed fewer players than any other Division One side. Only 21 had the pleasure of wearing Port Vale colours, providing an enviable stability which owed much to their injury and disciplinary record, or perhaps it was because we were so skint we couldn't afford any more on the payroll. The team was practically the same one that finished the previous season, with the addition of Matt Carragher from Wigan, on a free obviously. But HRH John Rudge is a wily old fox, the sort of bloke you'd take to a car auction, he can sniff out bargains from miles away. Matt was to prove a useful player, being voted Young Player of the Year at season's end. More importantly, John McCarthy, our flying winger and thoroughly good bloke, was still in black and white, although we knew that when an offer of £1m plus came in he would be gone, just as Steve Guppy, Ian Taylor and Robbie Earle had before him.

After a mediocre start and our usual first round exit from the Coca-Cola Cup (well done York City), we eventually got the three points in late August against Sunderland in a 3-1 thriller. But off the pitch, money was, as usual, tight and the new stand had to be in place by the start of the following season. To add to the financial problems, The Football Trust announced it had run out of money and so couldn't offer any assistance. It therefore came as no surprise when we learnt that 'Super John' was off to Birmingham City for a whole load of dosh in September. Before you could say "Lend us a quid," HRH swooped, bringing in Gareth Ainsworth from Lincoln City at £500,000 as a replacement. Yet again the main man bought wisely as 'Galloping Gareth' was to be voted Player of the Year and a nice earner was made for the club. Thanks Lincoln, but we wish he'd start driving a car instead of that wretched Massey Ferguson.

As winter approached, we learned that the award-winning Vale fanzine *The Memoirs of Seth Bottomley* was no more. Meanwhile, the local press was full of stories about dodgy goings on at the new (non) Community Stadium. A couple of councillors had resigned in protest over the taxpayer having to foot the bill for the opening match slap-up meal, entertainment and all the business. With invitations printed on a certain football club's headed notepaper, they'd initially thought the football club would be paying. The ensuing saga dragged on for weeks in what became known as the 'Britannia Beano'. So, when we decided to start a successor to *Seth*, we thought we'd have our own Beano, and Issue 1 appeared in early November.

Back to the footy. Mid table, non stop rain, a trip to Highbury in the cup, resulting in a well deserved draw and a near sell-out replay lost on a penalty shoot out. "Why didn't you just belt it son?" is a phrase that comes to mind. Came the New Year, and not a Happy one. The bad weather continued and we realised that not only do fanzines get wet in the rain, but our strikers lose their ability to strike. Having such a small squad was not now such a good idea with injuries taking their toll. We were now stuck in the relegation zone with seven successive defeats. We just couldn't win (Reading and Manchester proving to be the exception). Eventually we approached the end of season run-in with matches against Middlesbrough and Charlton which were undeservedly lost. Thankfully, those in a similar position in the league did likewise, and come the last match we had to win to stay up. Luckily our opponents were Huddersfield away. The McAlpine Stadium had yet to see us lose in three visits and somehow we had beaten them 4-1 early in the season. The result was never in doubt with a deserving 4-0 victory ensuring that Division One football would be seen at least somewhere in North Staffordshire next year. Miraculously, even The Football Trust came up with some money guaranteeing the development would take place, in spite of the injunction still in force.

Yes, all's well in Port Vale Land. Long live HRH John Rudge and well done Bill Bell. But please don't leave it so late next time.

VOICE OF THE VALLEY

Charlton Athletic

No 80   April 1998   £1.50

The famous Charlton Athletic fanzine

Mark gets to play in green at last!

You may have seen that film *Sliding Doors*, where the girl does - or doesn't - make it on to an Underground train and her subsequent life unfolds in two dramatically different ways. I can relate to that just now. If Michael Gray of Sunderland hadn't scuffed a weak penalty at Sasa Ilic with the last kick of the domestic season, Charlton wouldn't be in the Premiership.

And maybe, with the way the game is going, they never would have reached it. It's going to take more than you, me and a box or three of fanzines to hold back *that* particular sliding door.

But Gray, the 14th penalty taker after eight conventional goals over 120 emotionally draining minutes at Wembley, *did* scuff his shot. And in that split second of disbelief - well, several hours, if I'm being honest - Charlton Athletic were reborn. All the seasons of underachievement, mismanagement and mediocre football melted away before our eyes. After an interval of 41 years, Charlton really were going to play top-flight football at The Valley again. Never mind *you* having to believe us, *we* had to believe us, ourselves.

It is the ultimate triumph of belief over reason, romance over realism and, while we obviously cherished it above all others, I know we were not alone. Most of you reading this won't support Charlton. But you might support Doncaster Rovers or Brighton or Hereford. And the message is that our victory could be yours.

The point is that there never was a cause more hopeless than ours when we were stranded at Selhurst Park ten years ago. And if we could turn our problem around then so can you. All you need is stamina, determination, spirit and just a slither of luck. Having neither Paul Ince nor David Batty in your side might just help too. But I digress.

The key moment of the Addicks' '97-98 promotion campaign was the summer signing of Clive Mendonca from Grimsby Town for a paltry £700,000. It was one of those rare moments at clubs like Charlton when they actually buy a player that you have always admired wistfully from afar. His 28-goal haul was better than any by a Charlton striker since Derek Hales menaced his way to 31 in 1975/76.

"If it wasn't for a Mackem you'd be shite" sang the Sunderland hordes at Wembley. Not quite. But we couldn't have made it without him. Mark Kinsella not only won the Player of the Year, but finally got the attention of Republic of Ireland boss Mick McCarthy, otherwise a much-celebrated figure in the red corner of SE London. It was a season to savour in so many ways.

Arguably the funniest moment was the chant which rang round The Valley at the FA Cup third round clash with Nottingham Forest. "We only paid eight quid!" chorused a gleeful Covered End at the visiting supporters who'd parted with £20 to see their side stuffed 4-1. Of course, we wouldn't normally applaud fellow football supporters being ripped off. But in Forest's case the Charlton board were simply responding in kind to the despicable treatment handed out to every set of visitors to the City Ground.

As if that show of solidarity wasn't enough, on Easter Monday the club paid to lay on coaches for 4,000 fans to travel free to Port Vale. Charlton won - outrageously against the run of play - and Vale officials sulked because the Addicks wouldn't pay their car park fees after putting thousands through the turnstiles. The rapport between fans and board spilled over into the raucous party mood which characterised home games in the second half of the season.

Once sober to the point of prohibition, The Valley fairly bubbled its way to promotion. Stockport were the only visiting team to win a First Division game there all year. It's hard to believe, in hindsight, but in a dodgy patch as winter turned to spring, manager Alan Curbishley was about as popular as a Des O'Connor record at a rave. And Carl Leaburn... no, life's too short.

Curbishley set his side the task of winning their final nine games of the season to go straight up, and incredibly the Addicks proceeded to do just that. Well, almost. They drew the last one 0-0 at Birmingham. But results elsewhere determined that it didn't matter anyway. Play-offs loomed. In an engagingly nutty finale, goalkeeper Sasa Ilic ended a run of nine consecutive clean sheets by letting in four at the Twin Towers and central defender Richard Rufus scored his first goal in 165 senior outings to take the game into extra time.

Of course, the doom-mongers were soon out predicting that Charlton would 'do a Barnsley', as if in some mysterious way this was worse than 'doing a Wolves', a 'Manchester City' or a 'Birmingham'. Truth is, they'd all swap places with the Addicks now, at least while we're still level on points with Arsenal. And above Man United (in alphabetical order). We're realists at The Valley. We've had to be. But the reality of summer 1998 is pretty sweet from where I'm sitting, which is in an office looking out at the towering structure of the new 8,000-seater west stand.

Yeah, the editor of *Voice of The Valley* finally sold out, following a clutch of Charlton's most prominent fans on to the staff. I knew the writing was on the wall when the directors came out to a standing ovation at Vale Park. You just can't argue with that. Brighton, Doncaster, Hereford, it could be you. But for now, it's us. And don't we just love it!

WAKE UP BLUE

Birmingham City

It's amazing what can happen in the strange footballing reality that Birmingham City dwell in: dramas, tantrums, walk-outs, walk-back-ins, God complexes, mobile phone throwing and on the footballing side pure 'bad luck'. Just your average season at Blues. If Shakespeare were alive today, his quill would be on fire as he documented one of the world's greatest dramas: *Birmingham City: Ye loads of years of shite and panic.*

The season started with a good run of results which gave the fans optimism, even though the team wasn't playing particularly well. A change of system to 3-5-2 looked to be paying off; Peter Ndlovu was taking teams apart, doing his best impression of a greyhound on a motorbike, while Devlin and Furlong were sticking it in the back of the net. All was well and good. The fans got the beers in and danced about in silly hats, before falling on their faces with cheesy grins. Could this be the season when they finally stopped pulling our hosepipes and actually fulfilled some of the comatose giant's potential? No. Come mid-October things fell apart quicker than a leper at a disco.

After the defeat of Wolves (Ha Ha Ha Ha) the team obviously caught something from the Black Country and forgot how to play football. A run of seven games without a win began to take its toll on everybody, as small cases of insanity broke out. Trevor even started to dress like Puff Daddy in a poor attempt to look hard and ignore the criticism.

A massive revolt against the manager began. It became clear that he had made a lot of mistakes; he tried to incorporate an Italian-type system into the club, with player rotation and the use of a defensive back three with wingbacks, which did not suit the players. Some of his player management was also causing a stir, in particular his verbal battles with the striker Paul Devlin. So started the undercurrent of voices calling for his head. The feeling was that he'd been given a chance and messed up. The media had already lined up a successor in the shape of Steve Bruce, and Trevor's bags were waiting at the back door. It looked like Francis had one more game to save his job, the game at West Brom. We lost.

However, rather than ending his reign, this game seemed to have the opposite effect. The Blues had battered them for 90 minutes only to lose to a single shot on goal. More importantly, Trevor did something he had never done before; he showed passion and emotion. By kicking and punching the air throughout he showed us, for the first time, his true feelings for the club. Our usually reserved millionaire boss was at last excited by something other than the size of his bank balance.

Phasing out the squad system and reverting back to a 4-4-2 soon paid off and results quickly turned round. Unbeaten over the Christmas period and playing some great football, you could see the confidence returning. Except for a certain Paul Devlin who, in the greatest tradition of Christmas spirit, decided to start a war of words with Trevor, which amounted to public rattle-throwing and, behind closed doors, shouting of the word 'wanker'.

The first game of 1998 was a shocker for every Blues fan and a nightmare for Stoke. We produced one of our all-time greatest performances, stuffing them 7-0 and creating a frenzy of beer-drinking and silly hat-wearing across the West Midlands. A buzz started around the ground, the fans getting the feeling that something big was around the corner (again).

Slowly creeping up the league, three great things happened in January: Michael Johnson scored his first ever league goal, the ultra talented Dele Adebola signed (much to the annoyance of Crewe fans) and we beat Wolves. Doing the double over them appeared to cause Mark McGhee to have a breakdown as he continued to claim that we were still 'crap'. It was all too good to be true.

How right we were. After the home win against QPR, Tricky Trev quit after his family were abused by supporters using a suite which was supposedly reserved for players and their wives. (Also, the salmon sandwiches weren't quite as tasty as they used to be). The shock was unbelievable. Fans were in uproar over the incident. How could a situation arise where drunken individuals where able to mix with the manager and his players? The answer? Karren Brady.

The underbelly of the club was in conflict. Team management and the commercial department did not like each other. They did not speak. Trevor was fed up with the unprofessionalism. And Karren was out to make a quick buck from anywhere (her club-name-changing idea being a perfect example, Readers' Wives United anybody?). But the fans rallied to get him back, while Karren issued statements claiming 'I'm the boss, I will control the world and lead you all the way to the promised land, hail me, hail me, I am the chosen one'. After a few days, Trevor came back because of 'fan power' and reassurances that Karren would not speak to him.

With normality restored, it was back to the task of reaching the Premiership. After beating West Brom in injury time to the chant of "One chance, we only need one chance," the race was on to beat Sheffield United to the last play-off berth. They had to slip up and we had to keep on winning.

Sheffield started to lose, while we missed a barrage of opportunities to overtake them; it was going to the wire. Finally, it all boiled down to us having to beat Charlton and United losing to Stockport. A chance to make it into the top six meant a full house at St Andrews and a wonderful atmosphere. But in the greatest of Blues traditions we failed in great style. Stockport beat Sheffield, but we couldn't put the ball in the back of the net. *Typical* Blues!

Source: *Spitting Feathers*

WAR OF THE MONSTER TRUCKS

Sheffield Wednesday

A pessimist, ask anyone, is never disappointed. The start of the '97-98 season brought us Di Canio, predictions from the pundits of a seventh or eighth place finish for Wednesday, and our sadly unloved band mastering the intricacies of *The Great Escape*. Seasoned watchers of the blue and white stripes knew, even then, that the most relevant of these three was probably the last, and started digging the tunnel.

Never off my wall at work is the league table as it looked after the first four games of '96-97, with Wednesday proudly sat atop the whole pile. A big memory from those giddy days is David Pleat's head appearing in that football shaped screen on *Football Focus*, appearing totally mystified at how it could all have happened.

A Sheffield Wednesday Fanzine

WAR OF THE MONSTER TRUCKS

The Voice of Boothy Bolshevism

Hello hello I'm back Again !!

BLIMEY ! - IT'S THE KING OF GLAM

Issue 17 - Year Zero Edition. Price £1.00

Four matches into the latest campaign we had one point from 12 and the hapless Pleatster wore exactly the same look. But if we could have predicted the misery, we couldn't have dreamt of the drama of it all.

Come the start of November we suffered a clinical 6-1 dissection at the pitchfork of the Red Devils, and our beleaguered boss was gone. Shortly afterwards, I was in bed struggling to wake up for work when the 'phone rang. "Any comments about Atkinson?" "Dunno, what about him?" It was surely a dream? But no, the charismatic/fat hero/Judas (delete as appropriate) was back, and several portions of hell broke loose. Not even Trevor Brooking could have found a fence to sit on as Wednesdayites decamped to one side or the other. Even our three person editorial board was divided. Ron Atkinson had delivered us a silver cup and the best day of our lives. He had also flushed us down a claret and blue toilet.

First time out with Ron at the controls against Arsenal (funny to think back now...) and Hillsborough was awash with conflicting emotions. The *Barmy Army* chant banged around, but only the very brave dared to whisper "Atkinson's" at the front of it. But when the Arsies were vanquished, good times peeped from around the corner and a tidal wave of forgiveness washed over the multitude.

And notwithstanding a splendid win at L**ds and a glorious home rout of Man U, that was it for Wednesday's season. We won some, we lost a few more, our cup run once again turned into a limp, we grubbed around the ocean floor, and we escaped the relegation mire with two matches to go. And Crystal Palace did the double over us.

Ron had just about done the job he was brought in to do. After which he didn't get his contract renewed and got all mardy, both at the board and at - of all people - 'portly' 'keeper Kevin Pressman; hugely harsh after the lettuce untroubling one had kept us in more games than Ron has pairs of Ray-Bans.

But written into the footnotes of a season where even with the early doors presence of Atkinson, we finished up as anonymous as Barry Venison's style consultant, there were a few notable happenings.

One of Pleat's last acts was to let go of the talismanic hero David Hirst. A legend in his own pub lunchtime. The oft knackered but enormously talented Hirsty had recently had an on the field slap hands fight with Beni Carbone (after which the feisty Italian had run sobbing from the pitch only to be forced back by Peter Shreeves). As a result the next game brought the unthinkable: the booing (by some at least) of the Barnsley Behemoth. And then, unbelievably, he was gone.

And, of course, he straightaway reverted to being a top-line striker who, biggest surprise of all, was almost completely injury free. The curse of Wednesday strikes again. People round these parts will tell you to joke about the curse at your peril. In the run-up to the 1998 World Cup, Andy Hinchcliffe (England), Petter Rudi (Norway) and Dejan Stefanovic (Yugoslavia) were all in the frame to take part, but all mysteriously failed to make the cut. The curse of Wednesday.

Then there was the strange case of Patrick Blondeau. Pleat signed the defender from Monaco in the summer of 1997 after the player had been recommended by Arsene Wenger (as if he knows anything). Shortly after this, the wily Mr Wenger signed two other Monaco players himself, presumably ones not recommended to us. Our Patrick played a handful of matches where (to use the official phrase) 'he had some difficulty adapting to the pace of the English game'. Subsequently he got dropped, and gave the French press one of those "Merde, Sheffield she is 'orrible and Wednesday don't start training until 9.04 in the morning" stories. He went through the charade of saying he had been taken out of context, and then he was gone.

But the big, big thing about this season and what will surely remain when all the managerial malarkey and piss-poor lack of progress is long forgotten is Paolo Di Canio. We don't care that all our beer money is being used to pay the bloke. We don't care that he and compatriot Carbone between them spent half the season suspended. We don't even care that he talks 100% proof bollocks about the symbolism of his tattoo. Paolo is the real deal. He popped in a hatful of top solo goals, usually involving him strolling effortlessly around a helpless 'keeper and stroking the ball in. But if when he was good, he was very, very good, when he was mad he was... well, a joy.

Best of all was his tubthumping tantrum of temperament in the cup game against Watford. Learn it well, youngsters. The ball goes off our hero for a throw-in (subsequently shown to be the case on telly). He rants crossly at the linesman along the lines of the ball never having touched him, prompting the affronted official to call across to the ref to slap the sideboarded one's legs. This he does, complete with yellow card. At which Paolo goes ballistic and in seconds has traded in the yellow card for a nice red one (although in fairness one of our Italian speaking correspondents (!) says that he was quite clearly only asking the question "Why?" But when you ask it two millimetres away from the ref's face, whilst trying to stick your finger up his nose, you're dancing on the thinnest sort of ice). Brilliant.

That particular tantrum cost us an hour's drinking time as Watford forced extra time and penalties, but we just didn't care. Here, at a stadium where recently passion has been about as rare as Gary Lineker saying 'bloody', here at last was somebody with proper Latin passion. Ron, as only he could, gave Paolo a run as captain towards the end of the season. This involved him ranting on at the officials just the same, but as the last rant left his lips, turning round and geeing on his colleagues. New chants about our hero seemed to be born every week but, unsurprisingly at a time when Full Montyism afflicted the people's republic of Sheffield from every side, we shamelessly bellowed out the one to the hot 70's tune of *D.I.S.C.O.*. If it was good enough for legions of hard Glaswegians, it would do for us.

And as a back-drop to a season of toil and turmoil, there were the inevitable Wednesday bit parters so beloved of *Sky* and top of the vitriol pops for opposing supporters everywhere. First, the Uncle Fester-like Tango, whose star has waned a bit this season as even he seems to have got a little fed up with leading the charge. And second, the Wednesday Kop Band, parping away like the NDO at the back of the Kop. Love 'em or loath 'em (and there are plenty either way), they have been responsible for this season's major tune (you know, that continental one) and were signed up by Richard Branson to do one of the 30 million official World Cup tunes. We may be shite at football but we do see life.

Sheff Utd, bless 'em, have at least been able to, as usual, put our suffering into perspective - cup semi, play-offs, nul points. But it's a hollow consolation. Yes, all in all, it's been a nothing of a season, where our tykey neighbours up the road seem to have won a lot more friends than us just by managing to be relegated with a smile on their faces. And it's left us facing yet another new dawn where the pessimists, never disappointed remember, expect the sun to set in pretty much the same place.

THE WATER IN MAJORCA

West Ham United

"Roll up, roll up! Guess the weight of John Hartson and win a year's subscription to *The Water in Majorca*." To say that business was slower than Ian Bishop in diver's boots would be like suggesting that Steve Lomas did not look the epitome of cool with his ginger goatee.

Whether the reluctance of Hammers fans to partake in our little game was due to the dubious quality of the prize on offer or the fact that Super Johnny Hartson's waistline was increasing at an exponential rate comparable to that of inflation in 1920's Germany is open to debate.

Not that we really minded because his goals tally was increasing

just as quickly as his girth. We're not elitist at the Boleyn Ground - we can't afford to be, having suffered Iain Dowie in and out of the team for the past three seasons. We'd have no objections to Bernard Manning leading the line if he knew where the back of the net was. As lizard-tongued ska-icon Buster Bloodvessel sang on *Lip Up Fatty* in the early eighties, "There's nothing wrong with being fat is there?" You need only look at those one-time giants of Saturday afternoon pantomime, Big Daddy and Giant Haystacks. Even their mums would have struggled to describe them as lean, mean, fighting machines. And what self-respecting footballer's CD collection would be complete without the soulful crooning of the walruses of love, Luther Vandross and Barry White? There's even quite a good book about the fattest.

No, it was unanimous that they could wheel John Hartson on and off the pitch on a trolley if he could lead us to some long overdue silverware. And in the glorious Autumn it looked as if he could become the first man to fire 20 top-flight goals at the Boleyn Ground since Tony Cottee's heyday. Seventeen goals by the first week in December made Hartson the Premiership's top scorer and made it the most prolific start to the season by a Hammers striker since the days of the legendary Mike Small. We even laughed off the minor indiscretions that were beginning to surface. An incident at an Essex hotel which meant he was taken to a local police station - just letting off steam. An FA disrepute charge after calling Mike Reed a 'homer' - just a heat of the moment comment summing up what the rest of us were thinking.

But then things - Hartson's finishing *and* his backside - started to go pear-shaped. In the next 13 games he found the net only twice - against the footballing giants of Emley and Barnsley. His work-rate was suddenly on a par with that of French air traffic control and watching him lumber red-faced around the pitch was strangely reminiscent of one of the residents of Noel's Crinkly Bottom. Supporters in the Chicken Run were even said to be overcome by alcohol fumes every time Hartson ventured near the touchline. Chunky, cuddly or big-boned - call it what you want but the fact was that the Premiership's top scorer, a man earning in the region of £10,000 per week, had a physique which wouldn't have looked out of place on Hackney Marshes on a Sunday morning.

And then the inevitable happened as John snapped at his inability to recapture his early-season form and was sent off for a flailing elbow at the Reebok Stadium. As strange as it may sound, most Hammers fans were quite relieved at the three match ban he received as new signing Trevor Sinclair reminded us of what a decent striker should be. It was during his three week holiday that the uncanny parallels between Hartson's and the aforementioned Small's first seasons in the claret and blue prompted an investigation by the *TWIM* fraud squad as to whether they were in fact the same person. The evidence did seem to be conclusive. Both started the season like trains and were top scorers in the division by November, before going off the rails for supposedly overindulging in substances that are not regarded as performance-enhancing. And neither had a clue what the offside law was! When somebody pointed out that Small and Hartson had never been seen in the same place at the same time we were convinced that we were in the midst of a unique footballing déjà vu. Conspiracy theories were soon sweeping the Boleyn Ground whilst we waited for the big man's return, with everyone mindful of the fact that Small's Autumn goalfest had ultimately ended in relegation.

In the meantime, news filtered through of an incident in an Ascot pub involving Hartson, Vinnie Jones and a barmaid which ended with a quick bout of fisticuffs with the locals. We were beginning to wonder if Hartson's suspension had been cunningly planned so that he could indulge in some of his other passions.

His perfectly timed comeback coincided with our biggest game of the season, an FA Cup quarter final replay against Arsenal. A sylphlike Hartson (well, perhaps Mick Quinn-like as opposed to Michelin Man-like) appeared on *Sky* to inform viewers that he had lost 11 lbs during his enforced absence. There was even a rumour doing the rounds that Hartson was about to publish the secret of his success: the H-Plan Diet, a revolutionary weight-loss programme which involves only the daily drinking of 15 pints of a special hop-flavoured 'tonic', with the only solids allowed being the occasional packet of pork scratchings and a chicken vindaloo on a Friday night. Suddenly the Ascot incident began to make sense. Hartson was obviously introducing Jones to his diet and the fracas occurred when followers of a rival diet turned up.

Despite a goal in the Arsenal match, Hartson still looked more Ronald McDonald than Ronaldo and he hadn't found the net again when it was time to renew acquaintances with old friend, Derby's Igor Stimac, on Easter Saturday. After wrestling each other to the ground, Hartson proceeded to throw a punch at Stimac within six yards of the referee's assistant. A red card was the only option, although on this occasion the general feeling was that Hartson's only crime had been to miss with his haymaker. The striker left the pitch with the applause of the Boleyn Ground ringing in his ears, the crowd strangely oblivious to the fact that Hartson's actions had cost him the chance to be the Premiership's top scorer as well as more than likely costing us our first taste of European football for 18 years.

A fortnight later Hartson signed off with two goals against Blackburn, a performance reminiscent of his early-season form, leaving us with the task of securing a minimum of seven points from our last four matches. In typical West Ham style we began the run-in with only our second home defeat of the season. If losing 4-2 to Southampton wasn't embarrassing enough, watching Carlton Palmer as the main tormentor didn't bode well for the following week's trip to Liverpool. Now anywhere north of Arsenal can be considered a bogey ground for West Ham (in our past 47 visits to Newcastle, Everton, Leeds, Manchester United and Blackburn we have won only four times) but Anfield makes these look like happy hunting grounds. Our last victory was in September 1963 and it was nine years to the month since we last scored a goal there (albeit in a 1-5 defeat that relegated us!). But surely this was going to be the year our hoodoo would end. Liverpool were already assured of a UEFA Cup place and were missing McManaman, Fowler, Redknapp and Jones. With the scales tipped so firmly in our favour we weren't too disappointed with a 0-5 defeat, particularly after having been 0-4 down at half-time.

Other results ensured that our destiny was still very much in our own hands. Our mission, if we chose to accept it (which we usually didn't), was to win our last two matches, which would guarantee us seventh place in the league and a place in next season's UEFA Cup if Chelsea won the Cup Winners Cup. First up was a trip to Selhurst Park to face a Palace side with only one home win all season and who had just been relegated the previous Saturday. A goal in the fourth minute confirmed that it was just a case of boosting our unimpressive goal difference against a demoralised side. An hour later we were 3-1 down and only a last minute equaliser saved us from the ignominy of defeat.

The final match of the season against Leicester became almost an irrelevance. If Newcastle failed to win at Blackburn or Arsenal got at least a draw at Villa we couldn't qualify for Europe, regardless of events at the Boleyn Ground. Despite Tony Cottee's best efforts to put one over on his old mates we scraped a 4-3 win, but for the fourth time during the season - they had already beaten us 4-0 in the league and knocked us out of both cups - Arsenal did us no favours and lost at Villa Park.

After the match it was time for the annual extravaganza that is the Hammer of the Year Awards. Hartson was awarded third place - hardly impressive considering that when the votes were cast he looked like being the first Hammers player to be the top division's highest scorer since Pop Robson in 1973 - and shuffled out onto the pitch to collect his trophy. Afterwards, whilst the rest of the team undertook a lap of honour, Hartson mooched around a 15 yard circle sweating like a man in a sauna wearing a sleeping bag, before deciding he had something far more interesting to do and headed back up the tunnel.

And that was that. West Ham's most successful season for 15 years - success in E13 is relative and not a very close relative at that; in genealogical terms, perhaps second cousin twice-removed - was over and a new tin of Silvo polish could once again be crossed off the board's summer shopping list. All we had to look forward to now was the price of our season tickets increasing by 40 per cent. Oh yes, and the 'Hartson to Manchester United in exchange for Teddy Sherringham and £5 million' rumours.

Still, as they say, every cloud has a silver lining and at least we were spared having to cheer Chelsea on against VFB Stuttgart.

THE OLD TRAFFORD HOME DRESSING ROOM

Schmeichel and Berg were getting increasingly pissed off with Poborsky's pre-match warm up routines

Source: *War of the Monster Trucks*

WE ARE LEEDS

Leeds United

I could never hope to start this season's contribution to *Survival of the Fattest* without mentioning this. So, if you will allow me, I would like to dedicate this review to the epitome of a football hero. To a captain who led his players to glory, and led his supporters in their daily lives in the schools and factories of Yorkshire. If not for him, Kevin Keegan would have retired without that one tiny blemish on an otherwise goody-two-shoes career. If not for him, the reverse pass would remain forever undiscovered and a whole generation of Leeds fans would have grown up without knowing just how good life can be. The late and very, very great BILLY BREMNER: 9/12/42-7/12/97.

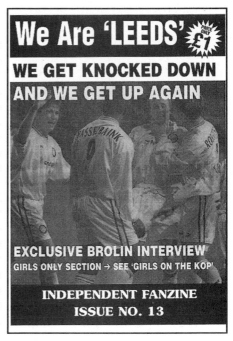

During the close season, George Graham promised us that the campaign ahead was going to be much better that the one we had just endured. For those literary aficionados amongst us, '96-97 was something akin to reading Dylan's *Tarantula*. Now we had a promise of better, with a team of cheap imported nobodies. It seemed that Georgie was assembling a squad of hundreds as cheaply as a penny-pinching Scotsman could. We got Dutch men, Portuguese, Norwegians, Scots and a man from Surinam called Hasselbaink, all the time avoiding absolutely anyone that we might have heard of.

Scorn was heaped upon this promise of improvement from all angles, including myself. Let me admit once and for all, George Graham has never spoke a truer word. OK, OK, I never said that we were not poor at times, but as the season progressed, it became more and more clear that things were definitely looking up. In fact at time times during '97-98 Leeds United were something else, something we hadn't been for a long time.

The first (and for some time only) team to beat Manchester United in the league; we taunted the mighty (not) Newcastle that they were s**t without Shearer, as we beat them 4-1. When he returned later in the season it became apparent that they were s**t with him too. Throughout the season, early pacemakers Blackburn were a very good side. We put four past them, too.

TWICE. Not many teams had even scored at Pride Park, and Derby were still unbeaten at home when we hit town in March. We turned them over 5-0 in front of the *Sky* cameras without breaking sweat.

However the performance of the season has to be the game at Chelsea, just a couple of days after Billy died. Chelsea did everything they could: they attacked constantly. The referee did every thing he could: he was booking and sending Leeds players off like it was going out of fashion. Yet our nine men held on for three quarters of the game to draw 0-0. Of course, the media dwelt only on the fact that we'd had so many bookings and totally forgot that their beloved Chelsea had also had players booked, or that they couldn't beat nine men.

That game at Stamford Bridge was just part of our purple patch. From the beginning of November to Christmas we were beating teams for fun. As Chumbawamba topped the charts with *Tubthumpin'* it was us who got knocked down and got up again. We gave West Ham a goal lead then turned them over in the second half 3-1. We gave Derby a three goal head start then beat them 4-3. We had the Oakwell (un)faithful dancing in the aisles when they led us 2-0 then crying in their beer when we beat them 3-2.

As we stood proud and topless in third place, just three points behind the leaders, we were regretting losing those silly points. Giving Everton a point at home and losing to Palace and Leicester were bad enough; giving Aston Villa their first win of the season when we absolutely buried them was painful. We could have been contenders; as usual, we never missed an opportunity to miss an opportunity.

By now the fiascos that were Brolin and Yeboah were sorted out. Whichever side of the fence you stood on, you had to agree that the team were showing a far more commendable spirit than previously. So Christmas, third place and feeling invincible. Then we went to Anfield and found out how good we really were. As the season progressed, one or two of our players were catching the eye. If Lucas Radebe hadn't been away in South Africa so much, of or if he played for a team with a higher profile, we would be making Manchester United look rather foolish for parting with ten million for a Dutch centre half that nobody had really heard of before. Then there's Harry Kewell. If Ryan Giggs was that good at that age, so was I. Darting back and forwards between Leeds and Australia for meaningless Mickey Mouse tournaments was ruining his season. When he pulled out of yet another of these, in true anti-Leeds fashion the spiteful Australian FA, led by our very own Terry Venables, got Harry barred from playing our next game at West Ham. Well, he wasn't fit anyway. Strangely, they overlooked the fact that Stan Lazaridis was on the other team.

The embarrassing defeat at West Ham brings us nicely up to the next couple of talking points. On the return trip from Stansted, our entire team, ex-players, most of the staff and board and a select band of journalists were involved in what can only be described as being seconds away from a major air disaster. How the pilot managed to safely land the burning plane, nobody knows, but Captain John Hackett and his crew will remain heroes of Leeds United for ever.

On a positive point, the air crash did one good thing. It made Leeds fans review the situation and it temporarily put a stop to the sick Munich chants. Temporarily that is, until those above criticism, those who have always found the Munich songs so disgusting, yes, those wonderful Manchester United fans, taunted us with "You should have died at Stansted." For God's sake, don't get me wrong; I'm not saying two wrongs make a right, but a phrase containing the words black, pot and kettle springs to mind.

If there's anyone out there who doubts that Manchester United hate Leeds, or who thinks that the dark days of the football hooligan are behind us, they should have been at that match. Yes, I know there was trouble at Leeds, but the otherwise impartial press blew it all out of proportion. What happened to Leeds fans (including many women and children) at Old Trafford will never be forgotten. Escort after escort of supporters were constantly pelted with bricks, bottles and full cans by what can only be described as around two thousand screaming savages. They were not there for the football, and they stopped some from getting into the ground till around half time. Leeds fans are no angels, and the scum of both sides has spoiled these games for long enough, but this was the worst I've ever seen. Of course, the whole sorry episode was totally ignored by the otherwise impartial press.

Next season we are going to contact Mulder and Scully. There is definitely something spooky about Leeds United and the FA Cup. Let's face it, there has to be something going on at any club who've won something less times than Sheffield Wednesday... It seems that the easier it falls into our laps, the quicker we drop it. (Just like the FA drop misconduct charges against England captains.) All the big guns were dropping like flies: Chelsea, Liverpool and Blackburn were dumped early on. Then Barnsley beat Manchester, and that left just Arsenal and Leeds from the top half of the table in the quarter finals, and we had drawn Wolves at home.

A mediocre First Division side stood between us and the semi-finals. In his infinite wisdom, George Graham picked a team of defenders. He was going for 1-0 and he got it. Unfortunately, as befits such tactics, it was Don Goodman of Wolves who scored. I know we can't get it right every time, but when we get it wrong, it goes wrong man fashion. We never miss an opportunity to miss an opportunity.

Still, we have got Jimmy Floyd Hasselbaink. Anonymous and then dropped as he struggled to adapt in the first half of the season, by Christmas he had just four league goals to his credit. At the end of the season he was only two strikes behind Hartson. Our youth team reached the final of the Northern Intermediate Cup and the semis of the FA Youth Cup, and our reserve team is made up of last year's Youth Cup-winning side. You have to take into consideration that apart from the odd first teamer, this bunch of 18-year-olds were competing against the second teams of clubs like Liverpool and Man United, and they won the Pontin's League.

When coupled with the first team's qualification for Europe, things are definitely looking up. The future's bright, with a few more quality imports, the future's Leeds United.

WHAT A LOAD OF COBBLERS

Northampton Town

The '97-98 season was supposed to be one of transition. Having been promoted in the 93rd minute of the Division Three play-off final the previous year, the fans and local media were looking for some consolidation, while the bookies had us as favourites for a swift return to the basement. Even the fanzine editor (OK, me!) had predicted a 16th place finish in *FourFourTwo*. At 4.45 on Saturday 9th August, most fans were agreeing with bookies as Bournemouth ripped us to shreds in the second half. Comments on leaving the ground that day were along the lines of "it's going to be a long hard slog" and "what's the lowest points a team has been relegated with?" Four days

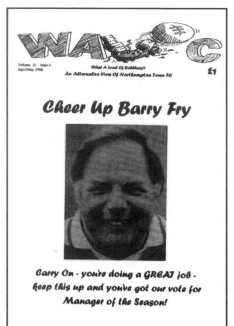

Cheer Up Barry Fry

Carry On - you're doing a GREAT job - keep this up and you've got our vote for Manager of the Season!

later against Millwall in the Coca-Cola Cup, half time opinions hadn't changed. Then John Gayle entered into the fray, getting amongst the Millwall defence and turning the game around for us. We won 2-1, but more importantly it seemed to give the whole team a lift. We could compete at this level, we thought, and suddenly the fans who'd booed Gayle on his arrival as sub now hailed him as "Super Johnny Gayle." Football fans - fickle?

We didn't lose a league game thereafter until October 11th with the trip to Grimsby. The Codheads played their best football of the season, thrashed us 1-0 and denied us top spot in the division. Had the bubble burst? Well, no, but it was a bit up and down. We only won one of the next six league games (but only lost one as well). We recorded back-to-back away wins in August and September (Walsall and Carlisle) but our growing band of away fans had to wait until March for the next rendition of *Jingle Bells*. We threw away a 2-0 lead at Luton on Boxing Day, which didn't help the nerves, but we were generally difficult to beat away from Sixfields, accumulating the division's most number of draws on our travels.

We also became probably the most hated team in the division. Opposition managers came to Sixfields, slagged off our style, claimed their team was the only one to play football, but still left on the end of a defeat. The words 'grapes' and 'sour' spring to mind. A telling quote came from a Fulham player following the 1-0 win at Sixfields in our final home game. He suggested, and I paraphrase, that "Northampton play that way (the long ball game) to win their games 1-0." Hmmm, this was April 25th and our previous 1-0 win had been on September 20th. I wonder who'd been feeding him those lines - probably that master tactician Kevin Keegan.

We were constantly in the table's top half dozen all season. We were getting altitude sickness, but still no-one was really giving Ian Atkins or the players credit for being there. Opposing managers grudgingly acknowledged our achievements in their programme notes and then whinged like mad after we'd drawn with or beaten them.

There were disappointments along the way: the failure to dispose of non-league Basingstoke without resorting to penalties in the FA Cup and the disappearance of team spirit and aggression (except for Ian Clarkson on Muzzy Izzet) in the FA Cup Third Round v Leicester both spring to mind. The foul count said it all that day. Leicester had five free kicks; we had none! (Perhaps the ref was a homer!)

Our Jekyll and Hyde personality returned in the latter stages of the season. One week we'd lose at home - Wrexham - and then we'd record *that* first away win since September - Bristol Rovers. We then went to play a poor Brentford side, there for the taking and who we'd hammered 4-0 at Sixfields, and played for (and obtained) a 0-0 draw. Yet the following week at Watford we'd battled our way to another point thanks to a late (and deserved) Dean Peer equaliser. Strange events at Watford - Graham Taylor has done away with the ball-boys. Fair enough, you might say, but when the ball goes out the players sometimes had to go 40 yards to retrieve the ball, at which point the Watford crowd jump on *your* players' backs for not sprinting after the thing. Yeah, right!

We were well on course for a return to the play-offs, but then lost two on the trot: relegation-threatened Burnley did us 1-0 at Sixfields (Carl Heggs was sent off for hacking at a defender and was suspended for the last three games plus the first play-off game if we reached it), Chesterfield came back from a goal down (and this was Ian Clarkson's first goal in over 250 professional career appearances) to win 2-1 and then Preston grabbed an injury time equaliser. Other teams had caught us up, and things were looking decidedly shaky, but once again the team and Ian Atkins surprised us all with a Chris Freestone hat-trick inspired victory at Plymouth... We were back in the frame. Up next was moneybags Fulham - at least they'd taken over the title of most hated team in the division! This was one of the sweetest wins of the season, and meant we only needed a point from our final game at York to confirm a play-off spot. Over half of the crowd of 6,688 were there from Northampton to see the side achieve what none of the us had expected - another play-off spot and the possibility of another Wembley experience. We anxiously awaited the other results to see who we'd be playing. Bristol Rovers were the first hurdle and if we disposed of them then it looked like Fulham. Yeah, that would do.

Our 1,700 ticket allocation for the Memorial Ground was gone in a flash. We'd already won there, but Rovers were going into the game as the form side. After starting well, the referee changed the whole course of the game with a penalty decision that only he saw. Then our normally ever-so-reliable defence gave Bennett yards of space in the penalty area to head home from a corner, which again, only the referee had seen fit to give. Two-nil down at half-time and we had to do something. We did. We went 3-0 down to a piece of Hayles magic. Then Rovers should have had another penalty, then they hit the post. Oh well, who wanted to go to Wembley anyway? But wait - John Gayle's onto a through ball, he's got his foot to the ball and lobbed the 'keeper. Three-one, a consolation or real hope? This raised the team and suddenly Rovers were rocked. We pressed hard but couldn't grab a second. The feeling as we left the ground was that thanks to 'Super' Johnny's goal we had a chance; we had an away goal. And let's face it, 2-0 was what we would have needed if we'd only lost 1-0.

Wednesday 13th May was without doubt the greatest night in the short life of Sixfields Stadium. There was real hope born of the feeling that the tie was by no means over. Sixfield's largest crowd (including 1,350 Gasheads) was at its noisiest. The volume didn't drop for 90 minutes and I left the ground emotionally drained, not really believing the whole night: the atmosphere, the performance and most of all the result. Carl Heggs returned from suspension and looked so hungry that night. He gave the Rovers defence a torrid time, but they held out for over half an hour. We hit the woodwork and there was a slight tremor of worry - was this going to happen after all? But from a corner Heggs was eventually found totally unmarked and he swept the ball home. One-nil at half time. The volume was cranked up an extra notch for the second half, and after 20 minutes, with the Cobblers in total command, Heggs brilliantly beat the full back and drove in a low cross. Clarkson, with one goal in 250+ appearances, hammered home from a couple of yards out. Level on aggregate! Could we hold out until 90 minutes and then extra time? We didn't need it. Ray Warburton rose high at the far post and powered a downward header past a now demoralised Rovers' defence. Three-nil and ahead over the tie. The last 13 minutes were both a blur and a nail-biting climax as Rovers tried to get the goal to take it to extra time. As the final whistle went the pleas of the announcer to keep off the pitch and allow the team to do a lap of honour were never going to be listened to. We were going back to Wembley!

The omens were in place. Last season we had played a team in the play-off semi-final who wore blue and white in the first leg, and yellow in the second. Rovers had worn the same. The final was on the same date (May 24th). We were allocated the same end of Wembley Stadium. The referee was the same. It was all there. Even more amazing was that we were taking even more fans this time around. Last year we'd created the record for the biggest gate and most fans from a single club, 32,000 Cobblers, at a Division Three play-off final. This season we took a record 42,000, the most *any* club has ever taken, in the largest gate for a Division Two play-off.

Oh and we lost 1-0.

WHEN SKIES ARE GREY

Everton

You've got to laugh, haven't you?! Yes, once again our loveable, witty, salt-of-the-earth, red neighbours have been forced to take off their paper hats and burst their balloons as the many 'Everton going down' parties planned around the city were cancelled at extremely short notice.

You see, contrary to popular opinion, Everton and Liverpool aren't those happy scouse, convivial, side-by-side buddies. They hate us and we hate them. And long may it continue.

Needless to say, one of the more relieved groups of people in our divided soccer city were those stout-hearted chaps at Merseyside police, as the threat of mass

WHEN SKIES ARE GREY
THE EVERTONIAN FANZINE

#64
one english pound

insurrection was averted at a tension-filled Goodison on May 10th, when the Blues limped to safety. Now don't get me wrong. There are a lot of Liverpudlians who see Man United as the big enemy and aren't bothered about Everton or local rivalry, but then again there *are* a lot of reds fans in Wiltshire...

Joking apart, relegation was on most people's minds for much of the season; a scenario that has been depressingly familiar for Blues for much of the nineties. For a club of Everton's magnitude, that is simply inexcusable.

Now to football fans at large, especially the nauseous post-Italia '90/ *Fever Pitch* types, Everton are an irrelevance; a horrible Northern club that plays boring long-ball football, attracts inexplicably large attendances and wastes big money on poor players, and thoroughly deserves to be relegated instead of plucky Bolton or Barnsley. Whilst there's more than a grain of truth in the above observations, they don't tell even half the story.

As far as Evertonians are concerned, there is no bigger club than ours. From the inception of professional football Everton have been major players. No club has spent longer in the top division. Very few can match our history and trophy haul and I would argue that no one can match the fervour and loyalty of the Goodison fans. And unlike most major clubs, Everton FC still draw the majority of their support from the immediate locality. So while Liverpool and

Man Utd can pull in fans nationwide, Everton FC is every much a city of Liverpool institution, and while nationally we may be unfashionable at the moment, in the city of Liverpool, Everton FC is a major part of everyday life.

I've often heard it said by outsiders that they had no idea how big a club Everton is until they actually visited Goodison, and I'm sure that any neutrals (or indeed Coventry fans present on the final day) could fail to be moved by the unbearable tension and unrestrained relief felt by 38,000 hysterical scousers when the final whistle blew. All of this makes the current struggles all the more galling. For too long the Goodison politburo has taken the incredible support for granted and sat on their hands whilst Goodison burned.

Throughout '97-98 Everton consistently proved that they were not good enough to get themselves out of trouble. Ultimately it was only due to the fact that there were three even poorer teams than us that saved the Blues. Not that it wasn't close. Even when gifted a comedy penalty in the last five minutes of the last game, by a referee who gave the best 'Homer' performance at Goodison for many a year - the scoring of which would almost certainly guarantee our Premiership status - we missed, and almost managed to lose the game in those frantic, nerve-strewn final minutes. Couldn't make it easy for ourselves, could we?

Still we survived, again, and considering that we're making a habit of this, comparisons with our previous last-day escape are both inevitable and enlightening. In 1994 the feeling was one of uncontrollable fear and disbelief, but in the aftermath our new chairman was making big promises and our new manager, the hapless Mike Walker, seemed to be getting to grips with his new charges. Blues fans on the surface had good reason to be quietly confident about the future.

This year, survival gives us nothing to celebrate. In fact the mood among the faithful is one of anger. Peter Johnson, on the few occasions he opens his mouth these days, is still making ridiculous promises about anything from big money signings to state of the art new stadia. However, we've learnt from bitter experience that it pays to be a little less trusting of our Pete. What he says and what he does are not always the same thing - sometimes they're not even in the same ballpark.

Now some readers will be wondering why team boss Howard Kendall is not coming in for more stick; after all, he picks the team. Granted, on occasions Howard's tactics have been a little Jekyll, but in general the fans understand the constraints under which 'the dome' is working. Howard Kendall is one of the greatest figures in the illustrious history of Everton Football Club, and to most Blues in my age bracket (early 30's) he is the nearest thing we have to a hero. Howard knows the game inside out and has done it all, but at the moment he's being asked to produce the proverbial silk purse from a sow's ear. After watching the Blues all season, the majority of fans are of the same opinion, and even a goat herder in the Peruvian Andes could tell you that the squad needs large scale investment.

Unfortunately, sat on his yacht, lazily surveying the sun-kissed regal splendour of Monaco, Peter Johnson doesn't see it that way. It's not about money, he says, it's about getting the blend right. Sentiments which, let's face it, are merely camouflage for signing First Division journeyman, and so Howard is forced to trawl the bargain basement. Consequently, I fear that most Blues can only see more of the same next season; there is not even a false dawn on the horizon. Johnson owns 68% of the club, so even the growing voices of dissent from both shareholders and ordinary supporters is unlikely to bother the hamper magnate. Johnson is rumoured to be tiring of the continual abuse he is receiving from the faithful, but reportedly won't settle for less than £60 million to relinquish his control of the Blues.

So with no high profile backer on the horizon, it looks like some Park Ender will have to win the lottery 12 weeks on the bounce. Then again, maybe we're all being a little too cynical. Who knows; maybe we'll all be 'pleasantly surprised' by events next season. Erm... where have I heard that before?

WHEN YOU'RE SMILING

Leicester City

In the great scheme of things, Leicester City's second successive season in the Premiership was another poke in the eye with a shitty stick for those who believe in the 'those who come up must go down' theory. Yes, we just might be a glittering example for all those languishing in the lower reaches of the First Division. And yes, we might even be the exception that proves the rule. But all these underdog attitudes and conspiracy theories... it's all getting a little tiresome. After all, even sheepshit floats! Just look at Derby County's inflated position over the past couple of seasons. In my first draft of this article I started believing in our own paranoia. I actually tried

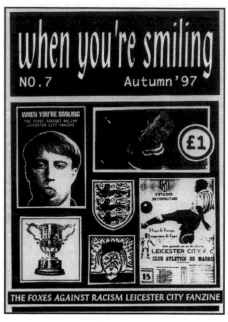

to make out that we began the season as one of the favourites for relegation. Well, I'm afraid that even in the murky, crack-influenced, ranting mind of the fanzine writer could you really believe that Bolton, Barnsley and Crystal Palace weren't dead certs for the drop? So after radical detoxifying treatment and some cold turkey (or should that be Eagle!) I was brought round to the cold and stark reality - everyone thinks we're Wimbledon!

By Martin O'Neill's standards this was a quiet one (and I did say by *his* standards). For instance, not even a sniff of Wembley... and the manner of our cup exits suggests that normal service has been resumed! However, some bizarre and downright illegal activity on the part of several referees, a couple of players and a whole travelling support will keep us talking in the beer gardens all summer.

On the playing side it was a carpet slippers by the fire sort of a year - total safety. You could count on the fingers of one hand how many times we were out of the top ten. But it didn't look like a slippers sort of a season when we started collecting points like we were contenders in *Fun House*! We were class! We were unstoppable! We had Tony Cottee... and Graham Fenton... and Steve Claridge... and a whole host of other completely ineffectual strikers! By the end of the campaign it was shown that we were fourth in the Premiership for stinginess in the defensive region and yet heading for relegation in terms of

---

goals scored! What the hell, we all knew we couldn't keep winning all the time, so we settled for drawing and losing throughout autumn and winter. We even came close to claiming the Fair Play League - which only goes to show that we were without the sterling services of injured Stevie Walsh for a good portion of the time.

In between our sporadic bouts of genius and good fortune, we were largely kept hugely entertained by the media's portrayals of a couple of fracas at Filbo. First was the anti-Ian Wright campaign, following his end of match show-down with Walshy, after he had just equalised in about the 54th minute of injury time. Then, just to spice things up a bit, we became embroiled in the 'is Shearer just a mindless thug with an arm-band and a charisma bypass?' debate. This followed his 'accidental' attempt to kick Neil Lennon's face off. But these weren't the only matters involving Leicester City that took the media's eye.

Two factors threatened to undermine our entire season. We managed a comfortable consolidation of our Premier status, and we even had a fair crack at getting into Europe again in the end. However, it was the manner of our Euro exit that brought an abrupt end to our winning ways. A Marshall away goal and a dodgy penalty had set the scene for the home leg. With a Madrid defender sent off and City beginning to dominate, we looked set to net some glory... That was until the ref sent Garry Parker off for taking a free kick too quickly! Demoralised and confused, that little tosspot Juninho took advantage and that was that. Such a shame about that broken leg of his! Our Blue Boys never managed to come to terms with this disaster. As if the county's psychotherapists weren't busy enough healing the players' mental scars, the media circus turned the whole city into manic Prozac addicts as they taunted every fantastic result and performance with 'O'Neill going' or 'Heskey/Elliott transfer requests'. Every good result seemed to be another nail in the coffin for City's continued revival. Victories against Man Utd away, Chelsea, and our mighty (and immortal) 15 minute demolition of Derby County ('Four nil! Four nil! Four nil...!') were all cases in point. At times, it looked as if there were definite advantages to fighting the relegation dogfight. After all, I don't see anyone exactly queuing up for Howard Kendall, his defenders or strike force.

Well, winning at Upton Park was never seriously on the agenda, so we missed out on Europe by a handful of points, and then watched as O'Neill's position became more and more uncertain. How could this be? Pierpoint (our Mr Boss - *he'd* like to think) said he was happy with the board's late season restructure... Ah, but then he's a scheming, conniving little prat with 'wacky' glasses and a self-confessed dislike of football. Then the PLC chairman (I didn't mention our flotation did I? Well now I have) stepped in and Martin has been persuaded to stay put. We all breathed a huge sigh of relief and settled down to watch the World Cup. Christ only knows what NEXT season will have in store!

WHERE'S THE MONEY GONE?

Darlington

Usually, Darlington are either challenging for promotion (or at least we did once a couple of years ago), or battling against relegation to the Pox-hall Conference. However, this season for the Quakers was like a pin with no sharp bit: pointless. Despite manager Dave 'Dodgy Hodgy' Hodgson managing to say, "We can still make the play-offs" even more times than I did in *SOTF3*, we were never higher than 15th in the Nationwide League Division Three. And of course, due to the sad plight of Donny Rovers, we were never threatened by relegation either.

Rather than give you a thrilling statistical rundown of every wretched match - recalling in vivid

detail how Darlo defenders gifted so many soft goals that other teams' fans would laugh as if Vic Reeves were pulling stupid faces on *Shooting Stars* (more about the Darlington-born 'comedian' later) - I will pick out the vital parts of the season and then clear off home for my tea.

Funnily enough, almost all of the incredibly important things happened off the pitch. Which was lucky really, because not a lot was going to happen on it. You see, the 'pitch' was rubbish, it was like a cheap pair of scissors - cut up badly. But it wasn't the groundsman's fault, he had no equipment and the soil was upside down - really! Our first game was on Colchester United's no doubt superb field of dreams. We lost 2-1. However, since one of their goals was a controversial penalty and we'd had Lee Brydon sent off, it didn't give our optimistic fans any headaches.

By the end of the month, however, the Feethams Faithful were screaming for their Paracetamol. We were without a win, had already been knocked out of the Coca-Cola Cup, and were third from bottom of our poxy league. Our opening cover had screamed 'Hope Springs Eternal!' with a picture of super duper defender Richard Hope doing some very untypical bouncing around. But *WTMG's* prediction of a 13th place finish now seemed like it had been made by a bunch of drunkards with a brain even smaller than little Phil Brumwell's.

There was some relief in October, though, as Darlo clinched the signing of Austrians Mario Dorner and Franz Resch. Mario was an ex-U21 international, while Resch had represented the full national side. They were, at least on paper, excellent acquisitions. Dorner made his debut as a sub in a 5-1 win over Doncaster, and looked impressive. Franz Resch sat in the stand muttering away in German. Come the end of this damned season, Super Mario was attracting £800,000 bids from Premiership clubs, while Franz didn't live up to the hype and was released.

After scraping past Dr Martens' Midland Division side Solihull Borough on penalties in the first round of the FA Cup, amid unfounded allegations that the referee had been slipped a few quid by Borough officials, Darlo were drawn against noted giant-killers Hednesford Town. "Nothing to worry about there," I hear you quip, "Darlo aren't giants! Ha ha!" Okay, if you must. Anyway, their ground is about as small as the average Hartlepool fan's brain, so there were less than 200 tickets on sale to Darlo. "Hey! Rather than give priority to fans who pay upfront for season tickets, why not draw the names of people who can go to Hednesford out of a hat?" thought some idiotic blunderer who has somehow managed to get on the Darlo board. So they did, depriving many loyal supporters of a ticket.

As it happened, Darlo won 1-0, with Darren Roberts scoring and then getting sent off for allegedly kicking the Hednesford goalie in the head during the celebrations. The red card was subsequently changed to yellow after the referee studied video evidence. Still, the win meant we'd reached the third round for the first time in ages. A draw against Wolves was a good result; they'd rake in the money for the Quakers and they were struggling in the First Division, which would give us a chance to cause an upset.

The original game was called off, and we were very unlucky to lose 4-0 in the re-arranged fixture. Daz Roberts missed an open goal, we hit the post, had shots cleared off the line, saw goalie David Preece make a bad mistake and conceded two of the goals in the last minute. In other words, typical Darlo!

It was probably this cup run that kept Dave Hodgson his job. The league form was still poor, although we did reach 15th after a 1-0 win over Brighton (the old Doncaster). This game nearly brought some very unwelcome news: Mike Peden, who was supposed to pay hated majority shareholder Reg Brealey for his 83% shareholding in the club, was not at the game. The sceptical chaps and chappets amongst us reckoned his absence added fuel to the fire of a rumour that the Scottish businessman had lived up to his country's tradition of being tight !£$%^&*s and hadn't bought the club. It didn't help when the club claimed that Peden had just had 'flu. Thankfully, our scepticism, on this occasion, was unfounded and he did take over a few weeks later.

It may have been a useless excuse of a season, but Darlo did actually win some silverware. After two draws with Hartle-fool United (1-1 at Feethams and 2-2 at the Norwegian Oil Tanker), Darlo won the Comcast Challenge Cup on away goals. The aforementioned highly prestigious trophy is awarded to the aggregate winner of the two league derby matches. Can't be bad...

It was obvious to everyone, even Hodgy, that our main problem was in defence. Not only did Darlo fans have to put up with reading *WTMG*, they were also subjected to a host of horrible gaffes both home and away. The loan signings of Steve Tutill and Craig Liddle from the Grand Old Duke of York City and Middlesbrough respectively steadied the ship. Tutill was signed permanently, while we even offered some money for Craig Liddle (this is unheard of for Darlo - so he must be good!).

Finally, after a 2-1 home defeat by Torquay - Ambrosia Devon Rice - United and with Darlo in 18th place at the end of March, Dave Hodgson gave us an almighty shock. No, he didn't do the decent thing and resign - it was even more surprising than that. HE ADMITTED THAT WE WOULD BE HARD PUSHED TO MAKE THE PLAY-OFFS!

A couple of days later, Darlo sold youngsters Jamie Coppinger (England U16 international) and Paul Robinson (who, to be honest, was no great shakes) to Newcastle for a deal worth a possible £1.2m and more, with international appearances, over time. Steady on Hodgy, that was almost a shrewd piece of business. No chance of promotion but raking in a million quid for two youngsters, one unblooded in league football... I'll be calling you a good manager next.

Things look promising for next season, especially off the re-turfed Feethams pitch. The fantastic new East Stand is finished and generating a host of new commercial opportunities like the 'Wall of Fame'. A new kit deal with an Italian firm is in place and Super Mario Dorner has pledged his future to the club.

One thing the club could do with is a celebrity fan. A survey carried out by some sad stattos revealed that Darlo are one of a select band of clubs who don't have any famous faces getting into games for free. And there's a few potentials: superstar Vic Reeves, actress Wendy Craig (whose brother played for Darlo once), Coronation Street star Glen Hugill and the totally not famous Arctic explorer Robert Swan all come from Darlo. But none of them want to be associated with a club whose highlight was *WTMG* finishing runners-up in Cardiff fanzine *The Thin Blue Line's* fanzine of the year award (and that was for "achieving the difficult task of being so awful it's bloody brilliant"). But wait, Middlesbrough's Neil Maddison claims his hero is ex-Quaker David Comer, *and* he's a Darlingtonian... Does he count?

WHITE LOVE

Bolton Wanderers

It's all gone Pete Tong!

A previous incarnation of this fanzine was called *Here We Go Again!* and after this season's startling performance it would be easy to see why!

Two things happened in the summer months of 1997 that would have a critical bearing on our forthcoming season. First, deep in the bowels of our spanking new erection - the gloriously named Reebok Stadium, our guide and mentor Colin Todd opened his copy of *Too good to go down - the thoughts and tactics of Bryan Robson* and devoured every paragraph and every sentence with relish. Second, even deeper in the bowels of Lancaster

Gate, the men in black, and a whole host of shady characters, lone gunmen and one particular chap who smoked like a beagle, decided which teams would stay in the Premier League and those who would not get an invite to the next season. You can guess which three names were on this list can't you?

Spirits were high during another baking summer back in Lancashire. The club seemed to be doing things the right way for a change. After going on a shopping expedition in the North East, Toddy brought in Neil 'Nobby' Cox and Robbie 'Robbie' Elliott to provide what we hoped would be a solid defence, and Peter 'Beardo' Beardsley in some sort of midfield-general-cum-striker role to bring experience to the heart of the team.

In the blazing heat of August, Bolton opened their account with a 1-0 win down at Southampton. You would have thought we were capable of winning the World Cup if you had seen the Super Whites supporters dancing and singing all the way up the A34 back to sunny Lancashire, and when Toddy announced better things to come, well, for once you had to believe him. Rumours were beginning to spread that Todd had lined up South African Mark Fish for a major role with the Wanderers. Things were looking good!

The Coventry game saw a debut performance from Peter Beardsley in a Wanderers shirt after his on/off £500,000 transfer from Newcastle. Beardo for his part set up two goals for Nathan Blake to clinch a point. But if you looked closely, the bad omens were already there: Bolton had a nasty habit of conceding goals early on in a game, and Nathan Blake had a dreadful habit of missing some absolute sitters, despite scoring twice on the day itself.

When those loveable Tykes from the wrong side of the Pennines rode into town, they found Bolton in charitable mood. In a scrappy game we gifted them the points after Jamie 'Rambo' Pollock had given the Barnsley 'keeper a dose of hospital food following a clattering early in the game. Blakey for his part lived up to expectations and managed to hit the woodwork on numerous occasions to deny us a share of the points.

At the start of September the team made its debut performance at our new palace of glittering delights. And before you ask, yes the toilets did have toilet paper, yes they did flush properly, yes the food was still crap, and no, we couldn't find a Ladbrokes inside the ground! That Everton game has become famous for the goal that never was, when 'Mad' Gerry Taggart headed the ball past Eddie Yeats, sorry, Neville Southall, only to see Terry Phelan clear the ball from a good yard or so behind the line! 'Mad' Gerry was a tad miffed at not being awarded the honour of scoring the first goal at 'The Reebok' as it became known, but more worryingly, our record signing from Newcastle, Robbie Elliot, was stretchered off with a broken leg and would miss the rest of the season.

The game away at Arsenal was something else, with Ian Wright needing one goal to equal some miserable record or other for the Gooners. We silenced the Highbury crowd for all of, oooh, ten minutes, as young Tommo nipped a cheeky goal past an outstretched Seaman to claim first blood. Then in another act of Corinthian charity, so as not to upset him and have him go home in one of his famous sulks, we gave Wrighty a few shots on target to make his day (he scored three of them).

Showtime came when we entertained our neighbours from Stretford at home. The lads were up for it, so to speak, so much so that Nathan Blake, despite his lack of shooting accuracy, took out Gary Pallister with a good slap when the spineless wonder tried a spot of on-the-field intimidation. Both of them had the first of what would be many early baths at the stadium. Maybe the players had heard they were filled with champagne and Melanie Sykes would be on hand to towel them down afterwards! That's the only explanation we could think of for so many of the Premier League's finest wanting to leave the Reebok pitch early! The team battled for a goalless draw and left the pitch to a standing ovation and a deafening chant of "Stand up if you hate Man U!" It brought a tear to many an eye.

The last time Spurs played Bolton we gave them the thrashing of a lifetime, and given their dismal start the feeling was that we could do the same again. But no, we were denied once again as Tommo scored the first goal at the stadium from the penalty spot, only for Chris Armstrong to undeservedly equalise. Again, Blakey should have had a goal or two - his errant targeting was quickly becoming a cause for concern. The month finished with Beardo rescuing a point against Palace in a 2-2 draw at Selhurst Park.

Orient had managed to get past the first hurdle in the Coke Cup and their reward was Premiership Bolton. After an unconvincing 3-1 first leg defeat, the Londoners had little, if any, reason to bother turning up for the second leg at the Reebok Stadium. And so all credit goes to their supporters for bringing a World Cup atmosphere to the ground, while no credit goes to our club for insisting on full admission prices and thus keeping the ground half-empty. The Corinthian spirit once again prevailed as time and again Orient clawed themselves back into the game in a 4-4 draw. Our defence was springing leaks faster than the Titanic.

Red Card fever took over the following Saturday in our first home defeat against Aston Villa, Dean 'Deano' Holsdworth debuting for the Whites. Andy 'Son Of Colin' Todd displayed a bit of his old man's spirit when he absolutely floored Stan 'The Man' Collymore with the best right hook we have ever seen after a bit of fisticuffs with the work-shy Brummie. Referee Graham Poll commented that it was the best punch-up he had ever seen. Well, at least we won the fight!

'Mad' Gerry was the next to see the Red Mist when he floored West Ham's Craig Forrest after being provoked in the Upton Park goal-mouth, and he became the third player to serve a three-match ban for rucking on the pitch. Equally worrying was the fact that living legend 'Supa-John' McGinlay was being shown the exit door at the Reebok Stadium after a barren start to the season.

When Ruud Gullit ran onto the pitch during the home match against Chelsea he received a standing ovation from all four sides of the ground, yet incredibly the *Daily Express* chose to kick up a stink and interpret such a gesture as a mass racist chant against the man. For the record we were actually chanting "Feeesh" at our South African defender! Dean Holdsworth grabbed his first goal for the club, a late winner, to start the goal spree that would instantly repay the record £3.5m splashed out on him!

Liverpool scored the fastest ever goal at the Reebok, and once again, no surprises this time, the Whites had a bit of a kicking match to get things on a level pegging. This time Robbie Fowler took the short walk back to the changing room in an all-too-familiar scenario after bringing down Per Frandsen with his elbow. Bolton took full advantage and secured a draw late on.

Many Wanderers fans dubbed our next match 'Black Saturday' when bottom of the table Sheffield Wednesday put five past a stunned Wanderers team. Many of us were on the long road home over the Pennines well before half time! To cap it all, 'Supa-John' was prized away from the club and he duly took his drinking boots to Bradford City after a protracted bout of horse-trading over his signing-on fee. It left a gap in many Wanderers fans' hearts and many relieved landlords when he went!

Another local derby against Blackburn, and Tommo walked for allegedly tw*tting Jeff Kenna. Blakey missed another sitter in injury time to deny us an equaliser and once again proved that when it matters the lad couldn't hit a cow's arse with a banjo!

Christmas brought little joy as we scabbed a home draw against Derby County and lost away at Elland Road. The Boxing Day encounter against whipping boys Barnsley saw one of the best goals ever when Gudni 'Iceman'

Bergsson thundered home a stunning strike past a disbelieving Tykes' defence. However, embarrassment prevailed as Barnsley held out for a point. 'Drunken Duncan' only added to our seasonal woe with a hat-trick when we lost 3-2 at Goodison, and then days later we were dumped out of the FA Cup by... Barnsley!

The Southampton match was enlivened only by Frankie Benali's early exit and the first appearance of Bob 'Super Bobby' Taylor in a Wanderers shirt. While the rest of the Premier League were scouring the continent for fresh legs, Toddy continued to proclaim that we still had what it took to survive in the Premier League, and baffled and amazed us by taking on (supposedly) over-the hill players from the lower leagues. Bob quickly showed all the qualities to be found in the First Division as he missed two sitters and hit the bar from just three yards out!

Coventry were involved in 'Black Saturday - The Sequel!' Emotions were running high in the crowd as the Sky Blues liberally took the piss, spanking us 5-1, and the pro and anti Todd factions in the East Stand came to blows as tempers frayed. The following Saturday in Stretford, or is it Trafford, 'Super Bobby' Taylor scored his way into Wanderers folklore with a superb goal against Man Utd. The press, as usual, had whipped up some serious hysteria about the game. Their claim that supporters were out to spoil the pre-match Munich party or whatever it was with their paper planes, proved inaccurate, as usual. The gap between truth and fiction in the papers was cruelly exposed as the fans behaved impeccably, and were jolly good sports. We let the football do the talking that day!

With points slipping away and every match taking on a sh*t-or-bust mantle, the theme tune from *The Great Escape* had its premier at the Reebok after the late equaliser against West Ham (John Hartson opting to join the growing red card brigade during the second half).

The relegation battle at White Hart Lane was dogged by an appalling first minute foul on Dean Holdsworth, well inside the box, and an equally appalling decision by Peter Jones not to award a penalty which would have earned us a share of the points. Young Tommo in midfield took to showing the strikeforce how to find the back of the net with a stunner at Anfield, while Keith Branagan twice had to acquaint himself with the back of the net.

Then came what must have been the dilemma of the season. Did the team lie down and let Arsenal get a step closer to the Championship, so denying the Rags, or did they go for the kill? A draw would have seen honour satisfied if Keith Burge had pointed to the spot when Blakey was brought down inside the box, and Martin 'Urko' Keown became the tenth member of the red card brigade at the Reebok. A scoreless draw at Selhurst Park was surely our nadir; Wimbledon were basically inept yet Blakey couldn't find the net and Deano was booed off by *both* sets of fans!

"Hey Roy, I hope you've brought some red cards with you. We've run out of 'em here in Bolton," said one supporter to a grinning Roy Hodgson as he got off the Blackburn team coach. A backs-to-the-wall display including a long awaited goal from Deano, an outstanding performance from Jimmy 'Maldini' Phillips and a great winner from 'Super Bobby' Taylor gave us a 2-1 win. But Derby County took us to the cleaners on Easter Monday, winning 4-0, and Todd astounded us all with his superior grasp of tactics by leaving our best defenders Jimminho and Gudders on the bench!

With four remaining matches we needed maximum points, but the trip to Villa Park didn't promise much until 'Super Bob' took matters in his own hands and thundered home a cracking shot from well outside the box. Three-one to the good and yes you guessed it, *The Great Escape* was sung throughout the borough all night long!

The final home game provided a 5-2 thrashing of Crystal Palace and saw us leapfrog Everton and leave the drop-zone for the first time since before Christmas. So the stage was set for a cracking final game as Bolton took their Premiership campaign to the wire. A win would guarantee our survival and condemn the bluenoses to their long awaited fate. Chelsea were more bothered by the up and coming European Cup Winners Cup Final in Sweden and would be a push-over; their ranks would be swelled by a few Chelsea pensioners and groundstaff. Or so we thought! It was a tearful end to the season as Vialli reluctantly scored and Bolton snatched defeat from the jaws of victory at Stamford Bridge. Relegation is much harder to swallow a second time around especially as 'the goal that never was' could have kept us in the top-flight and sent the bluenoses into a derby match that didn't involve Liverpool! Life is sh*t, football is cruel; get used to it. Hmmm, we'll have to.

A week later the club showed what they thought of us and added an average of £60 to the price of a season ticket!

YELLOW BELLY

Lincoln City

At last. Wonderful. Deep joy. Orgasmic bliss. And other euphoric expressions. After years of not much, if not sod all, we've actually done something special and gone and got ourselves promoted. A season of incident, controversy, and highs and lows climaxed (sorry about these sexual references but they are almost appropriate bearing in mind the pleasure these events have given us) with the last game at home to Brighton. City won 2-1 and, with Torquay losing, the highly improbable had happened and we were promoted to the Second Division. No failure to get over, no play-offs to fret about, we'd got automatic promotion to the same league as Man City, Stoke, Reading, Fulham *et al.* Wonderful!

THE YELLOW BELLY

Issue No. 4. £1.00

A Lincoln City and Football in General Fanzine

Your Stars

Gareth Ainsworth

Footy Diary

It wouldn't be right to describe to you the ins and outs of every single game throughout the season, although it has to be said that the 0-0 draw at Rochdale on a cold wet Tuesday night in November was surprisingly entertaining. Better therefore to relate the other important events of a rollercoaster season.

City had an ordinary start, the highlight being a 2-1 win at Notts County. This was a controversial victory with ex-Imp Devon White getting sent off, Phil Stant scoring the winner from what they thought was an off-side position, and the referee being attacked by a home fan. In other words a good day out for us City fans, then. The midweek game at Rotherham followed soon after, and we performed pretty badly, going down 3-1. Personally I had an inkling that things weren't going to go well that night when the stewards bollocked me for selling the fanzine inside the ground, and then when the roof of my mouth had been removed on encountering the nuclear heat of one of their meat and potato pies. The most significant thing about this game though was that, unknown to the supporters, it was to be Gareth Ainsworth's last match for the Imps, the club having already agreed to flog him to Port Vale for half a million. Gareth was the best player to have played for City since Darren Huckerby and he was a real favourite. Under John Beck most players looked like they were prepared to run through a brick wall for the cause if they were asked to, and no-one personified this more than him. On top of that he was skilful, fast, and scored goals. Although the fee was a good one for us, Port Vale had surely got a bargain. Most Lincoln fans will support Gareth wherever he is, and he will undoubtedly play at the very top level.

So after an indifferent start, an early exit from the Coca-Cola Cup, and the sale of our best player, things were looking a bit bleak to put it mildly. As if to confirm what a fruitless pastime predicting football events is, City then amazingly embarked on a 16 game unbeaten run, and went to the top of the division. Highlights included a 1-0 win at near-neighbours Scunny, where Dean Walling leapt salmon-like to bury a header in their net, and another 1-0 victory at Colchester that put us on top of the pile. Nose-bleeds all round.

Although the Beck system was effective, and no-one could complain when it had got us where we were, it was non-league opposition in the FA Cup that found out how to handle it, giving City their hardest challenges for some time. The two games against Gainsborough were excellent entertainment with one team totally outplaying the other. Sadly though it was them doing the outplaying across both games and City were very lucky to go through, mainly due to the Gainsborough lads becoming knackered towards the end. At home to Emley it was a similar story, with the Unibond side playing all the football, and their fans were very disappointed with only a draw. The replay at the McAlpine stadium was another dramatic game with City going out on penalties. The mutterings of discontent at Beck's rigid style of play increased a bit with this result. Generally, we couldn't see the sense in conceding possession with endless punts up the pitch, especially when we were two up with a few minutes left. A thrashing at Peterborough and defeat at home to Rotherham on Boxing Day turned these polite complaints into something much more audible (and basic) as the games went by and City slipped down the table.

By now there were distinct pro and anti-Beck factions. In early February, City featured live on *Sky* when they televised the Friday Nationwide game at Cambridge. To us it was a fairly routine 1-1 draw, made more memorable by the award-winning bacon rolls, but to the impartial viewer it must have been pretty dire stuff. Alan Brazil said, "After seeing this, watching Wimbledon will be like watching Real Madrid," along with other such quips. Although his comments were far from malicious they were leapt on by the 'Beck Out' brigade. A few games later following a couple of crappy home draws he was gone, with coach Shane Westley and senior player Stant taking over for the rest of the season. While it was easy to criticise John Beck for his manner and his tactics, he also deserved a lot a praise. He saved City from another relegation to the Conference in '96, brought in some excellent players, and got the team to the top of the league in November. If he'd allowed the players more (or should that be some) freedom the team would have done even better, the supporters would've been happier, and he'd probably still be here now.

To their credit, Westley and Stand realised what was needed and they fine-tuned the system just enough. Lee Thorpe, so often isolated on the right touchline, played as an out-and-out striker with Colin Alcide to great effect, and the results improved a lot. At Shrewsbury for example, City were superb, and once again promotion was being talked about.

And then there was Macclesfield. As we stood drenched on the uncovered away terrace near the disgusting bogs, some of us wondered how Stevenage had been refused entry to the Football League. On top of this, their stewards were heavy-handed and their lion mascot made obscene gestures to our fans, before the police led him (or it) away. Actually this was dead funny even if he was a pillock. To be fair though, they are a good team with a good manager, and City would have been well chuffed if they had got away with a draw. After a brawl between about 15 players, Imps 'keeper Barry Richardson and home player Sedgemore were sent off and we were sunk by a late goal.

Around this time, Lincoln MP and City fan Gillian Merron introduced her Football Sponsorship Levy Bill in the Commons, aimed at getting a fairer deal for smaller clubs in the distribution of *Sky TV* money. It is amazing to supporters of clubs in the lower leagues how the Premier League can be awash with cash and have no concerns at all about the effect this imbalance will have on the football pyramid. Surely the system should be designed so that the funds are spread out more responsibly, and hopefully this bill will go some way towards achieving that.

City by now were hovering around the edge of the play-off zone with crunch home games against Peterborough and Exeter to come. After losing to the Posh at their place 5-1, the pessimists amongst us feared the worst, but needn't have as City romped (what a lovely word) to a 3-0 win. The Exeter game was much tighter but another hard-earned win put the Imps in fourth spot. Away at Darlington, Dennis Bailey's last minute equaliser kept us in the hunt and denied Torquay automatic promotion. Then it was quite simple. On the last Saturday of the season we had to beat Brighton, and Torquay had to lose at Orient for the Imps to go up. And in front of a crowd of 10,000 fans on an afternoon of high drama and emotion that's exactly what happened.

Fellow supporters of lower league clubs will know that following your team isn't easy, and the highs are usually easily outnumbered by the lows. So often you find yourself slouching out of the ground muttering obscenities, as some smart-arse away team gathers in front of their jubilantly grinning fans. Or you travel hundreds of miles to watch a dismal defeat at some windswept dump with only miles of motorway and bloody David Mellor on the radio to look forward to. Every so often though, something brilliant happens and you beat a 'name' club in the cup or the team strings together a decent unbeaten run. When the ultimate happens and your club does what City did this year it makes it all the more worthwhile. You can stick two fingers up to all the suckers who walk about the town wearing Premier League shirts and to the clever sods who take the piss out of you for going every week. And you can savour every moment. Like I said at the start ... Wonderful!

YELLOW FEVER

Oxford United

What a tragedy for Manchester City. A club of that stature with all those fans turning up in such numbers every week. They are a credit to the club and they deserve more. And playing Macclesfield next season at their fabulous ground! Gosh! And, of course, three cheers for Forest, back where they belong. It's so brilliant for the 'Boro, especially after all their heartbreak of late. What a good manager Robbo is - he has clearly learned his lesson. No more over-paid, over-rated slobs for him in his Cellnet-Teesside revolution. With all that money invested in the team and the stadium they *deserved* to go up, Sunderland too. It's the *passion* of the North East. *Real* fans up there, you know. Through thick and thin, etc. Plucky Charlton. Community club. So brave. Ooh! Charlton went up... they'll do a Barnsley. It's the *widening gulf*. When will Wolves get the promotion their *super* stadium deserves?

Better Looking than Shotts - but not nearly as good!

£1

WELCOME BACK SHOTTS!!!

FREE! Minchery Farm Calender

Yellow Fever Issue Three. £1. February 1988. Mal's Moustache Special. The other Oxford Fanzine.

S.O.S. - Shave Our Shotton!

All the usual crap - Dr. Dave, Gilly's Poems, Denis Smith-a-plenty, Massey...

...Carry On Up the Manor, Boreland Bros, Rumours, Leeds, Cheese, etc...

Shotts' 'Tache has got to go. It's got to go, it's got to...

And there concludes the round-up of the Football League this year, as read in every paper, and seen occasionally on telly if the Premiershit was having a night off. What, other teams exist? Surely not. Oxford? What division are they in? Mid-table in the first. That's good. A nice quiet season, eh?

Well, actually, no, but thanks for asking. We've perhaps just experienced one of the most extraordinary seasons ever, even by our most turbulent standards. For the record, we've got debts running at somewhere between £6m and £21m, depending on whose guestimations you believe. We've been days away from closure. We've got a one-third built new stadium decomposing in Oxford's brown belt (it's next door to a sewage farm) that hasn't seen a builder in 18 months. We've had to sell three of our best players from a poor squad to pay the other players' wages. We've had three managers this season, two chairmen, a thrashing at the hands of our hated rivals, and a team that languished in the *'relegation-threatened'* end of the division all season. Oh, and by the way, we've also witnessed a miracle. Read this and take heart, anyone who thinks their club is doomed.

The start of the season had all the ingredients for a long, dreadful relegation campaign. The words every fan dreads were not long in coming when our then manager Denis Smith, flushed with the success of a pre-season win over Aldershot announced: "I'm going to play a wing-back formation this season." Memories of Brian Horton's post-1990 World Cup announcement that Steve Foster was going to play *Il Libero* (shudder) came flooding back. Our 'exciting new forward' to replace cult hero Paul Moody turned out to be all-year-round tan man Nicky Banger, released by relegated Oldham. You get the picture...

Sure enough, come September, we were struggling. Then the bombshell: our chairman stood down, and the club announced it was in big financial trouble. I'll let *Rage On* (elsewhere in this book) explain the full details because they are cleverer than I, but basically, building the new ground (all one-third of it) had crippled us, and using the only accounting term I know, we were fucked. The club never quite put a figure on our debts, so the local paper did: £21 million, considerably more than the board were hinting at. How did we get into that sort of mess? Maybe free transfer Nicky Banger was in fact £20m Ronaldo. Perhaps not.

A home defeat against Ipswich in the Coke Cup soon followed, just when we most needed a cup run, and lo! every player was put up for sale the next day. Within hours our talented midfielder Bobby Ford was sold to Sheffield United for £250k, an absolute steal, but enough to pay our players' wages for a while. The club then announced it was going to start budgeting. Not a bad idea at all, but perhaps just a trifle late in the day. We'd gone past the stage when buying Tesco tea bags was going to make a difference. Add a 1-0 up, 4-1 down thumping at the hands of hated rivals Swindon in the midst of this chaos and you start to realise the despair Oxford fans were feeling at the time.

Every match provided a new wave of rumours about who was leaving next. Most centred around Joey Beauchamp, who was enjoying a good season, Nigel Jemson, and Darren Purse. Nicky Banger was also attracting the scouts in numbers, but that was more to do with his ability to tie reef knots. Then a good rumour started: Denis Smith, our highly-rated (by himself) manager, was linked with the vacant West Brom job. Vacancy being his trademark, we knew he was definitely going to get it.

At this point, a fan wrote to Oxford and suggested that should Denis leave us, the best man to appoint would be our ex-skipper Malcolm Shotton, moustachioed porn star icon of our eighties glory days. The fan sent a copy of the letter to Shotton, then coaching at Barnsley, and was delighted to receive a phone call the following evening. "I'll tell you what," Shotton said, "I'd crawl from here to Oxford if I thought I had a chance of the job. I *love* the club."

The next day, Denis left for West Brom. Oxford's board acted swiftly, and taking on board the fans' views, appointed Malcolm... Crosby, Smith's trusty assistant. Our next six games fluctuated between us being dreadfully unlucky and just plain dreadful. After a sickening defeat by Charlton, a rumour started sweeping the terraces that Crosby was not enjoying it much as manager, and he wanted to join Denis at West Brom. This spurred our letter-writer into action once more. "If we are ever to get ourselves out of this mess," he wrote, "it has to be Shotton, and soon."

Days later, at a lively Open meeting, Crosby resigned. The following day, Malcolm Shotton was, at last, paraded as the new manager. He was meant to sit in the stand, like new managers always do, for his first game - a relegation clash with Portsmouth. After 20 minutes he was on the touchline, bellowing instructions, urging the team on, and getting everyone going. After a stirring half time team talk (and it has been a few years since we've been able to say that), we bombarded the Portsmouth goal, and in the last minute, Super Joey Beauchamp scored the game's only goal. It was our first win in ages, and the first 90th minute winner for nearly a year.

The next week was described by the players as being "hell on earth," as Shotts decided he was going to get them fit. It worked. The following Saturday, we went away to top of the table Forest and thrashed them with a performance described by those present as simply sublime. I stayed at home, priced out by the £20 admission charge into The Shitty Ground (it's their *Premiership ambition*). And, with a few blips, we carried on for the rest of the season. Revenge was taken out on Swindon, the double was completed over West Brom, we won at Maine Road and Reading, and Stoke were demolished... It was an awesome three and a bit months, inspired by a man who simply cared for the club and who possessed an ability to motivate and get the best out of his players. Are you watching Denis Smith?

Having looked utterly doomed in February, we finished in the top half of the table, well above Swindon, who'd been top of the table in November, and just behind West Brom who'd been top until Smith arrived. Darren Purse was sold for £700,000 to keep us afloat, and Nigel Jemson was sold because he didn't take kindly to the thought of afternoon training. "I only want people here who want to play for Oxford," Shotts announced. It's not often you get to say this about football managers, but honestly, the man is a dream. He genuinely loves the club, and we love him, moustache and all.

While Shotton deserves huge credit, so too do the players who worked their socks off for the cause. Big Kevin Francis instantly became a star, and interestingly, Steve Davis - a slow, ginger, but thoroughly good defensive player - proved astute signings. Joey Beauchamp, bless him, scored 19 goals from the wing, full-back (Sir) Les Robinson was knighted, and defensive rock Phil Gilchrist won a Booker Prize for his poetry. Even the less able among the squad improved beyond recognition. The best aspect of our revival, however, was the youth players who came into the team and shone. After a stunning performance at QPR, Simon Marsh and Paul Powell were called into the England under-21 squad. Denis Smith had tried to sell Marsh to Brentford for £50k just months earlier. Every player has given their all since Shotton took over, and for that they can all be very proud, because we are of them. Thanks, lads.

So, in all, quite a story. But because we're small Oxford and insignificant, you will not have had the chance to read it before today, because our game is covered by trendy reporters who think the all-seater Premiershit and its flag-waving, half-time mascot, corporate box bollocks is what it's all about. Not Oxford's extraordinary turnaround, nor the community-owned Bournemouth miracle, Southend's slide, or the arse of a chairman who resided over the Doncaster disaster. Not even a mention for Swindon's inspirational Steve McMahon, who led his expensive team from the top of the table in November to 18th by the season's end. If the season was a fortnight longer, he might have saved Manchester City. If it isn't a big name team, the trendy media folk who claim to '*understand*' football don't give a flying shit.

Finally, congratulations to the reporter in the *Guardian* who covered our last game of the season at Middlesbrough and failed to use the word 'Oxford' once in his 600+ words. A credit to his profession.

Moments from Oxford's distinguished history
No. 1: Furious after his unfortunate sending off at Leeds, Martin Gray aimed a kick at the dressing room door.

YOOO REDS

Barnsley

In our first ever spell in the top flight we won more friends than points and our stay was about as short as a Doncaster FC golden goal video.

What didn't win many friends was this fanzine. Towards the end of the season, I received threats from Man Utd fans for writing disparaging words about their club and players. Typical! They want everything - to win every trophy *and* to win friends. They want everybody to stand back in awe of them and applaud 'em for everything and kiss their feet until their heads get bigger than a German penalty taker's.

As soon as we won promotion, even before the

previous season had ended, they said that we were down. But as soon as we knew we were relegated from the Premiership, we sung "We're going up, we're going up!" And this is from a club that's renowned for staying in the same league for years and years without moving. In fact we've moved divisions on fewer occasions than Man Utd fans are allowed to move in their seats... (Oops, there I go again.)

At the start of the season the bookies had manager Danny Wilson as one of the favourites for the chop. But there's no way we would have got rid of him. Anyway, the only other job he could take would be the next monarch! Of course this would be just a part-time occupation because being God is a full time commitment...

Everybody thought that Bolton had a much better chance of staying up than us. Just because they finished way ahead of us in the First Division didn't make 'em an ounce better than us. OK, perhaps a few pounds better... And most of them came from one bloke, ex-Barnsley man Gerry Taggart - he must weigh about 18 stone. But he's nothing compared to our giant mascot, Toby Tyke. If Taggart is 'lighter' than Toby Tyke it's only because he spends most of his time out of the sun and in the pub.

We enjoyed our time in the Premiership and all the money that *Sky* threw at us, because it meant that we could buy great players such as Ashley

Ward and Jan Ageing Fjortoft. We spent that much money, you'd think it was falling from the sky! But no script about Barnsley would be complete without mentioning our number one enemy (do we have a sense of affinity with Leicester and Reading?), and this is Mark 'mouth' McGhee. He slagged us off, saying we didn't deserve to be in the Premier League and Wolves had more to offer! Well look, big-mouth: so what if we came straight back down? At least we've won a promotion. Full stop.

It wasn't all doom and gloom though. Arjan de Zeeuw and his wife decided to name their baby boy after Danny Wilson (they called him Daniek, which is the Dutch version). We're all hoping that in 20 years he will follow in his father's footsteps and play down at Oakwell. As coincidence would have it, Steve Bull of Wolves also had a son. He too has named the child after his manager. The boy is called Shithead. His middle name is Terry, which comes from the way Steve plays football. This makes his full name Shithead Terry Bull. I know it's a bit of a terrybull name but it's Steve's son I feel sorry for.

Going back to Arjan, he seems to have one of the strongest accents at the club - and he's not even English! When he first arrived in the town he was a little mystified and in an interview he said: "When I first got here I thought, My God - where am I? I didn't know I was in England then because people were speaking in a language I couldn't understand. But I'm used to it now. In fact everybody keeps telling me that I've picked up the accent too. I was down in London and a shoe saleswoman asked my wife where she was from. When she replied that she was Dutch, the response came: 'Holland! - And you're married to this Yorkshireman?'." So the next time tha hears sumbdy talk wi a Yorkshire accent, just remember, he could be a foreigner really.

Speyking, I mean speaking of foreigners, last season Barnsley FC saw more overseas players than the entire number of foreigners seen by Barnsley Tourist Office in the last ten years! And yes, we do have a Tourist Office. How else do you think stragglers who've lost their way around Yorkshire are supposed to find their way home? They can't ask a local can they? Some of these have never been outside the town. It would go something like: Tourist: "Vich vay to ze airport?" Local: "Erm, tha guz darn ere and darn Sheffield Rd, then tha comes to the edges of the world and then keep going and tha there, allreight?".

OK, so I've lost the plot a little but this is nothing to how Barnsley FC lost their way half-way through the season (not that we knew where we were going at the start of the campaign, like). Still, towards the end we picked ourselves up and played some outstanding stuff.

Some might say that it was a touch embarrassing losing 6-0 at home to Chelsea whilst singing, "We're gonna win 7-6." I'll say; I mean, it's bad enough for a side to be out-sung when they're 1-0 up, but Chelsea were an absolute disgrace. Six goals to nil up, and they were still out-sung by us? They should be ashamed of themselves! Some of 'em even went home before the final whistle - and I'll tell you why: they believed our song. The moral of the story is that come hell or high water, one thing was for sure in the Premier League:

nobody was going to get us down; nobody was going to hurt our pride. We might sound like the losing contestants on *Bullseye* but it's true: we came wi nothing, wiv hed a good day and wiv enjoyed ourselves.

If you want to know whether or not we can come up again, watch this space - and you'll never know, so put the book down and go and find out from reading a newspaper! Let me guess... As you read this, we are currently in... fifth position? I guess I must be psychic. You know, everybody always said I was telepathetic.

At least, that was the cry of one or two fans who read my material and thought it was in bad taste. Most of 'em didn't even pay for it either (they were given away free because Barnsley folk don't have much money). Even when I dropped the price to 50p at the Arsenal match I still only sold about 30 copies, making a total loss of £1122 in one season! And this is a fanzine in the top ten, according to *Total Football* magazine. So do Barnsley fans want a fanzine? Yes! Well, 30 of them do, but since the other 18,970 don't, in deference to democracy, it's goodnight from me and I will leave you with the following Barnsley anthem: *God save our gracious team, God save our noble team, God save our team. Happy and glorious, Reds are victorious, God save our team.* (For the last sentence I would like to request that the song by Frank Sinatra, *My Way*, should ring in your ears. *And now the end is near...* RIP *Yooo Reds* Fanzine: 1997 - 1998.)

The Zulu

Birmingham City

Over the years you eventually come to terms with following the Blues. You don't ask for a lot, but still end up with fuck all. Each season you build your hopes up, only to have them dashed. And each season you come back for more. Why? Because the blood in your veins is Royal Blue and fuck the rest of the world. Right now I'd settle for a team of battlers who gave 100%. Trevor Francis kept telling us that his players would run through a brick wall for him. Great, let's brick up the goalmouth. Maybe then they'll score the goals to get us out of this poxy division.

The highlights of the season were Savo Milosovic gobbing on the sad bastards, and the falling out between Trevor Francis and Karren Brady. It was handbags at 40 paces with Karren winning on points. And I doubt we'll ever know the truth of what really happened with Trevor's son. OK, abusing Trev's family was not on, but come on, his son is 18 and a big lad; if he can't cope with football culture and all it entails, then he should stay at home with the babysitter.

David Sullivan has been very quiet this season, slagging us off just the once about the disappointingly low gates. Well David, I can recall you proclaiming after we won promotion from Division Two that we were going to win promotion again, finish in the top six of the Premier and win a major trophy. Maybe you were just a little optimistic. Just give us a team near the top of the league, and we'll fill the ground for you.

David Gold has told Trevor there's no more money available for new players, and though the team is screaming out for a midfielder of quality, I'm in complete agreement with him. Trevor has bought in some 25 players in the two seasons he's been in charge, and I think that it's high time he and his coaching staff start getting the job done; the ingredients are there, the recipe isn't. Half-way through the season, Trevor told us he wanted to build a squad, when we still hadn't got a team. Then at the end of the season he talked of building a dynasty when he hadn't got a squad. All this grand talk is very well, and one day it may even turn into something real, but first things first. You

---

ALSO AVAILABLE FROM RED CARD PUBLISHING

Back Issues of 'SOTF'

Limited numbers of these back issues are still available - order now to avoid disappointment!

ISBN 0952 6610 04

ISBN 0952 6610 12

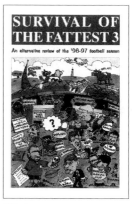

ISBN 0952 6610 20

Dicks Out 2 - the unique Guide to British Football Songs

ISBN 0952 6610 39

A tongue-in-cheek and hard-hitting book which chronicles the history and lyrics of the British football song. An honest look at terrace culture (including the language!), this book contains all of the terrace anthems, and many, many more, including:

Newcastle's *Blaydon Races*, Norwich's *On The Ball City*, Leeds' *Marching On Together*, Wolves' *Yogi Bear Song*, Bristol City's *Drink Up Thee Cider*, Cardiff's *He's A Swansea Jack*, Tottenham's *Show Me The Way To Go Home*, Chelsea's *Celery Song*, and from Scotland, Celtic's *The Soldier's Song* and Rangers' *Follow, Follow*.

can't put the cart before the horse, you have to start on the pitch with a team - a good team - and use that as the base to build on. Great clubs like Man United, Liverpool and Arsenal are dynasties but they all started out by doing it where it mattered - on the pitch.

Just look at the Golden Tit up the road. He's tried to build a dynasty in reverse at Molineux. They have a great stadium, excellent facilities, their own training pitch and a first class youth policy, but unfortunately for the Golden Tit they have a c**t for a manager and a team of tossers. Ask any Wolves for their preference: what they've got now, or the old run-down Molineux and a bloody good team.

At the start of last season I wrote that anything less than finishing in a play-off place would be a failure. Well, as Cilla would say, Surprise, Surprise! We fucked up again (OK, Cilla wouldn't say the last bit). Forget all that shit about 'if only'... If only Ndlovu had scored from that penalty... If only Portsmouth hadn't equalised in the last minute... the same at Sunderland, and if only we'd scored against Charlton. If only my Auntie had a pair of balls, the silly cow would be my uncle. 'If onlys' never have and never will win fuck all.

Our chances were wanked away in October and November, when we took only 11 points out of a possible 36, lost five, drew five, won only two and scored just eight goals. But far worse was Trevor telling us that the team had played great football and were unlucky. Bollocks, we were shit. What a difference the mentality at a club makes. Look at Old Trafford: Alex Ferguson fully expected his team to win the European Cup. Liverpool fans were very pissed off for only finishing third in the Premier (while all us Bluenoses would have got pissed *up* if we'd finished sixth in the fucking First Division). While over at Villa Park, thanks to Chelsea, the sad bastards are back in Europe.

And what prospects for this coming season? I honestly think we'll do it, no doubt about it. Trevor will have promotion in the bag by Xmas; then we can have a go at winning the Coca-Cola Cup and the FA Cup. Yes, this season it's going to be all sunshine and roses. I'll have to sign off now - there's two men in white coats at the door.

P.S. Keep the faith, but keep taking the tablets